CONNECTED & DISCONNECTED
IN VIET NAM

Remaking Social Relations in a Post-socialist Nation

CONNECTED & DISCONNECTED

IN VIET NAM

Remaking Social Relations in a Post-socialist Nation

EDITED BY PHILIP TAYLOR

Australian
National
University

PRESS

VIETNAM SERIES

ANU PRESS

Published by ANU Press
The Australian National University
Acton ACT 2601, Australia
Email: anupress@anu.edu.au
This title is also available online at press.anu.edu.au

National Library of Australia Cataloguing-in-Publication entry

Title:	Connected and disconnected in Viet Nam : remaking social relations in a post-socialist nation / editor Philip Taylor.
ISBN:	9781925022926 (paperback) 9781760460006 (ebook)
Subjects:	Social interaction--Vietnam.
	Vietnam--Social conditions--21st century.
	Vietnam--Social life and customs--21st century.
Other Creators/Contributors:	
	Taylor, Philip, 1962- editor.
Dewey Number:	959.7044

Cover design and layout by ANU Press. Cover photograph: *Monk on Sam Mountain with iPad* by Philip Taylor.

Contents

Preface

Thirty years after the launch of economic liberalisation and global reintegration policies in the mid-1980s, Vietnamese are experiencing profound realignments in their social relationships. Revolutions in industry, consumption, exchange, and governance have transformed people's relations with each other and have fostered new social identities and networks. New media technologies, communications infrastructure, and education opportunities have widened cultural horizons and nurtured new ambitions and outlooks. Millions of Vietnamese are on the move as students, industrial workers, and marriage migrants have taken leave of home communities, and forged new links to people and places. In the process, divisions have opened up between city and countryside, the old and the young, and people of different regions and ethnicity. Vietnamese mobilise existing connections of various kinds to bridge the gaps, but also find themselves unequally situated to build new relationships or take advantage of new opportunities. Social relationships once considered backward or obsolete are being re-evaluated as resources for development, and practices and places that were once deemed marginal are assuming new centrality.

This book explores the dynamic processes of connection and disconnection that are remaking Vietnam's social landscape. It features essays by scholars from Vietnam and abroad who draw on research conducted in diverse Vietnamese localities. The essays were first presented as papers at a Vietnam Update conference held at The Australian National University (ANU) in December 2014. This is an annual conference series that discusses a theme of contemporary relevance to Vietnam's socioeconomic development. The theme selected for the 2014 Vietnam Update was 'connection and disconnection'. Conference presenters engaged with topics such as social capital, development from below, socially inclusive growth, and the new subjectivities emerging in Vietnam's globalised, market-based society. The essays selected for inclusion in this book share a common research methodology and disciplinary approach. As ethnographic reflections on connection and disconnection, they offer a unique perspective on how Vietnamese in a great variety of circumstances relate to each other and redefine what it means to be Vietnamese.

The 2014 Vietnam Update conference was opened by ANU Chancellor Professor Gareth Evans. His informative speech reflected on changes in Vietnam and in Australia's relationship with Vietnam since 1990, when he presented a paper at the inaugural Vietnam Update in his capacity as Australian Minister for Foreign Affairs. Carl Thayer and Suiwah Leung provided an overview of recent political and economic developments to contextualise the thematic papers. Attending the 2014 Update were representatives of the Australian Department of Foreign Affairs, the Embassy of Vietnam, the US Embassy in Vietnam, and the Japanese development agency. Many Australian aid-funded PhD scholarship students attended the Update, along with numerous other academics and students. The participants also included representatives of commercial, non-government, religious and community organisations, and many individual Vietnamese-Australians. The audience members took an active part in discussions, and their feedback to the presenters has been incorporated into the chapters in this volume.

The 2014 Vietnam Update was hosted by ANU College of Asia and the Pacific. The organising committee comprised ANU scholars David Marr, Li Tana, Ben Kerkvliet, Sango Mahanty, Greg Fealy, Peter Chaudhry, Ha Viet Quan, and myself. They took responsibility for paper selection, program design, and the funding and running of the conference. A large share of the conference organising work was shouldered by administrative staff in the Department of Political and Social Change of ANU College of Asia and the Pacific. The organisers wish to thank, in particular, Kerrie Hogan, Kate Hulm, Allison Ley, Phạm Thu Thủy, Luke Hambly, Melissa Orr, Daniel Striegl, Beverly Williams, and Sean Downes They helped to ensure that the conference was well-attended, vibrant, friendly, and professionally run, as noted by many conference participants.

The Vietnam Update organisers would like to express our gratitude to the Australian Government Aid Program of the Department of Foreign Affairs for generously providing funding for the 2014 Vietnam Update. This support enabled us to fund the participation of a large number of paper presenters from Vietnam, along with other international specialists, and to help cover some of the costs of running the conference and publishing the results. Also making a significant financial contribution to the Update and the production of this book were the School of Culture, History and Language and ANU College of Asia and the Pacific. The series organisers are grateful to these sponsors for helping to disseminate this new research on Vietnam.

As editor of this book, I would like to thank the many individuals who contributed to its production. For their timely and constructive advice on the chapters, I thank the peer reviewers Philippe Le Failler, Ken Maclean, Erik Harms, Jean Michaud, Truong Huyen Chi, Keith Taylor, Kirin Narayan, David Chandler, Catherine Earl, Alexandra Winkels, Catherine Locke, Assa Doron, Martha Lincoln, Linh Khanh Nguyen, Oscar Salemink, Rupert Friederichsen, Oliver Tappe, John Marston, John Kleinen, Li Tana, Nir Avieli, and Margaret Bodemer. Diana Glazebrook did a magnificent job with the first round of copy-editing, and Duncan Beard provided prompt and professional assistance with editing and formatting the manuscript for publication. I thank the editorial board of the ANU Press Vietnam series for their support, encouragement, and critical advice in every stage of this book project. The board consists of Kim Huynh, Sango Mahanty, David Marr, Ben Kerkvliet, Li Tana, Judith Cameron, Nola Cooke, and Ashley Carruthers. Finally, my thanks go to Jim Fox for supporting the establishment of the Vietnam book series, and to Lorena Kanellopoulos, Sascha Villarosa, Emily Tinker, and all others at ANU Press for their help in bringing this book to fruition.

Philip Taylor
Canberra
December 2015

Introduction: An Overture to New Ethnographic Research on Connection and Disconnection in Vietnam

Philip Taylor

Connections are the source of life in Vietnam. The tangible and intangible ties that bind Vietnamese people to their families and compatriots are characteristically rich and are constitutive of self, community, and nation. In traditional Vietnam, the person was enmeshed in relations (*quan hệ*) of hierarchy and reciprocity that structured family life and the thicket of mutual exchanges that typified the traditional village. The Vietnamese polity has long drawn metaphorically on relations of this kind, as rulers have utilised idioms of kinship and debt to secure legitimacy, command loyalty, and promote social cohesion. History has been made by people who were able to inspire a following and call on the resources of their entourage to repel an enemy or found new settlements and alliances. Vietnamese from all walks of life have long cultivated social relationships to deal with the authorities, form martial unions, make a living, and gain promotion. As social certitudes have dissolved and been recast by the experience of revolution, war, and market-based global integration, one constant has been the role played by such relationships. As the nation has changed, connections have remained central to what it means to be Vietnamese.

Although it remains true to speak of the ubiquity of connections, it is important not to overlook the diversity and dynamism of social relationships in Vietnam. Ethnographic research reveals that the mode and intensity of social connections available to contemporary Vietnamese vary according to class, region, gender, and ethnicity.

Seen as 'social capital', connections are often viewed as a resource to be augmented for the benefit of self and society, however, it should be recalled that not all connections are equally efficacious or desirable, and some may come at a steep cost to the individual and society. Social disconnection, too, is a recurrent theme in Vietnamese life, be it in the form of death, demotion or exile, or disavowal of one's personal ties and background. Vietnamese frequently have sought social reclusion in pursuit of ends as varied as moral integrity, ritual potency, tranquillity, and status. When existing relations are severed deliberately or unavoidably in times of life transition or social upheaval, people find themselves drawn by circumstances into new connections and in that moment new social intimacies and identities are born.

The theme of disconnection has been central in Vietnamese history. Repeatedly, Vietnamese have found themselves divided or uprooted in times of war, political separation, or societal crisis. The very idea of what it has meant to be Vietnamese has been repeatedly reset in moments of historical rupture: when the indigenous peoples of the Red River plain came under Chinese rule around two millennia ago; when Vietnamese formed their own polity after living for 10 centuries as Chinese imperial subjects; when peoples from disparate cultural and historical traditions were incorporated into Vietnamese social space; and when the nation was reborn successively in encounters with colonial, neo-colonial, socialist, and market-based orders. The historian Keith Taylor has proposed that Vietnamese identity be regarded as fundamentally discontinuous: comprised of numerous distinct orientations that have arisen at different conjunctures in time and space (K. Taylor 1998, 2013). Portrayals such as this have been drawn in rebuttal of a nationalist past that assigns Vietnam with a singular, unified, and continuous history. Yet Vietnamese historians also have emphasised discontinuity, for instance by downplaying the country's debts to China or stressing division, conflict or contradiction as themes in the country's history.

Perhaps the most commonly debated instance of disconnection in contemporary Vietnam is the situation of Vietnam's numerous 'national minorities' (*dân tộc thiểu số*), many of whom are said to have had, until recently, at best tenuous connections to the lowland state. These peoples are often characterised as suffering disproportionately from poverty, isolation, social exclusion, and cultural deprivation, while at the same time being subject to the intrusive and paternalist development policies of the ethnic majority–dominated central state. However, relatively little is known about whether those deemed as minorities regard themselves as marginal, or how they might turn participation in the nation-state to their own advantage. More research is required to determine to what extent the intensive state-building activities in the periphery have their origins in the national capital or arise out of the desires and relations of residents of the periphery themselves. Also in need of further investigation is whether nation-building initiatives integrate, or alternatively parochialise, their intended beneficiaries, and what vernacular development paths have been forged by the people inhabiting Vietnam's multifaceted and continuously re-imagined internal frontiers.

This volume offers a series of ethnographic explorations into the themes of connection and disconnection in contemporary Vietnam. The essays provide detailed accounts of connecting and disconnecting that put these processes into context, show how they are experienced by social actors and reveal their consequences and meanings. The cases demonstrate that the nature and significance of social connections are diverse with regards to region, class, gender, and ethnicity. The approach adopted is practice-oriented in that it does not assume these relations are governed by universal rationality or inalterable cultural templates, but that they are imbued with explicit and tacit meanings made consequential through action and in context. The accounts emphasise agency and dynamism in showing how connections are forged and broken by actors, without implying that all people enjoy equal capacity in this regard or that connections are a panacea that can enable the individual to overcome the constraints of circumstance. The essays investigate the diverse attempts by state authorities to prescribe and regulate the ways citizens connect and disconnect; however, they also show that state intentions are not always realised. To understand how and why Vietnamese citizens connect with each other, and the world around them, requires close investigation of local and personal histories, conditions, and meanings.

This opening essay frames the contributions with a review of research on the numerous realms of life in Vietnam that have been shaped by connection and disconnection. It then broaches the themes addressed in the first four chapters in this volume, which investigate disparity and disconnection in the lives of contemporary Vietnamese of the lowlands. Moving next to the relationship of ethnic minorities to the Vietnamese national project, it outlines the research agenda taken up by four of the contributors who explore agency and diversity in the ways minority populations engage the state. In a concluding section, which reflects on the volume's final two chapters, it examines the profound realignments in people's orientation to heritage, history, and place that are consequent on Vietnam's integration into the international order.

Into a Vietnamese Landscape of Social Connection

Both connection and disconnection have been prominent topics in the study of Vietnamese society and history. Nevertheless, rarely has the attempt been made to trace in a systematic manner how such processes interact in diverse arenas of life in Vietnam. This review of the scholarship in select disciplines examines the significance of connections and their absence in a variety of contexts, endeavours, and events. I commence by exploring the interplay of connection and disconnection in the formation of modern Vietnam's social and political landscape.

The density of the social networks that characterise the nucleated villages of northern Vietnam is well documented (Gourou 1936; Toan Ánh 1968; Nguyen Tu Chi 1980; Jamieson 1995:28–36). Several scholars consider the cohesion fostered by this mode of social organisation to have been a resource enabling the flourishing of the Vietnamese people. For instance, cooperation in rice production and collective defence was a factor in the Vietnamese polity's demographic strength and its ability to expand into new lands at the expense of more loosely structured Southeast Asian neighbours (Gourou 1936:133; Lieberman 2003:393). At the same time, the relative autonomy of villages — in relation to the court and to each other — is said to have given the Vietnamese social system resilience in times of crisis (McAlister and Mus 1970; Woodside 1976). As Hy Van Luong has observed, indigenous models of social relatedness offered formidable resources in dealing with the power inequalities of colonialism and capitalism. Political leaders were able to draw on the gender and age hierarchies and the insider/outsider distinction characteristic of Red River Delta villages to mobilise the population against enemies, while sentiments of trust and mutual obligation of the kind generated in village gift exchanges helped cement cooperation in arduous struggles. Such cultural resources were crucial to the mobilisation of villages in revolutionary action in the French colonial period and again in anti-corruption protests in the 1990s. Since the *đổi mới* reforms of the 1980s, kin connections have been used as a resource for accumulating economic resources (Luong 2003, 2005, 2010).

Nevertheless, the very tightness of these social relationships and their hierarchical and autarchic nature also posed threats to the construction of a national society founded on socialist egalitarian principles. Much of the work of socialist nation-building under the Democratic Republic of Vietnam (1954–76) was dedicated to undermining traditional modes of relatedness and reattaching individuals to the nation and ideals of modern socialist citizenship. State cultural authorities intervened in social and ritual life in northern Vietnam to simplify life cycle rituals; curtail extravagance in feasting and gift exchanges; undercut deference to local landlords and village elites; and prescribe appropriately modern, civilised, and cultured modes of living (Kleinen 1999; Malarney 2002; Luong 2010). In tandem, the Democratic Republic of Vietnam state promoted egalitarian gender roles and marriage practices while also criticising romantic and individualist ideals of personhood that had become prevalent among the urban middle class since the late colonial period (Pham Van Bich 1999; Ninh 2002; Werner and Bélanger 2002; Phinney 2008). Intriguingly, the receding of the socialist state from many aspects of social life since the late 1980s has been accompanied by the revival of traditional life cycle rituals, marriage practices, gift exchanges, patrilineages, and village festivals. However, the simplified, modest, and egalitarian aspects of these revived practices show that the period of socialist reforms did leave some mark on northern Vietnamese cultural life (Luong 2003; Malarney 2003).

The fabric of society in southern Vietnam, by contrast, is renowned for being more loosely woven, with a higher preponderance of what the sociologist Mark Granovetter (1973) calls 'weak ties', as well as being more open, mobile, urbanised, and globally interconnected (Hickey 1964; Rambo 1973; P. Taylor 2001; Biggs 2010; Luong 2010; Harms 2011). From early in the history of Vietnamese colonisation, this new frontier was associated with a regionally distinctive social structure and governance style that was personalistic, egalitarian, and informal (Sơn Nam 1997; Li 1998; K. Taylor 1998; Choi Byung Wook 2004; Dutton 2006). In the French colonial period, this looseness, openness, and mobility was associated with the rapid development of high levels of land concentration, social inequality, itinerancy, and social banditry (Brocheux 1995; Engelbert 2007; Biggs 2010:23–125). Cultural and societal changes in the colonial and postcolonial periods were also highly sensitive to global currents and trends (Ho Tai 1992; Brocheux 1995; Jamieson 1995; Do Thien 2003; Peycam 2012). With the dismantling of socialist command and control policies in the late 1980s, the south quickly gained national predominance in commodity production, trade, and business, and it continues to be associated with high levels of cultural innovation, social differentiation, and mobility.

However, southern Vietnam is also home to several important folk movements that have reorganised society along communitarian lines. Markedly localist and religious in inspiration, and coalescing around charismatic authorities, these movements have been seen as a compensatory response to the anomie and chaos of the southern frontier and the inequalities engendered under colonialism (Wolf 1969; McAlister and Mus 1970). Each of these particularist groupings forged a unique response to the challenges of frontier society. The Hòa Hảo Buddhists (who are also inspired by Confucianism) emphasised charity over ritual ostentation; their prophet mocked people's reliance on the spirits for patronage, and promoted a conception of the person as indebted for his or her existence to the ancestors, nation, Buddha, and humanity (Ho Tai 1983). The Cao Đài synthesised numerous strands of religious and philosophical learning into a grand and eclectic canon, and assembled a formal pantheon of spirit teachers to whom believers had access via their mediums (Hoskins 2015). The Cham Muslims reorganised life around mosques that served as hubs for a markedly cosmopolitan community, in which local authority and prestige stemmed from prowess in long-distance trade and religious travel (P. Taylor 2007a). Khmer society in parts of the Mekong Delta assumed the form of a Khmer cultural archipelago in a broader Vietnamese milieu, with each Buddhist temple operating as a civilising centre and miniature polity unto itself and offering its affiliated lay community a great variety of services (P. Taylor 2014).

The communist-led revolution represented a different response to the challenge of colonialism, one in which the theme of disconnection is clearly evident. Historians of the revolution trace its inception to the assault on tradition and the embrace of the new that characterised Vietnam's nationalist ferment in the first decades of the twentieth century (Marr 1981; McHale 2004). Some scholars have drawn attention to the extraordinary youth of the leaders of the revolution whose social radicalism was more in tune with global modernist currents than with the hierarchical and conservative mores of their parents. This radical orientation was in turn replaced by an expectation that revolutionaries conform to the discipline of a party whose policies were aligned with strategic shifts in the international communist movement (Ho Tai 1992, 2010). However, the unity on display in the proclamation of independence from France in 1945 was superficial, for the party itself was divided, and struggles within the party over the correct revolutionary path persisted over subsequent decades (Brocheux 1995; Marr 1997, 2013). More significantly, the party's rise to power alienated a plethora of non-communist nationalist groups and hardened the resolve of many Vietnamese to fight against it (Guillemot 2010; Chapman 2013).

Although fought in the name of national unity, Vietnam's wars were a time of grievous division between Vietnamese of different backgrounds and political allegiances. The character of the wars as a civil conflict was already evident in the First Indochinese War (1945–54), which pitted people of different political, ethnic, religious, social, and regional affiliations against each other (Le Failler 2011; Lentz 2011; Keith 2012:213–241; Chapman 2013; McHale 2013). Two Vietnamese states — the north and the south — emerged out of this war, with different social and political systems, and alliances to rival international power blocs (Fall 1967; Jamieson 1995). Divisions internal to each of these states also were on display during the long war they fought with each other from the late 1950s to the mid-1970s. Such contestation was particularly tumultuous in the south of the country, where the 'Vietnam War' exacerbated, and in turn was shaped by, numerous conflicts based on religious, ethnic, class, generational, regional, and urban–rural divisions (Hickey 1993; Topmiller 2006; Hunt 2008; Miller 2013). Sadly, the curse of conflict continued to afflict Vietnam as it was drawn almost immediately into another decade-long war with neighbouring Cambodia and China, countries with which Vietnam's socialist leaders previously had entertained warm and supportive fraternal relations (Nguyen-Vo Thu-Huong 1992; Goscha 2006).

Nevertheless, social connections featured prominently in Vietnam's wars. The trust, loyalty, and cohesion born out of shared suffering and confinement in colonial prisons and long residence in remote guerrilla bases were decisive to the ability of Vietnam's communist leaders to survive and coordinate a nationwide resistance in a context of intense surveillance and repression (Zinoman 2001; Nguyen T. Lien-Hang 2012:17–47). Việt Minh agents cultivated a network of civilian supporters in the cities who supplied the rural-based resistance with goods and information (Goscha 2013). The communists' major opponent in the south, President Ngô Đình Diệm, was often accused of being inflexible and non-accommodating towards the religious, ethnic, and localist affiliations that structured society in this region. Nevertheless, he put siblings and other family members in key government positions and made use of his Catholic connections to mobilise support and advance his political interests (Miller 2013:41–53). At the grassroots level, Heonik Kwon describes how in Central Vietnam there was more to the experience of war than that of being helpless victims caught in an arbitrary clash between impersonal and alien forces. Even in the region that witnessed some of the Vietnam War's most brutal battles, war was waged and its disastrous effects were mitigated against by virtue of peoples' membership of a fine meshwork of numerous small interlocking social networks (Kwon 2008:69–71).

Many of the policy shifts that occurred in the post-war period were made possible owing to social connections. For instance, the liberal market reforms announced in the mid-1980s have been analysed as a response to a combination of economic crisis, ideological conversion/confusion, and bottom-up resistance (Fforde and de Vylder 1996; P. Taylor 2001; Kerkvliet 2005). However, several scholars also emphasise the role played by senior party leaders with long-standing ties to local areas and authorities who encouraged and protected a variety of 'spontaneous' economic activities that contravened official policy. These leaders' ties to local authorities and other party leaders at the national level were instrumental in getting these local initiatives endorsed as formal policy (Dang Phong 2004; Rama and Vo Van Kiet 2008). Connections also facilitated reform in the field of cultural policy. In a vivid illustration of networking politics in Vietnam, Thaveeporn

Vasavakul shows how networking between state officials, researchers, popular organisations, mediums, and local followers was critical to the official rehabilitation of the mediumistic cult of the Holy Mothers in the 1990s and early 2000s in northern Vietnam (Vasavakul 2003:35–42).

In his provocative analysis of Vietnam's political system, Martin Gainsborough sheds light on the centrality of social connections to state power and policy. Senior state officials stand at the apex of patronage networks. Individuals who win high office are put upon to channel the spoils of office such as licences, contracts, exemptions, and investment to their network members, to the exclusion of others, and are reciprocated with loyalty, money, and shares, among other gifts (Gainsborough 2010:146–147). Gainsborough acutely observes that patronage shapes the major political event in Vietnam: the five-yearly party congress. The significant policy shifts that are often announced in these closely followed events are less the outcome of experimental policy development, ideological struggles between factions, or the rise and fall of sectoral, regional or generational interests, but rather are centrally the result of struggles between the influential members of patronage networks. The formulation of policy at such events consists less of adherence to ideology or principles than the jockeying for position among individuals who, if successful, will be able to share the spoils of office with his or her network of clients (Gainsborough 2010:135–155).

In an era of market socialism, connections nourish economic life. Nguyen-Vo Thu-Huong provides a cogent ethnographic analysis of post-socialist business practices, which she describes arrestingly as the 'hooking economy'. In an economy characterised by uncertainty, the privileging of state enterprises, informational deficits and regulatory laxity, private entrepreneurs gain resources and contracts by establishing personal relations of patronage with state and quasi-state economic managers. Many deals are struck in entertainment venues, including those that offer a variety of prostitution services. The sex industry thus features both as a metaphor and the context for the practices of 'hooking', which are integral to post-socialist business (Nguyen-Vo Thu-Huong 2008:3–24).[1] Gainsborough too has reported on the links between Hồ Chí Minh City entrepreneurs and local

1   Kimberly Hoang illustrated similar processes in her ethnographic study of Hồ Chí Minh City's night life (2015).

administrative authorities. By establishing bonds with highly placed officials, with whom the proceeds of business are shared, companies can negotiate opaque and treacherous legal terrain with reduced risk of political or legal repercussions, while making life difficult for their competitors, who the authorities might move against (Gainsborough 2010:38–39).[2]

Although connections mitigate risk, they may also in themselves pose a threat to security and social cohesion. In the early 2000s, exposure of the octopus-like network built by the gang boss Năm Cam brought to light the collusive relationships that existed between criminal syndicates and highly placed officials and powerful departments such as the police (Gainsborough 2010:48–49). Researchers have exposed the corrupt relationships between timber traders and state authorities that facilitate the illegal timber trade across the Lao–Vietnam border (To Xuan Phuc et al. 2014). Special interest groups (*nhóm lợi ích*) linked to powerful officials also highlight disparities between rich and poor. As Bill Hayton observes, businesses and individuals strive to put themselves under the umbrella (*ô dù*) of protection provided by connections to high-ranking state and party leaders. The cultivation of such relationships can confer immunity from prosecution and leeway in a complex and competitive business landscape, along with specific benefits such as jobs, promotions, and scholarships. Meanwhile, people without an umbrella are extremely vulnerable to harassment and prosecution. These patronage practices have fostered a small and privileged elite who owe their fortune to birth, marriage, and fortuitous connections. Their wealth and privilege in a country where substantive poverty is still widespread jars uncomfortably with the socialist rhetoric coming from the country's leaders who stand at the apex of the elite (Hayton 2010:22–25).

---

2   In their study of land investment in rural Vietnam, Thomas Markussen and Finn Tarp infer that people who have relatives in the government are able to draw upon those kin links to secure tenure over land and avoid the expropriation of their land by the state. Having such favourable connections to the authorities, they contend, gives people the confidence needed to make investments in their land (Markussen and Tarp 2014).

The Dynamics of Disconnection and Reconnection

Ethnographic studies of connection from below show that social relationships provide a means by which Vietnamese people can moderate the excesses and iniquities of market-driven development. In his study of community environmental regulation, Dara O'Rourke shows that linkages within local communities and between community activists and the authorities are beneficial in changing the behaviour of serious environmental polluters (O'Rourke 2004:68). Linkages to extra-local actors such as the media enable community demands to reach higher level authorities.[3] Social ties between a firm and its workers, consumers, suppliers, or neighbours influence the way it responds to complaints about pollution. Social relationships are also at the heart of regulation, and agencies with strong linkages to the community are successful in implementing state policies. Nevertheless, O'Rourke warns that social relationships between factory managers and authorities, or between individuals in state agencies, can also enable environmental polluters and decrease the responsiveness of authorities to community demands (O'Rourke 2004:224–227).

People in socially precarious circumstances may intensify relations of mutuality to reduce the risks of market-based society and fill the gaps left by the shrinkage of the once omnipresent state. In her research in rural Hà Tĩnh, Pam McElwee observed that poor farmers experienced hardship and uncertainty as a result of their production of rice and other goods for global markets. In response, they partook of a moral economy which was similar to that described by James Scott (1977) in his study of Mekong Delta peasants under French colonialism (McElwee 2007). People at the margins of subsistence in Hà Tĩnh spread risk by exchange relations with each other and with wealthier community members, upon whom they exerted moral pressure to distribute their wealth, effectively enforcing a social price on private accumulation. The farmers also criticised the heartlessness and lack of social responsiveness of officials who made their lives,

---

3   Andrew Wells-Dang's study of networked civil society politics in Vietnam similarly reveals that relationships between environmental activists, the press, scientists, retired officials, local residents, and the authorities have been key to efficacy in environmental activism (Wells-Dang 2012).

and that of their families, difficult with overbearing enforcement of regulations. In protesting against official indifference and malpractice, poor farmers in the 1990s and 2000s were influenced by norms of fairness and sufficiency (McElwee 2007). Nguyen Van Suu (2007), Ben Kerkvliet (2014) and John Gillespie (2014) similarly have noted that protests against corruption and land confiscations frequently have been motivated by these kinds of moral economy concerns.

Faced by the inadequacy of officially prescribed social and cultural relationships, numerous communities in Vietnam make recourse to a variety of vernacular translocal connections. Such decentred networks are particularly evident among members of ethnic minority groups whose integration into the national community has not always been equitable and harmonious. The transnational networks of minority actors include commodity chain networks maintained by Hmong people in the northwest of the country with China (Turner, Bonnin, and Michaud 2015), transnational business and cultural associations of the ethnic Chinese in urban areas (Yu 2006), and the cross-border networks mobilised by Cham Muslims in Vietnam's southwest for work and religious travel in Malaysia (Tran 2016). Other translocal linkages are controversial or divisive, such as the mass conversion to evangelical Christianity of minority groups like the Hmong (Ngo 2015), the rejection among some groups of official ethnic labels (Nguyen Van Thang 2007), or the appeals made by diasporic actors for ethno-nationalist solidarity among Central Highlanders (Salemink 2006:39–42). As discussed by Oscar Salemink in his chapter in this book, these decentred forms of ethnic reconnection create dilemmas for the government which, in order to reassert authority over its minority citizens, has begun to backtrack on its modernist reform agenda and rehabilitate identities and practices that were once criticised as backward, elitist, and autarchic.

In Vietnam, social relationships are never merely received or static but are dynamic and constantly being actively managed. For the women who dominate Vietnam's marketing sector, success in livelihoods comes from proficiency in the arts of self-representation. Ann Marie Leshkowich shows that much of the work done by traders in Bến Thành market, as they represent themselves to customers, their peers, and market regulators, consists of the agentive enactment of social identities. Market women often essentialise themselves, claiming to be — as women — naturally adept at their trade; construing themselves as struggling working class; distancing themselves from the state; or claiming ties of kinship with their customers and paid workers. However, rather than treat this self-essentialism as simply a strategy to grasp advantage as opportunities arise, Leshkowich regards it as a form of historically constituted political and economic subjectivity. She shows that their profession or trade has been alternatively stigmatised, romanticised, dismissed, and celebrated in shifting state policies that have created uncertainty, anxiety, and risk. By essentialising themselves as women, as traditional, as kin, or as workers, the traders of Bến Thành make themselves legible within the discourses employed in the regulation of their behaviour. Through such enactments, they are able to experience control, predictability, and meaning in their profession and lives (Leshkowich 2014).

The practices of performative sociality exemplified by market traders are among the variety of practices by which Vietnamese have been shown to mould and shift their social relationships. Anthropologists and linguists have demonstrated how Vietnamese gender and age hierarchies, along with relations of parity and sameness, are reproduced and situationally modified through modes of address and self-reference, as well as in discipline and at play (Luong 1990; Rydstrøm 2003; Sidnell and Shohet 2013). In his ethnography of culinary practices in the town of Hội An, Nir Avieli shows how dishes consumed at a variety of meals communicate subtle messages about the character and significance of social relationships. Intriguingly, his study reveals that commensality may not only create kinship and generate bonds, it may also divide and distinguish (Avieli 2012). Vu Hong Phong demonstrates how, through alcohol consumption, men in a multiethnic frontier context bond with their male peers (Vu Hong Phong 2008:148–149). Analysing relations between hostesses and their clients in the bars of Hồ Chí Minh City's sex industry, Kimberly Hoang describes how performances of masculinity and femininity in such sites affirm and contest global racial and class hierarchies (Hoang 2015). Markus Schlecker shows how, by returning to their home villages to take part in feasts and festive occasions, people in Hà Nội materialise a new post-socialist orientation to the 'ancestral village' as a place of traditional relatedness and belonging (Schlecker 2005).

Several studies explore the active limiting of one's sphere of relatedness. In the context of middle-class Hà Nội, Alexander Soucy (2014) describes the management and pruning of social relations that takes place during the issuing of wedding invitations. Catherine Earl shows how, through work, leisure, consumption, and marriage choices, women in Hò Chí Minh City secure urban middle-class membership and distinguish themselves from their lower-status compatriots (Earl 2014).[4] Erik Harms examines the socially destructive urban redevelopment practices that demolish and scatter existing residential communities, and replace them with exclusive, high-class enclaves that promise to separate their new residents from the undistinguished urban masses (Harms 2012, 2014). Perhaps the most disturbing practices of social truncation take place in reproductive health clinics, where technologies such as ultrasound are routinely used to detect foetal abnormalities and unwanted female gender in foetuses. Subsequently, abortions are commonly prescribed and undertaken, sometimes illicitly, to secure desired reproductive outcomes and interdict the formation of socially undesirable persons and relationships (Bélanger and Khuat Thi Hai Oanh 2009; Gammeltoft 2014).[5]

The dynamics of social disconnection and reconnection are especially pronounced in the experience of migration. Vietnamese have been subject to many varieties of coerced migration, be they conflict-induced refugee movements, de-urbanisation campaigns, official programs to open new economic zones in remote border areas, or environmental refugee flows (Hardy 2003). Migrants who have moved voluntarily or under compulsion have often found themselves transplanted into an unfamiliar or unpleasant social setting where they experience tense and brittle relations with their new neighbours (McElwee 2008; Hansen 2009). In other cases, they may feel socially isolated and excluded from the opportunities for connection or advancement in their new social environment (Huong 2004; Nguyen Minh 2015). In such cases, social connections play a key role in enabling movement and re-emplacement. Research on migration in Vietnam has demonstrated the value of family and homeland networks in facilitating chain migration to new economic frontiers and urban spaces (Carruthers and Dang 2012; Winkels 2012), nurturing children who have been left behind (Locke et al. 2012), and gaining empowerment in the cities (Karis 2013).

---

4   For a collection of insightful essays on practices of middle-class distinction in contemporary Vietnam, see Van-Nguyen Marshall, Drummond and Bélanger (2011).
5   A detailed account of sex-selective abortion is provided in Tran Thi Minh Hang (2011).

The work of reconnection is a key theme in the Vietnamese diaspora's relationship with the homeland. Formed largely out of processes of disconnection and rupture, the large community of Vietnam-origin people who live overseas has been visiting home and sending remittances for at least three decades (Small 2012; Schwenkel 2014). Transnational flows of cultural and entertainment content, via DVDs, television, internet, and social media, connect the diaspora with the old country, although in both contexts the reception of these influences is met with controversy and surveillance (Carruthers 2008; Valverde 2012). Return gifts of money express obligation and relatedness; however, the gifts also create social distance within transnational families (Nguyen-Akbar 2014). Such gifts court the risk of being seen as insufficient or, alternatively, excessive, having the capacity to humiliate and wound both the recipient and giver alike (Thai 2014). The inflow of foreign currency also can express counter-cultural forms of non-official relatedness that transcend nation-state boundaries and the borders between the living and the dead. Allison Truitt shows how remittances in US dollars express the debt of overseas Vietnamese to their relatives in Vietnam and how in turn the living repay their debt to the ancestors through counterfeit versions of the same currency (Truitt 2013:83–103).

Connections to the spirit world are enacted in dynamic and multiform ways, and occupy a prominent place in Vietnam's post-revolutionary social landscape (Malarney 2003; P. Taylor 2007b). Through their offerings to the ancestors and the potent spirits of the land, Vietnamese repay their debts to the proximate yet otherworldly beings who guarantee security, enforce morality, and make life possible (P. Taylor 2004; Pham Quynh Phuong 2009; Jellema 2007). The sanctified gifts that worshippers bring back home from pagodas and shrines spiritually nourish their families and materialise the relations of mutual care that bind the spirits to the living (Endres 2011; Soucy 2012). By being inducted as a spirit medium, people who are marginalised, ill, socially anomalous, or dogged by misfortune may secure healing and social reintegration as the follower of a master or a child of the spirits (Fjelstad and Hien 2006; Norton 2009; Salemink 2010). The links maintained with the spirit world are multilateral and mutually generative: with offerings, worshippers might rehabilitate a ghost as an ancestor and thereby transform their own social identity (Kwon 2008; Marouda 2014); via afflictions visited upon their kin, a war martyr might signal their need to be recovered from the oblivion of national history (Malarney 2001; Gustafsson 2009). The ties between spirits and their earthly Vietnamese adepts today span the globe, with both mediums and the religions that institutionalise interactions with the spirits found in the many locations around the world where Vietnamese people have made a home (Fjelstad and Hien 2011; Hoskins 2015).

A final illustration of the generative power of connections highlights the role of social networks in assembling the knowledge that Vietnamese have about themselves and their own society. Many of Vietnam's leading intellectuals and academics belong to lineages of intellectuals. Despite the socialist emphasis on mass education and the production of expertise, both kinship and kin-like relationships have been essential in nurturing intellectual capacities and dispositions in the face of criticisms about elitism and the levelling tendencies of socialist academic culture (Bayly 2007). In contemporary Vietnam, Eren Zink found that the academic field is constituted out of connections. Institutes and departments can be filled with people from the same kinship network or birthplace, and a tangle of personal relationships cross-cut institutional and national boundaries. People in one's network positioned in departments and ministries can enable an institute to secure project funding or access sensitive information that gives cogency to an analysis (Zink 2013:157–171). Scholars who lack or fail to nurture such ties may find their careers thwarted, irrespective of their talent and hard work. The work of scientific production relies crucially on the cultivation of relationships, and the history of the emergence of a new idea is very much the story of the connections activated and the debts incurred in the process of its assembly and articulation as new knowledge.

Making Connections and Disconnections

This review of scholarship demonstrates that connections are a pervasive and influential dimension of Vietnamese life. Important insights into Vietnamese politics, society, and culture come from research that has carefully traced the social linkages and disconnects that have shaped events in these domains. The essays in this volume take these findings as a point of departure as they explore issues that call out for more rigorous scholarly treatment, and uncover new stories about connection and disconnection.

One of the most fundamental questions about social connections is the degree to which these resources are equally available and useful to people from different social backgrounds. Hy Van Luong observes in his contribution that Vietnamese from all walks of life consider social connections to be a reliable way to resolve all manner of daily problems, ranging from medical care for a family member to credit for business expansion. However, he also shows that the extent to which contemporary rural Vietnamese have recourse to social capital varies considerably in relation to their economic status and their regional location. His study sheds light on the inequitable distribution of a set of social resources whose subtlety and significance have previously not been adequately described by researchers attempting to measure inequality in Vietnam. While it may be true that gifts have the power to bind people together, Luong reminds us that not everyone has the same capacity to give gifts.

Hy Van Luong's chapter draws upon fieldwork data from two villages — one located in the Red River Delta and the other in the Mekong Delta — which was collected in 2005–06 and 2012–14. It shows that the social relationships upon which people rely are sustained and strengthened by meals, drinks, gifts, and favour exchanges. As incomes rise, many households and individuals spend more on these gifts and exchanges to sustain and expand their social capital. However, he finds that the poor are much less capable of doing so than the rich and the powerful, especially considering that the monetary value of 'standard' gifts has increased significantly at life cycle ceremonies. He also identifies variation between the two rural regions. Northern Vietnamese villagers have strengthened various forms of associational ties, complete with their life cycle ceremony gift obligations, to a greater extent than their southern counterparts. The rich evidence martialled in this chapter demonstrates that although social connections may matter to all Vietnamese, the quantity and quality of connections to which people have access, the benefits they bring, and the costs imposed in the effort to maintain them, are not evenly distributed. Paradoxically, Vietnamese of different regions and classes are divided by social connections in a way that is both shaped by and continues to shape profound differences in their social circumstances and cultural identities.

The capacity of gifts to sustain relationships between people who have been separated spatially and by class is the focus of the chapter by Nguyen Thi Thanh Binh. It focuses on the case of a successful business migrant who returned to her Red River Delta village from the south of Vietnam after a long absence. Like many Vietnamese return migrants, her initial intention was to make bequests to her family and ancestors, however, her giving soon also extended to non-kin, such as the village poor, and sponsoring communal feasts and the refurbishment of communal buildings. Her actions earned her accolades from the villagers for her generosity of spirit, and this adulation exerted moral pressure upon her to give more and more. The extraordinary and unexpected dynamics that led her to accelerate her rate of giving not only drained her financially, they also aroused intense debates about her motives and background. Assessments of her character ranged from views of her blessed fate and Buddha-like qualities to dismissive and disparaging comments about her capability, personality, and family morality. Ultimately, the tensions and ill feelings unleashed by her charitable actions caused this return migrant to rethink her plans to re-establish herself in her native village.

This story of a failed return offers a timely treatment of the dislocating experiences of migration. Told from the perspective of a returned migrant, it shows how nostalgia for the homeland arising out of the disappointments of migration can precipitate the desire to return and reconnect. When acted upon, however, such sentiments can lead to disenchantment, serving instead to underline the change in subjectivities brought about in the experience of migration, as well as the gulf in moral expectations between rural and urban localities. Seen from the perspective of the villagers who hosted her return, this case illustrates the value of migrants to marginal rural communities both as a link to new worlds and opportunities, and as a source of remittances and models for social reinvigoration. At the same time, it reveals how the joyful anticipation of attending a homecoming may easily deteriorate into dissension and mutual mistrust, showing how the gap in status and experience that divides migrants and their home villages is not easily bridged by acts of good will or by sentiments of belonging to a common ancestral homeland.

The chapter by Nguyen Khanh Linh provides a graphic illustration of how divisive social connections can be. She studied a rural locality near Hải Phòng City that is distinctive for its very high rate of transnational marriages. Women from the fishing commune of Hải Thành enter into more marriages with foreigners than any other locality in Vietnam, many of them marrying men from wealthier rural localities in China and Korea. At the same time, a great number of the women who marry into Hải Thành come from other generally poorer rural localities in Vietnam, in a sense 'replacing' the local women who have married out. Significant realignments in social status and subjectivity are occurring among the women of Hải Thành owing to their involvement in these very different marital alliance networks which connect them to East Asia and elsewhere in Vietnam.

As Nguyen Khanh Linh's chapter reveals, the flows of female marriage migrants into and out of Hải Thành make it a remarkable node in a vast hypergamous chain that links numerous far-flung rural localities in Vietnam and overseas. However, just as the passage of women into and out of Hải Thành makes visible stark differences between rich and poor rural localities, it also brings about yawning gaps between the women themselves. The study examines the marked difference in class and status between the out-marrying and in-marrying women. These distinctions are marked on the bodies of the two classes of women and are interpreted in local discourses as innate differences of race, ethnicity, and morality. The sharpening and essentialising of distinctions between women and between ruralities that occurs as a result of these translocal marital alliances offers a sobering example of how connections can accentuate inequalities in extreme and diverse ways.

Yen Le's chapter ventures into the little-known world of leprosy sufferers in Vietnam, where it uncovers valuable insights into the power of disconnection. Drawing on the author's ethnographic fieldwork in Quy Hòa, a segregated village for leprosy-afflicted people in South Central Vietnam, the chapter tells the villagers' stories about social exile and reintegration. It traces the cases of elderly villagers who contracted leprosy between the 1940s and the 1980s, showing how the stigma provoked by a leprosy diagnosis and the disability caused by the disease brought about a form of social death and induced them to seek refuge in this isolated settlement for leprosy sufferers. Shifting to the ethnographic present of 2011, it elucidates why 'sameness' is such a salient discourse in the village and how, as a defining characteristic of the community, it has reconfigured the villagers' lived reality of leprosy. The notion of 'sameness' determines boundaries between leprosy-affected residents and 'healthy' people, and between 'inside here' and 'out in life'. It reveals a strong sense of connection shared among community members based on perceived commonality and equality on the one hand, and, on the other, disconnection from the outside world engendered by persistent leprosy stigma and sufferers' self-stigmatisation.

Through examining the ontologies of leprosy sufferers' connections and disconnections, Yen Le sheds light on the construct of leprosy and the lived reality of people affected by the disease in contemporary Vietnam. In doing so, her chapter also seeks to answer why exclusive communities for people with leprosy still exist long after leprosy has been declared medically curable, and when outpatient treatment has replaced segregated institutional care as the preferred public health approach to treatment. Her chapter shows that while the medical rationale for segregation no longer exists, the existential problems leprosy sufferers continue to endure provide justification for their continuing attachment to segregated communities such as Quy Hòa.

Debating Disconnection in Vietnam's Minority Worlds

As noted in the preceding discussion, the ultimate symbols of disconnection in present-day Vietnam are the minority nationalities. Much of the international development literature on Vietnam focuses on the socioeconomic gap between the majority Kinh and ethnic minority groups. Studies seek out the drivers of the 'ethnic gap', which are believed to include factors such as remoteness, lack of connectivity, poor land and water quality, low schooling, weak market access, and poor governance (Imai and Gaiha 2007; Baulch et al. 2010). The attention of policymakers is fixed on the cultural traits, language deficits, and customary practices and beliefs that are said to keep people poor and hold them back. Stereotypes proliferate in popular discourses about minority people's backwardness and insularity, and their lack of awareness of what it takes to prosper in the modern world. The incapable and needful minority other is very much the central figure of the present-day era of high development in the national periphery. Such a figure not only functions as a pretext for development but may indeed have been produced by it.

In marked contrast, many anthropologists hold to the view that Vietnam's minority others suffer from an excess of connection to the state project. It is not difficult to find critiques of the harm done by state development policies, which are deemed to be utopian, arbitrary, inflexible, paternalist, and all-encompassing. Scholars who adhere to the view that redemptive agency comes from below, or from the periphery, find signs of resilience in activities that are resistant, evasive, transcendent, or resourcefully recombinant; in short, inspired by a logic of disconnection from the state.[6] In the terms coined by James Scott, such tactics consist of 'the art of not being governed' (Scott 2009). A logical implication of this perspective is that the only scope available to ethnicised actors to remain true to themselves exists beyond the realms of what the state has set in train for them as its subjects (for a critical discussion, see Salemink 2015). Such an interpretation would disqualify the state itself as an arena in which minority actors might exert authentic agency. This may be a major oversight given that the state is such a significant presence in the lives of its minority citizens and has shaped the agenda for continuity and change in their traditional homelands for well over a half century in most localities.

Four essays in this volume show how the state may serve as a vehicle for minority self-assertion, each in unique ways. The chapter by Nguyen Thu Huong examines the dynamics of political disconnection among the minority peoples of Vietnam's Central Highlands. Her research reveals that the Bahnar, among other groups in Kon Tum Province, are under-represented in state employment and service provision positions. Relative to the Kinh, most of whom are migrants, the indigenous people of this highlands province appear to suffer from a low level of inclusion in state structures and lack influence in political decision-making. In part, such inequalities reflect discrepancies in social and cultural capital. They also give expression to disparities in political capital, which are rooted in differential war experiences. However, Nguyen Thu Huong proposes that an alternative explanation for this situation is that the highlanders may be disinclined to take office. She illustrates this proposition with comments by Bahnar

---

6   Jean Michaud's notion of 'Hmong infrapolitics' forcefully articulates this perspective (Michaud 2012). These themes also are apparent in many of the essays in the book edited by Philip Taylor, *Minorities at Large*, as well as in an article by the same on vernacular rural development (P. Taylor 2011, 2007c).

individuals that show how they discount themselves from responsible office and state-orchestrated rituals on the grounds that such pursuits are incompatible with their own distinct morality and identity as minority peoples.

Such an approach resonates with James Scott's analysis of upland lifeways in historical Southeast Asia as structured around purposive avoidance of the lowland state's embrace. However, Nguyen Thu Huong's analysis is more nuanced than this in showing that such orientations are not universal among the peoples of the Central Highlands, but rather are contingent upon the complex historical relations that groups and individuals have had with state-building initiatives in this locality. She also avoids homogenising state–ethnic relations by showing within one select group the markedly gendered nature of their practices of state evasion. Moreover, in a way that appears to fundamentally depart from the state evasion paradigm, she discovers that acts of selective withdrawal are linked to projects of cultural exceptionalism, moral purification, and gender differentiation, which themselves draw upon discourses employed by the state to mobilise and govern its ethnic minority subjects. Hence, far from being an entity that minority peoples must artfully avoid in order to obtain authentic self-realisation, the state itself provides the stage and the script through which people may enact their ethnic difference.

In studied contrast with the tactical retreats staged by the Bahnar, the Hmong and Nùng residents of the northwest commune of Vĩnh Thủy actively engage the state by assertively deploying its categories and programs. When Peter Chaudhry conducted his fieldwork in this mountainous commune in Lào Cai Province, he found that the majority of its residents were categorised as poor and had long been reliant on state handouts. One possible interpretation for commune residents' entrenched poverty status would be to link it to their marginality and lack of opportunities to better themselves. An alternative approach would be to view it as a sign of local people's subjugation to the state's upland development project. However, Chaudhry soon came to observe that to be designated as poor had obvious value to local residents themselves, and was a status that locals actively strove for and contested. Far from being an index of disconnection or disempowerment, locals assertively manipulate and milk for maximum benefit this category of disadvantage assigned by the central state.

Vĩnh Thủy is thus a prime exemplar of what Peter Chaudhry refers to in his chapter as an 'agentive periphery'. However, what he has uncovered in this border commune is not a pure and resilient modality of local power that flourishes at the limits of the modern state's reach, for it is the central state that furnishes the resources for peripheral actors to act in such an autonomous manner. Nevertheless, poverty is a resolutely local project, as evidenced by the local relational categories, moral economy considerations, and status and schisms at stake in the designation of households as poor. Local officials build patronage and create legitimacy in local eyes by exercising discerning judgement in the allocation of poverty alleviation resources. Householders are strategically ingenious in pressurising officials to decide in their favour and presenting themselves as eligible for the handouts. Poverty is a hybridised category of subjectivity that proliferates at the interface between local and central state criteria and needs. Chaudhry describes this as an example of political *metis*, whereby modern state biopower is reworked through local circuits of meaning and relatedness into a biopolitical project with strikingly local characteristics.

What degree of autonomy is open to ethnic minority actors under a state known for its centralising efficacy and assimilatory bent? Surprising answers to that question can be found by examining the case of Thai elites in northwest Vietnam. In his research among high-ranking Thai state cadres in a Thai-dominated province of the northwest, Ha Viet Quan found that a number had formed around them an elaborate entourage of clients, subordinates, partners, and allies. Exploring these political networks through participant observation, he found them to be personalistic, hierarchical, flexible, and assimilatory, and held together by performance and mutual obligation. Moreover, these social formations were politically significant. The Thai cadres exercised power through their personalistic networks: implementing state programs and initiatives; securing appointments, promotions, and contracts; and fending off assaults on the prestige of the leader from the leader of rival networks. In sum, the mode of power embodied by these senior Thai cadres very much resembles the traditional model of entourage politics characteristic of the Tai culture area in the era before the rise of centralised bureaucratic states. Remarkably, Ha Viet Quan found it thriving openly among the political class in a region that, for over 60 years, has been under the rule of a socialist state.

Ha Viet Quan concludes from his evidence that the mode by which the state exerts power in Vietnam is not as uniform as is often assumed by scholarly observers, or, indeed, is evident in the state's own rhetoric. Rather, the case of the Thai northwest suggests that the state is amenable to heterogeneous modes of authority and indeed is comprised by such heterogeneity. An additional implication is that this mode of personalistic rule is not threatening to the projection of state power in the uplands but is precisely the means through which the state prosecutes its agenda in such regions. The central state is reliant on powerful Thai elites to effect its writ, and the elites in turn reproduce their power through their favourable connections to central authority. Another revelatory implication of this study is that the incorporation of culturally and politically distinct groups into the Vietnamese national project does not necessarily come at the expense of those groups' identity and authority; to the contrary, those unique qualities may be enhanced in the process of political integration. Minority autonomy is thus obtainable without eroding the authority of the state project; in fact, to the contrary, the state's prestige is burnished as its power is exercised through such means.

Although participating in state structures enables minority actors to advance their own interests, when the government prescribes how they may do so, the results can be unpredictable. The chapter by Philip Taylor focuses on the efforts by the Vietnamese government to control the educational mobility options available to the Khmer monastic population in Vietnam. Khmers in Vietnam have a highly developed vernacular education network based in their Buddhist monasteries. The socialist government not only permits the operation of this religious-based education network, it recently has supported the development of a Buddhist institute in Vietnam as the peak educational destination for Vietnamese Khmers. Like elsewhere in Southeast Asia, this intervention in monastic education was designed to consolidate national identifications among local Buddhists. However, the effort was far from successful, as Khmer monks continued to travel to centres of monastic learning outside of Vietnam. The state-prescribed option has been bypassed by Khmer monastics, who are determined to pursue far more expansive educational alternatives.

The determination of Khmers in Vietnam to chart their own monastic education routes illustrates the tensions between the territorialising nation-state and the decentred itineraries of citizens who are inspired by their own spatial imaginaries. Having historically migrated to monastic centres in Cambodia to pursue higher education, Khmers in the Mekong Delta found their traditional avenue of social mobility blocked by the rise to power of socialist states in both Vietnam and Cambodia. In time, the Vietnamese government developed its own Khmer vernacular higher education system, modelled on the Buddhist university system found in Theravada countries. However, the option failed to satisfy Khmer people's desire for cosmopolitan self-realisation and experiential immersion in a Khmer-language educational milieu. Resisting parochialisation within Vietnam, Khmers trod other paths, including educational migration to Burma, Sri Lanka, Thailand, and post-socialist Cambodia. Their sometimes illicit journeys illustrate the challenges posed to states by the demotic aspirations for connection unleashed by globalisation. The official response, which has been to actively police educational returns, exemplifies the pitfalls minority citizens face in an era of aspirational transnational travel.

Disconnected and Reconnected in History and Space

Much hope for social betterment is invested in Vietnam's global integration, yet with it has come a sense of anxiety about the threats that powerful international processes and actors pose to Vietnam's very identity. One of the ways the state has responded to this sense of threat has been to confer on certain cultural practices and objects the status of being part of a Vietnamese cultural canon. Similarly, the contemporary concern to register and protect strategically significant places, such as national parks, borderlands, and historical sites, responds to official apprehension about unregulated change and threats from without. However, these efforts to fix the meanings of items and practices as iconic heritage run counter to dynamic popular processes of modification and re-signification, and may serve to undermine or obscure their value to local populations. Equally, the rush to secure certain sites for the benefit of the Vietnamese nation risks removing them from the realm of everyday use and ironically may render them less accessible to local people. These contradictory processes of securing and losing control over culturally significant practices and sites are topics explored by the final two essays in this volume.

As Oscar Salemink observes in his chapter, Vietnam is experiencing a rapid heritagisation of its cultural legacy. Numerous cultural and ritual sites, objects, and practices have been formally recognised as national heritage by the state in line with UNESCO criteria. Taking place in tandem with these developments is the transformation of heritage into spectacle, as state authorities and tourist companies stage festivals that celebrate a variety of local practices as ancient and distinctive, thereby securing possession of them as icons of Vietnamese national identity. However, as Salemink shows in his chapter, this ritualised connection with the nation paradoxically comes at a price of local disconnection from the cultural site, object, or practice that is officially labelled cultural heritage. He contends that, especially for religious sites, objects and practices, heritage recognition casts a secular gaze on cultural life. Among other things, it effectively disenfranchises attempts by locals to modify and reinterpret their ritual practices and cultural identifications in meaningful alignment with the profoundly altered conditions they experience as subjects of marketisation and global integration. In other words, when sites, objects and practices are inscribed as heritage, the dynamic values invested in them by various constituent communities risk being obscured and discounted.

Focusing on the transformation of the cultural traditions of Vietnam's Central Highlanders into heritage displays, Oscar Salemink's chapter shows these processes at work. The use of ceremonial gongs was once widespread in the Central Highlands, and traditionally was embedded in the ritual and social lives of numerous highland peoples. Powerful forces have rapidly marginalised these practices, ranging from social and ritual reform in the socialist period to the major economic and social changes occurring under conditions of capitalist commoditisation. Highlanders have responded to these ruptures by embracing Christianity as an autonomous form of vernacular modernism, while their diasporic representatives have promoted alternative identifications for highlanders as members of a collectively oppressed people. In an attempt to counter these new identifications, state cultural authorities have moved to endorse fading practices such as gong use as authentic, and stage cultural festivals that celebrate their status as cultural heritage. Oscar Salemink argues that, through this process of secularisation, local communities' own cultural responses to their contemporary predicament are effectively disqualified, while outside players — cultural experts, state agencies, tourist companies — effectively take over the management and staging of highland heritage for their own benefit.

The final chapter, by Edyta Roszko, looks through the lens of a dispute between Vietnam and its large neighbour China to examine the territorial and historical recentring of a once marginal island off the Central Vietnamese coast. China's expanding political and military influence in the South China Sea to secure the supply of natural resources has recently led to numerous maritime confrontations with Vietnamese sea users. Its attempt to enclose virtually the entire sea has been a focus within Vietnam of public anger and political contestation. One location where we can see some local consequences of this contestation is Lý Sơn Island, which is considered as a historic and contemporary stepping stone to the Paracel island chain and a border zone in Vietnam. China's seizure of Vietnamese vessels, and the arrest and months-long detention of Lý Sơn fishermen have been widely covered in Vietnam's mass media, adding fuel to a heated debate about disputed areas in the South China/Eastern Sea, and stirring new imaginings about the role of the sea and its islands in the nation's history.

Against the backdrop of the South China Sea dispute, Edyta Roszko analyses how the small and marginalised coastal location of Lý Sơn has become central to the state's sociocultural project of redefining Vietnam from a rice-growing culture to a maritime nation. Responding to media discourses, Vietnamese people have come to see the contested waters and islands as inalienable national territory and, through their practices of patriotic tourism to Lý Sơn Island, they demonstrate a new identity as citizens of the sea. While such attention brings new status and economic opportunities to a once peripheral place, it also has required from Lý Sơn people a shift in subjectivities in response to the state's re-territorialising project. Moreover, the growing national interest in the island's historical and cultural heritage comes at the cost of obscuring from consciousness islanders' cosmopolitan legacies of travel and trade, including, indeed, their relations with China. In the context of conflict and contestation, islanders have been disconnected from key aspects of their identity and history as they simultaneously have been recentred as heroic subjects of a new maritime nationalism. Offering lessons that reach far beyond the study of Vietnam, the dilemmas confronted by Lý Sơn Islanders highlight the global stakes entailed in local experiences of connection and disconnection in even the most obscure lives and places.

References

Avieli, Nir 2012, *Rice Talks: Food and Community in a Vietnamese Town*, Indiana University Press, Bloomington.

Baulch, Bob, Hoa Thị Minh Nguyễn, Phương Thu Thị Nguyễn and Hùng Thái Phạm 2010, *Ethnic Minority Poverty in Vietnam*, Working Paper No. 169, Chronic Poverty Research Centre, Manchester, UK.

Bayly, Susan 2007, *Asian Voices in a Postcolonial Age: Vietnam, India and Beyond*, Cambridge University Press, Cambridge.

Bélanger, Danièle and Khuat Thi Hai Oanh 2009, 'Second-Trimester Abortions and Sex-Selection of Children in Hanoi, Vietnam', *Population Studies*, vol. 63, no. 2, pp. 163–171.

Biggs, David 2010, *Quagmire: Nation-building and Nature in the Mekong Delta*, University of Washington Press, Seattle.

Brocheux, Pierre 1995, *The Mekong Delta: Ecology, Economy, and Revolution, 1860–1960*, Centre for Southeast Asian Studies, University of Wisconsin–Madison, Madison.

Carruthers, Ashley 2008, 'Saigon from the Diaspora', *Singapore Journal of Tropical Geography*, vol. 29, no. 1, pp. 68–86.

Carruthers, Ashley and Trung Dinh Dang 2012, 'The Socio-spatial Constellation of a Central Vietnamese Village and its Emigrants', *Journal of Vietnamese Studies*, vol. 7, no. 4, pp. 122–153.

Chapman, Jessica 2013, *Cauldron of Resistance: Ngo Dinh Diem, the United States, and 1950s Southern Vietnam*, Cornell University Press, Ithaca.

Choi Byung Wook 2004, *Southern Vietnam under the Reign of Minh Mạng (1820–1841): Central Policies and Local Response*, Cornell University Southeast Asia Program Publications, Ithaca.

Dang Phong 2004, 'Stages on the Road to Renovation of the Vietnamese Economy: An Historical Perspective', in Melanie Beresford and Angie Ngoc Tran (eds), *Reaching for the Dream: Challenges of Sustainable Development in Vietnam*, ISEAS Publications, Singapore, pp. 19–50.

Do Thien 2003, *Vietnamese Supernaturalism: Views from the Southern Region*, Routledge Curzon, London.

Dutton, George 2006, *The Tay Son Uprising: Society and Rebellion in Eighteenth-Century Vietnam*, University of Hawaii Press, Honolulu.

Earl, Catherine 2014, *Vietnam's New Middle Classes: Gender, Career, City*, NIAS Press, Copenhagen.

Endres, Kirsten 2011, *Performing the Divine: Mediums, Markets and Modernity in Urban Vietnam*, NIAS Press, Copenhagen.

Engelbert, Thomas 2007, '"Go West" in Cochinchina: Chinese and Vietnamese Illicit Activities in the Transbassac (c. 1860–1920)', *Chinese Southern Diaspora Studies*, vol. 1, pp. 56–82.

Fall, Bernard 1967, *The Two Viet-Nams: A Political and Military Analysis*, Frederick A. Praeger, New York.

Fforde, Adam and Stefan de Vylder 1996, *From Plan to Market: The Economic Transition in Vietnam*, Westview Press, Boulder, Colorado.

Fjelstad, Karen and Nguyen Thi Hien (eds) 2006, *Possessed by the Spirits: Mediumship in Contemporary Vietnamese Communities*, Cornell University Southeast Asia Program Publications, Ithaca.

Fjelstad, Karen and Nguyen Thi Hien 2011, *Spirits Without Borders: Vietnamese Spirit Mediums in a Transnational Age*, Palgrave Macmillan, New York.

Friederichsen, Rupert 2012, 'The Mixed Blessings of National Integration: New Perspectives on Development in Vietnam's Northern Uplands', *East Asia*, vol. 29, pp. 43–61.

Gainsborough, Martin 2010, *Vietnam: Rethinking the State*, Silkworm Books, Chiang Mai.

Gammeltoft, Tine 2014, *Haunting Images: A Cultural Account of Selective Reproduction in Vietnam*, University of California Press, Berkeley.

Gillespie, John 2014, 'Social Consensus and the Meta-regulation of Land-taking Disputes in Vietnam', *Journal of Vietnamese Studies*, vol. 9, no. 3, pp. 91–124.

Goscha, Christopher 2006, 'Vietnam, the Third Indochina War and the Meltdown of Asian Internationalism', in Odd Arne Westad and Sophie Quinn-Judge (eds), *The Third Indochina War: Conflict between China, Vietnam and Cambodia, 1972–79*, Routledge, London, pp. 152–186.

Goscha, Christopher 2013, 'Colonial Hanoi and Saigon at War: Social Dynamics of the Viet Minh's Underground City', *War in History*, vol. 20, no. 2, pp. 222–250.

Gourou, Pierre 1936, *Les Paysans du Delta Tonkinois:* Étude de Géographie Humaine, Éditions d'Art et d'Histoire, Paris.

Granovetter, Mark 1973, 'The Strength of Weak Ties', *American Journal of Sociology*, vol. 78, no. 6, pp. 1360–1380.

Guillemot, François 2010, 'Autopsy of a Massacre: On a Political Purge in the Early Days of the Indochina War (Nam Bo 1947)', *European Journal of East Asian Studies*, vol. 9, no. 2, pp. 225–265.

Gustafsson, Mai Lan 2009, *War and Shadows: The Haunting of Vietnam*, Cornell University Press, Ithaca.

Hansen, Peter 2009, 'Bắc Đi Cú: Catholic Refugees from the North of Vietnam, and their Role in the Southern Republic, 1954–1959', *Journal of Vietnamese Studies*, vol. 4, no. 3, pp. 173–211.

Hardy, Andrew 2003, *Red Hills: Migrants and the State in the Highlands of Vietnam*, ISEAS Publications, Singapore.

Harms, Erik 2011, *Saigon's Edge: On the Margins of Ho Chi Minh City*, University of Minnesota Press, Minneapolis and London.

Harms, Erik 2012, 'Beauty as Control in the New Saigon: Eviction, New Urban Zones, and Atomized Dissent in a Southeast Asian City', *American Ethnologist*, vol. 39, no. 4, pp. 735–750.

Harms, Erik 2014, 'Knowing into Oblivion: Clearing Wastelands and Imagining Emptiness in Vietnamese New Urban Zones', *Singapore Journal of Tropical Geography*, vol. 35, no. 3, pp. 312–327.

Hayton, Bill 2010, *Vietnam: Rising Dragon*, Yale University Press, New Haven.

Hickey, Gerald Cannon 1964, *Village in Vietnam,* Yale University Press, New Haven.

Hickey, Gerald Cannon 1993, *Shattered World: Adaptation and Survival among Vietnam's Highland Peoples during the Vietnam War*, University of Pennsylvania Press, Philadelphia.

Hoang, Kimberly Kay 2015, *Dealing in Desire: Asian Ascendancy, Western Decline, and the Hidden Currencies of Global Sex Work*, University of California Press, Berkeley.

Hoskins, Janet 2015, *The Divine Eye and the Diaspora: Vietnamese Syncretism Becomes Transpacific Caodaism*, University of Hawaii Press, Honolulu.

Ho Tai, Hue-Tam 1983, *Millenarianism and Peasant Politics in Vietnam*, Harvard University Press, Cambridge, Mass.

Ho Tai, Hue-Tam 1992, *Radicalism and the Origins of the Vietnamese Revolution*, Harvard University Press, Cambridge, Mass.

Ho Tai, Hue Tam 2010, *Passion, Betrayal and Revolution in Colonial Saigon: The Memoirs of Bao Luong*, University of California Press, Berkeley.

Hunt, David 2008, *Vietnam's Southern Revolution: From Peasant Insurrection to Total War*, University of Massachusetts Press, Amherst.

Huong, Nghiem Lien 2004, 'Female Garment Workers: The New Young Volunteers in Vietnam's Modernization', in Philip Taylor (ed.), *Social Inequality in Vietnam and the Challenges to Reform*, ISEAS Publications, Singapore, pp. 297–324.

Imai, Katsushi, and Raghav Gaiha 2007, 'Poverty, Inequality and Ethnic Minorities in Vietnam', *International Review of Applied Economics*, vol. 25, no. 3, pp. 249–282.

Jamieson, Neil 1995, *Understanding Vietnam*, University of California Press, Berkeley.

Jellema, Kate 2007, 'Returning Home: Ancestor Veneration and the Nationalism of Đổi Mới Vietnam', in Philip Taylor (ed.), *Modernity and Re-enchantment: Religion in Post-revolutionary Vietnam*, ISEAS Publications, Singapore, pp. 57–89.

Karis, Timothy 2013, 'Unofficial Hanoians: Migration, Native Place and Urban Citizenship in Vietnam', *The Asia Pacific Journal of Anthropology*, vol. 14, no. 3, pp. 256–273.

Keith, Charles 2012, *Catholic Vietnam: A Church from Empire to Nation*, University of California Press, Berkeley.

Kerkvliet, Benedict J. Tria 2005, *The Power of Everyday Politics: How Vietnamese Peasants Transformed National Policy*, Cornell University Press, Ithaca.

Kerkvliet, Benedict J. Tria 2014, 'Protests over Land: Rightful Resistance and More', *Journal of Vietnamese Studies*, vol. 9, no. 3, pp. 14–34.

Kleinen, John 1999, *Facing the Future, Reviving the Past: A Study of Social Change in a Northern Vietnamese Village*, ISEAS Publications, Singapore.

Kwon, Heonik 2008, *Ghosts of War in Vietnam*, Cambridge University Press, Cambridge.

Le Failler, Philippe 2011, 'The Đèo Family of Lai Châu: Traditional Power and Unconventional Practices', *Journal of Vietnamese Studies*, vol. 6, no. 2, pp. 42–67.

Lentz, Christian 2011, 'Making the Northwest Vietnamese', *Journal of Vietnamese Studies*, vol. 6, no. 2, pp. 68–105.

Leshkowich, Ann Marie 2014, *Essential Trade: Vietnamese Women in a Changing Marketplace*, University of Hawaii Press, Honolulu.

Li, Tana 1998, Nguyễn Cochinchina: Southern Vietnam in the Seventeen and Eighteenth Centuries, Cornell University Southeast Asia Program Publications, Ithaca.

Lieberman, Victor 2003, *Strange Parallels: Southeast Asia in Global Context, c. 800–1830: Volume 1, Integration on the Mainland*, Cambridge University Press, Cambridge.

Locke, Catherine, Nguyễn Thị Ngân Hoa and Nguyễn Thị Thanh Tâm 2012, 'Struggling to Sustain Marriages and Build Families: Mobile Husbands/Wives and Mothers/Fathers in Hà Nội and Hồ Chí Minh City', *Journal of Vietnamese Studies*, vol. 7, no. 4, pp. 63–91.

Luong, Hy V. 1990, *Discursive Practices and Linguistic Meanings: The Vietnamese System of Person Reference*, John Benjamins Publishing, Amsterdam.

Luong, Hy V. 2003, 'Gender Relations, Ideologies, Kinship Practices and Political Economy', in H. Van Luong (ed.), *Postwar Vietnam: Dynamics of a Transforming Society*, Rowman and Littlefield, Boulder, Colorado, pp. 201–224.

Luong, Hy V. 2005, 'The State, Local Associations, and Alternate Civilities in Rural Northern Vietnam', in Robert Weller (ed.), *Civil Life, Globalization, and Political Change in Asia: Organizing Between Family and State,* Routledge, New York, pp. 123–147.

Luong, Hy V. 2010, *Tradition, Revolution, and Market Economy in a North Vietnamese Village, 1925–2006*, University of Hawaii Press, Honolulu.

Malarney, Shaun Kingsley 2001, '"The Fatherland Remembers Your Sacrifice": Commemorating War Dead in North Vietnam', in Hue-Tam Ho Tai (ed.) *The Country of Memory: Remaking the Past in Late Socialist Vietnam*, University of California Press, Berkeley, pp. 46–76.

Malarney, Shaun Kingsley 2002, *Culture, Ritual and Revolution in Vietnam*, University of Hawaii Press, Honolulu.

Malarney, Shaun Kingsley 2003, 'Return to the Past?: The Dynamics of Contemporary Religious and Ritual Transformation', in H. Van Luong (ed.), *Postwar Vietnam: Dynamics of a Transforming Society*, Rowman and Littlefield, Boulder, Colorado, pp. 225–256.

Markussen, Thomas and Finn Tarp 2014, 'Political Connections and Land-related Investment in Rural Vietnam', *Journal of Development Economics*, vol. 110, pp. 291–302.

Marouda, Marina 2014, 'Potent Rituals and the Royal Dead: Historical Transformations in Vietnamese Ritual Practice', *Journal of Southeast Asian Studies*, vol. 5, no. 3, pp. 338–362.

Marr, David G. 1981, *Vietnamese Tradition on Trial, 1920–1945*, University of California Press, Berkeley.

Marr, David G. 1997, *Vietnam 1945: The Quest for Power*, University of California Press, Berkeley.

Marr, David G. 2013, *Vietnam: State, War, Revolution, 1945–1946*, University of California Press, Berkeley.

McAlister, John T. and Paul Mus 1970, *The Vietnamese and Their Revolution*, Harper and Row, New York.

McElwee, Pamela 2004, 'Becoming Socialist or Becoming Kinh?: Government Policies for Ethnic Minorities in the Socialist Republic of Vietnam', in Christopher R. Duncan (ed.), *Civilizing the Margins: Southeast Asian Government Policies for the Development of Minorities*, Cornell University Press, Ithaca, pp. 182–213.

McElwee, Pamela 2007, 'From the Moral Economy to the World Economy: Revisiting Vietnamese Peasants in a Globalizing Era', *Journal of Vietnamese Studies*, vol. 2, no. 2, pp. 57–107.

McElwee, Pamela 2008, '"Blood Relatives" or Uneasy Neighbors?: Kinh Migrant and Ethnic Minority Interactions in the Trường Sơn Mountains', *Journal of Vietnamese Studies*, vol. 3, no. 3, pp. 81–116.

McHale, Shawn Frederick 2004, *Print and Power: Confucianism, Communism, and Buddhism in the Making of Modern Vietnam*, University of Hawaii Press, Honolulu.

McHale, Shawn 2013, 'Ethnicity, Violence, and Khmer–Vietnamese Relations: The Significance of the Lower Mekong Delta, 1757–1954', *The Journal of Asian Studies*, vol. 72, no. 2, pp. 367–390.

Michaud, Jean 2012, 'Hmong Infrapolitics: A View from Vietnam', *Ethnic and Racial Studies,* vol. 35, no. 11, pp. 1853–1873.

Miller, Edward 2013, *Misalliance: Ngo Dinh Diem, the United States, and the Fate of South Vietnam, Harvard University Press*, Cambridge, Mass.

Ngo T. T. Tam 2015, 'Protestant Conversion and Social Conflict: The Case of the Hmong in Contemporary Vietnam', *Journal of Southeast Asian Studies*, vol. 46, no. 2, pp. 274–292.

Nguyen Minh T. N. 2015, *Vietnam's Socialist Servants: Domesticity, Class, Gender and Identity*, Routledge, London.

Nguyen T. Lien-Hang 2012, *Hanoi's War: An International History of the War for Peace in Vietnam*, University of North Carolina Press, Chapel Hill.

Nguyen Tu Chi 1980, 'Le Làng Traditionnel du Bac Bo, Sa Structure Organisationnelle, Ses Problems', *Études Vietnamiennes*, vol. 61, pp. 9–131.

Nguyen Van Suu 2007, 'Contending Views and Conflicts over Land in Vietnam's Red River Delta', *Journal of Southeast Asian Studies*, vol. 38, no. 2, pp. 309–334.

Nguyen Van Thang 2007, *Ambiguity of Identity: The Mieu in North Vietnam*, Silkworm Books, Chiang Mai.

Nguyen-Akbar, Mytoan 2014, 'The Tensions of Diasporic "Return" Migration: How Class and Money Create Distance in the Vietnamese Transnational Family', *Journal of Contemporary Ethnography*, vol. 43, no. 20, pp. 176–201.

Nguyen-Vo Thu-Huong 1992, *Khmer-Viet Relations and the Third Indochina Conflict*, McFarland & Company, Jefferson, NC.

Nguyen-Vo Thu-Huong 2008, *The Ironies of Freedom: Sex, Culture, and Neoliberal Governance in Vietnam*, University of Washington Press, Seattle.

Ninh, Kim N. B. 2002, *A World Transformed: The Politics of Culture in Revolutionary Vietnam, 1945–1965*, University of Michigan Press, Ann Arbor.

Norton, Barley 2009, *Songs For the Spirits: Music and Mediums in Modern Vietnam*, University of Illinois Press, Champaign, Ill.

O'Rourke, Dara 2004, *Community-driven Regulation: Balancing Development and Environment in Vietnam*, MIT Press, Cambridge, Mass.

Peycam, Philippe 2012, *The Birth of Vietnamese Political Journalism: Saigon, 1916–1930*, Columbia University Press, New York.

Pham Quynh Phuong 2009, *Hero and Deity: Tran Hung Dao and the Resurgence of Popular Religion in Vietnam*, Silkworm Books, Chiang Mai.

Pham Van Bich 1999, *The Vietnamese Family in Change: The Case of the Red River Delta*, Curzon, Richmond, Surrey.

Phinney, Harriet 2008, 'Objects of Affection: Vietnamese Discourses on Love and Emancipation', *positions: east asia cultures critique*, vol. 16, no. 2, pp. 329–358.

Rama, Martin and Vo Van Kiet 2008, *Making Difficult Choices, Vietnam in Transition*, International Bank for Reconstruction and Development/The World Bank, Washington.

Rambo, Terry A. 1973, *A Comparison of Peasant Social Systems of Northern and Southern Viet-Nam*, Southern Illinois University Center for Vietnamese Studies, Carbondale, Illinois.

Rydstrøm, Helle 2003, *Embodying Morality: Growing up in Rural Northern Vietnam*, University of Hawaii Press, Honolulu.

Salemink, Oscar 2006, 'Changing Rights and Wrongs: The Transnational Construction of Indigenous and Human Rights among Vietnam's Central Highlanders', *Focaal: Journal of Global and Historical Anthropology*, vol. 47, pp. 32-47.

Salemink, Oscar 2010, 'Ritual Efficacy, Spiritual Security and Human Security: Spirit Mediumship in Contemporary Vietnam', in Thomas Hylland Eriksen, Ellen Bal and Oscar Salemink (eds), *A World of Insecurity: Anthropological Perspectives on Human Security*, Pluto Press, London, pp. 262–289.

Salemink, Oscar 2015, 'Revolutionary and Christian Ecumenes and Desire for Modernity in the Vietnamese Highlands', *The Asia Pacific Journal of Anthropology*, vol. 16, no. 4, pp. 388–409.

Schlecker, Markus 2005, 'Going Back a Long Way: "Home Place", Thrift and Temporal Orientations in Northern Vietnam', *Journal of the Royal Anthropological Institute*, vol. 11, no. 3, pp. 509–526.

Schwenkel, Christina 2014, 'Rethinking Asian Mobilities', *Critical Asian Studies*, vol. 46, no. 2, pp. 235–258.

Scott, James C. 1977, *The Moral Economy of the Peasant: Rebellion and Subsistence in Southeast Asia*, Yale University Press, New Haven.

Scott, James C. 2009, *The Art of Not Being Governed: An Anarchist History of Upland Southeast Asia*, Yale University Press, New Haven.

Sidnell, Jack and Merav Shohet 2013, 'The Problem of Peers in Vietnamese Interaction', *Journal of the Royal Anthropological Institute*, vol. 19, no. 3, pp. 618–638.

Small, Ivan 2012, '"Over There": Imaginative Displacements in Vietnamese Remittance Gift Economies', *Journal of Vietnamese Studies*, vol. 7, no. 3, pp. 157–183.

Sơn Nam 1997, *Cá Tính Miền Nam* [*The Southern Character*], Youth Publishing, Ho Chi Minh City.

Soucy, Alexander 2012, *The Buddha Side: Gender, Power, and Buddhist Practice in Vietnam*, University of Hawaii Press, Honolulu.

Soucy, Alexander 2014, 'Wedding Invitations and Relationship Management in Hanoi', *The Asia Pacific Journal of Anthropology*, vol. 15, no. 2, pp. 141–157.

Taylor, Keith 1983, *The Birth of Vietnam*, University of California Press, Berkeley.

Taylor, Keith 1998, 'Surface Orientations in Vietnam: Beyond Histories of Nation and Region', *The Journal of Asian Studies*, vol. 57, no. 4, pp. 949–978.

Taylor, Keith 2013, *A History of the Vietnamese*, Cambridge University Press, Cambridge.

Taylor, Philip 2001, *Fragments of the Present: Searching for Modernity in Vietnam's South*, University of Hawaii Press, Honolulu.

Taylor, Philip 2004, *Goddess on the Rise: Pilgrimage and Popular Religion in Vietnam*, University of Hawaii Press, Honolulu.

Taylor, Philip 2007a, *Cham Muslims of the Mekong Delta: Place and Mobility in the Cosmopolitan Periphery*, NUS Press, Singapore.

Taylor, Philip 2007b, 'Modernity and Re-enchantment in Post-revolutionary Vietnam', in Philip Taylor (ed.), *Modernity and Re-enchantment in Post-revolutionary Vietnam*, ISEAS Publications, Singapore, pp. 1–56.

Taylor, Philip 2007c, 'Poor Policies, Wealthy Peasants: Alternative Trajectories of Rural Development in Vietnam', *Journal of Vietnamese Studies*, vol. 2, no. 2, pp. 3–56.

Taylor, Philip (ed.) 2011, *Minorities at Large: New Approaches to Minority Ethnicity in Vietnam*, ISEAS Publications, Singapore.

Taylor, Philip 2014, *The Khmer Lands of Vietnam: Environment, Cosmology and Sovereignty*, NUS Press, Singapore.

Thai, Hung Cam 2014, *Insufficient Funds: The Culture of Money in Low-Wage Transnational Families*, Stanford University Press, Stanford, CA.

To Xuan Phuc, Sango Mahanty and Wolfram Dressler 2014, 'Social Networks of Corruption in the Vietnamese and Lao Cross-border Timber Trade', *Anthropological Forum*, vol. 24, no. 2, pp. 154–174.

Toan Ánh 1968, *Nếp Cũ: Làng Xóm Việt Nam [Old Ways: Vietnamese Villages]*, Nam Chi Tùng Thư, Saigon.

Topmiller, Robert J. 2006, *The Lotus Unleashed: The Buddhist Peace Movement in South Vietnam, 1964–1966*, University Press of Kentucky, Lexington.

Tran, Angie Ngoc 2016, 'Weaving Life across Borders: The Cham Muslim Migrants Traversing Vietnam and Malaysia', in Kwen Fee Lian, Md Mizanur Rahman and Yabit bin Alas (eds), *International Migration in Southeast Asia: Continuities and Discontinuities*, Springer, Singapore, pp. 13–37.

Tran Thi Minh Hang 2011, 'Global Debates, Local Dilemmas: Sex-selective Abortion in Contemporary Vietnam', PhD thesis, The Australian National University, Canberra.

Truitt, Alison 2013, *Dreaming of Money in Ho Chi Minh City*, University of Washington Press, Seattle.

Turner, Sarah, Christine Bonnin and Jean Michaud 2015, *Frontier Livelihoods: Hmong in the Sino-Vietnamese Borderlands*, University of Washington Press, Seattle.

Valverde, Kieu-Linh Caroline 2012, *Transnationalizing Viet Nam: Community, Culture, and Politics in the Diaspora*, Temple University Press, Philadelphia.

Van-Nguyen Marshall, Lisa Drummond and Danièle Bélanger (eds) 2011, *The Reinvention of Distinction: Modernity and the Middle Class in Urban Vietnam*, Springer, Dordrecht Heidelberg.

Vasavakul, Thaveeporn 2003, 'From Fence-breaking to Networking: Interests, Popular Organizations, and Policy Influences in Post-socialist Vietnam', in Benedict Kerkvliet, Russell Heng and David Koh (eds), *Getting Organized in Vietnam: Moving in and around the Socialist State*, ISEAS Publications, Singapore, pp. 25–61.

Vu Hong Phong 2008, 'Male Sexual Health Concerns in Muong Khen, Vietnam', *Culture, Health and Sexuality* vol. 10 (supplement), pp. 139–150.

Wells-Dang, Andrew 2012, *Civil Society Networks in China and Vietnam: Informal Pathbreakers in Health and the Environment*, Palgrave Macmillan, New York.

Werner, Jayne and Danièle Bélanger (eds) 2002, *Gender, Household, State: Đổi Mới in Việt Nam*, Cornell University Southeast Asia Program Publications, Ithaca.

Winkels, Alexandra 2012, 'Migration, Social Networks and Risk: The Case of Rural to Rural Migration in Vietnam', *Journal of Vietnamese Studies*, vol. 7, no. 4, pp. 92–121.

Wolf, Eric 1969, *Peasant Wars of the Twentieth Century*, Harper and Row, London.

Woodside, Alexander 1976, *Community and Revolution in Modern Vietnam*, Houghton Mifflin, Boston.

Yu, LiAnne Sandra 2006, 'The Re-emergence of Vietnam's Ethnic Chinese Community through Local, National, and Transnational Structures', PhD thesis, University of California, San Diego.

Zink, Eren 2013, *Hot Science, High Water: Assembling Nature, Society and Environmental Policy in Contemporary Vietnam*, NIAS Press, Copenhagen.

Zinoman, Peter 2001, *The Colonial Bastille: A History of Imprisonment in Vietnam, 1862–1940*, University of California Press, Berkeley.

1

Social Relations, Regional Variation, and Economic Inequality in Contemporary Vietnam: A View from Two Vietnamese Rural Communities

Hy V. Luong

The salience of social connections or social capital in Vietnam is summed up in a contemporary Vietnamese saying regarding different factors of importance in the Vietnamese labour market: '*nhất hậu duệ, nhì quan hệ, ba tiền tệ, bốn trí tuệ*' ('Of first importance is descent; second are social relations; third is money; and fourth is the intellect'). Such a saying may over-simplify reality, but it is a fact that ethnic Vietnamese from all walks of life think first and foremost of social connections in their search for the solutions to various problems in their daily lives: from the purchase of a motorcycle and many other consumer durables, to medical treatment for a family member, to securing a job, a loan, or a business contract.

In both the quotidian maintenance and cultivation of social relations, and in their mobilisation in moments of need, ethnic Vietnamese usually invoke 'sentiment' (*tình cảm*). Notwithstanding the strong local ideological emphasis on 'sentiment', the maintenance and cultivation of social connections or social capital require the investment of time and material resources; time and material resources needed in offering advice, giving gifts, doing favours, or in hosting death-anniversary meals and wedding banquets, among others. In this context, people from different social strata are far from being on a level playing field. This is reflected in my research data over the past decade from two Vietnamese communities, the village of Hoài Thị (2012 pop. 1,141) in the northern Red River Delta, and the community of Khánh Hậu (2012 pop. 14,213) in the southern Mekong Delta, which have both experienced good growth in income in this period.[1] However, my field data show not only some impact of wealth and socioeconomic stratification on the cultivation of social capital, but also of a major regional variation in social capital configuration. Northern villagers' social connections include many relations formalised through the establishment of patrilineages and numerous voluntary associations, in contrast to the pattern in rural southern Vietnam. Northern villagers also mobilise their social connections more effectively, at least in terms of material assistance from people in their networks. Towards the end of the chapter, in reference to the larger debate on the salience of social connections in the political economy and sociocultural fabric in some other East Asian societies (for example, Gold et al. 2002:10–17; Walder 1986; Yang 1994, 2002), I argue that it is problematic to attribute the salience of social connections in Vietnam solely to the shortage of goods and services, the weakness in the Vietnamese formal institutional framework (lack of strong commitment to institutional rules),

---

1   Khánh Hậu is well known in the literature on Vietnam as it was studied in the late 1950s by three American social scientists and their Vietnamese research collaborators (Hickey 1964; Henry 1964). In 2006, although most of its land was still used for agriculture, Khánh Hậu was incorporated into the municipality and provincial capital of Tân An due to its proximity to Tân An, and divided into two 'urban' wards (phường), Khánh Hậu and Tân Khánh. In this chapter, I use 'Khánh Hậu' to refer to both of the recently created wards and their population (7,863 in Khánh Hậu and 6,350 in Tân Khánh in 2012). Khánh Hậu is located at about 55 kilometres from Hồ Chí Minh City, while Hoài Thị is situated about 30 kilometres from Hà Nội. In 2012, Khánh Hậu's population was 12.5 times larger than Hoài Thị. Khánh Hậu's area was also 21.8 times larger than that of Hoài Thị (1,073 hectares in contrast to 49.3 hectares). Hoài Thị villagers have a very strong sense of identity and live in a nucleated settlement, quite distinct from the five other villages (thôn) in the commune of Liên Bão. This strong village identity, below the commune level, is typical of the Red River Delta of Northern Vietnam. In contrast, Khánh Hậu is a spatially dispersed community, with no clear boundaries among its hamlets (ấp) and no strong identity among the population of any hamlet.

I first conducted research in Hoài Thị and Khánh Hậu in 1990–92. I have carried out systematic and comparative research on these communities three more times in the past decade and a half, with primary funding from the Social Sciences and Humanities Research Council (SSHRC) of Canada, and with the collaboration and assistance of Vietnamese researchers at the University of Social Sciences and Humanities in Hồ Chí Minh City, the Southern Institute of Social Sciences, the Ethnology Institute, and the National Institute of Cultural and Arts Studies.

the subsequent uncertainty in the social environment, and people's mobilisation of social capital for problem solving. This salience is also partly and deeply rooted in local models for and of social reality.

Social Connections in Local Sociocultural Fabric: A View from Two Rural Vietnamese Communities

To the extent that ethnic Vietnamese consider social connections or social capital a fundamental aspect of their lives, these connections are not only mobilised in daily life. These relations are also ritualised in the attendance and gifts at life cycle events such as weddings and funerals, and, to a lesser extent, in the invitation to and attendance at the annual death anniversaries of relatives and acquaintances. As average income has significantly risen in the past three decades in Vietnam, the financial investment in the cultivation of social connections has increased correspondingly. This increased investment is partly reflected in the size of weddings, funerals (Figures 1 and 2), death anniversary feasts, and, in northern Vietnam, in the revitalisation and creation of patrilineages and numerous voluntary associations to strengthen social capital.

In Hoài Thị and Khánh Hậu, the average number of visitors at funerals in studied households increased respectively by 66 per cent and 88 per cent over three-and-a-half decades (respectively from the average of 160 in 1976–85 to 265 in 2006–12 in Hoài Thị, and from 146 to 274 in Khánh Hậu).[2] As a widely shared Vietnamese practice, one pays respect to the deceased not only when the deceased is one's relative, friend, co-worker, or a member of the nuclear family of one's

---

2   As Hoài Thị had a small population, a census was conducted in the entire village in 2000, 2005, and 2012, focusing on household economy and social capital. A survey using the same instrument was carried out in Khánh Hậu in 2000 using a random probability sample of 340 households. This sample increased to 367 households in 2005 and 411 in 2012 in order to include households splitting off from the original sample and to reflect the increase in population. In 2005, in the research project on gifts and social capital, the Dinh hamlet in Khánh Hậu was also chosen for in-depth research on gifts and social relations, in comparison with Hoài Thị. The method of participant observation was also used in 81 of the surveyed households (40 in the Dinh hamlet of Khánh Hậu; 41 in Hoài Thị) for two months in 2005 and for a shorter period in 2012. Most of these households also recorded their gift flows from February 2005 to January 2006. In-depth interviews were also conducted with 111 of the surveyed households (40 in the Dinh hamlet; 30 in other hamlets of Khánh Hậu; 41 in Hoài Thị) in 2005 and 2012.

friend/co-worker, but also when the deceased is a parent or parent-in-law of one's friend and co-worker (*tứ thân phụ mẫu*), even when the deceased did not reside in the same household with the latter. These funeral visits are made without invitation from the family or relatives of the deceased. Visitors routinely present cash gifts to help defray funeral expenses, unless, as an option among the well-off in southern Vietnam, the family of the deceased publicly announces the non-acceptance of cash gifts. (When the family of the deceased in Khánh Hậu or in southern Vietnam does not accept cash gifts, visitors usually bring incense and fruits.) In native discourse, the visit and the gift reflect the sentiment (*tình cảm*) of the visitor towards the deceased and/or his/her family members. They also help to reaffirm a visitor's social bond with the spouse, or parents, or descendants of the deceased.

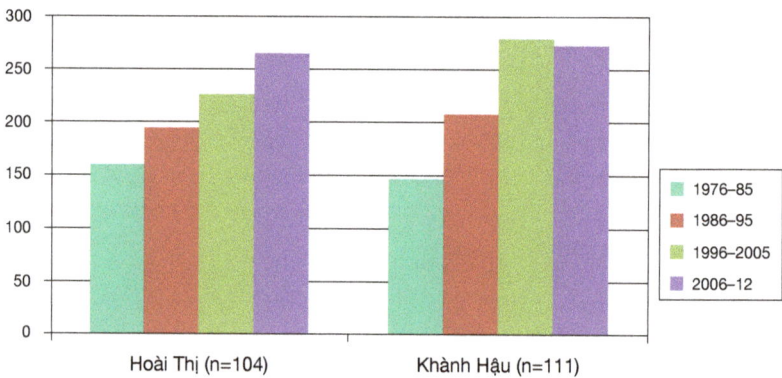

Figure 1: Average number of visitors to funerals in surveyed households since 1976.
Source: Author's research.

At weddings, the invitation list is determined not only by the bride and the groom, but also by their respective family members. (In both of the studied rural communities, the bride and groom's families normally hold separate banquets and have independent invitation lists.) Besides relatives, friends, and co-workers of the bride/groom, and friends and co-workers of the parents of the bride/groom, very close friends of the bride/groom's adult siblings are also usually invited. Invitations reaffirm not only the social relations of the bride and groom, but also those of their parents and adult siblings. This extension of invitation to people in the social circles of the bride/groom's parents and adult siblings is facilitated by the widespread use of kin terms among speakers of Vietnamese to address the (close) friends of one's parents and siblings.

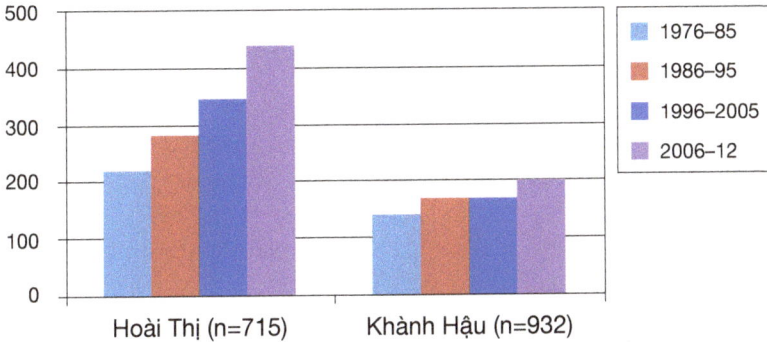

Figure 2: Average number of wedding guests in Hoài Thị and Khánh Hậu, 1976–2012.
Source: Author's research.

Nowadays, wedding guests routinely make cash gifts which normally cover or exceed estimated meal costs. However, special relations with the bride/groom and with his/her parents and siblings are symbolised by much larger gifts, if guests' economic conditions allow them. More specifically, the bride/groom's grandparents, aunts and uncles, first cousins, and close friends normally make much larger gifts than other guests, and may choose to make gifts in gold (necklaces, bracelets, earrings, etc.) instead of cash. The size of the gift also depends on the giver's economic circumstances, as one informant in Khánh Hậu explained to me regarding the cash gifts by his siblings to his daughter at her wedding in 2004:

> HL: I would like to ask more about [the gifts from] the maternal aunts and uncles of the bride [interviewee's daughter] … I see here that Mr Năm gave 200,000 VND; that Mrs Bảy in Thủ Tửu [hamlet] gave 500,000 VND; that Mrs Tư … gave only 50,000 VND; that Mr Tám gave 100,000 VND. Those four people are full brothers and sisters. Why were their gifts so different?

> Male Interviewee: Let me tell you … Mrs Bảy gave 500,000 because she was wealthy. Mr Năm gave 200,000 because although he was fairly well-off, he was less wealthy than Mrs Bảy. Mr Tám gave 100,000 VND because he had to take care of ancestral worship in his

house, and because he was not that well-off. Mrs Tư was poor. She was married, but lived without a husband. She [consequently] gave 50,000 VND. When her children get married, I will give gifts of 50,000 VND ... And when a child of Mrs Bảy who gave 500,000 VND gets married, I will give back 500,000 VND ... It [the gift] depended on the giver's circumstances. Whatever he/she gave, I will give back the same amount. (Hy V. Luong's interview with the male head of Household 9 in Khánh Hậu)

However, the principle of strict reciprocity in the above excerpt is more applicable among non-relatives and distant relatives than in close friendship and kinship relations. In the context of close relations, the size of the gift also depends on the circumstance of the recipient. When I asked the male head of Household 48 in Khánh Hậu why he had given a wedding gift of 300,000 VND ($18.91 USD) to his nephew (deceased elder brother's son) and only 100,000 VND ($6.30 USD) to his wife's nephew (wife's elder brother's son) in the early 2000s, he emphasised his sympathy for his nephew growing up without a father in contrast to the much wealthier household of his wife's brother.

Vietnamese families in Hoài Thị, Khánh Hậu, and, in fact, throughout the country, carefully keep the lists of gifts at weddings and funerals for one to three decades for the purpose of reciprocity. The act of reciprocity does not have to be performed on the same occasion (a wedding gift for a wedding gift, a funeral gift for a funeral gift); it can be for a variety of events or occasions. It also does not have to be in the same form of gift (cash gift for cash gift); a generous cash gift can be partially reciprocated by such favours as more attentive or expedited services (sales, medical, bureaucratic, etc.) or service fee reduction (discounted prices, waived fees, etc.). Favours can also be reciprocated by generous cash gifts at weddings, funerals, and other ritual events. More generally, gifts not only reflect social relations but also actively structure social relations, giving advantage to those people who can afford generous gifts.

Annual death anniversary feasts are less elaborate and smaller in scope than weddings and funerals. To the extent that the death anniversary organiser's economic resources allow a more extensive invitation list, death anniversary feasts are not restricted to the spouse, children, parents, siblings, and other close relatives of the deceased. Also invited are close friends of the deceased and their spouses, fairly close friends of the event organiser and of the organiser's children, parents and possibly some siblings of the organiser's children-in-law, among others. Some death anniversary feasts in Hoài Thị and Khánh Hậu have 150–250 people in attendance, especially the first major one after the funeral. In Hoài Thị, as local authorities have taken a stand against feasting visitors at funerals, as a symbol of gratitude families of the deceased invite funeral gift givers to the first major death anniversary on the 49th or 50th day after the passing of the deceased. The invitation lists to first death anniversaries in Hoài Thị usually comprise more than 100 names. Beyond first death anniversaries, it is not uncommon for Khánh Hậu and Hoài Thị households of some means to host 60–150 guests at their most important annual death anniversaries. In Hoài Thị, death anniversary guests nowadays usually bring incense and cash gifts, a controversial departure from the once prevalent practice of not giving gifts to fellow villagers at death anniversaries (see Luong 2010:408–409).[3]

The controversial and quickly spreading practice of cash gifts at death anniversaries in Hoài Thị was reportedly started by young villagers, many of whom had not reached a life stage of being responsible for organising death anniversaries of ancestors. Unable to reciprocate the death anniversary feast invitations by their relatives and acquaintances, they felt the need to make cash gifts at death anniversaries. An elderly Hoài Thị village leader commented on this new practice:

> The cash gift practice at death anniversaries started with young people just three to four years ago [around 2010–11] … For a long time, we had instituted the rule of no gift whatsoever when villagers attended death anniversaries within the village … People followed this practice for a while … Then, as living conditions improved, people began bringing fruit to death anniversaries. One year, at the death anniversary of the mother of a retired official whose children all lived far away, there was so much fruit that this retired official's wife decided to re-sell it afterwards, as the fruit could not be given to her children and grandchildren, this was not well received in the community … We consequently instituted the rule of no fruit gifts and re-affirmed the rule of no gifts at all at death anniversaries. It was observed for a few years. Then younger villagers began giving cash gifts, as they felt awkward coming empty-handed to a death-anniversary feast. As some people made cash gifts, those without gifts felt awkward and made cash gifts too … Nowadays, a family may spend a few million đồng a

---

3   In my ongoing re-study of seven rural communities in three regions of Vietnam, Hoài Thị is the only one where gifts at death anniversaries can take the form of cash.

year on gifts on those ritual occasions, because for a funeral, the gift is 100,000 đồng at a minimum, to be followed by a 100,000-đồng gift at the 50th-day death anniversary.

The practice of cash gifts at death anniversaries started with younger Hoài Thị villagers because few of them had entered the life stage when they could host death anniversaries for deceased parents. Among middle-aged and older villagers in both Hoài Thị and Khánh Hậu, it is a common practice for brothers to divide the hosting of feasts on the death anniversaries of parents among themselves so that they can reciprocate relatives and friends who have invited them to death anniversary feasts and other events (see Luong 2013).

Regional Variation in Social Relational Configuration

Many similarities between Hoài Thị and Khánh Hậu notwithstanding, wedding banquet data (Figure 2) show an important difference in the social relational configuration between the two communities. More specifically, Hoài Thị villagers have invested considerably more time and resources to cultivate social connections, informal or formal, than people in Khánh Hậu.

The self-recordings from February 2005 to January 2006 by 64 households (23 in Khánh Hậu and 41 in Hoài Thị) regarding the ritual events where gifts were (potentially) exchanged and social connections strengthened, reveal that Hoài Thị households on average attended many more such events in a year than their Khánh Hậu counterparts (55.8 events on average in Hoài Thị, compared with 32.8 in Khánh Hậu).[4] The average number of death anniversaries and weddings attended by Hoài Thị households was twice as many as that attended by those in Khánh Hậu; and 11 times as many house construction celebrations (see Table 1). These household self-recordings are congruent with the data on household-organised and invitation-based events such as weddings, showing that the size of these events has

---

4   In Khánh Hậu, only 29 of the 35 households agreeing to self-recording for one year recorded the events with gift exchanges attended by the members of their households. In my interviews with 35 Khánh Hậu households in November and December 2006, I determined that the self-recordings by six of 29 households were far from complete, and that we had reliable data from only 23 of the 35 self-recording households.

increased much more significantly in Hoài Thị than in Khánh Hậu over the past three-and-a-half decades. They confirm that Hoài Thị villagers made stronger efforts to cultivate social ties.

Table 1: Average number of gift-exchange events attended over a 12-month period by studied households in Hoài Thị and Khánh Hậu, 2005–06.

	Hoài Thị	Khánh Hậu (Dinh hamlet)
Number of events attended	55.8	32.8
Of which:		
Death anniversary	27.8	13
Wedding	21	11.4
Funeral	2.8	4.5
House construction	2.2	0.2
Other	2	3.7

Source: Author's research.

In the northern village of Hoài Thị, the more noticeable increase in the size of wedding banquets over three-and-a-half decades and the greater attendance at events with gifts reflects a very different social capital configuration than in Khánh Hậu. More specifically, Hoài Thị villagers have made significantly greater effort to organise voluntary associations and to revitalise patrilineages in order to strengthen social ties which involve obligations at life cycle ceremonies and death anniversaries.

In 2005, when comparative data on kinship and voluntary association ties in the two communities were systematically collected, the striking differences in social relational configuration between Hoài Thị and Khánh Hậu became evident. More specifically, within the kinship domain, the kinship network in Hoài Thị was much denser than in Khánh Hậu. Due to the relatively high degree of community endogamy across generations, every Hoài Thị villager was related consanguinally or affinally to numerous others in the village (see Luong 2010:401–402). Of equal importance was the establishment or re-creation of numerous associations in Hoài Thị, a process which has intensified over the past two decades. They ranged from patrilineages to voluntary associations, the most important being same-age associations (*hội đồng niên*). Through these institutions, in which Hoài Thị villagers invested considerable time and financial resources, they strengthened their social networks and social capital — social capital as defined by Bourdieu as 'the aggregate of the actual or potential resources which are linked to possession of a durable network of more or less institutionalized relationships' (Bourdieu 1986:249). The strength of Hoài Thị villagers' social capital is partly reflected in the higher number of events involving gift exchanges which they attended.

Kinship

Hoài Thị patrilineages were revitalised from the 1980s onwards. They played an increasingly important role in both rites of solidarity and rites of passage. For example, at the village tutelary deity's procession during the village festival in the first lunar month, many lineages presented their offerings to the deity and had them carried in the procession in order to assert their identities. Many also organised the worship of lineage founders and established 'education-encouragement funds' (qũy khuyến học), recognising the educational achievements of students in their lineages. At funerals, patrilineages made their own offerings to deceased members and organised their male members in order to assist with funeral processions and grave digging. A Hoài Thị villager related how the patrilineage of her husband raised funds for funeral offerings:

> Female interviewee: The [Nguyễn] Sỹ patrilineage specifies that the patrilineal kin who [according to customs] wear [white] mourning head bands would each contribute 10,000 [VND to the funeral gift from the patrilineage to the household of the deceased]. So, when the mourning head bands are distributed to a household, the household gives the money. Three bands, 30,000 VND; 2 bands, 20,000 VND. (Nguyễn Tiến Lộc's interview with Household 480 in Hoài Thị)[5]

In Khánh Hậu, the descendants of Nguyễn Huỳnh Đức organised themselves into the only patrilineage in the community, whose activities centred on the death anniversary of the lineage founder on the ninth day of the ninth lunar month. The activities of the Nguyễn Huỳnh patrilineage in Khánh Hậu were more limited in scope than those of the patrilineages in the village of Hoài Thị: it neither had an education-encouragement fund, nor was it actively involved in the

---

5   Nguyễn Tiến Lộc was a member of one of the two field teams in my research project. So were Tạ Hữu Dực, Nguyễn Anh Tuấn, Nguyễn Thị Nhung, and Huỳnh Ngọc Thu whose names are mentioned at the end of some other interview excerpts.

funerals of its members. In the larger context of the Mekong delta, patrilineages were rarely established, and when they existed as in Khánh Hậu, the scope of their activities was considerably more limited than observed in the Red River of North Vietnam. The reciprocal obligations among the members of the same patrilineage in Hoài Thị in particular, and in the Red River Delta in general, strengthened their relations and enlarged their social capital.

Non-kinship

In Hoài Thị, the strengthening of kinship ties through patrilineages was a part of the larger institutional framework for enhancing social capital. Hoài Thị villagers had established numerous non-kinship associations with formal rules for mutual assistance. Most notable were the same-age associations (*hội đồng niên*). About two-thirds of Hoài Thị men between the age of 18 and 60 belonged to the same-age associations whose membership was village-bound. Same-age associations had strict rules regarding gifts and mutual assistance on major occasions in association members' households: wedding (a major collective gift to an association member), house construction, and funeral (of members, members' spouses and parents; with collective offerings and labour assistance at the ceremony). (Only 24 of the 319 Hoài Thị women in the 18–60 age range joined same-age associations.) One villager explained the importance of same-age association ties:

> When asked about whether they were happy with the membership in the same-age association and whether the membership had led to a good amount of mutual assistance, the whole group concurred that a same-age association was better than a same-school-class association (*hội đồng học*). A same-school-class association did not bring together all the friends of the same age from the village. If the same-school-class association was formed among classmates from a senior secondary school, some members would be from other communes. Such fellow association members could not understand one another as well as childhood friends of the same age and from the same village. When one joined a same-age association, one's household, although having only one son, would have ten sons [from a same-age association with ten members]. When one's household had a house constructed, all association members would come to help without pay and need to be fed only. Even when an association member was absent, his younger or elder brother would come to help as a replacement [for the absent association member]. Or when a member's household had a wedding, fellow [same-age] association members came

to help set up the banquet area. Those who worked away from the village and could not help before the main wedding day would make an effort to be at the wedding. (Fieldnotes of Tạ Hữu Dực about Household 383 in Hoài Thà)

The remaining voluntary associations in Hoài Thị, while less important than same-age associations, were numerous: education-promotion associations (hội khuyến học), elderly male group at the communal house, elderly female Buddhist association, all-women incense-offering team (đội dâng hương), adverse-circumstance women's group with incense burners at the pagoda (nhóm bát hương), same-military-service association (hội đồng ngũ), same-circumstance women's associations (hội đồng tâm), alumni associations, same-occupation associations, parallel-verse singing (quan họ) club, spirit medium group (nhóm con nhang), and a retired state worker group. Male villagers participated more in the formal voluntary associations than their female counterparts (Figure 3) because, according to many female informants, married women had more domestic duties (including the care of children and grandchildren).

In contrast, voluntary association membership was much less common in Dinh hamlet of Khánh Hậu,[6] despite a population size three times greater than Hoài Thị. In 2005, the number of voluntary association memberships for every 100 persons aged 16 or above was 112 among men and 70 among women in Hoài Thị, and 17 among men and 7.6 among women in Khánh Hậu (Figure 3).[7] By 2012, this difference had widened. Specifically, in Hoài Thị, eight neighbourhood associations had been

---

6   Khánh Hậu also had a poetry club and traditional music club whose activities were partly sponsored by the local government. But relatively few Dinh hamlet residents were members of these clubs. The three Cao Dai temples in Khánh Hậu, however, formed three communities within which there was mutual assistance in the form of praying at funerals.

7   These statistical figures for villagers above the age of 16 do not include rotating credit associations, which involve mostly households and household budgets. There was an average of 0.56 rotating credit association memberships per household in Dinh hamlet of Khánh Hậu compared with 0.4 in Hoài Thị. In terms of gender, in the northern village of Hoài Thị, both men and women participated in credit associations, while in the southern community of Khánh Hậu, it was mainly women who participated in credit associations. Since data on credit association membership were collected not at the individual level but at the household level, they are not used in the calculation of the number of association memberships per 100 adult men or 100 adult women.

In both Hoài Thị and Khánh Hậu, there were also state-organised associations, such as women's association, peasant association, elderly association, youth association, and trade unions (only in Khánh Hậu). In 2005, the rate of membership for every 100 residents above the age of 16 was 44 in Hoài Thị and 11 in Khánh Hậu for women's association; and, for other state-organised associations, 84 for both men and women in Hoài Thị, and 14 for men and 9 for women in Khánh Hậu.

formed, covering 37 per cent of village households. Women going through the same Buddhist ceremonies (*lễ quy y*) had also formed mutual aid associations. Membership of the Buddhist association also increased from 75 in 2005 to 157 in 2013. The *quan họ* club membership doubled from 22 to 44. Declining membership of same-circumstance women's associations (*hội đồng tâm*) was due to their transformation into rotating credit associations, requiring contributions beyond the capacity of a number of members. The number of other voluntary association ties remained essentially unchanged. In general, the number of voluntary association ties per 100 adults in Hoài Thị increased from 2005 to 2012, while it did not increase in Khánh Hậu. The difference between two communities in voluntary association membership thus widened during this seven-year period.

Table 2: Voluntary association membership in Hoài Thị and Dinh hamlet of Khánh Hậu, 2005.

	Hoài Thị	Khánh Hậu
Population	1,032	2,894
Association membership		
Communal house association/group	41	42
Buddhist (prayer) association	75	40
Ritual teams	48	7
Spirit medium group	8	
Cao Đài children's team		6
Education-promotion association	86	6
Same-military-service association	41	2
Same-occupation association/group	7	13
Same-age association	240	
Same-circumstance women's association	45	
Adverse-circumstance women's group	21	
Alumni association	24	14
Retired state worker group	14	9
Quan họ singing club	22	
Gymnastics club		5
Traditional medicine philanthropy group		22
Rotating credit association	100	385

Source: Author's research.

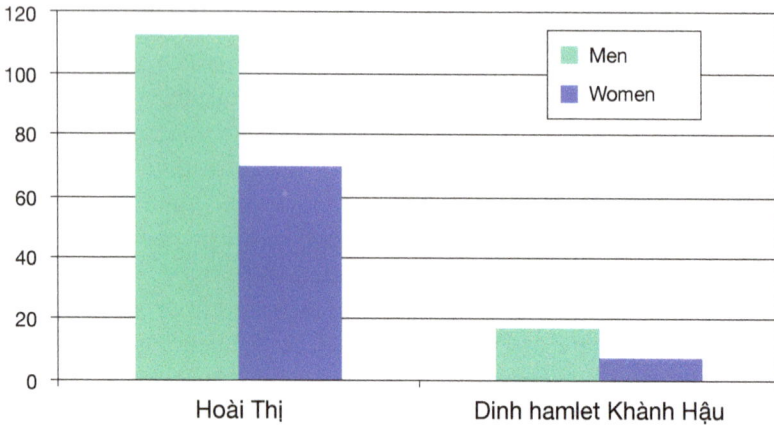

Figure 3: Voluntary association membership — number of memberships per 100 residents above the age of 16 in 2005.
Source: Author's research.

The northern–southern difference in social relational configuration is a major feature not only in the rural landscape, but also in big cities such as Hà Nội and Hồ Chí Minh City. In Hà Nội, numerous same-village associations (*hội đồng hương*) exist among people born and raised in somewhat distant villages in rural northern Vietnam, but in Hồ Chí Minh City, same-village or even same-commune associations among people migrating from rural southern Vietnam are unheard of. Even same-district associations are rare. Only same-province associations exist with very limited membership among people coming from the same province. While southerners do draw upon their ego-centred informal networks in urban contexts, northerners establish formal voluntary associations much more often.

If the high frequency of endogamous marriages rendered kinship ties in Hoài Thị multiplex in that the same two persons had different kinship roles vis-à-vis each other, depending on the tracing path (see Luong and Diệp Đình Hoa 2000:50–51), the formation of numerous voluntary associations, mainly in the past two decades, rendered social relations in Hoài Thị considerably more so. At major events such as weddings and funerals, many villagers had to present multiple gifts, many through their associations, because of these villagers' multiple relations to the household with such an event. In the context of intricately tight intra-village social networks and multiplex relations, it was difficult for any Hoài Thị household not to be fairly heavily involved in gift exchanges within the village.

From a diachronic perspective, the proliferation of voluntary associations accounted for an important part of the significant increase in the number of guests at such ritual events as death anniversaries and weddings in Hoài Thị, as explained by a villager:

> Male interviewee: When I got married, we served about 35 trays of food [to about 175 guests]. [In those days] … a wedding was attended by close relatives like first patrilineal cousins. Nowadays, [given the] same-age and same-school-class associations (*hội đồng niên* and *hội đồng học*), invitations are sent out to a larger number or even to the entire village … Not in my day … It is only in the past few years when same-age associations proliferate, [there are] more wedding invitations. (Nguyễn Anh Tuấn's interview with Household 412 in Hoài Thà)

From a synchronic perspective, both the tighter kinship network in Hoài Thị than in Khánh Hậu and the proliferation of social ties through voluntary associations in Hoài Thị also underlay the more frequent attendance of Hoài Thị villagers at ritual events with gift exchanges. The larger number of events attended by studied Hoài Thị households reflects their generally larger social capital by which, as discussed below, they successfully mobilise material assistance on numerous occasions, ranging from job introduction (heavy concentration of villagers with non-agricultural incomes in the alcohol retail trade and in the construction industry in Hà Nội) to easier access to interest-free loans and to house construction in Hoài Thị itself.

The material assistance mobilised through social capital can be examined in greater depth through three cases: one well-off household in Khánh Hậu in 2006, and two relatively poor households, one in Khánh Hậu and one in Hoài Thị, undertaking household renovation in 2003 and 2005 respectively. Both of the poor households were in the second (below-average) income quintile in their respective communities, with the Hoài Thị household earning an annual per capita income of 4.7 million VND ($317 USD), compared with 3.7 million VND ($250 USD) in Khánh Hậu. The Khánh Hậu household received house construction gifts from only 11 households, worth 1 million VND ($63 USD), while the Hoài Thị household received cash gifts from 106 households (85 from Hoài Thị) totalling 5.1 million VND ($328 USD) on the occasion of its house renovation in 2003. These gifts added to the flow of interest-free loans for house construction (see below), enabling the Hoài Thị household under analysis to spend more on its house renovation than otherwise possible. In Hoài Thị, cash gifts and labour contributions came not only from kin and neighbours, but also from same-age association members, among other people whose social ties were formed or strengthened in the past two decades.

Among better-off Hoài Thị villagers, material assistance for the purchase of property and house construction was also quite substantial. A 37-year-old trader in Household 379, whose per capita income of 45 million VND ($2,300 USD) in 2012 placed it in the top income quintile in Hoài Thị, related the material assistance that he had received:

> When I had the house built in 2006, it cost 260 million VND ($16,227 USD). My friends lent me a good part of the money, interest-free … When I asked a friend for a loan of ten million VND ($625 USD), he told his wife to get a tael of gold and gave it to me. A tael of gold was 19 million VND ($1,186 USD) at that time. He said, 'How come only ten million VND? Take this. Give the house a good paint instead of leaving it unpainted …' I chose to pay him back in three instalments, two-tenths of a tael, half a tael, and three-tenths of a tael. He said, 'No hurry. Take your time and make sure that you have enough money for other things.' When I bought a piece of land in the village, 85 square metres, for over 700 million VND ($35,700 USD) later, I had to borrow over 300 million VND from my friends, all interest-free. 100 million VND from one friend, and scores of million VND from each of some other friends. And $3,000 USD from my elder brother's daughter. (Excerpt from Hy V. Luong's interview with Household 379 in June 2014)

The reciprocal gift/labour exchange and interest-free loans allowed Hoài Thị villagers in particular, and northern Vietnamese rural dwellers in general, to build more expensive brick houses, even when they had very limited resources of their own. In contrast, in the southern Mekong Delta, many poor rural dwellers constructed simple and less expensive houses with thatched roofs, wooden walls and earthen floors.

Because of the aforementioned difference between Hoài Thị and Khánh Hậu in social capital configuration, despite the higher annual per capita income in Khánh Hậu than in Hoài Thị (31 million VND ($1,482 USD) versus 23 million VND ($1,094 USD)), in 2012 the average number of people from whom surveyed households could borrow at least five million VND interest-free for at least one month was 15 in Hoài Thị and 5.5 in Khánh Hậu. In other words, social capital could be mobilised more easily in Hoài Thị than in Khánh Hậu.

However, social capital is a double-edged sword (Portes 1998; Geertz 1963). It can be mobilised for the purpose of resolving various problems in daily life. But it also involves obligations to people in one's social network. In the context of lower per capita income in the northern village of Hoài Thị than in the southern community of Khánh Hậu, and in the face of larger numbers of kinship and non-kinship ties with gift obligations in the former, Hoài Thị villagers have introduced rules and practices for limiting ritual expenditures and gift expenses. By 2012, beer flowed without limit at death anniversary feasts and wedding banquets in Khánh Hậu, while in Hoài Thị, the number of beer cans offered at ceremonies was restricted. As cash gifts at weddings minimally covered the cost of the meal, these usually amounted to 100,000 VND (about $5 USD) in Hoài Thị in 2012 in contrast to 200,000 VND (about $10 USD) in Khánh Hậu. Despite the larger number of events attended by Hoài Thị villagers, the annual per capita spending on ritual events such as weddings, funerals, death anniversaries, among others, remained lower in Hoài Thị than in Khánh Hậu, both in 2005 and in 2012 (see Table 2). Hoài Thị villagers succeeded in holding down their gift and ritual expenses and simultaneously increasing their social capital, more than people in Khánh Hậu.

Table 3: Per capita spending on gifts in 2005 and 2012 in million of VND (in constant 2012 value of VND).[8]

	Hoài Thị		Khánh Hậu	
Year	2005	2012	2005	2012
Number of surveyed households in community	(n=247)	(n=280)	(n=367)	(n=411)
Annual per capita income	14.72 ($450 USD)	22.97 ($1,094 USD)	16.785 ($513 USD)	31.12 ($1,482 USD)
Annual per capita spending on gifts	1.99 ($61 USD)	2.49 ($119 USD)	2.22 ($68 USD)	3.1 ($148 USD)
% of income spent on gifts at ceremonies	13.5%	10.8%	13.2%	10%

Source: Author's research.

Class and Social Capital

Although ethnic Vietnamese of all social strata attach great significance to social connections or social capital, opportunities for maintaining and expanding social capital are not equally available to all members of society. While the poor can express their sentiment through advice, support, and sociality, those with wealth and political power, forming a dominant class, are in a much stronger position to cultivate social relations by organising more events, inviting more people to these events, and by offering financial support and interest-free loans to people in their social networks.

Survey data (Table 4) indicate that in 2012, in both communities, the average net per capita expenditure on rituals (mostly on weddings, funerals and death anniversaries) and gifts at these rituals hovered in the range of 1.75 to 2.5 million VND for the first (lowest), second, third, and fourth income quintiles. These expenditures are both

---

8   As average incomes rose during the period between 2005 and 2012, gift and social relational expenditures per capita, controlled for inflation, also increased in absolute amount (by 25 per cent in Hoài Thị and 40 per cent in Khánh Hậu). There is thus no evidence that, as wealth increased, villagers became less involved in the gift economy. However, in both communities, the percentage of income spent on gifts and social relations dropped from over 13 per cent in 2005 to the range of 10 per cent in 2012. The declining percentage of income spent on gifts and social relations probably resulted from a greater investment in education, among other items. In our general household survey in 2000, with 207 households in Hoài Thị and 340 in Khánh Hậu, we did not ask about gift/ritual spending. Data are only available for 40 households in Hoài Thị and 70 households in Khánh Hậu in 2000 on the basis of a different research instrument, making 2000 data not strictly comparable to 2005 and 2012 ones.

for gifts in attending those rituals in other households, and for net expenditures for the organisers, after deducting the cash gifts from guests. Many poor households in the bottom income quintile in both communities had to spend annually (almost) as much per capita on ritual event gifts as those in the middle income quintile in order to maintain their social relations. For households in the bottom income quintile, these ritual expenses to maintain social capital amounted to an average of 23 per cent of income in the southern community of Khánh Hậu and 31 per cent in the northern village of Hoài Thị. At the opposite end, although households in the top income quintile clearly spent more on ritual expenses to cultivate social relations and obtained more benefits from their larger social capital (reflected in the much larger number of possible interest-free loans), on average, their ritual expenses amounted to less than 10 per cent of their income.

Table 4: Per capita income and ritual expenditure by income quintile, 2012 (income and expenditure in million of VND; USD equivalents appear in parentheses).

Income quintile		1 (lowest)	2	3	4	5 (highest)
Hoài Thị	a. Per capita income	7.74 ($369)	15.12 ($720)	19.33 ($920)	25.15 ($1,196)	47.4 ($2,257)
	b. Per capita ritual expenditure	2.4 ($114)	1.95 ($93)	2.26 ($108)	2.48 ($118)	3.35 ($160)
	% of income spent on ritual expenditure	31%	13%	12%	10$	7%
	Average no. of possible interest-free loans at or above 5 million VND ($238)	10.7	9.9	16.4	15.8	21.7
Khánh Hậu	a. Per capita income	8.66 ($412)	16.4 ($781)	23.22 ($1,106)	32.1 ($1,529)	75.22 ($3,582)
	b. Per capita ritual expenditure	1.97 ($94)	1.75 ($83)	2.22 ($106)	2.4 ($114)	7.2 ($343)
	% of income spent on ritual expenditure	23%	11%	9.6%	7.5%	9.6%
	Average no. of possible interest-free loans at or above 5 million VND ($238)	2.3	3	5.8	3.4	11.7

Source: Author's research.

Why did the poor in both Khánh Hậu and Hoài Thị tend to accept the burden of ritual expenses, which took up a relatively high percentage of their income, and which caused considerable tension in intra-household relations? As seen in two of the three cases below, the burden of ritual expenses was accepted by households in order to reciprocate assistance received in the past (at weddings and funerals, among other occasions) and to maintain their social relations, which would increase the likelihood of future assistance from people and households in their networks.

In 2005, Household 91 in Khánh Hậu comprised a 73-year-old woman living with her granddaughters, aged six and 12. Household income was derived mainly from the remittances from her youngest son and daughter-in-law (the parents of her granddaughters) who had received 1.5 hectares of cultivable land in the Plain of Reeds as a part of the resettlement of landless cultivators in the late 1980s. The elderly woman's mother had a long ancestral root in Khánh Hậu, while her father came from a neighbouring commune. Her deceased husband's family had settled in Khánh Hậu for at least one generation. Her daughter-in-law came from a neighbouring commune located in Tiền Giang Province. In 2005, the daughter-in-law returned to Khánh Hậu during slack seasons to help take care of the two granddaughters, while the son stayed in their new village to take care of the land. With an annual per capita income of 3.1 million VND ($196 USD) in 2005, Household 91 fell into the bottom income quintile in Khánh Hậu. However, it had ancestral worship duties to five deceased persons, including the elderly woman's husband, parents-in-law, and grandparents-in-law. Due to its limited financial resources, it annually organised only one big death anniversary banquet (that of the elderly woman's husband), which cost about 2 million VND ($125 USD). The elderly woman in Household 91 reportedly attended 53 events in a 12-month period in 2005–06, presenting gifts worth approximately 2.3 million VND (about one-quarter of the total income of this household, equivalent to $146 USD). They included 26 death anniversaries (mostly among the elderly woman's relatives and acquaintances in Khánh Hậu), 12 weddings, eight funerals, four birth celebrations, three visits to sick acquaintances, and one house construction party. The overwhelming majority were organised by the elderly woman's relatives, children-in-law's parents, and neighbours. Although some of the elderly woman's gift money came from remittances from her oldest son living in another province and occasional gifts from her four married daughters in Khánh Hậu, the bulk of the gift expenses, as well as more than half of the big death anniversary expenses, had to be covered by her youngest son and daughter-in-law. (It is customary for youngest sons in the southern third of Vietnam to inherit their parents' houses, a greater portion of their parents' land, and to assume a greater responsibility for ancestral worship, in contrast to the pattern in the Red River Delta, where the oldest son tends to assume this role.) The gift burden on the youngest son and his family was a major source of conflict between the elderly woman and her daughter-in-law, to the point that they were barely on speaking terms with each other during our fieldwork in 2005:

> Mrs C. [daughter-in-law in Household 91] said that she would be ready to pass on her family affairs to whoever was willing to take them over ... that the family had no savings year in, year out ... that money was heavily spent on ritual gifts ... [She referred to Mrs K., her mother-in-law, in the front room with] another reminder [to her] about the need to go to the funeral of Mr Tư in Thủ Tửu [hamlet]. Mrs Sáu [a neighbour of Mrs C.] also made a similar complaint that it was a heavy burden getting married to a youngest son and living in a family with ancestral worship obligations, and that earnings were heavily spent on ritual banquets.

> Mrs Sáu went home to go to bed. I continued talking to Mrs C. until 10 p.m. Mrs C. complained and talked about all sorts of things centring on the conflict with her mother-in-law and the costly ritual banquet expenses in a household with ancestral worship duties ... Her mother-in-law [reportedly] spent a lot of money [on gifts to be brought to ritual banquets]. [Mrs C. said] no matter how hard she worked, money was always short, and that they were regularly in debt. Her mother-in-law readily accepted invitations, and spent 100,000 VND on a wedding gift [above the normal figure of 50,000 VND for a wedding in 2005] and 50,000 VND on a funeral gift. Occasionally, Mrs C. suggested [to her mother-in-law] to scale down the gifts. Her mother-in-law reportedly said that she could not behave like a dog. [When Mrs C did not give the money for a ritual banquet gift], the mother-in-law, after changing her clothes [to go to the banquet], kept repeating: 'Maybe I am a dog.'

> Mrs K [the mother-in-law] would attend the funeral as the in-law of the deceased's in-law. Mrs K called Ms Sáu [nicknamed] the Fatso in to give the money, but Mrs C understood that it was her obligation to give the money to Ms Sáu. Mrs C. talked quietly to Mrs Sáu, and the latter left with no money. Mrs C left to visit a neighbour.

> Mrs K. [the mother-in-law] walked in and out of the house and told me: She [C.] did not care about funerals, as if I would not die [implying that C. did not care about the future reciprocation of acquaintances at Mrs K.'s funeral] … Mrs C said that [her mother-in-law] said that a gift of 50,000 VND was not adequate [at the funeral]. Because Mrs K. would go with the mother-in-law of her children, she reportedly wanted to give a 100,000 VND gift. (Fieldnotes of Nguyễn thị Nhung on Household 91 in Khánh Hậu in August 2005)

The large number of events attended by the elderly woman in Household 91 was due partly to her strong integration in the local social and kinship network, the need to reciprocate past gifts, given at her husband's funeral in 1994 and her five children's weddings over the years, the formal gift-exchange relations with her children-in-law's parents, as well as the anticipated need for a good and large future funeral for herself attended by people in her network and those of her children, including the recipients of her ritual gifts. Despite its relative poverty, Household 91 had an extensive social and kinship network and thus more social capital than many richer households in Khánh Hậu.[9]

In 2005, Khánh Hậu Household 16 comprised five members, a couple (husband aged 44, and wife, 39), their two sons (aged 17 and 2), and the wife's mother, who was temporarily residing with them to help care for their two-year-old son. Although the husband was born elsewhere, due to his father's work assignment in another province, he had long-standing connections to Khánh Hậu, where his maternal grandfather had been a large and influential landowner before the political change in 1975, a change that adversely affected the maternal grandfather's landholding due to the new regime's collectivisation policy. The husband had numerous close relatives in Khánh Hậu, and the land on which his house was built was bequeathed by his maternal grandfather. The wife came from Tân Hội Đông, a neighbouring commune located in Tiền Giang Province. This household had

---

9   In 2012, the number of death anniversaries attended by the members of Household 91 increased to 34, and the total ritual expenses to 8.75 million VND ($417 USD), triple that of expenditure in 2005. (The ritual expenses per capita in this household were 2 million VND a year.) However, the tension between the mother-in-law and daughter-in-law subsided apparently due to the significant increase in the annual per capita income of the household to 33.6 million VND ($1,600 USD) compared to $196 USD in 2005 thanks to the greater agricultural income of the son and non-agricultural income of the daughter-in-law. The ritual and gift expenses of Household 91 took up only 6.25 per cent of the household income in 2012.

0.45 hectare of land on which the husband worked, and the husband also helped the wife in her *phở* (beef noodle) business in the provincial capital of Tân An (6 kilometres away). Their annual per capita income of 3.1 million VND ($210 USD) in 2005 put them in the bottom income quintile in Khánh Hậu. Despite the relatively limited income of the household, the husband had an extensive kinship network in Khánh Hậu, while his wife possessed her own in her native commune, as well as in Khánh Hậu, where one of her sisters had married into a Khánh Hậu family. Among the husband's close relatives were his parents and four brothers with their families in Khánh Hậu, one married sister in Khánh Hậu, and three sisters married to husbands in a neighbouring commune or in the nearby provincial capital. The husband also had a maternal uncle, some maternal aunts, and numerous first cousins on both his father's and mother's sides in Khánh Hậu. The wife had her parents and seven married siblings, as well as numerous aunts, uncles, and first cousins, in her native commune neighbouring Khánh Hậu. The husband and wife in Household 16 attended a total of 51 gift-exchange events in the 12-month period under study, including 25 death anniversaries, 12 weddings, two wedding-preparatory ceremonies, seven funerals, three birth celebrations, one visit to a sick acquaintance, and one other ritual. Among the 25 death anniversaries were four banquets held at the household of this husband's maternal uncle, each of which required gifts to be brought.[10] As the husband was not the youngest son in his natal household and as his parents were alive and living with his youngest brother, he did not have any death anniversary to take care of. He also reportedly cut back on the number of death anniversaries attended in 2005 out of concern for the cost of gifts and the need to support his elder son's possible university education. But in 2005, this household still spent 3.1 million VND a year ($210 USD), about one-fifth of the total family income, on gifts for 51 events organised by other households. This resulted from the couple's strong integration into the local social networks in Khánh Hậu and in a neighbouring commune.

---

10   As a reflection of his wealth, the maternal uncle organised four death anniversary banquets with significantly overlapping guest lists (about 100 guests at the death anniversary of his father; 40 at that of his mother; and 40 and 20 at those of his two sons). In Khánh Hậu, despite the widely reported pattern of dividing death anniversary duties among siblings and close relatives, it was not uncommon for a household to hold many death anniversary banquets in a year if it had the economic means to do so.

In 2009, the husband in Household 16 passed away. The wife had to sell a part of the family's landholding to pay off the husband's medical expenses, and her sister-in-law took over the *phở* (beef noodle) business. In 2012, the wife in Household 16 worked for the sister-in-law in the morning and the early evening. The wife also peddled roasted rice paper (*bánh tráng nướng*) in the afternoon to earn extra income in order to bring her monthly income to 3 million VND ($143 USD). With the elder son being an officer in the armed forces and her mother returning to the neighbouring commune, Household 16 had only two members. Its annual per capita income rose to 18 million VND ($857 USD), putting the household in the second income quintile (below average). In 2012, despite having a nine-year-old child to support, Household 16 had to spend 2.7 million VND ($129 USD, or 7.5 per cent of total household income) on ritual gift expenses, including at 19 death anniversaries. The wife in Household 16 talked about this ritual expense burden and the need to reciprocate people who had made cash gifts during her husband's illness and later at his funeral:

Interviewee: I sell [roasted rice paper] in Khánh Hậu to earn some extra money in the afternoon [besides assisting my sister-in-law with her *phở* and beefsteak business]. It costs a lot of money to cover ritual feast expenses and gifts ... So many of them. Cash gifts, for example, on the occasion of month-old celebrations (*đầy tháng*) and first birth days (*thôi nôi*) for kids. Next month, there will be two of these events for my husband's niece and nephew [sister's children]. I already made a 200,000 VND gift when the baby was born. Next month, 200,000 VND [$9.52 USD] more for his month-old celebration. My husband used to take care of such events. Now I have to deal with them all ... Gifts for nieces and nephews have to be 200,000 VND. For other kids, 100,000 VND ... I also have to visit sick people in my network and that of my husband ... Because when my husband was sick, they came to visit and gave gifts. They gave 50,000 VND, and now when I visit a sick person in their families, I have to give 50,000 VND. For funerals, the gift has to be 100,000 VND. 50,000 VND looks miserly.

...

Interviewer: When your husband passed away, did you accept cash gifts?

Interviewee: Yes. The cash gifts were sufficient to cover funeral costs … The gifts ranged from 20,000 VND, 30,000 VND, 50,000 VND to 100,000 VND. Money could buy more in those days [in 2009, thus gifts had a comparatively lower value]. The funeral gifts amounted to over 30 million VND [$1,650 USD].

…

Interviewee: I have to wake up at 4 a.m. in the morning. I have not had any rest until now [interview taking place at the *phở* restaurant owned by the interviewee's sister-in-law] … Now, I am roasting rice paper and going to walk around the community to sell it. I work so hard.

Interviewer: Any siesta?

Interviewee: No. I work hard to earn some money to host a death anniversary feast for my husband.

Interviewer: When can you go home?

Interviewee: Around 5 p.m. I go home to take a shower and burn incense for my husband, and return here to work until 8:30 in the evening, during which I also wash clothes for my sister-in-law and her children.

Interviewer: No washing machine?

Interviewee: No, all by hand.

Interviewee [crying]: It is a lot of hard work to earn money. But my sister-in-law provides meals for me and my son every day … A lot of hard work. I sell roasted rice paper to earn some extra money. Many times, in roasting the rice paper, I cry and cry … I try to earn some extra money and try to save for my son … I do not spend a lot of time during the day at home, because I feel so sad there … Now, I roast about 20 rice papers in over an hour, and then go around peddling them, and earn 20,000 VND for the work [one-fifth of her daily income]. (Huỳnh Ngọc Thu's interview with Household 16 in November 2012)

Some poor and elderly people, as in Household 543 in Hoài Thị, decided not to accept death anniversary invitations in order to hold down their ritual gift expenditures. Household 543 in Hoài Thị, comprising an elderly couple, had an annual per capita income of 1.33 million VND ($63 USD in 2012) mainly from government assistance, which put them among the poorest in the village of Hoài Thị.[11] They spent nothing on ritual gift expenses in 2012, as they felt that they could not afford to. Unlike most other Hoài Thị villagers, they also believed that they could not borrow 5 million VND interest-free from anybody in their social network. The elderly couple's social capital and the ability to mobilise it in the form of interest-free loans was greatly diminished due to their lack of spending on ritual expenses. This lack of spending on ritual expenses reflects the extreme poverty of this elderly couple (in contrast to Household 91 in Khánh Hậu, the first case earlier discussed). In 2014, when I asked about their lack of spending on ritual expenses, the elderly couple talked at length to me about their embarrassment in not being able to maintain their ritual and social relation obligations:

> HL: Do you still give cash gifts at death anniversaries, or are they waived, as you are now over 80 years old?
>
> Husband: For the elderly over the age of 80, the cash gift is only 50,000 đồng ($2.40 USD). It is all right not to give a cash gift [given the age], but it looks better if one is given.
>
> Wife: He does not give cash gifts at death anniversaries. That is why he said, 'if one is given'. Without a cash gift, we come and stay for a short time … It feels embarrassing.
>
> HL: When the two of you turned 80, did your children organise a feast for you and your acquaintances?
>
> Husband: No, they did not … if I organised a death anniversary feast for my father, inviting other people, then [I would feel better] attending the death anniversaries organised by the latter … As I do not host a feast on my mother's or father's death anniversary, I do not go to death anniversaries that much.

---

11   The social welfare net in Vietnam has expanded noticeably in the past few years, well beyond the anti-poverty program started in the 1990s. New programs include modest assistance of 2.16 million VND ($103 USD) a year and a free health insurance card to the elderly from the age of 80 onwards and to other single elderly without much income and without children as a source of support; and assistance to disabled people, including victims of Agent Orange, with annual payments varying with the degree of disability (see Lưu Quang Tuấn 2012:13–14). In 2012, the elderly couple in Household 543 had one person with a minor mental problem who was eligible for 2.18 million VND ($103 USD a year) under the program of assistance to the disabled. In summer 2014, the government assistance to this couple had tripled to 6.54 million VND ($310 USD) because the disability assistance amount was doubled, and because the other person qualified for assistance provided to people aged 80 years and older.

Wife: My children do not organise a longevity meal for us [and our acquaintances] … When other elderly people have longevity feasts, I do not dare to show up despite the invitations … My husband and I are old. We are not able to host a death anniversary feast [for either parent of his]. Neither are our children. The longevity celebrations [for us] are less necessary than death anniversary feasts. If we are not able to host a death anniversary feast, there is no need to talk about a longevity celebration … It all boils down to the eldest [son]. If the eldest son took the initiative, the three younger sons would follow and contribute … If the eldest said that I would organise a longevity celebration for the parent, no way would the other children dare not to move in tandem … It is embarrassing not to be able to host an annual death anniversary for a parent [of my husband]. Embarrassing not to be able to do what other households have done … My first cousin T. [in the village] hosts a feast on the occasion of the death anniversary for my uncle [T's father], and invites me … Another cousin of mine going to the same event asks me to go with her. I have decided not to go, but do not want to go into details with her … It would be a shame for me to say that because of our inability to host a death anniversary feast, I cannot go … I feel miserable … [Husband tells her to stop talking about this problem.] It is all right to stop talking about this issue, but we would be the laughing stock of the village if we just go and eat at death anniversary events without being able to host one at our place. We end up cutting ties with relatives, close or far. We do not dare to go to those events. Except for one recent event, I did show up. People filled my bowl with foods, but I felt so bad inside that I could not really eat. (Author's interview with Household 543, June 2014)

The cases discussed above, and the lack of significant variation in the average ritual gift spending per capita among the four lower income quintiles in both communities, indicate that the relation between ritual spending and household income is far from being linear. My preliminary analysis suggests that besides household wealth, many factors affect ritual and ritual gift spending:

a. Sibling rank: In Hoài Thị, the eldest son assumes official responsibility for ancestral death anniversaries and social relations with relatives, although he may allow younger siblings to host some death anniversary feasts. In Khánh Hậu and in southern Vietnam at large, it is the youngest son who is supposed to assume such a responsibility. As the youngest son of Household 91 in Khánh Hậu is not resident, his wife felt this responsibility as a heavy burden.

In contrast, without official responsibilities for family rituals and social relations with relatives, the male head of Khánh Hậu Household 16, as well as the male trader in Household 379 and the elderly male head of Household 543 in Hoài Thị, had lower ritual and social relation spending than those with such responsibilities.

b. Stage in life cycle:

   i. People in their 20s tend to have many friends getting married, leading to higher wedding gift expenditure.

   ii. People in their 30s tend to have fewer ritual gift obligations in general (the trader in Household 379 in Hoài Thị as an example).

   iii. People in their 40s and 50s tend to be responsible for the weddings of their children, and to reciprocate the wedding gifts received at these events with similar gifts at friends' children's weddings. Those who experience the death of a parent/s also begin assuming death anniversary duties.

c. Degree of integration into local social networks: Hoài Thị villagers have close-knit social networks and tend to be well integrated in their community. In contrast, in Khánh Hậu and many southern communities, where there is a higher degree of geographical mobility, a number of newcomers in a community tend to be not well integrated and to have fewer obligations (see also Luong 2010:417–418).

Those factors complicate the relation between household income and social capital and ritual expenditure; this relation is not statistically linear among lower- and middle-income households. The highest income households in both Hoài Thị and Khánh Hậu tend to spend more lavishly on social relations in order to strengthen their social capital, which results in significantly greater assistance actually or potentially received (see the data on interest-free loans in Table 4). However, the incapacity of the poor to spend much at all on social capital cultivation — as reflected in the case of the elderly couple in Household 543 in Hoài Thị — weakens social ties and results in less assistance received in the form of interest-free loans.

Conclusion

How can we explain the difference in social capital configuration between Hoài Thị and Khánh Hậu, a difference that, I think, is characteristic of the difference between the northern and southern Vietnamese lowlands in general? The difference in social capital configuration lies not only in the greater efforts of Hoài Thị villagers in cultivating and formalising social relations (partly through the establishment of patrilineages and voluntary associations), but also in the greater return from these efforts, as reflected in the considerably greater sources of interest-free loans that can be tapped by Hoài Thị villagers than by those in Khánh Hậu.

Beyond Vietnam, the importance of social connections has been attributed to shortages in political economy and formal institutional weakness, leading to greater uncertainty and people's reliance on social connections in order to reduce uncertainty (Guthrie 1998; Walder 1986). Can the greater efforts of northern Vietnamese to cultivate social relations result from more shortages of goods and services and greater institutional weaknesses in northern Vietnam than in southern Vietnam? There is no evidence that Hoài Thị villagers have recently faced more shortages and greater uncertainty due to institutional weaknesses than the people of Khánh Hậu. With the strong economic growth in Bắc Ninh Province in recent years, Hoài Thị villagers have no trouble earning steady and fairly good incomes in the private or informal sector, and finding quality goods and services. There is no clear evidence either that the conformity to institutional rules is weaker in northern Vietnam than in southern Vietnam, leading to greater uncertainty in the sociopolitical environment and, consequently, to greater reliance on social connections for problem solving in northern Vietnam. Beyond the case of Vietnam, Japan seems to have much stronger formal institutional frameworks than Vietnam and does not have any shortage of goods and services. Yet gifts and social connections remain a very important part of the Japanese sociocultural fabric and political economy. I would argue that it is simplistic to attribute the importance of social connections solely to shortages of goods and services and institutional weaknesses. A strictly institutional explanation of the importance of gifts and social capital would fail to do justice to their salience in Vietnamese or Japanese sociocultural life and political economy. I think that we also need to take into account different enduring models of and for reality in northern and southern Vietnam, enduring models that account not only for the greater investment in social capital, but also, among other things, for the greater strength of patrilineal descent in northern Vietnam than in southern Vietnam (cf. Yang 2002 in Yang's debate with Guthrie in the Chinese context).

I would suggest that the enduring northern Vietnamese model for social reality involves a greater formalisation of social relations, both in terms of obligations and organisation (patrilineage and voluntary associations, with their explicit rules), and, as a reflection of comparatively less commercialisation in a rural community, more mutual assistance in time, labour, and interest-free loans (see Table 4) and less monetary expenditure per event. In Hoài Thị and the Red River Delta of northern Vietnam in general, at the community level, social relations, whether kinship-based or not, also tend to be more centripetal, leading to considerably tighter social networks within the community. In contrast, in Khánh Hậu, social relations are less formalised in terms of organisation and obligations, with less mutual assistance in time, labour, and interest-free loans. In Khánh Hậu and the Mekong Delta of southern Vietnam in general, at the community level, kinship and non-kinship relations tend to be more centrifugal, leading to looser social networks within the community. In Khánh Hậu, ritual events such as death anniversaries are organised in a free-flowing spirit, with less effort made to control costs, leading to higher expenses per event both for organisers and gift-bearing participants. Thus, while social relations (*quan hệ*) are important in the social fabric of both northern and southern Vietnamese communities, they take on different configurations, with varying degrees of effectiveness in mobilisation. It is possible that the different social capital configurations and enduring models for reality in the Red River Delta and the Mekong Delta of Vietnam result from the long-standing greater spatial mobility in the latter in a frontier context, which renders formal organisations less stable and less effective. We can attempt to analyse long-term historical and environmental reasons for the difference in the model for reality between the northern Red River Delta and the southern Mekong Delta in Vietnam (see, for example, Rambo 1973). But it is not clear that this difference can be reduced to short-term differences in political economy and institutional contexts.

References

Bourdieu, Pierre 1986, 'The Forms of Capital', in John Richardson (ed.), *The Handbook of Theory and Research for the Sociology of Education*, Greenwood Press, New York, pp. 141–158.

Geertz, Clifford 1963, *Peddlers and Princes*, University of Chicago Press, Chicago.

Gold, Thomas, Douglas Guthrie and David Wank 2002, 'An Introduction to the Study of *Guanxi*', in Thomas Gold, Douglas Guthrie and David Wank (eds), *Social Connections in China: Institutions, Culture, and the Changing Nature of* Guanxi, Cambridge University Press, Cambridge, pp. 3–20.

Guthrie, Douglas 1998, 'The Declining Importance of *Guanxi* in China's Economic Transition', *The China Quarterly*, vol. 154, pp. 254–282.

Henry, James 1964, *The Small World of Khánh Hậu*, Aldine, Chicago.

Hickey, Gerald 1964, *Village in Vietnam*, Yale University Press, New Haven.

Luong, Hy V. 2010, 'Quà và vốn xã hội ở hai cộng đồng nông thôn Việt Nam' ['Gifts and Social Capital in Two Vietnamese Rural Communities'], in H. Luong et al. (eds), *Hiện đại và động thái của truyền thống ở Việt Nam: Những cách tiếp cận nhân học* [*Modernities and the Dynamics of Tradition in Vietnam: Anthropological Approaches*], Nhà xuất bản Đại học quốc gia TP, Hồ Chí Minh, Ho Chi Minh City, pp. 397–424.

Luong, Hy V. 2013, 'Giỗ tổ tiên và động thái kinh tế xã hội' ['Ancestral Death Anniversaries and their Socio-economic Dynamics'], in *Tín ngưỡng thờ cúng tổ tiên trong xã hội đương đại* [*Ancestral Worship Beliefs in Contemporary Societies*], Nhà xuất bản Văn hóa thông tin, Hanoi, pp. 344–361.

Luong, Hy V. and Diệp Đình Hoa 2000, 'Bốn cộng đồng nông thôn và thành thị Việt Nam: cảnh quan kinh tế, xã hội, và văn hóa' ['Four Rural and Urban Communities in Vietnam: Economic, Social, and Cultural Landscapes'], in Hy V. Luong (ed.), *Ngôn từ, giới, và nhóm xã hội từ thực tiễn tiếng Việt* [*Discourse, Gender, and Society in Vietnam*], Nhà xuất bản Khoa học xã hội, Hanoi, pp. 39–97.

Lưu Quang Tuấn 2012, 'Socialist Republic of Vietnam: Updating and Improving the Social Protection Index', Asian Development Bank, Technical Assistance Consultant's Report, Project 44152.

Portes, Alejandro 1998, 'Social Capital: Its Origins and Applications in Modern Sociology', *Annual Review of Sociology*, vol. 24, pp. 1–24.

Rambo, A. Terry 1973, *A Comparison of Peasant Social Systems of Northern and Southern Viet-Nam*, Southern Illinois University Center for Vietnamese Studies, Carbondale, Illinois.

Unger, Jonathan 1998, *Building Social Capital in Thailand: Fibers, Finance, and Infrastructure*, Cambridge University Press, Cambridge.

Walder, Andrew 1986, *Communist Neo-Traditionalism: Work and Authority in Chinese Industry*, University of California Press, Berkeley.

Yang, Mayfair Mei-hui 1994, *Gifts, Favors, and Banquets: The Art of Social Relationships in China*, Cornell University Press, Ithaca.

Yang, Mayfair Mei-hui 2002, 'The Resilience of Quanxi and Its New Deployment: A Critique of Some New Guanxi Scholarship', *China Quarterly*, vol. 170, pp. 459–476.

2

The Dynamics of Return Migration in Vietnam's Rural North: Charity, Community and Contestation

Nguyen Thi Thanh Binh

This chapter tells the story of a return migrant in Bắc Đồng,[1] a village in Hà Nam Province of northern Vietnam where I carried out extended anthropological fieldwork in the late 2000s.[2] From my first days in this village, I had heard stories about a rich village woman living in Hồ Chí Minh City whose life and career had become legend. According to these stories, she had been one of the richest people in Sài Gòn in the 1980s and 1990s, a room in her house was sometimes full of money, and hundreds of workers were under her command. People in the village had different ideas about this lady's path to success and the way she exercised her power. In some ways, she was magical for them. Even her name, Núi, evoked a sense of mystery about her life.

1   People and places in this chapter have been assigned pseudonyms for purposes of confidentiality.
2   This chapter draws upon ethnographic research conducted in Bắc Đồng village, Hà Nam Province from July 2007 to May 2008. While living with and taking part in the villagers' everyday lives, I interviewed and collected life histories from a wide range of villagers, including my main interlocutor, who I met at her home in Hồ Chí Minh City. I am grateful to Bà Núi and Bắc Đồng villagers for sharing their experiences, insights and time with me. I would like to thank Philip Taylor for his extensive feedback on chapter drafts, and thank Ben Kerkvliet, Hy Van Luong, John Kleinen, Andrew Kipnis, Diana Glazebrook, and the two anonymous readers for their constructive comments. Harvard-Yenching Institute and the Research School of Pacific and Asian Studies, The Australian National University, provided funds for this research.

In Vietnamese, Núi means mountain, and people imagined that she was a mountain of money. Moving to the south in 1975 after the American war, Núi maintained contact with the village through her family and a number of migratory villagers who went to work in or visited her enterprise. Since the 1980s, she had sometimes sent gifts to her relatives and made small donations to the poor, and larger donations for village affairs. Bắc Đồng people's memories and imaginings about Núi and her life in the south might have ceased there if, at the end of 2007, this mythical woman had not suddenly visited her old home after almost 20 years. Her return became an event in the village. People were curious about the way she looked, how she treated the surrounding people, and what she did in their village. They wanted to touch and get up close to this powerful figure who had returned from a far away and prosperous world. Núi aroused in the villagers various expectations and hopes.

Initially, Núi planned to stay in Bắc Đồng for a short time to fulfil her obligations to her family and ancestors. As people learned that Núi was happy to see them, however, more and more villagers gradually came to visit her. In response to the sentiment of her homeland fellows, Núi decided to stay longer, give more gifts to people, and donate more money to renovate ritual places in the village. Her 'heart' of giving to the village's spiritual places and to the poor generated debate among the villagers as to whether she represented a new model of personhood and ethics, or standard of behaviour for the local elite and the rich. Some Bắc Đồng people, especially women, wanted to build a new kind of patron–client relationship with Núi, and for a period of time it seemed that a new inclusive community of villagers, reliant on her generosity, was emerging. This dynamic interaction saw Núi give more in response to the villagers' warm reception and she began to imagine the village as a welcoming and intimate home in which she might find a place after decades of living far away. The story did not end well, however, as envy and criticism from a part of the village population undermined the trust and warmth of these relationships, dashing the dreams and hopes of all parties in these interactions. Chastened and confused, the protagonist Núi returned to her southern, urban home, perhaps never again to return to her home village.

The somewhat tragic story of Núi sheds light on the phenomenon of return migration. As a fertile terrain for migration studies, the experiences of Vietnamese migrants who return home have been examined by several scholars.[3] The comparative literature shows that return migration may, in some instances, be viewed as the outcome of a failed migration strategy or, conversely, as satisfaction of one's original economic or cultural goals (Cassarino 2004:255). Return migration may enable one to reinvest one's migratory earnings in a place where one has a comparative advantage, or convert them into forms of social or cultural capital that may not be attainable in the migratory destination (Bourdieu 1986; Carruthers 2002). Some studies emphasise the factors that 'push' migrants to return home: the hardship and stress of life as a migrant; poor health or personal crisis; or the legal, institutional, and cultural obstacles to integration in the migratory destination (Brettell 2000:100). Alternatively, migrants may be 'pulled' home by homesickness, family crisis, or out of a sense of familial obligation (Gmelch 1980; Jellema 2007). The return home can be conflict-laden and mutually disappointing, both from the perspective of the returnee and their kin and neighbours. Returnees may be the focus of admiration, envy or mistrust from neighbours and kin owing to their exotic status, their relative wealth or practices of conspicuous consumption (Khater 2001). The gifts borne by returned migrants may accentuate social distance between giver and receivers or communicate uncomfortable messages about status differentials just as readily as they might inspire sentiments of belonging and relatedness (Hung Cam Thai 2014; Nguyen-Akbar 2014). Migrants who return home to rural settings may feel torn between their 'old' insider status (with the weight of kin obligations this entails) and their 'new' status as an outsider or stranger, as well as between the pleasure of belonging to a close-knit community and the loss of autonomy that a return to rural living entails (Phillips and Potter 2005; Laoire 2007). Elements of each of these strands can be identified in Núi's story, which can be profitably explored to shed light on the meanings of home and of return for those Vietnamese migrants who have re-engaged with their homelands.

The phenomenon of return additionally casts into relief the circumstances of those who remain at home. Núi's home of Bắc Đồng is a rice-growing village in the southern part of the Red River Delta of Vietnam. Located in a marshy area of the delta where the soils are poor

---

3   See, for instance, Carruthers (2002), Jellema (2007), Dang Nguyen Anh et al. (2010), Hung Cam Thai (2014), and Nguyen-Akbar (2014).

and people struggle to make a living, the village has been the recipient of various rural development programs to increase connectivity, improve irrigation, increase rice yield, teach new trades, and diversify livelihoods. Nevertheless, at the time of my fieldwork in 2007–08, only 30 per cent of households in the village were considered well off, because they had made the switch from farming to non-farming livelihood activities. The majority of villagers lived at subsistence levels and about 10 per cent of households were categorised as poor (most of these households comprised elderly occupants). Migration has been the most common local livelihood strategy over time. Such journeys began in the late 1960s, with official population transfers to the uplands, and most recently migrants have flowed to urban and industrial zones in Hà Nội, Huế and Hồ Chí Minh City in search of jobs as industrial labourers and following small business opportunities. One of the most significant waves of out-migration occurred in the late 1970s, shortly after national reunification, as a stream of villagers flowed to the 'promised land' of southern Vietnam. As one of the pioneers of this southwards movement, Núi was an ambivalent figure. The business she set up in the prosperous urban south served as a bridgehead for her fellow villagers and earned her prestige for helping them to escape the poverty and hardship of their home village. Yet during her visits home when she dispensed lavish gifts, the villagers were both awed and disconcerted at the discrepancies between their own humble circumstances and the fortunes of this plump, white and wealthy stranger.

The fervent hopes and intense disappointments unleashed by Núi's controversial return home demonstrate how local sociocultural expectations powerfully shape the meanings and trajectory of return migration. Pertinent in this regard is the complex malaise that had taken root in her home village in the decades since her departure. Characterised by a sense of confusion and marginalisation, these sentiments can be linked to the dislocations experienced by the villagers during the transition to the market economy. Núi's fellow villagers had witnessed the retreat of the socialist state from a formerly all-encompassing social support role and the loosening of social bonds brought about by the disestablishment of collectives, the rise of individualistic economic competition, and the steady outflow of migrants. Not coincidentally, the same period saw the eruption of a number of new religious movements in the village, with many villagers placing their confidence in mediums, fortune tellers, faith healers, and in prophets who envisaged the prospective return of a saviour figure. These movements, which were widespread in the Red River Delta in the market integration era,[4] held out the promise of social restoration and cosmic re-integration to villagers who had been dislocated and disoriented by rapid sociocultural change. It was within this turbulent context that Núi's return home took place. The manner in which some villagers construed her as an almost otherworldly figure is indicative of the messianic expectations that structured her home visit. The envy, insidious rumours and blatant criticism she and her followers attracted also show the status and value conflicts and enmity that characterised life in the village. Not surprisingly, these powerful and contradictory sentiments put this return migrant on course for a stormy homecoming.

This chapter discusses the hopes and fears that the people of Bắc Đồng village invested in a returned wealthy migrant. By investigating responses to her prodigious charitable giving, it explores what local people made of her identity, life and motives for giving, and how they used her activities to reconstruct and critically re-imagine their relationships to each other. I show that in the context of new and old forms of social differentiation, elderly women and the poor in the village construed this village returnee as a Buddha-hearted person and turned her into a patron of the village community. The community of veneration that coalesced around this wealthy returned migrant sparked conjecture and controversy — unleashing status and value conflicts and generating a debate about the ethics of her charitable giving. The warm sentiments precipitated by her return visit momentarily inspired in Núi dreams of reconnecting permanently to her homeland, but ultimately the conflicts it provoked resulted in a homecoming that was temporary and mutually disappointing.

Mysterious Rich Woman

Like other people in the village, I was curious to know what Núi looked like. In the first days of her visit, only close relatives and people who had received her gifts and donations came to visit Núi at her brother's

---

4   See, for example, Đỗ Quang Hưng (2001) and Nguyễn Quốc Tuấn (2012).

house. Others were curious but reluctant to approach her to avoid being misunderstood as 'catching the rich to be relatives' ('*thấy người sang bắt quàng làm họ*'). They waited until they knew more about how she treated people. Gradually, they learned from each other that Núi behaved nicely and seemed close to everyone. Through her family members, Núi sent a message to all of the villagers that they were invited to come to her house. Many decided to visit her to show their homeland sentiment and take the opportunity to learn more about her. Núi welcomed all of the guests, talking to them a little to see whether she still remembered who they were, what their relationship was to her, or what memory they had of her. Afterward, she often invited visitors to see video tapes and photos of her family life. During that time, Núi told people stories about a prosperous and modern Sài Gòn, and explained the differences between the lifestyle in the south and the north. People were full of admiration when they saw photos of her big house or the imposing wedding party of her son at a five-star hotel in Sài Gòn. Many women found it interesting and exciting to gather at Núi's place in the evening, and they began to visit with increasing frequency.

Each evening, around 20 people gathered at Núi's brother's house. Several elderly women who were relatives and had received gifts from Núi decided to stay with her and take care of her. They cooked, cleaned the house, and gave massages to her, for she had developed rheumatism and experienced difficulty moving about. Núi became a centre of attraction for the villagers, attracting women in particular to gather at her place. However, in interaction and conversations, most villagers appeared self-conscious in front of Núi. People tried to be careful and polite, especially some of the ladies who lived with her and served her. They always addressed Núi respectfully, to the point of fawning over her. Everyone, including myself, became drawn into this hierarchical interaction — more because of Núi's majesty than her gifts or money. Some people who were ranked as elder sisters or aunts in her lineage wanted to greet and talk to Núi in the familiar way that they often did to other village fellows, but they had to change and adjust their mode of address when confronting Núi directly. This was partly because Núi was different from people in the village. To them, she looked white, plump and healthy, and was dressed in beautiful clothes and wore make-up. When some young women in the village saw Núi for the first time, they commented that she was as beautiful as a fairy queen that they had seen in a movie. Many people were awed by her regal manner and the decisive way she behaved and talked to them, which reminded them of her status as a business person and boss.

Her return aroused debate among Bắc Đồng people about her fate and wealth. Many villagers linked her success to the favourable orientation of her ancestors' graves. People surmised that someone in her grandparents' generation in the village had been well off and possessed some knowledge of classical Chinese script. He must have consulted a geomancer when building the grave for the ancestors. Some villagers believed that the direction chosen for the grave fortuitously brought success to the daughters of the family only. In Núi's parents' generation, one of her aunts had become the owner of a big farm in Thái Nguyên Province, where many villagers went to find jobs before 1954. Meanwhile, Núi's father had lived an ordinary life in the village. However, Núi's eldest sister advanced no further than becoming a local labourer, like her younger brother. Hence the villagers believed that Núi had a special fate (số) that was different from others. Some believed that the mystery to her fortune lay in her name. Some said that it had been given to her when her parents were evacuated from the village to a mountain to avoid a French mopping-up operation during the First Indochina War. Others believed that there must have been a mystically significant reason for her parents to give her that name.

Many villagers explained her career and richness in terms of good fortune (gặp may). Several people believed that when she had moved to the south after 1975, by chance she was able to buy the house of a family who had migrated to America and had found a pot of gold hidden inside. Afterwards, she used this capital to do trading and develop her enterprise. Another hypothesis was that she gained business success by manipulating her husband's reputation. As her second husband had been a southern revolutionary who became a cadre in the north after 1954, people believed that after he returned to Sài Gòn in 1975 he must have acquired a high position in the new government. Núi would then have received many gifts and bribes from people who came to ask for her husband's favour. Also thanks to his power, Núi could easily gain success in her trade and business.

Given these ideas, Bắc Đồng people rarely used the term 'talented' (*giỏi*) to describe Núi and her career. They tended to emphasise the words 'rich' (*giàu*) and 'lucky' (*may mắn*), and believed that many young people were now more talented than her in business. However, they still deeply respected Núi's special qualities. Some villagers told each other that Núi could quickly determine whether a newcomer was trustworthy simply by looking at him/her from a distance. That is why, they said, in her business in the south, Núi liked to see prospective employees face-to-face before offering them work. If they did not appear to her to be reliable and trustworthy, she politely declined to employ them and gave them money to find another job or to return home. When Núi returned to the village, she surprised people with her ability to quickly understand the situation of the people she met. The villagers told each other that she was very 'sharp-witted' (*tinh*). For all of these reasons, from the first days of her return, many Bắc Đồng people showed their respect to Núi. In all of the meetings or rituals in which she participated, even the village cadres and representatives of the elderly association in the village respectfully addressed her with elaborately polite speech. On the occasion of official rituals at the *đình*, the organisers invited her to sit on the same mat as the oldest men. People treated her as a distinguished guest, a daughter of the village returned home. During rituals at her lineage hall, Núi was invited to sit with the lineage elders. People in her lineage showed their happiness at having a daughter like her, who could bring fame to the family. The respectful title Bà Núi (Madam Núi) was used popularly by all Bắc Đồng people regardless of their gender or age.

Her Giving

Another intriguing aspect about Núi that generated much commentary among the villagers was her status as a generous benefactor. In just a short period of time she gave away an enormous amount of money, becoming one of the most generous patrons the village had ever seen. What is remarkable about this generosity is that it appears not to have been part of her original intentions for her return visit. Instead, it seems to have been elicited in the context of the villagers' interactions with her.

Like many emigrants in northern Vietnam, the practice of ancestor worship was the critical factor that brought Núi back to Bắc Đồng. As Kate Jellema (2007) has illustrated, in the midst of *đổi mới*, a quest to 'return to origins' transfixed the entire nation and ancestors exerted a strong pull on modern Vietnamese, wherever they resided. According to her, to '*về quê*' (return to the homeland) is a rite, an act of filial devotion, at once expected and demanded, forced and desired (Jellema 2007:58). Following this ideology of northern migrants, which also receives endorsement by the state, Núi initially intended her visit to fulfil her obligations to her family. She simply wanted to build a royal tomb for her parents and ancestors, and a new house for her brother, an ordinary labourer in the village. In this sense, she wanted to share her success with her family and meet her familial obligations.

At the beginning of her visit, Núi gave gifts only to relatives, as is the custom of Vietnamese who return to their homeland. When some poor villagers who had previously received Núi's charity via her family came to thank Núi for her kind heart, she responded compassionately by personally offering them further gifts. Gradually, it became Núi's routine practice — when confronted by relatives to whom she felt she should give something, or by poor and disabled people who had difficult lives — to give 100,000 *đồng* or more. Her close relatives and the old women who surrounded and served her every day often proposed to whom Núi should give her gifts and advised Núi of the recipients' circumstances. Núi's giving became a popular topic of discussion among the villagers, especially women, as to who had received her gifts.

The local government also decided to approach Núi after several weeks. Representatives of the village ritual committee[5] came to greet Núi and thanked her for the donation she had sent for the village festival the year before. They invited her to participate in rituals at the *đình* (the village communal house). Later on, Khôi — the village head — organised a meeting at the *đình* to express the gratitude of the village for Núi's previous contribution to village affairs and the poor. Khôi then went on to ask Núi for a donation to his project — already under construction — to rebuild the village road to the temple. In response

---

5   Like other Vietnamese villages in the Red River Delta, the committee of historical sites, which was later renamed the committee of rituals and festivals (*ban khánh tiết*), of Bắc Đồng was established in the early 1990s to take care of the village communal house and its rituals.

to this call and the sentiments demonstrated towards her by the cadres and villagers, Núi decided to contribute 20 million VND (about $1,000 USD) for the temple road and 20 million VND to renovate the *đình's* floor, which she thought made the temple look dirty and dark. Not long after that, Núi decided to spend another 20 million VND building a road to the ladies' temple to replace a path along the edge of a rice field after the elderly had complained to her about this path and she herself had experienced difficulty walking on it. In addition, Núi brought large quantities of fruit, cake and meat as offerings to the village temple and pagoda on significant occasions. After offering the food to the spirits, she shared it with the elderly, or sometimes with the whole village. By the end of the year, Núi again compiled a list of 60 poor families in the village and gave each of them a total of 30 million VND (about $1,500 USD) to celebrate the New Year. She also gave scholarships for poor and talented students and bought toys for the village kindergarten.

As Núi gave more and more, she became a hot topic in the daily conversations of the villagers, who paid attention to her every movement. Local cadres and representatives of the elderly association in the village made frequent visits to show their care for her, to present their plans and projects and to discuss village affairs in an attempt to gain her support. Influential people (*có máu mặt*) in the village, such as those who took care of the followers at the two shrines of the village and some mediums, also often visited Núi to talk to her about the possibility of investing in their groups' ritual interests. All the formal and informal social groups in the village considered Núi as a patron and tried to take advantage of her presence to invite her donations to their cause. Owing to her influence as a donor and her prestige, many villagers also expected her to be able to influence leaders to do a better job at managing the village. A woman recounted with satisfaction an occasion in which Núi had firmly chastised the village head:

> Once I heard Núi comment to Mr Khôi, the village head, that: 'You should not be strict about rituals. I myself was seized by the spirits so I shared with the mediums in the village. You should organise an annual festival and not make it bureaucratic. If someone makes a mistake, you should solve their problem yourself instead of sending them up to the commune. I used to manage hundreds of workers and I could solve all their problems.' Khôi could only nod his head. (Mrs Đặng, 68 years old, an elderly small trader and farmer in Bắc Đồng)

Although Núi denied that this exchange had taken place, circulation of the story indicated that people expected Núi to be able to change or have an influence on their local government. As her house became a centre where people, especially women, brought news of village daily life for discussion, Núi quickly grasped the situation of the village, the concerns of people and gossip about individuals. Some people came to ask her to mediate their personal grievances with other villagers, considering that her experiences of life outside of the village gave her the insight to offer judicious advice.

The esteem and honour that many Bắc Đồng people reserved for Núi encouraged her to give more, and nurture new ideas for the future. During the two months of her first return trip to the village, Núi contacted her family in Sài Gòn several times to order additional gifts and money to be sent to Bắc Đồng, since the level of demand had exceeded her expectation. When I asked them what they thought about her, most villagers said that Núi was ascendant (nổi lên) and venerated (được tôn sùng). The dynamics of the process show that her giving and other activities in the village were the result of an interaction between the demands and sentiments of Bắc Đồng people and her response to them — rather than any intentional plan.

Many women in the village thought that everyone who received something from Núi owed her a debt of gratitude (ơn), and thus felt compelled to fawn upon her (quỵ lụy). These explanations by Bắc Đồng people fit with the idea of the gift as an offering that inherently creates in the recipient an obligation to reciprocate (Mauss 1967). In reality, only a few Bắc Đồng people who received many gifts and favours from Núi tried to give her something in return, such as some fresh fruit from their garden or help with her housework. The majority of recipients felt that they could not give any equivalent material gifts in exchange, since Núi did not need anything they could give in return. Therefore, when a person accepted a gift from Núi, they also accepted that they were now indebted to her — but could only repay that debt through the expression of sentiment, respect or submission. Similar to the way that cash gifts given by returned overseas migrants to their relatives in Vietnam impose upon and burden those who receive them (Hung Cam Thai 2014:15), Nui's gifts aroused in her recipients a sense of obligation from which they could not easily extricate themselves.

Given this, some people in Bắc Đồng, especially the rich who were concerned about their manners (giữ ý), tried to keep their distance from Núi or avoid receiving her gifts. However, as Núi's giving became a phenomenon, most people were interested in receiving a gift which they viewed as a blessed token from a successful returned migrant that had the capacity to bring them joy and fortune. Her generosity to them was considered by many to be the result of their own fate, rather than Núi's own good heart. One old lady, who was the mother of some successful traders in the village and had no special relationship with Núi, told me that since she had witnessed Núi's gifts to many people, she also expected Núi to give her about 100,000 VND, the value of a health tonic that she sometimes took. By the end of Núi's visit, many people said that it was not only individuals who were indebted to Núi but indeed the whole village, for everyone in the village had eaten the pork meat and sticky rice that she had offered to the village deities during festivals and then shared out among the villagers, and on account of everything else she had done for the village. It was clear from their exhilaration that many people felt happy and proud to have been individually touched by her largesse.

Through giving, Núi was able to accumulate status and power. As more and more villagers received gifts from Núi and accepted the responsibility to show their sentiment for her, her prestige continued to rise. Many considered her generosity as the action of a fortunate person sharing with others the blessings (lộc) that she had received from the spirits. Her actions were similar to the wealth distribution practices of potlatch found among indigenous peoples of the American northwest coast, in which chiefs or the rich would build status by hosting lavish feasts and compete to give away food and property (Codere 1950; Jonaitis 1991). Closer to home, Núi's gifts were akin to the gifts distributed by Vietnamese spirit mediums to their following, whose largesse is motivated not simply by altruism or the imperatives of kinship or camaraderie, but by the obligations invested in those enjoying a status as masters — as spiritual patrons in a patron–client relationship (Endres 2011:13–36).

All of the villagers agreed that if Núi had no money or had not given it to people, she would not have been feted in the village. If a person gives only the average amount of charity to help the poor, they will receive esteem no greater than that enjoyed by ordinary people. In Núi's case, besides helping the poor she had also given her heart (tâm) to village affairs, thus she received the respect of local government officials and the esteem of the villagers. Before Núi returned to the south to celebrate New Year, Bắc Đồng village held a farewell for her. The event offered an opportunity for the village to evaluate her efforts and think about how to express their gratitude. After many days, at a meeting comprising all of the representatives of the village — the people, government and party (*hội nghị dân-chính-đảng*) — Khôi and the village leaders decided to present to Núi a classical Chinese script painting consisting of the word '*tâm*', meaning 'heart-mind'.[6]

In his speech at her farewell, Khôi tried to explain the meaning of this word and the reason the village wanted to give the script painting to Núi. Khôi understood *tâm* as the soul, spirit and heart inside the human person. Whoever had a good heart to do good things would be appreciated and supported by the spirits. However, to make sure that he and the villagers gave this award to Núi with a full understanding of its meaning, Khôi asked for advice from an advisor in Hà Nội, a journalist called Thức. Even though Thức had some knowledge of classical Chinese script and had been researching traditional culture and religion for a long time, he carefully spent several hours checking dictionaries and reference books before answering Khôi's question. He wanted to quote official books and classical texts. During a phone conversation with Thức, Khôi wrote down the meanings of the word that the journalist had summarised from various textbooks. According to his research, the main meaning of *tâm* was that whoever had a pure heart would be a Buddha. Thức wanted Khôi to emphasise that Núi had a valuable *tâm* because she helped the poor and gave offerings to the gods without any ulterior motive. Her *tâm* was not only recognised by human beings but by the spirits. Thus, she and her family would receive 'good fortune' (*phúc*). In response to this spiritual and meaningful gift, Núi thanked the village for giving her happiness beyond her imagination. Then she elaborated further the meaning of *tâm*. She explained that in the south she had learned from Buddhist monks that '*tâm* is Buddha and Buddha is *tâm*' (*tâm tức Phật, Phật tức tâm*). She understood that Heaven and Buddha gave birth to humans, and that Heaven can be characterised by benevolence, righteousness

---

6   In his analysis of the self in Vietnam, David Marr (2000) defined and translated *tâm* as 'heart-mind', meaning the bearer of inner awareness, sentiment, knowledge and moral judgement.

and morality (*nhân, nghĩa, đạo đức*), and behind the meaning of those three concepts is *tâm*. If a person has *tâm*, they can achieve anything they want (*muốn làm gì là làm được*).

These learned discussions about the meanings of *tâm* suggest that it is a broad and abstract concept. However, in the minds of many villagers with whom I talked, its meaning appeared to be less complicated. People simply thought that Núi had *tâm* because she believed in spirits, had Buddha in her heart, and tried to give to both living beings and the gods in order to receive good things for herself and family. As Marr (2000:770) notes, unlike most other concepts derived from the Chinese classics, *tâm* is not bound by hierarchy. The heart-mind of even the lowliest person in society is able to commune with other heart-minds, with nature, the spirits, and the universe at large. In the case of Núi, the villagers were compelled to admit that she was good, and gave and contributed to the community on these terms. Although she was not really talented or distinguished in terms of her 'merit' (*công*) to the country,[7] she deserved to gain the honour and esteem of the people. One elderly man said that,

> People do not esteem her [Núi] so much because of her talent [*giỏi*], social relationships [*quan hệ*] or morality [*đức*] ... but her *tâm* towards the village affairs. (Mr Lâm, 70 years old)

However, this gift of thanks was enough to make Núi feel happy before returning home to Sài Gòn, ending her first return visit full of passion and emotion. Meanwhile, for many Bắc Đồng people, her visit encouraged them to hope that their own situations and that of the village might continue to improve with ongoing assistance from this extraordinary benefactor.

Her Reasons for Giving

Although *tâm*, or heart, was how Núi's motives for giving were interpreted by Bắc Đồng village leaders, it only partially captured Núi's own reasons. For her, the role played by fate was more important. As a person whose life had once been as deprived as those villagers she had helped, and whose prosperity had come unexpectedly, she believed

---

7   For a discussion of the concept of *công*, see Jellema (2005).

that fate had played a crucial role in her success. She intuited that demonstrations of kindness to others might positively influence one's own fate. Additionally, she felt sympathy for people whose circumstances reminded her of her own difficult life. As her business career drew to a close, her health declined and relations with family members in the south became strained, she was particularly receptive to the warm homecoming that she received in Bắc Đồng village. Núi explained her actions with reference to her own life history and it is therefore useful to retell Núi's rags-to-riches story to understand what considerations influenced her actions.

Given her family's poor situation, Núi could attend only the first grade of school before dropping out to stay at home and help her parents take care of her younger brother. When Núi was 16 years old, she started to learn about petty trade. She travelled to northern mountainous provinces such as Thái Nguyên, Yên Bái and Lạng Sơn to practice buying and selling goods. During her trips to Yên Bái, Núi met and married the son of a landlord she often stayed with. One year after the wedding, when Núi was 20 years old, she gave birth to a son. At that time, her parents-in-law asked Núi to live with them and help with farming activities. But Núi disagreed. She decided instead to return to Bắc Đồng village with her four-month-old son. However, her own parents were not happy with her decision and did not invite Núi and her son to live with them in the family home, thus she moved again.

When Núi was 24 years old, on a trip to Thái Nguyên Province she met a southern military cadre who worked in a factory there. He was older than her by 20 years. She decided to marry him, for he was alone in the north while his family lived in Sài Gòn. Núi and her son then moved to live with him in a small apartment in Hà Nội. After she remarried, Núi had more children and became the primary breadwinner when her husband took early retirement soon after marriage. His pension was not enough to support a family in that subsidised period. Thus, she had to do various kinds of work to earn a living, including spinning silk for the ward's embroidery team and selling pork and chicken meat in the grey market (chợ đen). The 10-year period that she lived in Hà Nội — from the mid-1960s to the mid-1970s — was a hard and miserable time for Núi. Apart from economic difficulties, she also suffered from discrimination and prejudice from her family and neighbours about her marital life. She felt devastated when her team leader refused to advance her salary, despite her children being sick in the hospital and, on another occasion, when commercial management cadres confiscated 3 kilograms of meat — her whole capital — in spite of her explanation that her husband was a wounded southern soldier and her family was extremely poor. Such incidents made her recall the north as a land of harshness and poverty.

After unification in 1975, Núi followed her husband to Sài Gòn. In the beginning, she just sold fried bananas on the pavement. Later, she followed a friend into a business where she served traders who came from the north by helping to connect them with buyers. Thanks to her husband's position as a ward cadre, his connections, and her own efforts, more and more traders approached her for assistance and Núi earned a substantial income. Every day, several dozen traders resided in her house and sometimes she could earn a tael of gold in a single day. After three years in this business, she bought a big house in the city centre. From that time, Núi emerged as an influential trader in Sài Gòn.

In the early 1980s, her assets totalled more than 50 tael of gold. However, in 1982 Núi lost most of her capital through trading antique furniture. During that difficult period, by chance, a man from Đình Bảng village asked her to help him sell carved wooden furniture. At first, Núi earned a commission by selling the furniture in Sài Gòn but then expanded to Phnom Penh, Cambodia. In 1985, she opened an enterprise in her home to produce carved wooden furniture and by the 1990s she was exporting her products to Japan, Taiwan, and other eastern Asian countries. Included in her 100-strong workforce were around 50 people from Bắc Đồng. Some of them came to Sài Gòn with a letter of recommendation to Núi from their parents or relatives. Others asked relatives in the south to accompany them when they approached Núi for a job.

Núi thought a lot about training craftsmen, and in the mid-1990s she sponsored 10 boys from poor families in Bắc Đồng to learn the craft of furniture making in Nam Định Province. Núi also accommodated some young boys from poor families from Bắc Đồng in her home in Sài Gòn, where they were taught carving skills and, at the same time, sent to a local school to complete their education. Even from a distance, Núi remained connected to her village through such acts of patronage.

Núi's business thrived in the 1990s, when many of its products were exported. Each month, many container loads of goods were dispatched abroad and car loads of money were transferred back to her house. However, in 1999 her enterprise suddenly came to a halt. The intermediary companies between Núi's company and Japanese and Taiwanese buyers resented the large profits being derived by Núi and responded by establishing rival enterprises and enticing most of Núi's workers to work for them. Thus, her enterprise came to a standstill due to a shortage of labour.

Núi accepted this turn of events quietly and calmly, switching to real estate where she redirected her energy and capital into buying land. She purchased 5,000 square metres of agricultural land in Thủ Đức District, an undeveloped part of the city at that time. The subsequent urbanisation of this agricultural land rendered Núi's investment to be worth around 20 billion VND (close to $1 million USD). However, after that deal, her business career again came to a halt and she experienced a series of personal crises.

Since 2000, Núi has been ailing. Her leg developed a kind of rheumatism. She began to walk with a stick and sometimes needed assistance to move about. Her husband also died around that time. Most of her children were incapable of running the business, since they were used to depending on her. Three of them switched to small business, which only provided a subsistence income. The three youngest children continued to receive monthly stipends from their mother. Two of them had become drug addicts by 2008. In 1999, during her most prosperous period, Núi was able to send one of her sons to study in Canada. After graduating he remained in Canada and could have applied for professional employment and citizenship, but his ordinary academic performance led him to work in a field which provided no more than a subsistence income.

Looking back over her life, Núi was proud of her achievements. Although she was not as rich as the richest person in the south, what she had achieved was remarkable, given that she had left her home village and given birth to seven children in poverty. She was respected as a successful business person. It was in relation to her family that she believed she had failed. Extremely preoccupied with her business, Núi had been unable to take care of or teach her children well. Consequently, her children took life for granted and had no capacity to work hard as she had done. Núi reflected that the dependence of her children gave her power over them that other richer women do not have; she made all the decisions about the family and her property.

As previously noted, initially Núi planned to go home simply to build a house for her brother and grave for her ancestors before she got older and weaker. But Núi had not imagined how enthusiastically the villagers would welcome her. The emotion of the villagers encouraged Núi to stay longer and give more in the belief that this might be a decision made by the spirits. The spirits had led her back to the north to give and, as had previously happened in her life, they would give her other things in return. Explaining her giving, Núi said that the money gifted was like the blood vessels of the body. She had learnt from Buddha that only someone who cut a blood vessel without feeling hurt would not regret giving away their money. In her case, she did feel hurt but was compelled to do it in order to follow the spirit's call. In addition, Núi accounted for her actions in the village in terms of her compassion towards her natal village. Returning and being surrounded by many poor women made Núi feel sympathy for her fellow villagers who were in essence just like her — except for the intervention of fate. Witnessing people suffer hardship and poverty also made her feel less sad about her own family life and reminded her of her own good fortune/luck. Given her strong belief in fate and her sense that she was on the threshold of another major turn in her life, Núi gave liberally in the anticipation that something extraordinary was about to happen.

Contradiction and Misunderstanding

While Núi's generosity may not have been clearly understood by the villagers, her manner of giving stimulated a great deal of commentary and conjecture. For many Bắc Đồng people, Núi's giving was a strange and extraordinary phenomenon that they had never seen or heard of before. People not only wondered about how Núi had become rich but also about the source of her donations. Some people believed that most of her charitable gifts came from a Canadian charitable organisation. This idea might have derived from her son's residence in Canada, causing people to imagine that she had contact with such a network through him. Some villagers could not believe that she took money from her own pocket to give to others. As most knowledge about Núi came from villagers who had either worked for her or visited her in the south, her actions remained mysterious to most people. Even the way she gave surprised the villagers.

When offering charity, Núi carefully considered the situation of the poor to assess whether they genuinely needed help. If she found out that the children or close relatives of the poor people in the village were rich, she would not give them anything. Although hunger and poverty have existed in the village for a long time, Bắc Đồng people found it hard to grasp the concept and practice of charity that Núi introduced. At first, some people were reluctant to receive money from her. In other cases, children of the elderly objected to their parents receiving help. However, people gradually got used to Núi making a record of poor households' situations and her habit of taking documentary photos. She often made a detailed list of households and tried to understand clearly each of their circumstances in order to give them a suitable amount. Her gifts were flexible and fair but also arbitrary. I overheard women telling each other that Núi never gave gifts to people who complained about their difficulties but wore jewellery made from gold.

During her giving, Núi also set conditions on the contributions she made to poverty eradication or construction projects, which potentially threatened the authority of village officials. When Núi decided to give money to all of the poor households in the commune, she asked the local government to give her a list of poor households categorised according to her own criteria, instead of the official criteria and list. When donating money to build the temple road or repair the *đình*, she could easily calculate the cost of these works without the assistance of local cadres. People understood that it was difficult to swindle Núi. An elderly man on the ritual committee revealed that the local cadres had felt embarrassed when they calculated that a project to upgrade the road to the Lady's shrine would cost 24 million VND (about $2,200 USD). With her ability, Núi easily knew that it would cost less than that. But she politely responded that, given her limited budget, she would like to take over the construction work herself to reduce the cost. As a result, she only had to pay 17 million VND. This incident reminded Núi that the local cadres also expected something from her, at least for the time they devoted to village affairs. Núi shocked them when she offered them a gift of 10 million VND. She nicely explained that it was a reward for their hard work for the village. The fact was that Núi had to determine who was who in the village and find the best way to live with people. By being involved in the practice of giving, she wanted to help harmonise social relationships in the village.

Returning from a far-away world, Núi brought to Bắc Đồng many new values, most importantly the values of kindness, charity, and 'heart-mind'. Some old people said that they had never seen anyone as kind and giving as Núi. The villagers learned that Núi had practiced charity and giving for a long time in the south, where such activity was common. Apart from these charitable practices, Núi also represented a different way of life and thinking. People were surprised that she did not think exclusively about herself, her children, and her family. Núi claimed that whenever confronted with a decision to spend a lot of money on luxurious personal effects or expensive meals in a restaurant, she tried to limit her spending in order to save money for charity. Even though Núi owned property worth about $1 million USD, none of her children had a big house or expensive car. She gave each of them no more than a fixed monthly stipend. As noted above, Núi built a new house in the village for her only brother, gave him a monthly stipend, and gave other relatives larger and more frequent gifts than outsiders. But she never met her relatives' expectations, giving them just enough to live on and giving more to people who really needed it. By acting in this way, Núi said she could overcome the traditional Vietnamese ideology of 'family first' and think about others as well.

This way of thinking and behaving was strange to the villagers. Núi tried to make people understand that in the outside world, people acted beyond family obligations, beyond the concept of 'amoral familism' (Banfield 1967), and cared about other members of society. In the south, she said, individuals like her could take on the work of caring for the poor or victims of disasters, work that, in the village, was usually regarded as a responsibility of the government. Núi encouraged people to change their minds and act like people in the outside world. She advocated that the poor accept responsibility for their situation and try to overcome their poverty. If a person did not want their close relatives to be ranked as poor, they ought to take care of them and help them to better themselves. Núi criticised as hypocritical the egalitarian and communal discourses in the village by making people aware of the reality of social stratification and urging them to do something about it. She said people should love each other more and do more to help people outside their own family. Her advocacy of these values and ways of relating to others generated much debate among villagers as to whether this new form of personhood represented a good model or not.

From the outset, the rich doubted Núi's charitable intentions, claiming her to be motivated by self-interest and querying the morality of her wealth (Jellema 2005:233). Some hypothesised that in the past, Núi must have done something bad or evil to become rich and now she wanted to undertake charity to lessen her guilt. This hypothesis originated either from the idea in contemporary society that to be rich is immoral, or from the experiences of the rich in Bắc Đồng themselves, such as fierce competition among traders, sibling rivalry and fighting, exploitation of labourers, and rampant cheating by traders. Meanwhile, others surmised that Núi gave to have a peaceful heart and to forget about the fact that some of her children were drug users. Nevertheless, even though some rich villagers expressed their doubts about Núi's kindness and morality, they were prepared to admire what she had done for the village.

Some villagers whose children had previously worked for Núi in Sài Gòn ventured the observation that Núi had been a difficult boss. It was said that she favoured people who were clever with their hands and words and bestowed privilege on these, while lazy persons and those who did not know how to please her fell into disfavour. Núi stated that a clear distinction existed between boss and worker in the south. She liked labourers to refer to themselves as 'con' (children) in her presence, and address her formally as 'bà' (madam), regardless of how old they were or their kinship relationship with her. Villagers felt compelled to use this respectful mode of address (bẩm bà) in their interactions with her. Some people thought that this approach engendered politeness in villagers, while others thought of it as bossy (hách dịch). Many Bắc Đồng people felt it was difficult to submit to her in that way.

The way Núi had managed her workers in the past became a hot topic of discussion among villagers. It was claimed that her relationship with workers was a strictly patron–client one. It was a begging and giving relationship (xin-cho). She selected labourers carefully and implemented strict contracts and supervision. In order to retain her workers and to help them save money to bring home, Núi paid their full salary only at the end of the year. Every month, she gave them a small amount of money to buy necessities for personal consumption. If a worker needed an extra amount, they had to make a special request and provide a good reason. Workers were required to stay within the confines of their houses. Visitors had to seek the guard's permission to contact workers. Despite the fact that her management approach aimed to protect workers from social evils and assist them to save their remittances, many Bắc Đồng migrants decided to leave Núi's enterprise after a certain time. One former labourer who subsequently established his own enterprise compared Núi's management model to colonial-style capitalism. According to him, she exercised authoritarian behaviour (*cửa quyền*) over others. By contrast, modern young capitalists like him applied a model of 'agreement' (*thỏa ước*) based on the principle of 'two sides each have profit' (*hai bên cùng có lợi*). However, many parents in the village admitted that her strict rules had helped their children grow up and be successful.

After Núi came back to the village and began distributing money, some villagers complained about her being bossy and difficult. If anyone needed her help, they had to report to her in the manner of a subordinate (*thưa chuyện*). Only important persons such as Khôi, the village leader, were received formally by her. Usually, Núi let her nieces or some ladies help her serve tea for the guests. Some villagers did not feel respected when they were invited to sit at the table and talk to her while she was seated on the bed in the next compartment. For some, this arrangement resembled a colonial-era scene whereby the poor or subordinates came to ask favours from landlords or mandarins. It was unclear whether Núi treated people like this because it was her own way or because of her bad leg. Some villagers also questioned her morality since, according to them, Núi did not care enough for her family and relatives in the village. Even though Núi built a big house for her brother and gave him a monthly stipend and gave more to her nieces than to others, whenever she gave gifts to the poor, some of her more distant relatives claimed that she was not treating them fairly. Moreover, it was said she easily got angry and was prone to scold her brother and nieces if they did not follow her orders. As a result, some gossiped about her 'giving but cursing' (*cho rồi chửi*) without noticing that sometimes Núi felt tired and stressed due to her family members' reliance on her.

All of these dynamics show that local reaction to Núi's giving was extremely complicated. Most villagers acknowledged their esteem for her as a result of her giving and her 'heart'. Some intellectual men of Bắc Đồng told me that they had observed that it was labourers, who accounted for 60 per cent of the village population, who most welcomed and venerated Núi as their saviour. Her giving, according to those educated people, was like a capitalist giving to the poor. It made the poor feel less unequal and helped send a message to the rich in the community that they should not be selfish; instead, they should be kind and should share and give like Núi. On the other hand, her undisclosed motives and her rational approach to giving aroused controversy and disappointment in many people. Well-off villagers were the group most likely to raise questions: about her motives, her recent business 'failure' in Sài Gòn, her first marriage, and her 'immoral' background. Her failure to privilege her closest relatives served as additional ammunition for some villagers who, perhaps influenced by familial ideology or motivated by envy, used rumour and speculation, and their reserves of time and local connections, to try to cut Núi down for not caring adequately for her own family. Her potlatch-like generosity could not protect Núi from these barbs or put her esteem beyond dispute.

Limits of Giving

Despite these undercurrents, Núi's first return visit ended happily for both her and the villagers. Village leaders and people kept expecting and hoping that she would take the initiative and the main role in new rebuilding projects. Núi left the village with a vague promise that she would try her best to do more work for the village if the spirits let her. Returning to her big and quiet house in Sài Gòn, she missed the warm atmosphere in the village where she had been esteemed and surrounded by an entourage. Bắc Đồng village was scheduled to hold its festival two months after Núi's return to the south. On behalf of the village, Khôi tried to convince Núi to participate in the event, but Núi hesitated before making a decision. Since closing her furniture enterprise, she derived her main income from land trading but intended to sell most of her property and divide the profit between her children, as an inheritance. She would then keep a part of the profit for herself to enjoy her last days of life and to give to others in the form of donations. But, owing to the fall in the property market, she had not yet been able to put her plan into action. Thus, most of the money she had spent on living expenses and for giving had been borrowed with interest. However, the call from Bắc Đồng was so strong that at the last minute Núi decided to borrow more money and fly back to the village. Later on, she disclosed that this decision went against the advice of the spirits. As Núi often consulted with the gods before undertaking any significant action, she went to the temple to pray and ask the spirits whether she should return to Bắc Đồng a second time.[8] The two coins she cast to obtain the spirit's answer showed that she should not return, but Núi ignored this advice.

Responding to the expectations of the villagers, on her second visit Núi gave even more than she had during her first one. She gave 59 million VND to 59 poor households in the commune to help support their recovery from the coldest winter in recent history. The commune held a big official meeting at a hall to receive this donation. In this meeting, Núi gave a speech about how poor she had been and encouraged people to overcome their difficulties. Later, the district radio station conducted an interview with Núi. Subsequently, she decided to spend a further 100 million VND to rebuild a lotus pond in front of the village temple. During the village festival, Núi offered a big pig and a lot of sticky rice as offerings to the god, and gave the meat to the villagers.

Things became more complicated when Núi decided to buy a house for her own use in the village. She aimed to use it as a place to stay whenever she visited Bắc Đồng. After she died, it would be given to the lineage to use as their ancestor hall. This news caused wide discussion among villagers about whether Núi would stay permanently in the village or not, and why. Her decision reignited gossip that Núi had been forced to return to live in the village because she had gone bankrupt in the south, and because her children had become drug addicts, leaving no one to care for her.

Women in the village expressed excitement about her house purchase, thinking she had decided to return to Bắc Đồng. Some even visited Núi at her new house and asked her if she would stay permanently.

8   Mediums or followers of Tứ Phủ religion often practice 'xin đài' to seek a sign of the spirits' approval by throwing two coins. If they fall head and tails, it means the spirits approve.

Tired of her living arrangements being the subject of speculation, when two elderly women in the village asked her, 'Is it true that you will live here?', and added, 'Now then, stay here with us', Núi answered angrily: 'My god, do you want me to abandon my children and property? Would you ever do that to your children?!' The two ladies felt ashamed, saddened and surprised by Núi's response to them. They judged Núi's behaviour as improper and said that it showed an authoritarian attitude toward villagers. Explaining this incident, Núi argued that she was countering anyone who spread malicious gossip about her. When the two elderly women shared their version of what happened with others, most Bắc Đồng people showed no response or comment — they were caught between venerating Núi and judging her according to moral norms.

The story became more serious when a daughter of one of the elderly women, Thúy, decided to retaliate. One morning, when Núi was receiving the president of the commune's Women's Union, who had come to convince her to donate to her association, Thúy came to revile Núi with terrible words. Addressing Núi as a selfish old hag (*con mụ béo*), she claimed that Núi was a bad and immoral woman who had more than one husband and had used her wealth to shout at and scold villagers. Núi and the communal cadre sat quietly for an hour while they endured Thúy's verbal abuse. After this incident, Khôi and the village leaders sympathetically offered to send Thúy to the commune authorities for discipline. Many people who held Núi in high esteem came to console her and said that she should not bother about Thúy, that no one in the village wanted to touch Thúy, and that Thúy was a stubborn and undesirable (*thành phần bất hảo*) woman who had married and then divorced a strange man from the border area where she worked as a petty trader. Returning to the village, Thúy dared to heap insults on and fight with anyone. She even abused her own mother. However, in this case she wanted to defend her mother to redeem her own status. Commenting on what happened, the head of the village Elderly Association explained that when a person emerges as an economic power there will always be some who envy them. Further, no one dares to touch those with political power but people dare to abuse those with other powers, implying that economic power is not as strong as political strength. This incident made those who venerated Núi feel a bit discouraged. On the one hand, they were worried that Núi might abandon her role as patron. On the other hand, they did not want to get involved in a debate about their patron's morality, which had been questioned by some people who doubted her kindness and 'heart-mind'.

Around this time, Núi's relationship with family members in the village also soured. Her children in Sài Gòn never complained or intervened in Núi's donations. They had grown used to her practice of giving and charity in the south. However, when she returned to Bắc Đồng the second time, she met many objections from her close relatives and family in the village. While Núi had intentionally given more to her brother, sister, nieces and nephews than to outsiders in order to keep their relationship on a good footing during the first trip, family members now expressed disappointment and discontent when they compared what they had received with what outsiders were given. They wanted to receive much more than just stipends or small investments from her. They complained to their neighbours, and many villagers questioned whether Núi cared more about outsiders than her own siblings. Since her gifts could not reach all relatives and villagers, she also received subtle reminders from some distant relatives that she had forgotten to give to them. During the festival, when a woman who was possessed by the spirit at the Lady's temple saw Núi, she said obliquely that 'there is someone [she meant Núi] who only takes care of outsiders and neglects descendants and relatives'. Núi was perceptive enough to understand immediately that this woman's mother was one of her cousins to whom she had not yet sent greetings or a gift. Núi immediately arranged to send something to this cousin.

Things took a turn for the worse after Núi departed the village the second time. Two of her nieces abused some elderly women who had been staying with Núi in order to take care of her. Her nieces wanted these women to stop serving Núi in order to assume this task (and its rewards) for themselves. This incident led Núi to believe that her family in the village was hindering her work of giving and her good reputation. Subsequently, Núi phoned me and during our hour-long conversation she confessed her fear that people in the village would no longer come to her and that her entourage would abandon her. Núi called for my urgent help to mobilise her surrounding followers and encourage them to believe that she was able to handle what was happening. Núi's confession demonstrated to me that she was worried about losing the new identity and status that had been created through her interactions and acts of giving to the people and community.

After the incidents mentioned above, the villagers began to openly discuss Núi's popularity. Some men disliked and disagreed with the way many women in the village 'bootlicked' (bợ đỡ) and fawned upon on Núi. They criticised those ladies who looked after Núi more respectfully and carefully than they would their own mothers. It seemed that those men did not want to see manifestations of inequality and economic power in their community. Meanwhile, on their visits home or through their families, some successful young business people from Bắc Đồng working in Sài Gòn and abroad made it known, perhaps brashly, that they could do more giving than Núi in the near future. A competitive spirit emerged among other rich migrants from the village who claimed that they too could attain the kind of esteem and power held by Núi. At home, competitive young people working as traders also raised objections to the idea of venerating Núi, or indeed any rich person.

Following these interactions, Núi reflected sadly, 'homeland is a bitter fruit' ('quê hương là quả đắng').[9] Thúy's public scolding reminded her that people still remembered her past. The story of her miserable impoverishment in Hà Nội, her record of more than one husband, and marrying an older man and becoming his second wife were still recalled by people. It felt to Núi that her attempts to acquire a higher reputation in the village were the subject of obstruction and challenge, and that the villagers had not changed — northern people were still narrow-minded, selfish and envious. Their thoughts were extremely hard (tư tưởng nặng nề). The rich were despised and the poor disdained. While the villagers were talented, they were not prosperous and not happy due to their narrow-mindedness and limited horizons. After returning again to the south, Núi saw the northern delta as a place with limited prospects for development owing to its restricted area and poor markets. Núi reappraised southern people as broad-minded, tolerant and easy-going. Their hearts were like that of Heaven (lòng người như lòng Trời).

Nevertheless, from the remove of her home in the south, Núi persisted in safeguarding the esteem she had earned in her natal village. She pressured family members to continue giving to her followers in

---

9   Most Vietnamese are familiar with the famous line of poetry 'quê hương là chùm khế ngọt' ('homeland is a bunch of sweet star fruit'). In contrast, Bà Núi experienced homeland as a bunch of bitter fruit.

line with her previous plans. To patch things up at the village level, Núi thought about building a big gate for the *đình* and repairing the pagoda. However, these ideas could not be implemented as Núi was unable to sell her property due to the economic recession.

During that time, Núi chose to invite me to her house in Sài Gòn. She did not hide her aim of using me as a tool to remedy gossip about her in the village. Núi told me she thought that the villagers trusted me and would believe in what I saw and told them about her life in the south. She arranged several meetings for me with some of her children. She took me to visit one of the most famous temples in Sài Gòn where she was highly esteemed, and one of the biggest pagodas in the city where the master monk received her warmly and respectfully. She wanted to demonstrate that her wealth was real, that her children were under her command and taking care of her, and that the most honourable places and people in the south held her in esteem and acknowledged her good character. I felt nervous about Núi's expectations of me and wondered what I should tell the villagers about her life in the south. To my surprise, however, when I returned to Bắc Đồng, no one in the village asked me about my trip. I tried to mention my journey and Núi to encourage questions but the villagers tended to ignore my attempts. I wondered if they were trying to avoid debate or simply wanted to forget the sad story of a person in whom they had invested a lot of hope but who had become a lightning rod for contention and disappointment in their village.

Conclusion

The controversies surrounding this Vietnamese return migrant's efforts to reconnect with her home village offer revealing insights into the complex dynamics that shape homecomings and other projects of reconnection in migratory societies. In some respects, her return visit was in no way out of the ordinary, motivated at it was by a desire to return to her homeland to acquit her filial obligations at the end of a difficult working life that had brought both success and failure. Nevertheless, the direction and eventual outcome of her return journey was unpredictably shaped by the force of the imagination and the dynamics of class differentiation and status. The expectations invested by Bắc Đồng villagers in this rich return business migrant set her on a new course of helping the whole village and diverted her efforts away from her original intention to assist her own family. The difficulties villagers had in comprehending and contextualising her actions led to misunderstanding, conflict, and eventual mutual disappointment.

We can learn much from this story of conflicted return through the lens of social drama (Turner 1974), and by drawing out the perspectives of each of its key protagonists. Núi's own story shows that, like many migrants in northern Vietnam, she originally wanted to return to fulfil her culturally prescribed obligation to her ancestors (Jellema 2007). Return migration theorists might describe this motivation as the satisfaction of a migratory strategy, one that responded to the cultural 'pull' factor of familial obligation (Gmelch 1980; Brettell 2000; Cassarino 2004). However, what she encountered in her natal village made Núi feel sympathy and compassion for those suffering poverty and misery as she had in the past. She saw herself in her fellow villagers and this inspired her to give much more widely than familial obligation alone would dictate was necessary. Her emotional rediscovery of the village as a home in which she was esteemed was both epiphany and consolation for Núi, who had experienced harshness, hope and disappointment as a migrant trader under the socialist subsidy period, and again in a later phase of life as an urban capitalist trader. However, the reasons for her generosity were misunderstood and resulted in contradictory social, emotional and intellectual reactions. Instead of eliciting gratitude, her actions aroused envy and criticism among fellow village elites. In the end, the community of sentiment that had coalesced around her collapsed, brought down by the very familial ideology that had drawn her home in the first place.

In the context of increasing social differentiation in this rural setting, many of Bắc Đồng's poorest people spontaneously venerated this wealthy returned migrant and incited her to become a patron of the village. Many elderly women in particular aspired to form a community surrounding her, reliant on her generosity. Infused with sentiments of solidarity, mutual obligation and hierarchy, this following provided a space of refuge — not dissimilar to that provided by Buddhist pagodas or mediumistic followings in the northern delta — for people marginalised by the ideology of the patrilineal household (Luong 2006:382–383; Endres 2011:13–36). The villagers' construction of this homecoming migrant as a miraculous being also shows the important role of the religious imagination in creating a space of hope for the marginalised in the rural north. Conceptions of Núi as a Buddha-hearted person, a bringer of blessings, or a fairy queen illustrate the spiritual aspirations attached to her charitable acts. The village leadership also sought to acknowledge her contributions in these terms when they commended her as a 'heart-minded' person. Nevertheless, criticisms directed towards this spontaneous community of veneration also reveal the existence in rural northern villages of a vein of scepticism towards spiritual-based hierarchies that may derive from, or indeed pre-date, the ideological reforms of the high socialist era (Malarney 2003; Taylor 2007:29–36). The controversial homecoming ended in mutual disenchantment between Núi and the people who had expected so much of her. The story shows the power of the imagination and the limits of that power in the constitution of community in contemporary Vietnam.

The homecoming also provoked a number of ethical conflicts. One of the most heated stemmed from the familialist ideology of the village. Although motivated by a sense of filial reciprocation and the obligation to support her less fortunate family members, Núi's giving quickly escalated to include all manner of non-family members. As such, she was motivated by the universalistic ethics of Buddhism and an explicit critique of the orientation of 'amoral familialism' (cf. Banfield 1967) that limits ones sphere of ethical responsibility to the family. However, her behaviour was noted as an ethical violation by family members. Their objections to her generosity cannot be seen merely as examples of individual opportunism or greed, for this critique of her neglect of family members was voiced widely by other villagers, suggesting that she was in contravention of a more generalised norm. Núi's bewilderment at her fall from favour and the sweeping contrast she drew between the 'open-hearted' character of the south and the 'narrowness' and 'hardness' of the north can be read as a fundamental conflict between different ethical systems: the family-centric ethics of her northern rural birthplace and the Buddhist, modernist and capitalist ethics internalised during her long sojourn in the urban south.

A second plank of familialist ideology that became a source of contention were the traditionalist norms of feminine submission, fidelity and sacrifice (Ngo 2004; Pettus 2004). When Núi spoke harshly to a pair of elderly women, Núi suddenly found herself on trial by village gossips for her lack of wifely fidelity, and her inadequacies as a mother. In turn, her most vocal accuser was quickly silenced on the grounds that she too was severely lacking in feminine virtue. Núi shared these values, for it was her sensitivity to the implication that she had willingly abandoned her children that had caused her to speak out harshly against her elderly village dependants. Underlying all these attacks was an ideology of feminine submission. Women who asserted themselves too forcefully in public were prone to being disparaged as lacking in core feminine virtues. No amount of good will generated by Núi could immunise her against this assault on her character. Indeed, the very act of giving made her vulnerable to this angle of attack, for villagers themselves posited links between her wealth and her infidelity, and her generosity and her lack of support for her own children. These attitudes suggest that traditional gender ideologies continue to be mobilised to discipline women's involvement in the rural public sphere in northern Vietnam, for it was Núi's very influence and stature that made her vulnerable to the charge that she lacked feminine virtue.

The final set of serious conflicts was provoked by the challenge that Núi's charitable acts represented to local structures of authority and status in the village. Intriguingly, for this wealthy capitalist from the south, the elites who responded most warmly to her charity were the members of the village party and state administration. They hoped, perhaps naively, that her wealth could be channelled to support their village reconstruction projects, thereby elevating their own status. However, older educated villagers and men in particular objected to her sudden cult-like status on two grounds. The first was that it flowed almost entirely from the money she had accumulated from her business dealings, and hence did not connote talent or morality, indeed quite possibly the reverse. In these respects their critique of her status could be tied to the long-standing stigmatisation of commerce noted in northern Vietnamese rural communities (Malarney 1998). Second, they resented what they saw as a bossy and high-handed manner. In these respects she challenged status hierarchies in the village that prioritised age seniority, learning, and male gender.[10] Criticism directed at Núi's dealings with villagers may have reflected the

---

10   For an extended discussion of these hierarchies elsewhere in the rural Red River Delta, see Luong (2010:62–80).

influence of socialist ethics as much as a traditional discomfort for raw displays of great power and wealth. In short, her actions humiliated a section of the village elite, whose status was derived from tradition.

A different group of elites who resented her approach were Núi's fellow new rich. They did not so much resent her method as her success at it. These fellow elites were conflicted, for although she represented a new model of personhood and ethics for the local rich, she also represented a competitor. Their aspirations to outdo Núi in charitable prowess signify that this village is becoming an arena for status conflicts based on new criteria of externally derived wealth. Her case thus illustrates the complex terrain on which claims to status operate in contemporary northern Vietnamese villages. Although this wealthy migrant's charitable giving created new hierarchies between herself and marginalised village members, such hierarchies were unstable and prone to elicit contestation on both traditional and modern grounds. As such, this case reveals that far from merely enveloping all participants in warm sentiments of solidarity and concord, the charitable practices of returned migrants also have the capacity to promote invidious social comparison and dissension within rural communities, and to inflict harm on both charitable donors and recipients alike.

References

Banfield, Edward C. 1967, *The Moral Basis of a Backward Society*, The Free Press, New York.

Bourdieu, Pierre 1986, 'The Forms of Capital', in John Richardson (ed.), *Handbook of Theory and Research for the Sociology of Education*, Greenwood, New York, pp. 241–258.

Brettell, Caroline 2000, 'Theorizing Migration in Anthropology', in Caroline Brettell and James Hollifield (eds), *Migration Theory: Talking Across Disciplines*, Routledge, New York and London, pp. 148–174.

Carruthers, Ashley 2002, 'The Accumulation of National Belonging in Transnational Fields: Ways of Being at Home in Vietnam', *Identities: Global Studies in Culture and Power*, vol. 9, no. 4, pp. 423–444.

Cassarino, Jean-Pierre 2004, 'Theorising Return Migration: The Conceptual Approach to Return Migrants Revisited', *International Journal on Multicultural Societies*, vol. 6, no. 2, pp. 253–279.

Codere, Helen 1950, *Fighting with Property: A Study of Kwakiutl Potlatching and Warfare, 1792–1930*, Augustin, New York.

Dang Nguyen Anh, Tran Thi Bich, Nguyen Ngoc Quynh and Dao The Son 2010, *Development on the Move: Measuring and Optimizing Migration's Economic and Social Impacts*, Viet Nam country report, GDN and IPPR.

Đỗ Quang Hưng 2001, 'Hiện Tượng Tôn Giáo Mới: Mấy Vấn đề Lý Luận và Thực Tiễn' ['New Religious Phenomena: Theoretical and Practical Issues'], *Tạp Chí Nghiên Cứu Tôn Giáo* [*Religious Studies Review*], vol. 5, pp. 3–12.

Endres, Kirsten 2011, *Performing the Divine: Mediums, Markets and Modernity in Urban Vietnam*, NIAS Press, Copenhagen.

Gmelch, George 1980, 'Return Migration', *Annual Review of Anthropology*, vol. 9, pp. 135–159.

Hung Cam Thai 2014, *Insufficient Funds: The Culture of Money in Low-Wage Transnational Families*, Stanford University Press, Stanford.

Jellema, Kate 2005, 'Making Good on Debt: The Remoralisation of Wealth in Post-Revolutionary Vietnam', *The Asia Pacific Journal of Anthropology*, vol. 6, no. 3, pp. 231–248.

Jellema, Kate 2007, 'Returning Home: Ancestor Veneration and the Nationalism of Đổi Mới Vietnam', in Philip Taylor (ed.), *Modernity and Re-enchantment: Religion in Post-revolutionary Vietnam*, ISEAS Publications, Singapore, pp. 57–89.

Jonaitis, Aldona (ed.) 1991, *Chiefly Feasts: The Enduring Kwakiutl Potlatch*, University of Washington Press, Seattle.

Khater, A. 2001, *Inventing Home: Emigration, Gender and the Middle Class in Lebanon, 1870–1920*, University of California Press, Berkeley.

Laoire, Caitríona Ní 2007, 'The "Green Green Grass of Home"? Return Migration to Rural Ireland', *Journal of Rural Studies,* vol. 23, no. 3, pp. 332–344.

Luong, Van Hy 2006, 'Structure, Practice and History: Contemporary Anthropological Research on Vietnam', *Journal of Vietnamese Studies*, vol. 1, no. 1–2, pp. 371–409.

Luong, Van Hy 2010, *Tradition, Revolution, and Market Economy in a North Vietnamese Village, 1925–2006*, University of Hawaii Press, Honolulu.

Malarney, Shaun Kingsley 1998, 'State Stigma, Family Prestige and the Development of Commerce in the Red River Delta of Vietnam', in Robert Hefner (ed.), *Market Cultures: Society and Morality in the New Asian Capitalisms*, Allen and Unwin, St Leonards, pp. 268–289.

Malarney, Shaun Kingsley 2002, *Culture, Ritual and Revolution in Vietnam*, University of Hawaii Press, Honolulu.

Malarney, Shaun Kingsley 2003, 'Return to the Past?: The Dynamics of Contemporary Religious and Ritual Transformation', in Hy Van Luong (ed.), *Postwar Vietnam: Dynamics of a Transforming Society*, Rowman and Littlefield, Boulder, Colorado, pp. 225–256.

Marr, David 2000, 'Concepts of "Individual" and "Self" in Twentieth-Century Vietnam', *Modern Asian Studies,* vol. 4, no. 34, pp. 769–796.

Mauss, Marcel 1967, *The Gift*, W. W. Norton & Company, New York.

Ngo Thi Ngan Binh 2004, 'The Confucian Four Feminine Virtues (Tu Duc): The Old Versus the New — Ke thua Versus Phat huy', in Lisa Drummond and Helle Rydstrøm (eds), *Gender Practices in Contemporary Vietnam,* NUS Press, Singapore, pp. 47–73.

Nguyen-Akbar, Mytoan 2014, 'The Tensions of Diasporic "Return" Migration: How Class and Money Create Distance in the Vietnamese Transnational Family', *Journal of Contemporary Ethnography,* vol. 43, no. 20, pp. 176–201.

Nguyễn Quốc Tuấn 2012, 'Về Hiện Tượng Tôn Giáo Mới' ['On New Religious Phenomena'], *Tạp Chí Nghiên Cứu Tôn Giáo* [*Religious Studies Review*], vol. 1, pp. 11–15.

Pettus, Ashley 2004, *Between Sacrifice and Desire: National Identity and the Governing of Femininity in Vietnam*, Routledge, New York and London.

Phillips, Joan and Robert Potter 2005, 'Incorporating Race and Gender into Caribbean Return Migration: The Example of Second Generation "Bajan-Brits"', in Robert Potter, Dennis Conway and Joan Phillips (eds), *The Experience of Return Migration: Caribbean Perspectives*, Aldershot, Ashgate.

Taylor, Philip 2007 'Modernity and Re-enchantment in Post-revolutionary Vietnam', in Philip Taylor (ed.), *Modernity and Re-enchantment in Post-revolutionary Vietnam*, ISEAS Publications, Singapore, pp. 1–56.

Turner, Victor 1974, *Dramas, Fields and Metaphors: Symbolic Action in Human Society*, Cornell University Press, Ithaca.

3

Women as Fish: Rural Migration and Displacement in Vietnam

Linh Khanh Nguyen

This chapter discusses the pattern of rural-to-rural migration to and from a rural fishing community called Hải Thành[1] in northern Vietnam.[2] I unpack this double migration pattern in order to illustrate the intimate relationship of mobility, social class and displacement. Hải Thành is famous in Vietnam as the community that has sent the largest percentage, nationwide, of its young women abroad in transnational marriages to foreign men in East Asia (transnational women). Hải Thành men are also well-known offshore fishermen who travel away 20 days per month and who, due to the transnational marriages of local women, have had to look for wives from other rural communities (translocal women). By comparing the gendered, racial and social elements of migration by translocal women with transnational women in this community, my chapter centres on how different kinds of movement become coded with specific kinds of class status and subjectivities. In order to accomplish this, I explore the diversity of rurality, within and between countries, which is often conflated in much scholarship as 'the rural'. I investigate how

1   Hải Thành is a pseudonym.
2   I gratefully acknowledge support for preparing this chapter from the ZEIT-Stiftung Ebelin und Gerd Bucerius Foundation, which has funded the author for two years. I also thank the 2014 ANU Vietnam Update organisers, Philip Taylor, and two anonymous reviewers for their comments on this chapter.

migration from one rurality to another can be understood through the lens of social mobility. Ironically, this practice also engenders the social displacement of translocal women. This unwelcome ramification causes us to question the uncritical celebration of mobility and complicates the assumed linear, simplistic relationship between migration and social mobility. The case of translocal women in Hải Thành also illustrates that movement and non-movement are connected and mutually defining rather than dichotomised. Together, they create ongoing dynamics that characterise the lives of women in Hải Thành.

This chapter is based on 17 months of research in Hải Thành, from 2011 to 2014, including an 11-month period of intensive fieldwork from 2013 to 2014. During this time, I socialised with and interviewed local men, transnational women, and translocal women and their in-law families. I lived with two local families for more than a year, frequented Hải Thành people's homes and boats, ran errands with them, and attended local weddings and religious ceremonies. I took Korean classes with Hải Thành women and taught English classes for Hải Thành children. I also participated in the night life of Hải Thành, spending time in cafes and shops where young people hung out. These relationships and activities provided me with insights into the intimate and social life in Hải Thành, allowing me to understand their desires, values, prides, and struggles and disappointments as their lives are transformed by migratory forces, both internally and internationally.

Hải Thành in Motion: The Fishermen and the Women

Located near the Gulf of Tonkin, Hải Thành is a small rural fishing commune (*xã*) belonging to the Thuỷ Nguyên District (*huyện*) of Hải Phòng City in northern Vietnam with a population of around 12,000 people. Despite its small population and rural location, Hải Thành residents have a long history of movement and transnational migration. For example, Hải Thành men have been fishermen for generations and embark on monthly trips of 20 days to fish squid near Bạch Long Vĩ Island in the middle of the Tonkin Gulf (110 kilometres from home). Because the technique for fishing uses light attraction, Hải Thành fishermen are usually home every month from the 10th to the 20th day of the lunar calendar, for during this time the moon is bright, making prey harder to catch. Their monthly movement between the island and home is both circular and routinised.

The lucrative fishing industry of Hải Thành enables both the fishermen and the community to thrive. The majority of Hải Thành fishermen are boat owners who often hire workers from provinces in the centre of Vietnam to work on their boats because local labour cannot meet the demand of the growing fishing industry. Each boat worker gets paid 5 to 7 million VND ($250–350 USD) per trip, which is relatively high according to local living standards. The rest of the profit or loss goes to the boat owners, who can earn more than 100 million VND ($5,000 USD) on a good trip, but lose millions when hit by storms.

Although squid fishing is generally very profitable, it is certainly a laborious, treacherous and difficult job. Fishermen often talk about the long hours of work (12 hours or more per day) and how dangerous the job is, especially when the weather is rough (storms, cyclones, rain, high tides, etc.). The danger and hardship of the job, however, do not concern Hải Thành fishermen as much as the competition they face from Chinese fishermen. In December 2000, Vietnam and China signed an agreement concerning the delimitation of the continental shelf boundary in the Gulf of Tonkin in which Vietnam will occupy 53.23 per cent and China 46.77 per cent of the Gulf area. The two governments also established a joint fishing area between the two countries (BBC Vietnamese 2009; Uỷ Ban Biên Giới Quốc Gia 2000). While it is a joint fishing area, in reality only Chinese boats will fish in the area because Vietnamese boats cannot compete with them. According to Hải Thành fishermen, Chinese boats are at least five times bigger and 10 times more expensive, and their lights are so bright that they attract all the squid to their boats. It is only during 10 weeks in the summer (from April to June) when the Chinese government orders a yearly fishing ban (in an effort to rehabilitate marine resources) that Vietnamese boats will fish in the joint area. These two months are usually the most profitable of the year for the fishermen of Hải Thành.

While local men have been moving to the sea for generations, local women have been migrating to East Asia for marriages in the last decade. I refer to this group of women in my research as transnational women. In Vietnam, marriages between young rural Vietnamese women and Taiwanese and South Korean men are quite common. Socioeconomic changes in Taiwan and South Korea — such as changing gender expectations, outmigration of rural women, and the preferences for sons that result in more males than females — have made it difficult for rural Korean and Taiwanese men to find spouses and caused them to look to Southeast Asia and China for prospective spouses. Statistics show that Vietnamese women are the second-largest group of transnationals, after Chinese women, to marry Taiwanese and South Korean men. From 1995 to 2010, around 300,000 Vietnamese women married East Asian men (Bélanger et al. 2010). Hải Thành is the rural commune that has the highest number of transnational women nationwide, estimated to be around 2,500 (Duong 2013). In a community of only 12,000 people, 2,500 women is a significantly high proportion. Transnational marriages between local women and East Asian men started in Hải Thành in the early 2000s with only 12 marriages. Since 2005, the number of transnational marriages has escalated annually, peaking in 2008, when 600 local women migrated to Taiwan and South Korea, according to Ms Ngọt, the chairwoman of the local Women's Union. The statistics from the Hải Thành Youth Union in 2013 show that the number of Hải Thành single women over the (legally marriageable) age of 18 who remain in the community is fewer than 20 (Duong 2013). In fact, the number of transnational marriages is so large that, since September 2012, the city of Hải Phòng has banned transnational marriages in several communes, including Hải Thành, after facing increasing complaints that local men could not find prospective wives. This ban, however, has not succeeded in limiting transnational marriages in Hải Thành as Hải Thành people just pay to have their residential status (hộ khẩu) transferred to different provinces on paper without actually moving. After the marriages are finalised and migration completed, they transfer their residence back again.

The popularity and feasibility of transnational marriages in Vietnam relies in no small part on the family networks and the private matchmaking agencies that facilitate transnational encounters and subsequent marriages. Vietnamese women who have successfully migrated through marriage can act as a go-between to find a husband for their sister or cousin. As such, transnational marriages through family networks can offer greater security and trustworthiness than marriages arranged through a matchmaker agency. The matchmaking agencies, however, are able to bring many Korean and Taiwanese men to Vietnam, allowing more choice to women and lessening the waiting time for suitable potential matches. They are, consequently, more popular than family networks in orchestrating transnational marriages. Often, the men have to bear most of the cost for transnational marriages. As Wang and Chang (2002) explained, for example, when a Taiwanese man wants to seek a Vietnamese wife, he must pay a fee of between $7,000–10,000 USD. He then visits Vietnam where he is shown and introduced to a number of potential women at local hotels. All potential brides are brought together in a room and he moves from one woman to another, asking through a translator a few questions to whomever he finds attractive. He then selects a bride (this process usually takes less than an hour), a wedding is arranged soon after, and when the paperwork is done the bride migrates to Taiwan. To ensure a smooth process, the matchmaking industry includes sub-agents in both Taiwan/Korea and Vietnam who handle recruitment and paperwork. Information gained through my fieldwork indicates that transnational marriages between Vietnamese women and East Asian men cost around $10,000 USD.

The popularity of transnational marriages in Hải Thành has also dramatically changed the nature of the marital transaction. Since the majority of transnational marriages happen in southern Vietnam, until the mid-2000s few Taiwanese/South Korean men looked for wives in the North, where Hải Thành is located. As the supply of willing wives-to-be surpassed the demand, Hải Thành families paid large sums of money ($1,000–3,000 USD) to matchmaker agencies to make sure that their daughters were introduced to Taiwanese/South Korean men and that the required paperwork was completed. It is a common saying in Hải Thành that local women *bought* their husbands. But the situation has now changed: since 2007, the number of transnational marriages in the South is declining, while it is gaining momentum in the North, especially in the city of Hải Phòng (Trung Kien 2013). The supply of Taiwanese/South Korean men has exceeded local demand and local women no longer have to pay money to matchmakers and have significantly more choice in deciding which men they want to marry. This situation applies to transnational marriages arranged by both agencies and family members.

Since Hải Thành women opt to marry foreigners, Hải Thành men have no choice but to marry women from other places, usually remote places far from the community. Some local men who do not want to be fishermen have gone to big cities (such as Hồ Chí Minh city, Đồng Nai, or Hải Phòng city) to work in factories and have met their wives there. The division between the rural and the urban in Vietnam is clearly manifest in the fact that almost all of these women who marry Hải Thành men in big cities are themselves from rural places, having migrated to the cities for work. Once Hải Thành men get married and have children, most of them decide to return to Hải Thành, because the fishing industry there pays more, and because they have an extended family to care for and who will also help look after their own children. For the majority of Hải Thành men who are fishermen, their profession cripples their ability to find potential spouses. The long monthly trips away from home hinder their capability to court non-local women and maintain relationships. Many of them also have to resort to matchmakers. Ironically, their translocal marriages become very similar to the transnational marriages that they often criticise: there is often a matchmaker (an acquaintance of both sides), the bride and the groom meet briefly, and if they like each other a wedding will be held soon after. These women are often from rural areas poorer than Hải Thành and some are ethnic minorities (Thái, Nùng, Tày, and Hmong). The community at large and the women themselves consider translocal marriages as 'marrying up' for the women. Hải Thành, while still a rural place, is significantly wealthier than other rural localities thanks to foreign remittances and the profitable fishing industry. One can argue that, like transnational marriage, money also plays a role in translocal marriage. Additionally, once they get married, both the local and foreign husbands want their wives to stay home out of fear that they may become runaway wives.[3]

---

3   I personally only knew of two cases of runaway transnational and translocal women, but heard people say they knew of several women abandoning their husbands. When probed more closely, many of these stories were also second-hand. I suspect that the 'runaway bride' exists more as a cautionary tale than a common reality.

Women as Fish: Marriages in and out of Hải Thành

While Hải Thành is a rural place, its highly mobile population has impressively changed the face of this once poor community. Local people always proudly say that their lives are equal to those in the cities. They constantly reminded me of that fact by pointing out that their incomes rival those of urbanites and by showing that they have *nhà tầng* (houses of multiple floors), *xe xịn* (expensive scooters), *quán đêm* (a night life) and so on. Hải Thành has received support from the city of Hải Phòng to widen its local port, to build new roads connecting it directly to the centre of the city, and to turn half of its farming land into housing projects by 2025. But the most noticeable change created by the sudden wealth in Hải Thành is the lifestyle of young local people. Hải Thành people are famous for frequenting bars and restaurants, gambling, using drugs, dressing inappropriately and having carefree sexual relationships before marriage. The urbanites, of course, look down on Hải Thành people, taking these behaviours as proof that these rural yet financially able people lack cultural capital, are uncouth and insatiable. Urbanites in Hải Phòng often use the expression '*ăn chơi như người Thuỷ Nguyên*' (dress and party like the Thuỷ Nguyên people) to mock the uncultured status of the rural people of this district in general, and of Hải Thành in particular.

The changes in the lifestyles of the young people are often used to explain the pattern of out- and in-migration in Hải Thành. Young Hải Thành women choose to marry Taiwanese and Korean men because they do not want to marry badly spoiled local men who supposedly waste money on drugs, alcohol, and gambling. Local men want to marry women from other rural localities because these women are not spoiled like Hải Thành women, who have a reputation for being lazy, extravagant, and promiscuous. Thus, a double rural-to-rural migration pattern is created due to marriages: translocal women move from rural places in Vietnam to Hải Thành, and transnational women move from Hải Thành to rural places in Korea and Taiwan.[4] The internal rural-to-rural migration occurs to compensate for the transnational rural-to-rural migration.

While marriage is the driving force of the double rural-to-rural migration, to local people, especially fishermen, transnational and translocal women are viewed very differently. They are both described as fish, but while one can be caught, the other is elusive. The local way of fishing is to burn light bulbs at maximum capacity to attract squid and fish. After a while, the fish and squid become blinded by the lights, and that is when the fishermen pull the net up to catch them. Many fishermen told me that they use the same method to court translocal women: the fishermen show off their wealth and generosity while meeting the women, waiting for the 'blinded' moment to woo them into marriage. Of course, sometimes that tactic scares off women, but the majority of women in my research indicated that the financial difference between Hải Thành and their own community acts as an important factor in their marriage and migration.

Transnational women, on the other hand, are the good fish that get away. Similar to the way that Hải Thành fishermen complain that they cannot compete with Chinese fishermen over fishing, they also cannot compete with Korean and Taiwan men over local women. Moreover, the women, like the fish, have the ability to cross national borders while the (fisher)men are stuck within the border. The fish that gets away, as always, is seen as better. The fish that the Chinese fishermen catch are believed to be bigger, and the transnational women that the Korean and Taiwanese men marry are said to be better than translocal women.

The fish metaphor is very apt in showing that although very similar, translocal women are often judged to be inferior to transnational women. In the remainder of this chapter, I discuss how this comparison illustrates the intimate relationship of social class, migration and displacement.

---

4   Some transnational women reside in urban areas abroad and are considered luckier than those in rural areas. Urban residency is an increasingly important criterion for Hải Thành women when choosing their potential husbands.

The Rural as Destination: The Politics of Rural Migration

Mobility scholars have recently noted the conceptual and cultural shift in the refashioning of identity in which movement becomes the basis of new identity formation (Urry 2000). There is an understanding that 'not only one can be at home in movement, but that movement can be one's very own home' (Rapport and Dawson 1998:27). As such, Urry (2000) spoke of a mobile identity, Beck (2006) of a cosmopolitan identity, and Clifford (1997) of an uprooted identity. Moving away from the literature on migration and diaspora that views movement as a form of dislocation and displacement from home, Chu (2010) argues that to move is to belong in a desirable world where mobility is often considered a force of social reproduction.

However, not all movement is the same, and where one moves matters. Some directions of migration — such as rural to urban, and domestic to international — are deemed attractive and beneficial, especially in postcolonial countries, for they are often associated with increases in economic and social status and cultural-cosmopolitan values (Salazar and Smart 2012).[5] The consequences of these biases are twofold: rural-to-rural migration is often unnoticed, resulting in diverse ruralities becoming homogenous, and people who move from one rural locality to another, especially internally, are often excluded from the social and mobility capital associated with more desirable rural-to-urban or international migration.

Rural-to-rural migration is often ignored in mobility studies. Scholars tend to focus on rural-to-urban migration, both internally and internationally. Vertovec (2011) claims that the city is the foremost setting for the anthropology of migration because of its everyday multiculturalism and its large scale (see also Caglar 2010; Levitt and Jaworsky 2007; Brettell 2003; Bommes and Radtke 1996). As such, most recent research on migration and movement is based in big cities such as New York, Miami, Barcelona, Frankfurt, Manchester, London, and Beijing (Glick-Schiller and Caglar 2011; Foner 2010; Però 2007;

---

5   There is not always a preference for international migration over internal migration. Kalir's research shows that for small business entrepreneurs in booming China, moving abroad as construction workers actually means 'moving down' with respect to one's social mobility (Kalir 2013).

Stepick et al. 2003; Zhang 2002). This lack of attention to the rural as a migration destination fails to account for the significance of rural localities as accessible, desirable and transformative migration destinations for many rural people.[6] It also creates the biased assumption that only cities, and not rural places, are diverse, resulting in an unbalanced interpretation of migration.

It is the diversity of ruralities as well as the hierarchies among them that open up economic opportunities and contribute to the transnational and translocal marriages in Hải Thành. Most of the fishermen's wives are from relatively poor rural areas, ranging from the northern mountainous provinces (Bắc Giang, Bắc Kạn, Cao Bằng, Hà Giang, Lạng Sơn) to the provinces of the mid-north coast (Thanh Hoá, Nghệ An) and Central Highlands (Buôn Mê Thuột). This is how a woman in Hải Thành described the home place of her daughter-in-law in Thanh Hoá when she visited it:

> The road was small and very dark; there were not many lights like we have here. The houses were sparse and surrounded by forest. I jokingly told the in-law family that if they fought and the wife left, the husband would not be able to find her because she could easily hide anywhere. Their house was as big as the house I built for my chickens. It still did not have the concrete exterior layer and you could see the bricks in the wall. And there was no bathroom. Oh, if they had a bathroom like ours, it would have cost them a couple of hundred million.

The fact that their hometowns are poorer than Hải Thành is openly admitted by the translocal women themselves. They remark on the lack of jobs for young people and on the insufficient income from farming that creates hardship and distress for rural people. One translocal woman from Ninh Bình acknowledged:

> My hometown is very poor and the majority of people are farmers. Even though we toil away in the fields, we barely make anything. It is a little better now, but not much. When I was young, we were so poor that my two older siblings did not go to school but stayed home to help my parents. The whole family depended on a small plot of rice.

---

6   For studies of rural-to-rural migration in Vietnam, see Carruthers and Dang (2012), Winkels (2012), Taylor (2007) and Hardy (2003).

We also raised goats on the mountain, about 10. We only sold one or two of them when we were in dire need, not daring to sell more in case we needed money later.

The poverty of rural Vietnam and the insufficiency of farming have pushed most rural youths looking for jobs to the cities. Hải Thành, however, is different. Most translocal women recognise that, compared to their hometowns, it is easier to make a living in Hải Thành. Although the amount of land for farming in Hải Thành is so small that most families do not sell their rice or vegetables; the women have access to other job options. Near the commune, within the rural district of Thuỷ Nguyên, are three textile and shoe factories where women can find work. Within the commune, jobs such as mending and fixing fishing nets and traps become available whenever the fishermen are home. Women can also go to Cát Bà Island to raise farmed fish and clams, or trade and sell seafood. However, these kinds of jobs provided by the fishing industry are often limited to local people who grew up in Hải Thành and know the ins and outs of fishing. Some translocal women have set up street-side shops to sell food and drink because Hải Thành people, unlike many other rural folk, have money to spend. Little profit is generated by these ventures, and most translocal women, even if they work, are still dependent on the income of their husband and parents-in-law. What differentiates women in Hải Thành from those in other rural areas of Vietnam is that many women in Hải Thành do not *need* to work to sustain their families.

Not only are there differences between ruralities in Vietnam, but also between those in Vietnam and South Korea. Although Hải Thành is considered better than many other rural places in Vietnam, it trails behind in comparison to rural areas in Korea. Rural Korea is described in local discourses as cleaner, more beautiful, more sufficient, and more modern. One Hải Thành woman, after visiting her daughter in Changwon, Korea, said:

They have a huge amount of land but they are able to work on all of it because they have machines. That is why they can live comfortably as farmers. Unlike us here, we always struggle with not making enough. There are plenty of jobs even for older people like me. And everything is so clean, no dust. Even in the summer, the sun is not unbearable and in the winter, you work inside the greenhouses; you don't freeze like you do in Vietnam. You know, my complexion was so much lighter after a year there and there was no dirt stuck in my fingernails even after work. It is just so much better.

These economic differences, among other factors, motivate translocal and transnational marriages and migration, and make many women willing to marry outside of and far from their hometowns. These differences draw people to Hải Thành and rural Korea, turning them into rural places of great diversity. The literature on migration often fails to account for the differences among ruralities as they are conflated into 'the rural', and in so doing, little attention is paid to the rural-to-rural migration that is motivated by economic mobility. In my interviews and conversations with local women (before they marry transnationally) and translocal women, they express the hope that marriage will end their struggle to make ends meet and will help them achieve better lives for their children. Unfortunately, although economics are no longer much of a concern for both groups, translocal women do not necessarily reap the sorts of benefits of social mobility accorded to transnational women.

Connection, Hierarchy and the Politics of Race, Class and Gender in Migration

King and Skeldon (2010) have shown that a division remains in migration studies between internal and international migration, which form two almost entirely separate literatures with different conceptual, theoretical, and methodological standpoints that rarely talk to each other (see also Kalir 2013). Since the emergence of the 'migration-development nexus' in the 1990s, both scholars and policymakers have tended to focus almost exclusively on the relationship between development and international migration, overlooking the fact that, in most developing countries, internal migration is equally important (King and Skeldon 2010). This overemphasis on international over internal migration also stems from the intellectual bias that views 'nation' as the appropriate and significant unit of analysis (Wilding 2007; Hage 2005). The problem with the separation of internal and international migration is that it ignores many similarities in the migration processes between the two and provides only partial insights into the complex livelihoods of migrants and their communities (Glick-Schiller and Salazar 2013; Cohen 2011; King and Skeldon 2010).

In Hải Thành, both internal and international migration are crucial to sustaining the community in terms of economy, lifestyle, and population. Their interconnection is clearly seen in the relationship between translocal women and transnational women in Hải Thành: the in-migration of translocal women compensates for the out-migration of transnational women. More importantly, the identity and status of one group is defined against those of the other group.

While transnational women and translocal women are similar in many aspects (they both, supposedly, marry up and both migrate from one rural place to another rural place), most people in Hải Thành, including the women themselves, insist that there are no similarities between the two groups. The differences cited are numerous. First and foremost is the amount of money that transnational and translocal women respectively remit to their parents. The remittances from transnational women can reach up to $4,000 USD per year and can enable their parents to build new two-storey houses within three to five years, a major source of pride and social status in Hải Thành. After the houses are built, the remittances from transnational women are used to cover the living expenses of the parents and are put in the bank for investment. As a result, many parents of transnational women stop working and stay at home. They become a group of 'walking people': early morning or late afternoon, they (especially women) take a walk around the neighbourhood for daily physical exercise. Some even show off their comfortable lives by wearing 'modern' clothes and gold jewellery on their rounds. Local people told me that only 'walking people' have time to walk because they have transnational daughters; others are busy working. Wealth, in this community, is expressed through the body and having leisure time. More interestingly, even though both the fishermen and the walking people move in a circular manner (the former between home and Bạch Long Vĩ Island, the latter around the neighbourhood), fishermen have no choice but to move because their living depends on fishing. Urry wrote that *'unforced "movement" is power … for individuals and groups a major source of advantage'* (Urry 2007:51, emphasis added). Walking parents, by choosing to walk around the neighbourhood, show off their wealth and social status thanks to their daughters living abroad. Translocal women, on the other hand, mostly only give money to their parents at New Year, and the sum is small in comparison, ranging from $50–100 USD. That sum is not sufficient to help their parents build houses or quit working to take a walk every day.

Translocal women are also considered to be not as talented as transnational or local women. One Hải Thành resident summarised the commonly heard arguments:

> If they [translocal women] were talented [*giỏi giang*], they would not be staying at home all the time. Moreover, if they were so talented, why would they have to marry so far away from home? They would have been taken by local men already.

Both of these lines of reasoning are problematic, because they fail to acknowledge in-marrying women's understandable lack of familiarity with the fishing industry, as well as how common translocal marriages have become throughout rural Vietnam. As agriculture has become a sure way to poverty (Taylor 2004), many young Vietnamese have migrated from rural to urban areas looking for jobs. This is where they meet their future spouses who, most likely, are from different hometowns. Therefore, the phenomenon of translocal marriages in Hải Thành is not uncommon, although I believe it is exacerbated by this locality's atypically high number of transnational marriages. As opposed to the non-talented translocal women, transnational (and local) women are considered more accomplished, according to Hải Thành residents, because they can go anywhere (to the islands or foreign countries) and still manage to make a good living, sending money home for their parents and the community at large.[7] The difference in economic capacity translates into other status differences between the two groups. One of the translocal women from Nghệ An, Hoa, who married a local fisherman seven years ago, explained to me:

> Woman: They have money so they are, of course, different from me. They are foreigners now and that is so different from us. They have money to show off; I don't have money so how can I compare with them, like how dare I walk side by side with them. There are times when I talk to them and they don't even bother to answer. They only talk to people with money. Even when they talk to me, it is just some superficial and quick stuff. They go abroad so they are high and rich [*giàu sang*] while I am low and poor [*thấp hèn*].
>
> LKN: How do they show their differences?

---

7 See Thai (2014) for a study on why low-wage Vietnamese immigrants send home a large portion of their incomes and spend extravagantly on relatives during return trips.

Woman: By how they walk. The way they walk is so different. I don't have money so I walk like a normal person. They have money so they sashay like a supermodel. And they talk with airs and graces, lengthening the tone. Instead of saying 'I do this', they will say 'Iiiiiiii do thiiiiiiiiiis'. You know, instead of just saying it right out, they have to say it like it is so special. Then they will add foreign words to their conversations and talk with a foreign accent, like a Westerner speaking Vietnamese. How strange, you know, because they are Vietnamese. Even their gestures are for putting on airs. For example, if they need to get something from their pocket, their thumb and index fingers will touch each other while the other three fingers are extended up. Of course, not all of them are like that.

LKN: Are there any other ways you can tell that they are transnationals?

Woman: The most obvious signs are their clothes and their complexions. Their complexions are beautiful, lighter and pinkish because they do not have to work over there. And because they have gone abroad, they know how to dress really nicely. Their clothes look very different from the clothes you can buy here. We, on the other hand, just dress simply.

This dialogue shows how transnational women are perceived as having a high social status, and consolidate their status by acting like they are more refined and imbuing themselves with the qualities of foreigners. The translocal woman's choice of words suggests that even though transnational women are evaluated as fake and pretentious, owing to how they walk and talk, they are still envied because they embody certain qualities associated with life abroad (*cuộc sống Việt Kiều*) that are out of reach for translocal women: fashionable clothes, fairer complexion, and exemption from the dirty, hard agricultural work that makes women less attractive.

The attractiveness of the foreign in a postcolonial society such as Vietnam is often shaped not only by money but also by arrangements of power such as colonialism, capitalism, and modernity. As Gupta (1998) and Chakrabarty (2000) argue, the former colonial power and capitalism become the standard against which those living in the former colony are measured, and always fail. My conversations with Hải Thành people reveal that the West stands for everything that is desirable and in opposition to what dissatisfies them in Vietnam: capitalist (vs communist economy), industrial (vs agricultural), cosmopolitan (vs rural), democratic (vs totalitarian), offering opportunities to make money and travel (vs the lack thereof), and clean (vs polluted). Even though South Korea and Taiwan do not belong to the West, they are accorded all of the Western characteristics listed above. Korean and Taiwanese people are not white, but their skin colour is still much lighter than that of a Vietnamese person. South Korea and Taiwan, the so-called Asian dragons, have therefore become the Asian role models for the Vietnamese in their quest to catch up with the West. It is understandable then that the Vietnamese transnational women who have changed themselves into Koreans and Taiwanese are viewed as more modern, classy and wealthy than the simple rural Vietnamese in Hải Thành. The differences are shown in not only how translocal women view transnational women but also the other way around. A transnational woman remarked of her sister-in-law:

> I cannot clearly say why but the way she dresses just makes her look dirty [bẩn]. It's not that the clothes are unclean but she looks kind of dirty. She also does not have her nails done so her hands do not look nice. And she walks loudly; I can recognise her by the noise she makes. When we eat, I have the feeling that she just eats a lot. I don't know. I just do not talk to her much.

The body and lifestyle are once again used to delineate hierarchical status and class difference between translocal and transnational women. Besides economic differences, I believe that translocal women do not earn much cultural capital after moving because of the politics of migration, which favour the urban and the cosmopolitan. In the case of translocal women in Hải Thành, their marriage migration to a rural, internal place does not relieve them of the status of 'rural women'. Despite having mobile and uprooted identities, they are still regarded in Hải Thành as rural and backward, and are devalued by their unpleasant behaviours as well as their unappealing, unhygienic bodies. We see repeatedly the importance of dressing, maintaining beautiful hands, and hygiene (dirty vs clean, the white/black binary transformed into fairer/darker skin) as markers of social class among women. In other words, the body is a site where social differences are articulated.

As Jones (2001) notes, clothes are important elements of self-presentation and significant markers of class boundaries. In Hải Thành, clothes indicate conformity with different ideals of femininity. To dress 'like Koreans' or dressing 'simply' are modes of self-presentation that visibly separate transnational and translocal women, and signal different class affiliations (cosmopolitan vs rural). Similarly, Jiang (2014) argues that hand fetish and hygiene is the new class indicator, distinguishing the higher class from the 'dirty' working class. In Industrial times, the hands were associated with manual labour, a lower form of labour compared to the more advanced mechanical labour. As such, a measure of modernity is the extent to which the hands are freed from labour. Beautiful hands have, arguably, become the representation of civilisation and modernity (Jiang 2014). This global obsession with manicure is more than simply a question of women's unattainable beauty standards and oppression, but is also a tool for women to negotiate their social statuses (Kang 2010). In her study in New York, Kang concludes that the reasons women have their nails done vary from having higher self-esteem, attractiveness to partners, stress relief, bonding with other women, career advancement, and increased mobility (Kang 2010). Depending on their social positions, defined by race, sexuality and social class, the meanings and rewards of manicures and beauty differ among women. For example, airbrushed nails, while considered to be beautiful by many African American women, stigmatise them as belonging to a lower social class. At the same time, by choosing a more 'boring' middle-class nail style (French manicures and pastel colours), a working-class woman can elevate her status to that of a professional. As Kang convincingly shows, nails 'grow out of … bodies but also out of social relations and circumstances in which these bodies are embedded' (Kang 2010:132).

Manicure, for women in Hải Thành, is a ticket to an exclusive club of women who have the money and time to pay attention to beauty and pampering. Translocal women, who undertake agricultural and fisheries related work, considered both dirty and hard, and who do not have disposable incomes, cannot join this club. Few, if any translocal women in Hải Thành known to me have their nails done, yet all know where the nail salons are and the exact cost of each specific style. Their knowledge of manicures comes from listening to transnational and local women talking about manicures. Transnational women in Hải Thành, by having manicures done and criticising translocal women for not doing so, are essentially claiming their bodies as both special and normative, consequently reinforcing their class privilege. At the same time, translocal women's failure to keep their hands 'clean' and nice is understood as a personal defect rather than as a re/construction of marginality and disadvantage. Therefore, in the same way that the non-white body is the marked other against which the ideal woman is defined (Collins 2005; Bettie 2003), the rural woman's body becomes a spectre against which a cosmopolitan, urban ideal is defined. In other words, transnational women's beauty and privilege has no meaning without the failure of the rural translocal women to measure up against. The women's hands express both a privileged distance from hard labour and bind the articulation of class with the articulation of gender.

What is most surprising to me, however, is how the class hierarchy is mapped onto ethnic differences in Hải Thành. Often Hải Thành people told me that the in-marrying daughters-in-law of their neighbours are very rural (*quê*) because they are 'ethnic minority people' ('*người dân tộc*', commonly contracted in Hải Thành as '*tộc*'). The term 'ethnic minority' in Vietnam has such a negative meaning that it easily turns into racial categorisation, loaded with connotations of primitiveness and even savagery. Such connotations can be seen in the remarks made by one Hải Thành man about his daughter-in-law, who is an ethnic Thái woman from Thanh Hoá:

> She's very different from us here. Her true nature [*bản chất*] ... she argues all the time with her husband. If he says one sentence, she has to say another. If needed, she can physically fight her husband, unlike women here. Fight till the end! Before moving here, she lived in the mountains. From the road to her house on the top of the mountain, it takes more than an hour of walking. Their lifestyles are strange: they do not grow any food or raise any livestock. Instead, they just go into the woods and fetch whatever they can find for the day. Absolutely no long-term thinking. There is nothing to live on over there. It's exactly like how the TV portrays the ethnic life. I don't really understand her and I don't trust what she says yet. Because of her background, it is very hard for me to teach her.

The man implied that ethnic people are marginal, wild and primitive, both in their lifestyles and their personality. They are also dangerous and cannot be trusted, which makes them difficult to restrain and discipline. This representation is in line with the dominant discourses in Vietnam that fortify the binaries of majority–minority, modern–ancient, and civilised–barbarian (Michaud 2010).

Even though there are indeed minority ethnic women marrying local men, the number is small, and most translocal women who are assumed to be of ethnic minority background actually are not. When I questioned Hải Thành people about why they claimed these women to be ethnic minorities when they were not, they explained: 'We were just joking. It is because ethnic people are very honest, thus not very smart [*ngố*] even though they like money [*tham tiền*]. They also dress very rurally.' I witnessed how often the derived contraction 'ethnic' (*tộc*) is used in Hải Thành to talk about differences. When a grandmother jokingly told her five-year-old granddaughter, 'You must be ethnic [*tộc*] because you dress so funny,' she cried, 'No, I am not ethnic. My mum is ethnic but I am not because my Dad is not.' Her mother, a translocal woman, is a Kinh woman, not a minority. In other words, the 'bad' and 'backward' qualities of translocal women are mapped onto 'ethnic' inferiority. The ethnic mapping of class indicates a permeating but normalised hierarchy between the Kinh and other minorities in Vietnam. It is so normalised that Hải Thành people go about branding people they deem different and inferior to themselves as 'ethnic'. Here we see the categories of ethnicity and social class collapsed into one, which is conflated with the figure of the rural woman.

In Hải Thành, ideologies of race and class have combined to shape an ideal femininity that draws new forms of inclusion and exclusion along the rural/urban, local/global and majority/minority divide. Modern Hải Thành women fashion their identity by conforming to a Western/white ideal of beauty (fairer skin colour, being cosmopolitan, clean hands, nice clothes) and create their different other in the 'ethnic' rural women (dark skin colour, being remote, ugly hands, dirty clothes). As such, rural women are discriminated against because they are perceived to embody ethnic/racial inferiorities.[8]

The exclusion of rural women from modern Vietnamese society at large can be traced in the covers of books and magazines on women, in particular, how women can become modern, wonderful, and seductive. The female models on these covers are fairly similar in terms of styles and beauty (white stylish clothing, careful make-up, and accessories) (Figure 1). Take, for example, the book titled *Phụ nữ Hiện đại Thế kỷ XXI* (*Modern women of the 21st Century*) published by the Lao Động Press in 2011. The modern Vietnamese woman, shown on the cover, has her hair and nails done and wears jewellery and make-up. Her outfit

---

8   It should be noted that the politics of race, class and gender play out quite similarly for Vietnamese transnational women in Taiwan and South Korea. Vietnamese transnational women are also rejected in East Asia because they are rural women from a less economically developed country (Tsai 2011; Epstein 2008; Hsia 2007, 2008; Lee 2008; Sheu 2007; Wang 2007; Lee et al. 2006).

is a modernised version of a suit and she seems to be standing in front of a multistorey office building. It is noteworthy that she has a fair complexion and is wearing white clothing, reinforcing the Western beauty standards. In other words, the modern Vietnamese woman is a chic 'white' urban businesswoman rather than a plain, 'dirty' farmer.

Figure 1: The cover of *Modern Women of the 21st Century*.
Photograph by the author.

These perceived racial differences, along with social and economic differences, consolidate the hierarchy between transnational women and translocal women. This hierarchy reflects important differences between international and internal migration, demonstrating that not all migrations are the same and that the destinations of migration (rural or urban, local or global) are significant in the socioeconomic values and evaluation of migration. While mobility in the global world is usually accorded positive value, the marginal status of translocal women in Hải Thành challenges the simplistic and assumed relationship between migration and social, financial and cosmopolitan climbing.

Fish out of Water: Migration, Immobility and Displacement

Apart from generating social mobility, physical mobility has also been celebrated for its association with freedom, liberation, and resistance. The romanticisation of mobility in the image of the nomad is evident through the works of Mackinders, Deleuze and Guattari, and Bachelard, all of which connect mobility with power; specifically, they perceive in the nomad the ability to evade power and link mobility with freedom and liberty (Adey 2009). However, the case of translocal women shows that they are not only considered inferior but are also controlled and marginalised in Hải Thành. The marginalisation of translocal women in Hải Thành is revealed, first, in their physical immobility and confinement in the home. Unlike those who move to the cities for jobs, translocal women who have migrated to Hải Thành for marriages often find themselves unemployed. The lack of paid work for rural women in Vietnam in general, and the fact that most translocal women are under-educated, make many of them stay-at-home housewives. They might do some seasonal farming if their families do not rent out their plots or hire people to do the work. However, the amount of land for cultivation available to each household in Hải Thành is so limited that agricultural work does not take much time. Moreover, translocal women often reside with their parents-in-law and are financially dependent because the parents-in-law control the family budget.

Because of their ambiguous position as outsiders who are also now insiders, they are not trusted by local people.[9] Translocal women rarely visit their neighbours, as local people and their parents-in-law would view these visits as occasions for gossip. As I was told by local people:

---

9   For studies on the lack of trust and discrimination against migrants from other provinces and ethnicities in Vietnam, see Winkels (2012), McElwee (2008), and Hardy (2003).

> What else besides gossip will they talk about? They don't have jobs. They stay at home. They don't understand the politics and economics of the country or this community. What do they have to talk about besides gossiping?

In Vietnam, gossiping generally means speaking ill of your family and neighbours. In a small rural place such as Hải Thành, where everyone knows and is related to each other, the subject of gossip will spread like wildfire. Gossip is an unspoken taboo in Vietnamese face-saving culture (Hữu Ngọc 2004). Gossip is gendered, in the sense that men are said to talk about national and big ideas (*đàn ông bàn việc nước và việc lớn*) while women are considered to be only concerned with petty talk (*phụ nữ hay buôn dưa lê*).[10] The fear of gossip and its association with women explains why translocal women, when asked why they did not visit their neighbours, said they did not feel welcome. The fishermen, on the other hand, never said to me that they were not received warmly when visiting their neighbours or friends. It is as though men can talk outside of the confines of the home but translocal women cannot.

I witnessed this lack of trust in translocal women and the worry about gossip during my fieldwork. Most translocal women whispered when talking to me, for fear of their parents-in-law overhearing our conversations. Sometimes their parents-in-law would take over and answer my questions on their behalf. Even worse, many of my interviews and connections with translocal women were cut off after I happened to meet their parents-in-law in their houses. Then when I visited again, the parents-in-law would say to me that their daughter-in-law had gone elsewhere, or the translocal woman would text me and tell me not to contact her again. In some instances in which a woman had disclosed to me the details of her situation, I could speculate that, for example, the parents-in-law did not want me to know that they had lied to their daughter-in-law about having more money than they actually did, or that their son had been divorced by his first wife because he was a drunkard. In other cases, I had no grounds for speculation, as I was yet to know much about the woman's story. Given that I never faced a similar problem talking to other groups in Hải Thành, this abrupt disengagement reveals quite clearly the translocal women's status as outsiders who need to be controlled.

---

10 This belief is strongly linked to Confucian ideology that educated men are leaders both in terms of social morality and the formation of society (Luong 2010).

Besides the dreaded gossip, parents-in-law and husbands also like to keep translocal women inside the home for fear of infidelity due to the absence of their husbands for 20 or more days every month. To make matters worse, local women look down on translocal women and do not socialise with them. The reasons are various: we don't know them, they dress in an ugly and dirty manner, they do not know how to have fun, they are not generous. As a result, translocal women end up being socially and physically isolated, and their social network consists of only their in-laws and their cousins if they have married local men. Local people often say that they do not see translocal women much and do not really know who they are. The irony is that while the local people, especially the parents-in-law, often boast about the 'good' lives of translocal women (they really do not have to work much besides a bit of farming; they only stay home and look after their children; compared to women in other rural places, their lives are 10 times better), translocal women often feel constrained and inferior. One of the translocal women told me how much she enjoys working in the textile sweatshop. Even though she is poorly paid and works very long hours, the workplace provides her with a much-needed social network:

I have friends there, you know. People who I can talk to during lunch, people who I can hang out with. We eat together and we take a nap together. Sure, the hours are long and I have to stand on my feet all day — they are sore often. Sometimes, especially in the winter, I come home so late that the whole house has gone to sleep. I still have to make dinner for myself and eat by myself; I feel quite lonely.[11] But staying home is even lonelier.

The marginalisation of translocal women in Hải Thành is further demonstrated by their invisibility in local discourses. There is no term that describes translocal women as a group in Hải Thành. Hải Thành people use *Kiều Đài Loan, Hàn Quốc* (Taiwanese and Korean transnationals) to refer to transnational women, and *gái Hải* (Hải women), a shortened form of *gái Hải Thành* (Hải Thành women), to refer to local women. But translocal women are not assumed to belong to either of these groups. If they ever get talked about, it is usually as specific wives of specified fishermen, never as a group. Even though translocal women often distinguish themselves from local women,

11 Her husband is a fisherman, so he is not home most of the time.

Hải Thành people do not compare local women to translocal women, but to women in other places. In other words, translocal women rarely appear in local discourse. This linguistic absence indicates that translocal women have no identity outside of being defined in relation to men (being local men's wives). It seems that for translocal women there is no public acknowledgement of their life histories, struggles or identity outside of marriage. They are defined by heterosexual and patriarchal language that designates them as subject to male authority.

The denial of a place for translocal women in local discourse has other political implications. As Foucault noted, discourses are 'practices that systematically form the objects of which they speak ... Discourses are not about objects; they do not identify objects, they constitute them and in the practice of doing so conceal their own intervention' (Foucault 1972:49). Discourse, in creating the subject through marking the boundaries of exclusion, leaves behind the silenced group who, because of linguistic absence, have no way of articulating their subjecthood. Translocal women, in a Lacanian understanding, are a signified (a reality) without a signifier (a place in language) and are therefore 'real' but outside of the discursive reality.

Being made invisible, indeed, is one painful form of oppression, as Butler illustrated:

> Indeed, one can be interpellated, put in place, given a place through silence, through not being addressed, and this becomes painfully clear when we find ourselves preferring the occasion of being derogated to the one of not being addressed at all. (Butler 1997:27)

The invisibility of translocal women implies being ignored, devalued, rejected and not being heard. It also denies the independence and desirability of their identity, since they are neither attractive nor significant enough to even be identified. The displacement of translocal women is twofold: they are denied a linguistic place in the community of speakers, as well as a physical place in public spaces where they can participate in community life. They are, in short, refused a place of being and of having possibilities for human relationships. Their displacement is the problem of placelessness.

In many ways, translocal women are the fish that get caught from somewhere else and are out of water once in Hải Thành. The fact that they are young and relatively newly wedded matters much in how well they are integrated in the community. They have not been able to gain the trust and respect from their in-law families, neighbours, and people in the commune. They also have not made friends and social connections outside of their immediate families. Given how isolated translocal women are, I suspect that it will take them a very long time to feel accepted and comfortable in Hải Thành.

The question of belonging, writes Vijayasree, 'acquires an additional edge of urgency and poignancy in the case of female migrants, because, for them, the issue of self-definition can hardly be isolated from larger questions of gender' (Vijayasree 2000). Vijayasree talks about Indian writers in the West, but her comment also illuminates the predicament of translocal women in Hải Thành. Their migration is a re-entry into the northern Vietnamese patriarchal structure that excludes women as outsiders (ngoại tộc), by tracing descent through men, patrilocal residence, and an emphasis on male authority (Luong 2010). Their migration, instead of bringing freedom and social mobility, reinforces their female status as being displaced, invisible, and, ironically, immobile. Indeed, one does not need to migrate out of the country to be displaced; one can be displaced by being right at home and being a woman.

By focusing on the migration of translocal women and comparing this with the migration of transnational women, I join other mobility scholars in questioning the celebration of movement as a universal benefit (Glick-Schiller and Salazar 2013; Mai and King 2009; Partridge 2009; Ahmed 2004; Skeggs 2004; Tsing 2002; Tesfahuney 1998; Massey 1993). The displacement and confinement of translocal women in Hải Thành reveals that mobility can produce immobility, and that movement and non-movement are not fixed binaries. Instead, mobility and immobility are relative and interrelated. I have underlined that not all migrations are the same, and that the question of who moves where and under what conditions does matter. The focus in this study on diverse trajectories of migration sheds light on the hierarchy of mobilities that exists in Vietnam, and on the differentiations in status, personhood, and rurality that are implicated in these migrations. Only by paying attention to these complex dynamics of mobility, personhood, and place can we understand how marriage, migration, and social worth intermesh — like the often tattered and sometimes empty nets of the fishers of Hải Thành.

References

Adey, Peter 2009, *Mobility (Key Ideas in Geography)*, Routledge, London.

Ahmed, Sara 2004, *The Cultural Politics of Emotion*, Edinburgh University Press, Edinburgh.

BBC Vietnamese 2009, 'TQ tuần tra nghề cá ở Vịnh Bắc Bộ' ['China Performed Fishery Patrol in the Tonkin Gulf'], 31 May 2009, available at www.bbc.com/vietnamese/vietnam/2009/05/090531_china_fishery_patrol.shtml, accessed 14 August 2013.

Beck, Ulrich 2006, *The Cosmopolitan Vision*, Polity, Cambridge.

Bélanger, Danièle, Hye-Kyung Lee and Hong-Zen Wang 2010, 'Ethnic Diversity and Statistics in East Asia: "Foreign Brides" Surveys in Taiwan and South Korea', *Ethnic and Racial Studies,* vol. 33, no. 6, pp. 1108–1130.

Bettie, Julie 2003, *Women without Class: Girls, Race and Identity*, University of California Press, Berkeley.

Bommes, Michael and Frank-Olaf Radtke 1996, 'Migration into Big Cities and Small Towns: An Uneven Process with Limited need for Multiculturalism', *Innovation: The European Journal of Social Science Research,* vol. 9, no. 1, pp. 75–86.

Brettell, Caroline B. 2003, 'Bringing the City Back In: Cities as Contexts for Immigrant Incorporation', in Nancy Foner (ed.), *American Arrivals: Anthropology Engages the New Immigration*, School of American Research Press, Santa Fe, pp. 163–196.

Butler, Judith 1997, *Excitable Speech: A Politics of the Performative*, Routledge, London.

Caglar, Ayse 2010, 'Rescaling Cities, Cultural Diversity and Transnationalism: Migrants of Mardin and Essen', in Steven Vertovec (ed.), *Anthropology of Migration and Multiculturalism: New Directions*, Routledge, London, pp. 113–138.

Carling, Jørgen 2008, 'The Human Dynamics of Migrant Transnationalism', *Ethnic and Racial Studies,* vol. 31, no. 8, pp. 1452–1477.

Carruthers, Ashley and Trung Dinh Dang 2012, 'The Socio-spatial Constellation of a Central Vietnamese Village and its Emigrants', *Journal of Vietnamese Studies,* vol. 7, no. 4, pp. 122–153.

Chakrabarty, Dipesh 2000, *Provincializing Europe: Postcolonial Thought and Historical Difference*, Princeton University Press, Princeton.

Chu, Julie Y. 2010, *Cosmologies of Credit: Transnational Mobility and the Politics of Destination in China*, Duke University Press, Durham, NC.

Clifford, James 1997, *Routes: Travel and Translation in the Late Twentieth Century*, Harvard University Press, Cambridge, Mass.

Cohen, Jeffrey H. 2011, 'Migration, Remittances, and Household Strategies', *Annual Review of Anthropology,* vol. 40, pp. 103–114.

Collins, Patricia H. 2005, *Black Sexual Politics: African Americans, Gender and the New Racism*, Routledge, New York and London.

Duong, Yen 2013, 'Nơi đàn ông khó lấy vợ' ['The Village Where Men Have Difficulties Finding Wives'], 11 February 2013, Người Đưa Tin [*News Delivery People*], available at www.nguoiduatin.vn/chuyen-bi-hai-o-noi-dan-ong-kho-lay-vo-a67774.html, accessed 6 November 2013.

Epstein, Stephen 2008, 'The Bride(s) from Hanoi: South Korean Popular Culture, Vietnam and "Asia" in the New Millennium', *Citizenship Studies,* vol. 12, no. 1, pp. 9–25.

Foner, Nancy 2010, 'How Exceptional is New York?: Migration and Multiculturalism in the Empire City', in Steven Vertovec (ed.), *Anthropology of Migration and Multiculturalism: New Directions*, Routledge, London, pp. 39–64.

Foucault, Michel 1972, *The Archaeology of Knowledge*, Tavistock, London.

Glick-Schiller, Nina and Ayse Caglar (eds) 2011, *Locating Migration: Rescaling Cities and Migrants,* Cornell University Press, Ithaca, NY.

Glick-Schiller, Nina and Noel B. Salazar 2013, 'Regimes of Mobility across the Globe', *Journal of Ethnic and Migration Studies,* vol. 39, no. 2, pp. 183–200.

Gupta, Akhil 1998, *Postcolonial Developments: Agriculture in the Making of Modern India*, Duke University Press, Durham NC.

Hage, Ghassan 2005, 'A Not So Multi-sited Ethnography of a Not So Imagined Community', *Anthropological Theory,* vol. 5, no. 4, pp. 463–475.

Hardy, Andrew 2003, 'Migrants in Contemporary Vietnamese History: Marginal or Mainstream?', in Abu Talib Ahmad and Tan Liok Ee (eds), *New Terrains in Southeast Asian History*, Ohio University Press, Athens, Ohio, pp. 328–353.

Hsia, Hsiao-Chuan 2007, 'Imaged and Imagined Threat to the Nation: The Media Construction of the "Foreign Brides' Phenomenon" as Social Problems in Taiwan', *Inter-Asia Cultural Studies,* vol. 8, no. 1, pp. 55–85.

Hsia, Hsiao-Chuan 2008, 'Beyond Victimization: The Empowerment of "Foreign Brides" in Resisting Capitalist Globalization', *China Journal of Social Work,* vol. 1, no. 2, pp. 130–148.

Hữu Ngọc 2004, *Wandering through Vietnamese Culture*, Thtureii Publisher, Hanoi.

Jiang, Jing 2014, 'From Foot Fetish to Hand Fetish: Hygiene, Class, and the New Woman', *Positions: East Asia Cultures Critique,* vol. 22, no. 1, pp. 131–159.

Jones, Dorothy 2001, 'Defining Self and Others through Textile and Text', *Women's Writing,* vol. 8, no. 3, pp. 375–390.

Kalir, Barak 2013, 'Moving Subjects, Stagnant Paradigms: Can the "Mobilities Paradigm" Transcend Methodological Nationalism?', *Journal of Ethnic and Migration Studies,* vol. 39, no. 2, pp. 311–327.

Kang, Miliann 2010, *The Managed Hand: Race, Gender, and the Body in Beauty Service Work*, University of California Press, Berkeley.

King, Russell and Ronald Skeldon 2010, '"Mind the Gap!": Integrating Approaches to Internal and International Migration', *Journal of Ethnic and Migration Studies,* vol. 36, no. 10, pp. 1619–1646.

Lee, Hye-Kyung 2008, 'International Marriage and the State in South Korea: Focusing on Governmental Policy', *Citizenship Studies,* vol. 12, no. 1, pp. 107–123.

Lee, Yean-Ju, Dong-Hoon Seol and Sung-Nam Cho 2006, 'International Marriages in South Korea: The Significance of Nationality and Ethnicity', *Journal of Population Research,* vol. 23, no. 2, pp. 165–182.

Levitt, Peggy and B. Nadya Jaworsky 2007, 'Transnational Migration Studies: Past Development and Future Trends', *Annual Review of Sociology,* vol. 33, pp. 129–156.

Luong, Hy Van 2010, *Tradition, Revolution, and Market Economy in a North Vietnamese Village, 1925–2006*, University of Hawaii Press, Honolulu.

Mai, Nicola and Russell King 2009, 'Love, Sexuality and Migration: Mapping the Issue(s)', *Mobilities,* vol. 4, no. 3, pp. 295–307.

Massey, Doreen 1993, 'Power-Geometry and a Progressive Sense of Place', in John Bird, Barry Curtis, Tim Putnam and Lisa Tickner (eds), *Mapping the Futures: Local Cultures, Global Change*, Routledge, New York, pp. 59–69.

McElwee, Pamela 2008, '"Blood Relatives" or Unfriendly Neighbors?: Vietnamese–Ethnic Minority Interactions in the Annamite Mountains', *Journal of Vietnamese Studies,* vol. 3, no. 3, pp. 81–116.

Michaud, Jean 2010, 'Editorial: Zomia and Beyond', *Journal of Global History,* vol. 5, no. 2, pp. 187–214.

Ong, Aihwa 1999, *Flexible Citizenship: The Cultural Logics of Transnationality*, Duke University Press, Durham, NC.

Partridge, Damani James 2009, 'Travel as an Analytic of Exclusion: Becoming Noncitizens, and the Politics of Mobility After the Berlin Wall', *Identities: Global Studies in Culture and Power,* vol. 16, no. 3, pp. 342–366.

Però, Davide 2007, 'Migrants and the Politics of Governance: The Case of Barcelona', *Social Anthropology,* vol. 15, no. 3, pp. 271–286.

Rapport, Nigel and Andrew Dawson 1998, *Migrants of Identity: Perceptions of Home in a World of Movement,* Berg, New York.

Salazar, Noel B. and Alan Smart 2012, 'Anthropological Takes on (Im)mobility', *Identities: Global Studies in Culture and Power,* vol. 18, no. 6, pp. i–ix.

Sheu, Yea-huey 2007, 'Full Responsibility with Partial Citizenship: Immigrant Wives in Taiwan', *Social Policy and Administration,* vol. 41, no. 2, pp. 179–196.

Skeggs, Beverley 2004, *Class, Self, Culture, Transformations,* Routledge, London.

Stepick, Alex, Guillermo Grenier, Max Castro and Marvin Dunn (eds) 2003, *This Land is Our Land: Immigrants and Power in Miami,* University of California Press, Berkeley, CA.

Taylor, Philip (ed.) 2004, *Social Inequality in Vietnam and the Challenges to Reform,* Institute ISEAS Publications, Singapore.

Taylor, Philip 2007, 'Poor Policies, Wealthy Peasants: Alternative Trajectories of Rural Development in Vietnam', *Journal of Vietnamese Studies,* vol. 2, no. 2, pp. 3–56.

Tesfahuney, Mekonnen 1998, 'Mobility, Racism and Geopolitics', *Political Geography,* vol. 17, no. 5, pp. 499–515.

Thai, Hung Cam 2014, *Insufficient Funds: The Culture of Money in Low-Wage Transnational Families,* Stanford University Press, Stanford, CA.

Trung Kien 2013, 'Hỗ trợ phụ nữ lấy chồng nước ngoài tái hòa nhập cộng đồng' ['Support for Women who have Married Foreign Husbands to Reintegrate into the Community'], 12 August 2013, *An Ninh Hải Phòng* [*Hai Phong Security*], available at www.anhp.vn/phong-su/201308/ho-tro-phu-nu-lay-chong-nuoc-ngoai-tai-hoa-nhap-cong-dong-456058/, accessed May 2014.

Tsai, Ming-Chang 2011, '"Foreign Brides" Meet Ethnic Politics in Taiwan', *International Migration Review,* vol. 45, no. 2, pp. 243–268.

Tsing, Anna 2002, 'The Global Situation', in Jonathan Xavier Inda and Renato Rosaldo (eds), *The Anthropology of Globalization: A Reader*, Blackwell, Oxford, pp. 453–485.

Urry, John 2000, *Sociology Beyond Societies: Mobilities for the Twenty-First Century*, International Library of Sociology, Routledge, London.

Urry, John 2007, *Mobilities*. Polity Press, Cambridge.

Uỷ Ban Biên Giới Quốc Gia 2000, 'Hiệp định hợp tác nghề cá ở Vịnh Bắc Bộ giữa Chính phủ nước Cộng hoà xã hội chủ nghĩa Việt Nam và Chính phủ nước Cộng hoà nhân dân Trung Hoa' ['Agreement on Fishery Cooperation in the Tonkin Gulf between Vietnam and China'], 18 April 2000, *Bộ Ngoại Giao* [Ministry of Foreign Affairs], available at biengioilanhtho.gov.vn/vie/hiepdinhhoptacngheca-nd-e6a9f6ac.aspx, accessed 12 November 2013.

Vertovec, Steven 2011, 'The Cultural Politics of Nation and Migration', *Annual Review of Anthropology,* vol. 40, pp. 241–256.

Vijayasree, C. 2000, 'Alter-Nativity, Migration, Marginality and Narration: The Case of Indian Women Writers Settled in the West', in Ralph J. Crane and Radhika Mohanram (eds), *Shifting Continents/ Colliding Cultures: Diaspora Writing of the Indian Subcontinent*, Brill, Amsterdam and Atlanta, pp. 123–134.

Wang, Hong-Zen 2007, 'Hidden Spaces of Resistance of the Subordinated: Case Studies from Vietnamese Female Migrant Partners in Taiwan', *International Migration Review,* vol. 41, no. 3, pp. 706–727.

Wang, Hong-Zen, and Shu-Ming Chang 2002, 'The Commodification of International Marriages: Cross-border Marriage Business between Taiwan and Viet Nam', *International Migration,* vol. 40, no. 6, pp. 93–116.

Wilding, Raelene 2007, 'Transnational Ethnographies and Anthropological Imaginings of Migrancy', *Journal of Ethnic and Migration Studies,* vol. 33, no. 2, pp. 331–348.

Winkels, Alexandra 2012, 'Migration, Social Networks and Risk: The Case of Rural to Rural Migration in Vietnam', *Journal of Vietnamese Studies,* vol. 7, no. 4, pp. 92–121.

Zhang, Li 2002, *Strangers in the City: Reconfigurations of Space, Power, and Social Networks Within China's Floating Population*, Stanford University Press, Stanford.

4

'Here, Everyone is Like Everyone Else!': Exile and Re-emplacement in a Vietnamese Leprosy Village

Yen Le

One afternoon, I was sitting with Grandpa Thiện[1] in front of his house. He looked happy that afternoon, blissfully watching a whole new batch of chickens born a few weeks before. The quiet yard in front of his house was animated by cheerful, chirpy little chickens running around here and there. Grandpa Thiện was proud that his stock of chickens had increased remarkably with each batch of newborn chicks, and he was hopeful that the price of chickens remained stable, so that when they grew up, his wife would be able to sell them at a good price.

He told me about his niece, who was blind. She studied well and was able to become a teacher. She used to have a boyfriend who was not blind, but the relationship did not go anywhere because his family could not accept a blind daughter-in-law. The boyfriend broke up with her several years later to marry someone else. Then she met a blind man. Even though they could not see each other, they understood each other well. His family adored her too. They finally got married and lived very happily together.

---

1 Pseudonyms are used throughout this chapter.

Drawing upon his niece's story, Grandpa Thiện stated, 'You see, chickens stay with chickens, ducks stay with ducks. It should be that way.' He continued, 'Like here, people with leprosy should stay with people with leprosy. It's very difficult for chickens to stay with ducks.'

Grandpa Thiện is one of around 1,000 residents of Quy Hòa Leprosy Village in South Central Vietnam. Quy Hòa was established as a leper colony in 1929 by French Catholic missionaries. Located in a valley by the sea in the outskirts of Quy Nhơn, Bình Định Province, the leprosarium provided a sanctuary for people afflicted by the disease and a clinic for the administration of treatments. Until the introduction of sulphide-based drugs in the 1960s and more effective multidrug therapy in the early 1980s, treatment options for leprosy were limited (Monnais 2008). The disease progressed through the appearance of numb patches and skin rashes, lesions and ulceration, and disfiguration of the face and hands. Owing to the absence of sensation in their limbs, sufferers who engaged in everyday activities such as cooking, farming or sport were prone to injury and amputation was frequently required to deal with severe injuries and chronic infection. Perhaps even more significant side effects of the disease were the fear and stigma provoked by its symptoms. Many leprosy sufferers who came to leprosaria such as Quy Hòa for treatment settled there permanently, seeking a refuge from the shame and social ostracism that accompanied the disease. After national unification in 1975, the leprosarium was taken over by the state, becoming the Quy Hòa National Leprosy-Dermatology Hospital. As of 2013, the leprosy village, located adjacent to the hospital, is home to 426 leprosy-affected people and their families, who subsist on small-scale livelihood activities, a modest patient subsidy, and charity gifts.

Since the introduction of multidrug therapy in 1983, leprosy patients in Vietnam have been able to be medically cured after only six months to a year of treatment. Moreover, in tandem with improvements in early diagnosis, advanced cases of leprosy in Vietnam have consistently decreased since 1995 (Hồng Hạnh 2010).[2] Provided that they have been treated in a timely manner, people contracting leprosy have been able to avoid bodily residues and thus the social stigma

2   The new case detection rate decreased from 3.44 new cases in every 100,000 people in 1995, to 0.48 new cases in every 100,000 people in 2006. The leprosy prevalence rate also went down from 6.71 to 0.04 cases in every 10,000 people between 1995 and 2006 (Hồng Hạnh 2010).

attached to leprosy. New leprosy patients in Vietnam are now treated and monitored in their residential communities and are no longer isolated for treatment in segregated leprosy villages (*làng phong*), such as Quy Hòa. Nevertheless, there are still around 18,000 people living in leprosy villages across the country, who, although deemed to have been cured, are seriously disabled and unable to return to their original communities (Hoài Hương 2010). Most of the elderly people living in Quy Hòa had contracted leprosy before multidrug therapy was widely used in Vietnam. Although they have long been free of leprosy infection, most of them are afflicted with visible deformities and disabilities caused by advanced leprosy, and consistently expressed their wish to remain in the village.

'Here, everyone is like everyone else!' (*'Ở đây ai cũng như ai!'*) is the response I repeatedly received from villagers after asking them why they wished to stay in an exclusive leprosy village such as Quy Hòa. Members of the Indian leprosy-afflicted community of Bethany studied by James Staples (2007) referred to themselves as people of 'one disease, one caste, one religion'. Similarly, people of Quy Hòa leprosy village describe themselves as 'of the same kind' (*'cùng một thứ'*) and define their community by 'sameness'. Wherever I went in the village, people stressed their sameness — the same disease, the same life history, the same body, the same pain, and the same suffering. I came to understand 'sameness' as, first and foremost, the intrinsic factor that ties them all together.

This chapter tells leprosy-affected people's stories about sameness. It seeks to elucidate the conceptions of sameness held by residents of this exclusive village of leprosy sufferers, and how sameness as a defining characteristic of the community has reconfigured their lived reality of leprosy. It draws upon a year of ethnographic fieldwork conducted in Quy Hòa in 2011, during which I was welcomed into the homes and lives of numerous leprosy-affected villagers and their families. Over the course of my research, I collected life narratives of Quy Hòa residents afflicted with leprosy, while also observing and taking part in community events, meetings, rituals and daily activities. My research also took me to other communities of leprosy-affected people in southern Vietnam, and to the urban and peri-urban sites where people with enduring physical residues of the disease live and work.[3]

Drawing upon the villagers' conceptions of their own community, this chapter seeks answers to the question of why exclusive communities for people with leprosy still exist now that leprosy has been declared medically curable, and as only mildly contagious, and when 'community-based' and outpatient treatment has replaced segregated institutional care as the preferred public health approach to treatment. The chapter shows that while the medical rationale for segregation no longer exists, the existential problems leprosy sufferers continue to endure provide justification for their continuing attachment to such communities.

The chapter argues that community is a therapeutic antidote to the slights and injuries visited upon those with leprosy in the wider society. For people shunned and feared as threatening to the normal social order, such a community exists as a space of protection. For people displaced from their families and villages by their social invalidity and the emotions aroused by their physical disfigurement, the village provided an opportunity for social re-integration. For those gazed upon obsessively for their bodily difference, exclusive living continues to offer the powerfully redemptive experience of sameness. Such collective solutions have been arrived at through turbulent personal processes of banishment, degradation, withdrawal, re-emplacement, hope and reinvention.

The chapter illustrates these points by describing elderly Quy Hòa residents' experiences of intimate exile and the denial of relatedness with members of their own family. It describes the expulsion of leprosy-affected people from their communities and the social death meted out to so many with this disease — traumatic experiences that still haunt and unite those who endured them, irrespective of their social background. The chapter discusses how the value of 'sameness' arises out of newly discovered feelings of mutual sympathy

3   The fieldwork was conducted as part of my PhD in anthropology at The Australian National University. I wish to thank Philip Taylor for his guidance on my project and for his extensive comments on the argument of this chapter. I also am grateful to Assa Doron and Kirin Narayan for providing advice and encouragement in my writing, and to the anonymous readers who reviewed an earlier version of this chapter.

and love for those who are similarly social outcastes. The cases also demonstrate the empowerment and confidence that come from living in a community made up of people exclusively like oneself. I argue that the power of sameness, of being with identical others, and of living in a community where all people are alike, has a reassuring and healing effect that helps account for residents' attachment to life in this exclusive leprosy village.

Intimate Exiles

People in Quy Hòa come from all walks of life. While a large number of villagers are from poor rural areas, a few inmates of the leprosy village came from wealthy and illustrious families. One of them is an old man, Grandpa Tâm, the nephew of L., who stood out as the only Vietnamese general in the French colonial military among the many French generals and officials in the colony at that time. Needless to say, back then, this General's family was very well-known, highly respected, and powerful. Very few people, however, knew about his nephew, a leprosy sufferer sent into Quy Hòa.

One day, the inmates in the then Catholic-run Quy Hòa leper colony heard the news that the General, Grandpa Tâm's uncle, would be accompanying King Bảo Đại to visit Ghềnh Ráng, a beautiful beach area not far from Quy Hòa. Grandpa Tâm was coaxed by his fellow inmates into going there to meet his uncle. He escaped from the leper colony through the fence on the cemetery side, walking along the narrow trail around the hill that separates Quy Hòa and Ghềnh Ráng beach, and finally reached Ghềnh Ráng, where the King and the General were visiting. Grandpa Tâm bravely asked the entourage to let him come over and see the General, identifying himself as the General's nephew. However, the General rejected him, curtly denying having a nephew suffering from leprosy. As soon as this disavowal was uttered, members of the party severely chided the 'leper' and rudely told him to take himself someplace else.

After the trip with the King to Ghềnh Ráng, the General's rage continued to fester, and he vehemently reprimanded his sister, Grandpa Tâm's mother. He asked his sister to tell her leprosy-affected son to stay put in Quy Hòa, and never again come out and tell people that he was the General's nephew. He was such a powerful man in the French colony at the time; if people knew that he had a 'leper' nephew, it would be a big 'loss of face' (*mất thể diện*) and bring serious shame for not only him but the entire family.

The fury of the General and his family was conveyed to the leprosy-affected nephew, Grandpa Tâm, in a letter sent into the leper colony, which told him to henceforth stay within Quy Hòa. If he needed money, his mother would send more money for him, but he could not go out. Back in Quy Hòa, after the venture out of the leper colony and the humiliation of being disowned and sent away by his powerful uncle, Grandpa Tâm was very sad and felt pity for himself (*tủi thân*). Seeing him coldly rejected and expelled, his fellow inmates in Quy Hòa realised that even though they were born into very different backgrounds — he was from an extremely influential and prestigious family while most of them were poor peasants — once they became 'lepers', they all became the same. The spirit of egalitarianism encapsulated in the villagers' own words, 'Here everyone is like everyone else', has acted as salient rhetoric in this community's life since its inception. Regardless of how different they had been as individuals, as lepers they were bound to the same destiny. As Louisa Howe (1964) suggests, a community can be forged by symbolic understanding of a common destiny. In Quy Hòa, this strong sense of a shared fate, reflected through such stories as the one above, and also as regularly mentioned in villagers' self-description as people with the 'same lot' (*đồng cảnh ngộ*) or 'same fate' (*cùng chung số phận*), contributes to robustly sustaining the community.

Many people in Quy Hòa leprosy village shared with me their belief that most of the time they could only feel completely comfortable and open around people with the same disease. Many are very reluctant to enter social relationships with non-leprosy patients outside their exclusive network of leprosy sufferers. The family of my village friend, Hà, whose parents both had leprosy, is no exception. She proudly told me that she was very popular with boys when she was young. She had many followers, but she liked one man from a non-patient family in the upper village of Quy Hòa.

Hà was very happy when the man asked her to marry him. However, her leprosy-afflicted mother strongly rejected the idea and insistently advised her to choose the son of a leprosy-affected person, like her. Her mother believed that if Hà married into a non-patient family, her spouse's family would look down upon them. Her mother poignantly asked her, 'They can hold a glass of water in one hand, while I have to use both hands and yet barely manage to hold a glass. Just think, how could I ever talk on an equal level [*nói chuyện ngang hàng*] with them?'

Eventually, listening to her mother's advice, Hà did not marry the man from the upper village, but married the son of a leprosy-affected couple in Quy Hòa leprosy village. A few years later, the brother of the man from the non-patient family who used to be a love interest of Hà also married a daughter of leprosy sufferers in the leprosy village. His mother tried hard to prevent him from marrying someone from the leprosy village, but this was in vain, as the pair were very much in love and were strongly determined to get married, regardless of the parents' rejection of the idea. The man told his mother that he would die if he could not marry his intended. Finally, the upper village mother had to comply with the young couple's wish and reluctantly approved their marriage.

Soon after their wedding, the wife (the daughter of the leprosy-affected family) fell pregnant and gave birth to a boy. After giving birth to the first child, according to local custom, the daughter-in-law returned to her parents' house and the new mother and her infant were taken care of by her leprosy-affected mother during the first few months. The husband's mother was also excited about her new paternal grandson, the highly valued eldest son of the eldest son (*cháu nội đích tôn*). Nonetheless, what was frowned upon by people in the leprosy village was that whenever she came down to Quy Hòa to visit her new grandson, she always brought a clean bath towel from her house. Whenever the baby was handed to her, she put the infant onto the towel, and never let the baby's back make direct contact with her own arms.

People from the leprosy sufferers' community pointed out that this woman felt such aversion towards her own grandson because most of the time he was held by his leprosy-affected maternal grandmother and her daughter. That was why she never let the baby make direct contact with her own skin. Talking scornfully about that old lady from upper Quy Hòa, Hà's mother patted her daughter on the shoulder: 'You see, I was right to prohibit you from marrying that lady's son. She was disgusted even by her very own grandson, let alone us!'

After getting to know me well, my village friends revealed that their ultimate wish was to be seen as equal, or 'on an equal level' (*ngang hàng*) to other normal people. The utmost pain of having leprosy, as lived and told by villagers, is to be seen as lesser and to be denied full personhood. Grandpa Bảo told me with an angry tone, 'Once one gets this disease, one can never be the same as other people any more. People cannot treat you the same way as they treat normal ones.' To illustrate, he told me about Uncle Hậu, the head of the upper village, who is married to the daughter of a leprosy-afflicted couple in Quy Hòa leprosy village. Having lived in the upper village all his life and being married to a leprosy sufferer's daughter, he has long been used to leprosy-afflicted people. He is usually 'natural' around leprosy-affected people, Grandpa Bảo commented. Whenever Grandpa Bảo visited his house, Hậu was friendly and welcoming. However, once while Grandpa Bảo was visiting, another friend of Hậu's, a non-patient, dropped in to visit and his host's face suddenly changed. He looked confused and somehow embarrassed. Noticing Hậu's attitude, Grandpa Bảo quickly stood up from his chair, told Hậu that he would come again another time, and left. Grandpa Bảo resentfully realised that even though Hậu behaved very 'normally' to people with leprosy, he could not treat his leprosy-affected friend equally to his non-patient friends.

Grandpa Thiện once confessed to me that he only needs a (non-patient) person to look straight into his eyes and say 'hello' for him to be really happy. What people suffering from leprosy need, he implied, is normal treatment and respect without that stigmatising stare or shunning. My village friends' stories essentially demonstrate their profound wish to be the same, to be normal and to be equal, to stand 'on an equal level' (*ngang hàng*) as everyone else. Hà's mother, as described above, could not approve of Hà's marriage into a non-patient family, no matter how hard Hà tried to persuade her, because she could not accept a presumably unequal relationship with her daughter's prospective in-laws. The basis of this unequal relationship, she assumed, would be the inevitable focus on her defective and malfunctioning body in stark contrast to the intact bodies of the other family. Only when Hà married another village boy, who was also the son of leprosy sufferers in Quy Hòa, did Hà's mother feel equal to her counterpart. Her daughter's marriage would be more sustainable, she believed, if the two families were equal.

Some village friends emphasised to me that they only feel comfortable and equal within their exclusive community and interacting among fellow leprosy sufferers. 'Here everyone is the same' means that no one is seen as lower than anyone else. In such a 'normalising' social world (Kelleher 1988), leprosy-affected people's intrinsic desire to be seen equally as full, complete people can be fulfilled, spoiled personhood can be replenished and recovered, and dignity returned. Explaining the reason for villagers' willingness to convert and commit to Christianity, a senior nun of the Quy Hòa Franciscan convent said to me, 'These are the people who have suffered so much from society's maltreatment. First and foremost, Christianity sees them fully as a person, treats them with dignity [nhân phẩm] and cares for them while everyone else is scared of them and no one cares for them.'

Social Levelling

Quy Hòa villagers' description of their community — 'Here everyone is like everyone else!' — encapsulates a widely shared sense of sameness. This sentiment has been forged not only in the context of villagers' common physical suffering and their long-term relations with each other within the exclusive leprosy village, but even more poignantly in reference to the experiences of mistreatment that each had endured before entering the village. Listening to the life stories of Quy Hòa residents, one can trace that sentiment of sameness as borne out of a shared experience of social exclusion. I turn to the life stories of Grandpa Bảo and Grandpa Chân to illustrate this point.

Grandpa Bảo and Grandpa Chân both came from the same village in rural Quảng Nam, a province in Central Vietnam. Nevertheless, in colonial Vietnam, their lives were starkly different. While Grandpa Chân was the son of a wealthy and powerful landowner (địa chủ) family in their region, Grandpa Bảo was an impoverished landless peasant. Chân's family owned a very large area of land, which they leased out to landless peasants such as Bảo's family. Peasants worked on their rice fields, and were required to pay back a hefty amount of harvest to the landowner family as 'rent' for use of their land. Normally this rent was so unreasonably high that eventually the peasants were left with only a small portion of the rice that they had toiled hard to produce, while the landowner family increasingly became richer over time. Chân's elder brother was the deputy police chief of the province, an influential man who added to the family's power.

Meanwhile, Grandpa Bảo was far less fortunate. He lost both of his parents during his early teenage years and subsequently lost four of his five siblings. Eventually, there were only two members left out of his family of eight: himself, and the sister born right after him, Grandma Nga. As an orphan from a very young age, he had to struggle hard to survive and to support his younger sister. Despite always working very hard, Grandpa Bảo was an impoverished peasant.

The lives of Chân and Bảo were in such stark contrast, but they shared one thing in common — they both had leprosy, and their disease became known to villagers at around the same time. The experience of leprosy of an impoverished peasant and a son of a wealthy and illustrious landowner family significantly diverged. While Grandpa Bảo essentially experienced a 'social death' and painful humiliation as soon as his disease was exposed, Grandpa Chân was much better insulated by his family's wealth and power.

In rural Central Vietnam where Grandpa Bảo and Chân are from, agricultural work used to be based on mutual help and reciprocation. People in one community helped each other in labour-intensive farming tasks such as weeding, ploughing, and harvesting. If someone received help, they would be obliged to return that person's labour. Such contributions were calculated in labour days (*ngày công*) and one had to return exactly how much one had received. The reciprocal system (*đổi công* or *vần công*) worked well for most villagers; everyone could complete intensive farming work that individuals or families, working alone, could not have undertaken. However, those who could not contribute labour, such as the elderly, the sick, or the handicapped, were left out.

Leprosy sufferers were among those left out of the active labour-exchange circle. Debilitated by leprosy, Grandpa Bảo could not work in the rice fields anymore. He recalled the process of being excluded from the productive community:

> Before, a lot of people came to work for me. What fun it was! When I needed help, men, women and children, so many came. But when I fell ill and could no longer work for others, no one came to help me

anymore. At first, a few still came, but gradually there were less and less people. Finally my rice field became completely empty; there was no one. I could not work for anyone, so of course no one came to work for me.

Not only because of leprosy stigma but also due to his inability to reciprocate the agricultural work of others, Grandpa Bảo gradually became economically defunct and a social outcast in his community.

Faced with hunger, he had to wander around the village, wading in the flooded rice fields to catch fish, strolling along the village roads to pick star fruit or bananas, and looking for anything edible to satisfy his pressing hunger. His hands were already clawed and weak; in order to climb trees to pick fruit he had to press his chest hard against the tree bark for added grip. He did not feel that much pain owing to his numb skin, but his chest ended up being scratched, bruised and bleeding, which made him appear even scarier to other villagers.

A twist of fate saw his only surviving sibling, his sister Nga, also suffer from leprosy. One day while she was in the nearby market town of Hội An buying some herbal medicine believed to be helpful for leprosy, the villagers got together and destroyed her house so that she could no longer live in their neighbourhood. Having nowhere else to stay, she was forced to live in a tiny hut at the edge of the forest, far away from the village. Meanwhile, since Grandpa Bảo was now alone, he had to fetch water from the village well on his own, even as his skin injuries worsened. Each afternoon, he had to bathe in the river that flowed by their village. Grandpa Bảo had to expose himself on a daily basis to the villagers' eyes in order to undertake necessary activities such as foraging for food, bathing, and fetching water. Moreover, he had no other choice but to continue using the communal resources: fetching water from the village public well, bathing in the river, catching fish from the paddy fields in the village, and picking fruit from the trees that lined the village roads. His daily appearance in public spaces and his heavy reliance on communal utilities and natural resources, magnified by his debilitating illness, acted to intensify villagers' concern and anger at the 'leper'.

Meanwhile, as his family was very rich, Grandpa Chân never needed to work, to exchange labour with community members, or find food or fetch water by himself. He lived in a spacious two-storey house surrounded by a large garden. Since Chân developed leprosy symptoms, he stayed at home inside his family's big and well-insulated house. His own room on the second floor was far away from the villagers' eyes. Food was prepared and brought to him by the family's servants. If he needed something from the outside, he could ask one of the family's servants to fetch it for him. As the wealthiest family in the community, Chân's family had their own private well and bathing facilities, so he did not have to share the public well with others or bathe in the river. Even though the villagers were afraid of and gossiped about Chân's leprosy, he was not perceived by the community to be as intimidating as Grandpa Bảo.

Grandpa Chân's social experience of leprosy was also less confronting and torturing because of his family's power and influence in the region. While the villagers' banishment and exclusion was overt and was strongly directed against Grandpa Bảo and his sister, Grandma Nga, villagers whose livelihood heavily depended upon Grandpa Chân's family, the powerful landowner, never dared to explicitly exhort the banishment of Grandpa Chân. As Grandpa Bảo recalled, the villagers trying to expel him from the community called him 'that wretched leper' (*thằng cùi*) and directed their anger to him, saying, 'Send that wretch Bảo away! He stays here and pollutes our village. If we let him stay here, he will spread leprosy to us and our children!' Villagers added pressure on his relatives to send him away. However, Grandpa Bảo recollected that in a village meeting to discuss sending Grandpa Chân away, the most villagers could do was to generalise about leprosy patients in the area: 'The lepers living here are a source of illness and a threat to all of us. They are polluting our village. We should try to get them to go away.' Everyone attending that community meeting understood that the 'lepers' mentioned included Grandpa Chân, but no one dared to overtly name him as one of the polluting 'lepers' they wished to expel.

When Grandpa Bảo eventually left the village for Quy Hòa, he left in profound pain, shame, and anxiety. After one year, when he was allowed to come back for a short visit, he was shocked to see that his house had disappeared. As soon as he had gone, he was told, the village men — mainly his cousins and relatives — had immediately destroyed his house. All that was left of his previous house was the roof, lying on the small plot of land where his house used to be. When he asked about this, his cousins reluctantly explained that they had dismantled the house in order to preserve the wood, lest it be eaten by termites over time. However, he knew for sure that this was an excuse, because although they had dismantled the house they had left the roof out in the open where it continued to be eaten by termites. Ultimately, he understood that the destruction of the house was a collaborative expulsion plot by the villagers to ensure that he did not return to live in the village.

Meanwhile, as a high-ranked police officer, Grandpa Chân's elder brother was well-travelled and had a wide professional network. That was how he knew about the Christian-run leper colony of Quy Hòa. He decided to send his younger brother there. Grandpa Bảo still remembered the day when Chân left for the leper colony, around one year before he also left for the colony. He was among those who observed the departure of Chân and his entourage from afar. When Chân left, many family servants and villagers who worked on his family's land had to accompany him and send him off to the car. The family servants had to carry his suitcases to the police car that was sent to pick him up by his elder brother, while another was holding his hat. When he got into the car, everyone respectfully said farewell to him and wished him well.

Yet the respectful attitude of the servants and villagers did not mean that they were not scared or did not feel disgusted, Grandpa Bảo added. He knew that the villagers who were servants at Grandpa Chân's house, and who had to serve him, always washed themselves carefully after coming home. Sometimes the landowner family gave them some leftover rice from the family meals, wrapped in banana leaves. Although they felt nauseated, they never dared to reject the gift and always politely received the food. However, they would never eat the food from the leper's family and would feed it to their dogs at home, even though they were very poor and rice was seen as precious.

It was not true that Grandpa Chân did not feel sad and pained because of leprosy. Even though his family was wealthy and he had servants to help him, most of the time he was confined to the second floor of his house in order to avoid the eyes of villagers. Yet the most profound hurt for him was being abandoned by his fearful wife, who ran away after he contracted leprosy. No one knew where she escaped to, but many speculated that she had travelled very far away to the south, so that no one could find her. After Chân's wife left him, he was deeply saddened and felt very lonely, which eventually led to his decision to leave the family and enter the leper colony.

Being from the same community, Grandpa Bảo and Grandpa Chân had known each other since they were children. Yet at home in Quảng Nam, they had rarely talked to each other. At that time, Bảo was only a young orphan and a poor peasant, while Chân was the son of the most powerful and wealthy family in the region. When they happened to meet, knowing his superior position, Chân talked very little to Bảo, or domineeringly asked Bảo to do this and that for him. Being born and raised in an illustrious landowner family, Chân embodied superiority and arrogance over the other peasant villagers.

It was only since they came to Quy Hòa leper colony that they really became brothers (*anh em*), Grandpa Bảo recollected. Entering Quy Hòa, Grandpa Bảo was first horrified by the horrendous bodies surrounding him, but after some time, he realised that here everybody was the same. Grandpa Chân's previous life as a treasured son of an upper-class wealthy landowning family, and Grandpa Bảo's previous life as an orphan and an impoverished peasant, faded away. The socioeconomic gulf that divided them in their life outside suddenly did not matter anymore.

It was at the leper colony that Grandpa Chân started talking to Grandpa Bảo as an equal friend. He liked to talk and share things with Grandpa Bảo, probably because they had been neighbours back home and shared a lot in common. Now, two of them could sit together at the same table to drink some tea or share meals together, something that would have been impossible if they were still living back home, Grandpa Bảo commented. At first, Grandpa Bảo was even surprised when Chân invited him to his house for a death anniversary of one of Chân's ancestors (*đám giỗ*). But there, sitting on the same table and sharing the same meal, Chân openly affirmed to Bảo, 'Now, carrying this disease, I am like you, you are like me' (*'tôi cũng như anh, anh cũng như tôi'*). He stated their sameness and equality. As such, there was no one superior or inferior, since what connected them was the disease that they shared, and the same exclusive community in which they both took shelter. Here at Quy Hòa, the previous social hierarchy and status faded away; there was no longer landowner or peasant, since there were only leprosy-afflicted inmates, patients, or 'children' of the Franciscan 'mothers'.

Telling me this long story of his life, Grandpa Bảo expressed his genuine appreciation for Quy Hòa, which he called 'home'. Many times in our chats he repeated his hypothesis: 'If I hadn't come to Quy Hòa, I would have already died somewhere else. I wouldn't have lived for another 50 years as I have, and wouldn't have had a wife, children and grandchildren as I do now.' The nuns and their Quy Hòa leper colony provided him with shelter and rescued his life at a point when he felt most hopeless. By entering Quy Hòa, he left behind the social inequality of colonial Vietnam that had caused him pain and resentment as a landless, impoverished peasant. The previous social status of Quy Hòa villagers became erased and replaced by a homogeneous identity defined by their illness. Villagers' common description of their community — 'Here everybody is the same!' — not only speaks to their sameness but also underpins another important factor: their presumed equality and homogeneous identity.

Social Detachment

The stories of Bảo, Nga, and Chân demonstrate how the village of Quy Hòa acted as a safe haven for people afflicted by leprosy and who, in addition to enduring the debilitating physical aspects of the disease, had also suffered the blows of social devaluation and expulsion. However, not all people were so cruelly cast out from their families and social networks. A significant number of villagers I met had elected to leave their former lives of their own accord. Many did so having internalised their social invalidity as feelings of low self-worth and self-stigmatisation. Out of a sense of shame, they disengaged from social relationships and sought sanctuary in Quy Hòa as a community of self-exile.

The life stories of the elderly I met during my fieldwork in Biên Hòa City serve as examples. In Tam Hiệp, a neighbourhood in Biên Hòa crowded with leprosy-afflicted people, I got to know Grandpa Tùng, a nurse assistant to Father Thọ who has served this community since the day of its inception. Grandpa Tùng is also a leprosy-afflicted man;

his leg was amputated because of leprosy and replaced with a prosthetic limb. Besides that, however, he does not have other typical deformities caused by the disease, such as clawed hands.

Yet he always feels profoundly different as a leprosy-affected person. Those who knew his wife described her to me as a 'virtuous woman' who stayed loyal to him and took good care of him after he contracted leprosy. But several years after he was first diagnosed with leprosy, he was determined to leave her. She was broken-hearted and insistently tried to convince him to let her stay, but he adamantly rejected her. He left behind his wife and children, and went alone into a leprosy village in Sóc Trăng. Years later, he met Father Thọ, the founder of the 'Tam Hiệp leprosy neighbourhood' (*Xóm cùi Tam Hiệp*), as this area crowded with leprosy sufferers in Biên Hòa is known to city dwellers. Grandpa Tùng followed Father Thọ into Tam Hiệp, settled down and devotedly assisted the Father in simple day-to-day leprosy care for the residents, such as tending skin wounds, changing bandages, or sanitising ulcers and wounds. He has worked dedicatedly for the Father and for his community for decades. Father Thọ and this neighbourhood are his new family, he explained. Over the years, never again did he contact or go back to his wife and children.

Now that Father Thọ has become old and weak and is regarded as a symbolic fatherly figure to the community, rather than the proactive patron directly involved in daily care for the community that he used to be, Grandpa Tùng is planning to retire. Some of his elderly friends in the community tried to convince him to go back to join his family, who still wait for him and obtain news about him through his friends, but Grandpa Tùng refused. Instead, he wanted to enter a completely exclusive community for leprosy sufferers such as Bến Sắn, not far from their Tam Hiệp neighbourhood in Biên Hòa. Another elder commented to me that they felt pity for Tùng and his wife:

> He felt too serious about his leprosy, but he should not feel that heavy (*nặng nề*). He can easily go out and tell people he is a war invalid. His limbs are all very clean and look okay. He looks just like a war invalid with his prosthetic limb; no way are people able to know that he had leprosy. But he was determined to leave his wife, and now he even wants to move into Bến Sắn. His family love him but he always rejects them. Poor things!

Grandpa Hai, a respected elder in the Tam Hiệp community, also told me about his plan to move into an exclusive leprosy village such as Bến Sắn to spend the last years of his life and avoid 'causing trouble' (*làm phiền*) for his children. He always felt bad about his son and daughter, regretting that having leprosy-affected parents had brought great shame and trouble for them. His son had dated his wife for eight years, from high school until marriage, but not once did he take her back home to introduce to his parents. When their son decided to get married, Grandpa Hai and his wife were extremely anxious. Their son's girlfriend and her family did not know about Grandpa Hai and his wife. Grandpa Hai and his wife worried whether the girl and her parents would still want this marriage if they knew that the pair had leprosy. Grandpa Hai felt too ashamed of his leprosy-ruined body to appear at the wedding as the groom's father. His wife had milder leprosy than him, and when she covers the scars with long-sleeve tops and pants, few people could actually recognise that she had leprosy. Grandpa Hai has a higher level of deformities: his hands are clawed and lack several fingers, and one of his legs has been amputated and replaced with a prosthetic limb.

Grandpa Hai was extremely worried and could not sleep for weeks. Then he came up with an idea: they would lie to the bride's family and say that the father had already passed away. The whole family sat down together to discuss his plan, but his wife rejected it, saying it was ominous to say that he was dead. Finally, they decided to tell the other family that the father had run away with his mistress, leaving behind his wife and children, and that they had never heard from him since.

For their son's wedding, they asked a male relative to pair up with Grandpa Hai's wife to represent the groom's family. Half sulkily, half regretfully, Grandpa Hai told me about the weddings of his son and then of his daughter: 'Every time our children got married, my wife had to hurriedly pair up with a man!' On his son's wedding day, Grandpa Hai recalled, he nervously hid himself at home all day long, feeling pity for himself. Yet at the same time he felt happy, because his son could finally get married, something he had never even dared to dream of during his younger years when he had struggled with this illness. At that time, Grandpa Hai did not think he could ever get married, let alone have children. When their children were first born, he and his wife were worried about their marriage prospects. But in the end, Grandpa Hai was very happy that both of his children were happily married, and now he has little grandchildren who he adores very much.

Yet Grandpa Hai's family could not hide their secret forever. One day, a couple of years after his son got married, Grandpa Hai was genuinely astonished when his daughter-in-law's parents suddenly appeared in front of his door. They came to find him, to 'offer greetings', and to tell him they were happy to see him. 'They talked to me respectfully', he recalled, 'and told me I should not have hidden myself. They said we are *xui gia* [the parents of one's son's or daughter's spouse]; we are all connected.' Grandpa Hai told me he was so embarrassed that he did not know how to respond or what to do.

Grandpa Hai and his wife still live in Tam Hiệp neighbourhood because, as he said, his wife helps to take care of the grandchildren, who are all still very young. Thinking about the future, similar to Grandpa Tùng, Grandpa Hai and his wife plan to leave this neighbourhood for a completely exclusive life with other leprosy-affected people in Bến Sắn leprosy village. He is afraid that one day, no matter how much he tried to hide himself, his children's colleagues and friends could eventually find out about him, just like his son's parents-in-law had done. This would 'cause trouble' (*làm phiền*) for his children and disturb their careers, he believed. At the time we talked, his son had been promoted to the position of deputy head of his department in a state institution, and had just become a Party member, which would pave the way for his further promotion. Grandpa Hai was worried that his son's promising career prospects might be hampered if his colleagues knew about his leprosy-afflicted parents. Even though Grandpa Hai is living in a neighbourhood crowded with leprosy-afflicted people like him, he still feels somehow nervous of being discovered by his children's colleagues and acquaintances: 'You see, anyone can ride their motorbike into this neighbourhood. I want to enter a leprosy village and live there until I die, so no one can find me. I want them to regard me as an already dead person.'

In his research in Northern India, Ronald Barrett (2005:222) observes that sadness and resignation were pervasive emotions among the residents of the leprosy treatment centre where he did fieldwork. Predaswat (1992:54) cites a study on leprosy in Thailand (Leerapun 1989) in which the authors found that self-stigma precedes negative societal reaction. In her own research conducted in Noan Pa village, Thailand, Predaswat also observed self-stigmatisation among her leprosy-affected informants (Predaswat 1992:138). She found that sufferers' low self-esteem and social withdrawal stems from the cultural construction of leprosy in Thailand as impure and sinful. Because they know that leprosy results in social ostracism, they believe they are social outcasts (Predaswat 1992:138), which resonates well with Nancy Waxler's (1981) thesis that patients' response and adaptation to leprosy are primarily culturally conditioned.

Self-stigma is similarly prevalent among the leprosy-affected people in Vietnam who I met. Being sad and conscious about their difference, many have rejected relationships with families and friends, and have withdrawn into communities of people like themselves, in whose company they could find comfort. This withdrawal has its negative effects for it has hampered their social relationships and their prospects for reintegration. Nevertheless, the process of disengagement has not brought about their social death, for many have rebuilt relations and have found a new sense of empowerment and self-worth in their new community. This chapter will now examine these processes of personal reconstruction.

Love Among One's Own Kind

Grandpa Bảo told me about the day he arrived in Quy Hòa and was taken to his assigned house in the leper colony. On the village road he saw small groups of inmates sitting and chatting together. When they saw him arriving with two other patients, they blithely pointed at them, calling out, 'More of the same kind!' ('Rồi, cùng một thứ rồi!').

In the days after his arrival, he got to know more about the leper colony inmates who now became his neighbours. It was easy to mingle and befriend people here, the old man recalled. Seeing him strolling by himself on the village road, his fellow residents waved their hands and called to him to stop by. They asked him which province he came from, and how he found his way to the leper colony.

He quickly made a lot of friends in the leper colony. It had been very long, Grandpa Bảo recalled, since he had a friend or was approached by friendly people who wanted to talk to him and get to know him.

His bitter memories as a lone 'leper' back home in Quảng Nam Province were still clearly imprinted in his mind — as soon as people saw him at the other end of the village road, they turned their backs and started walking quickly in the opposite direction. As soon as he appeared at one end of the paddy field, the farmers dispersed, moving away from him. Grandpa Bảo remembered the profound feelings of hopelessness and of being completely alone, without any caretakers or friends, when his limbs were already curled and weak. Sitting in his house all day long, he sadly kept looking at the sun's rays moving from one corner of his little house to the other, from morning to afternoon, everyday. All he could think of at the time was — his tone lowered when he told me about those dark days — how to kill himself. He went out to the river, planning to jump into the water and let himself drown, but did not have the courage to do so, and ended up sitting on the bank, crying for himself and for his lot in life.

In contrast, here in the leper colony, when he walked up and down the village main road, people called his name and stopped him for a chat. He woke up in the leper colony, Grandpa Bảo added, to sympathetic people all around him: the nuns and his fellow inmates. His fellow inmates often affirmed to him, 'Here we are all the same!'

Grandpa Thiện also came to Quy Hòa after several years of being contained in his house and enduring the pain of leprosy by himself. At the time, having given up hope for a cure after desperately seeking help from different traditional healers, he thought that he was the only one in the country suffering from this strange disease. However, as soon as he arrived in the leper colony, he was astonished to see so many people with the same disease; many of them even had more severe physical symptoms than him. Seeing many other leprosy patients with abnormal bodies was intimidating at first, but in retrospect, he reflected, it was also somehow reassuring for him to realise there were many others suffering from the same disease, and that he was not alone in his arduous struggle with leprosy.

Similarly, upon his arrival, Uncle Phương was surprised to see the leper colony already crowded with many inmates who had the same disease. Not only did they have the same kind of bodies — the same physical symptoms as him — but once he started mingling with other inmates, he was amazed at how similar their experiences had been before coming to Quy Hòa. He found that they shared the physical pain caused by leprosy, and they had very similar experiences of being stigmatised, isolated or expelled from their communities of origin. Many felt deeply hurt by being shunned by their own family, banished by neighbours, excluded from the community, or even traumatised by a murder conspiracy aiming to eliminate the 'leper' peril. Here in the leper colony, people gradually found comfort and empathy in realising their shared pain as leprosy victims. Their ties, based on similar lived bodily experience and social reality of leprosy, were built and reinforced over time.

Uncle Phương, for instance, got to know a young lady called Sa in the leprosy village. At first, he was struck by her sad eyes. She had a very beautiful face, but her eyes were always clouded by sadness. When they talked, he was instantly touched by how similar their lives as leprosy sufferers were. She told him her life story, how she lost her legs because of leprosy, and mentioned many times that she was so despondent that she wanted only to die. He was struck by how her lived struggles were similar to his. Moreover, as a fellow amputee having to move around by wheelchair, he could understand profoundly the pain of losing one's body parts. They felt close almost immediately and often shared their stories, despite the age gap of more than 20 years. They now are married and live happily together in Quy Hòa.

Many village men stressed that it is important to live with 'the same' people and to find a partner similar to them, particularly when it comes to marriage. Uncle Hùng, a former tailor, for example, was first admitted for a lengthy period of leprosy treatment in the Franciscan leper colony of Núi Sạn, Nha Trang. In 1972, after being discharged, he lived outside for six eventful years. During those years, he joined the military of the American-backed southern regime and was relocated to Quy Nhơn with his regiment. More than once on their off-duty days, he recalled, his mates asked him to go for a brief visit to Quy Hòa leper colony, 'because they had heard that lepers' daughters are usually very beautiful'. However, he never agreed to go with them, since he was afraid people with leprosy in Quy Hòa would notice the marks on his body, which usually went unnoticed by people without experience of the disease. He was anxious that if the village inmates realised he also had leprosy, his secret about his past illness would be revealed.

After 1975, his family were among those relocated to the New Economic Zones under the new government's policy. There he happened to bump into two men he had previously trained as apprentice tailors. They were delighted to see him again, but he insistently denied having known them. They affirmed, 'You really look like our teacher, Hùng! You must be Teacher Hùng!', and invited him to come to their house. Yet he kept shaking his head, 'No, I am not Hùng!' Uncle Hùng wistfully told me that, once he had been admitted for treatment of the disease, he did not want to meet any old acquaintants who had known him before then. He was worried they would ask him where he had been during their separation; he would then have to tell lies. 'So many lies! I'm tired of telling lies', he explained. Uncle Hùng concluded by telling me that it is much better to be with 'similar' people, so one can have peace of mind, and not have to tell lies or think twice before saying something lest one's secret be revealed.

The turning point that catapulted Uncle Hùng back into an exclusive community for leprosy sufferers was a re-encounter with his ex-girlfriend, who had followed her family to settle down in the same New Economic Zone as Hùng. At first, he was happy to see her again and vaguely thought it might have been destiny that brought them back together. She was a gorgeous woman, 'but had a cruel heart', he reflected. After they had been casually dating for some time, she spread the news that he had leprosy among members of the youth association to which they both belonged. The rumours quickly spread through their neighbourhood. That night, as soon as he learned that his secret had been revealed, Hùng panicked, immediately packed his stuff, and ran out of the house. Now that people knew that he had leprosy, he dared not face anyone. The following day, he left the settlement well before sunrise so that no one could see him leave. Having nowhere to go, he decided to head for Quy Hòa, the village for leprosy sufferers he had known when his regiment was based in Quy Nhơn.

Uncle Hùng has remained in Quy Hòa, where, soon after he entered the leprosy village, he met his wife. He wanted to marry someone 'like him', he said, because he believed a wife who did not have this disease would look down upon (*coi thường*) him and his family and would not be loyal to him, causing his children to suffer.

After moving into the leprosy village, he rarely returned to visit his family. One of the few times he went back home was when his mother passed away. He arrived in time to attend the funeral, but he felt alienated outside his new community, surrounded by non-patient people. As the eldest son, he took on a major role in the funeral ritual. He was sitting, as was customary, in front of his parents' house to receive guests, but most of the guests ignored him. Few people came to greet him, and those who did so only briefly said, 'Oh you came back?' or 'Has your illness condition got better?', and then quickly stepped away from him.

The other time was when he returned for a family reunion during Tết, the Vietnamese Lunar New Year. He went back one week before the New Year to help his father repair the ancestors' grave, clean the house, and prepare for the rituals. Yet he eventually returned to Quy Hòa a few days before the New Year festival had started. Recalling that sad memory, he said he could not endure people's comments and attitude towards him. Everywhere in the neighbourhood, people told each other, 'that leper (*thằng cùi*) has come back!' Wherever he went, people stared at him 'in a weird way', and when he came close to anyone, they walked away and avoided him. When people walked past his family's house, they stared at him and whispered something to each other. He felt very sad and hurt, and decided to go away immediately, as he had done before. He had been looking forward to celebrating the Lunar New Year with all of his family for a long time, but he could not cope with people's attitude towards him. In the end, he had a lonely Tết back in Quy Hòa, but as he reflected, he felt much better, safe and free here with 'similar' people.

For leprosy-afflicted people, 'sameness' is ontologically defined against difference. In other words, the importance of 'sameness' as lived and told by leprosy sufferers reflects the weight of 'difference' in their lived realities. Consistently enthusiastic emphasis of 'sameness' reveals a clear-cut dichotomy in the mind — a clearly demarcated territory of 'people of the same kind', those affected by the same disease, in opposition to the outside world. The notion of 'sameness' determines boundaries and clearly defines 'patients' (leprosy-affected people) (*người bệnh/bệnh nhân*) and 'healthy people' (*người lành*), 'inside here' (*ở trong này*) and 'out in life' or 'out in the world' (*ở ngoài đời*). James Staples similarly observes strong delineation between the 'inside' and the 'outside' perceived by people affected by leprosy and living in an exclusive community in India (Staples 2004:77). Conversations with Quy Hòa residents are normally filled with anecdotes comparing and contrasting life inside and outside of the leprosy village. While 'inside here' signifies safety, security and familiarity, 'out in life' or 'out in the world' implies something intimidating, risky, and somehow other-worldly.

The Power of Sameness

Like Grandpa Thiện, Uncle Phương and Uncle Hùng, everyone I met in the village reported finding great spiritual strength and comfort in their 'sameness'. Sameness itself has great power, as Bauman writes: 'Knowing that one is not alone and that one's own personal cravings are shared by others has a reassuring effect' (Bauman 2001:63). In addition, community-living brings about the power of a collective and the comforting sense of belonging to a definite group. Community is a strategy to cope with the repercussion of stigmatisation, which Goffman refers to as 'in-group alignment' (Goffman 1963:112).

Quy Hòa reminds us of Robert Redfield's 'little community': a distinctive, small and self-sufficient community defined by homogeneity and sameness (Redfield 1960). In villagers' words and perception, Quy Hòa is first and foremost a community of sameness: a village 'of the like-minded and the like-behaving; a community of sameness' (Bauman 2001:64). Quy Hòa is where inmates can realise their commonalities in their illness and in past experiences, and thus, to borrow the words of Barry Adam (1978), commonalities are translated into a community that exists and lasts based on sameness.

For Grandpa Thiện, his body embodies shame; he always expressed honestly to me that he felt ashamed about his lacking body. Many times when we chatted, Grandpa Thiện stared fixedly at my fingers, thinking deeply about something. Whenever he happened to talk about fingers in our conversations, he always said 'fingers, like yours', as if he had never had them. For decades, it has been extremely rare for him to go out of Quy Hòa village. 'I felt too ashamed to go. How could I wish to go out with limbs like this?', he asked me, while slightly raising his deformed hands and glancing down at his toeless feet. He also never went back to his hometown because of fear that he would cause humiliation for his nieces and nephews:

Because they are my nieces and nephews, maybe they have no choice but to recognise me and call me their uncle no matter how they feel. But what would their husbands and wives think about me and our family? They would think this family has a leper uncle! They would despise [*khinh*] us, they would see my family as cheap [*coi rẻ*]. I would feel pity [*tội nghiệp*] for my nieces and nephews if their spouses look down on them because of me. So I never want to go back anymore.

Aunt Khanh, too, was immensely saddened by the changes to her body caused by leprosy. Around one year after abandoning treatment because of her mother's death, she was contacted by a nurse in the hospital who sent her a letter and advised her to come back in order to continue treatment, since there was a new type of therapy that had recently become available. In the period 1982–83, multi-drug therapy (MDT) was introduced to Vietnam, and leprosy patients were not only treated by a single type of antibiotics but by a combination of medicines, typically Dapsone, Rifampicine, and Clofazimine (World Health Organization 1998). With her family's encouragement, Aunt Khanh returned to Huế for treatment.

As a side effect of MDT, patients' skin can dramatically change colour to black or red during the period of treatment, and return to normal after stopping MDT. Aunt Khanh's skin tone radically changed to a deep shade of black after taking Clofazimine (most often called 'Lampren' by leprosy patients). When her father came to see her, he was surprised, too, teasing her: 'This dirty girl! Why are you as black as a smoked boiling pot?'

Multi-drug therapy was much more effective than the previous mono-drug therapy. Aunt Khanh was clinically free of leprosy bacteria after around one year of regular treatment. She now had the option of going back home or staying on to complete treatment until she fully recovered from the consequences of side effects. Looking at her body in the mirror, she found herself strange. Explaining her decision to remain in the hospital, she said:

> It looks very weird to be as black as an African. I thought I would be as dark as this forever because of the medicine's effect. I thought if I returned home, everyone would see that my face was as dark as a thickly burned pot [*đen như lọ nghẹ*] and the neighbours would gossip about my skin. I looked so strange, like no one else [*không giống ai*]! So at last, I made up my mind to stay.

At the time, the leprosy section in the Huế dermatological department was cramped with too many patients. The hospital decided to relocate a number of patients to Quy Hòa, which was supposed to have more space and a better natural environment — fresh air, cool breeze and pristine beach, very suitable for medical treatment. Aunt Khanh was among those who were moved from Huế to Quy Hòa in the mid-1980s, and she has remained there until now.

There was a point in time in the early 1990s when Aunt Khanh and her husband came very close to leaving the exclusive village and moving out to reunite with his sister. Aunt Khanh had met and fallen in love with her husband in Huế hospital. They married very soon after she arrived in Quy Hòa, where he lived. His sister, who was living and working in a state-run plantation (*nông trường*), insisted that the couple should come and join her, since at the time the plantation needed more people and they would be able to do farming on the plantation's huge area of land. The sister thought that it would be an ideal opportunity for them to reunite, because the plantation could offer land, work, and housing.

It was indeed a reasonable plan and Aunt Khanh seriously considered joining the plantation. By that time, she had already finished treatment; her skin tone had returned to normal and she did not have any explicit leprosy residues. However, her husband was very reluctant. He had an amputated leg, but, as they discussed, people might just think that he was a war invalid who had lost his leg during the war. What made him hesitate were some ulcers on his hands, which had deteriorated due to his work as a carpenter, making wooden furniture for the leprosy hospital and villagers. The hard work with saw, knife, hammer, and nails had affected his numb hands and exacerbated his hand injuries. Moreover, he felt uneasy and anxious about co-living in a shared house (*nhà tập thể*), the only accommodation option provided by the plantation, where they would live in very close proximity with and share common facilities with other workers' families. He was scared that the injuries would sooner or later reveal their secret; the neighbours would notice his wounds and realise he was a leprosy sufferer, and they would have to escape in humiliation. Eventually, he decided to reject his sister's offer and stayed on in Quy Hòa, rather than going out into the world with the risk of becoming known as 'lepers'.

Although their decisions to remain in an exclusive environment for leprosy sufferers took place at different points in time, both Aunt Khanh and her husband decided to do so because of their concern about bodily difference. For Aunt Khanh, her husband, and many village residents, the multiplicity of similarly defective bodies inside the community has a deeply reassuring effect. 'Community means sameness, while "sameness" means the absence of the Other', writes Bauman (2001:115). Inside their own world of sameness, community members do not have to worry about their difference or being seen as abnormal. Discussing life in leprosaria for Japanese leprosy-afflicted inmates, Susan Burns writes, 'for leprosy sufferers themselves, sites such as Yu no Zawa, offered up the hope of a "normal" life within the culture of exclusion, a life in which work, family and community might be possible' (Burns 2003:117). Within this distinct territory, and amid hundreds of 'people of the same kind', abnormalities are evened out and can be normalised; lacking bodies become normal, and illness becomes a matter-of-fact, albeit an important one. Village residents can enjoy the benefit of such a 'normalising' environment, as termed by Kelleher (1988).

For instance, the village men told me it is only in Quy Hòa where they could walk around freely without tops, as Vietnamese men usually do, particularly under the sweltering tropical sun. Outside the village, they would never be able to do so; when some villagers go back home for a visit, they do not even want to be seen by neighbours, let alone reveal their scarred and lacking bodies. Uncle Nghị told me that while he was still living with his family, his neighbours did not explicitly shun him. He remained mainly in the house without stepping outside. Yet he felt the occasional intrusive gazes, and the concerned stares from his neighbours through the small window were intrusive and unsettling enough for him to decide to leave his family for Quy Hòa. 'It is free [tự do] here. I don't have to worry about such things', he commented. Now in the leprosy village, he can bare his torso and limbs marred with scars to work all day under the sun at his little bicycle repair shop in front of his house.

My own introduction to the practical meanings for villagers of physical sameness and the tacit value they attach to being among people like themselves came when I first went to pay respects to Grandpa Thiện, who was to become one of my main interlocutors. He was among the first villagers I met in Quy Hòa because his house was the first near the village gate on the main road connecting the hospital and the village. Every day when I walked into the village, I had to pass by his little house.

When he first came to Quy Hòa, Grandpa Thiện was hopeful that his treatment would be finished soon so he could go back home. Yet it was when his body became deformed because of leprosy that he painfully realised that he could never return home. Moreover, during the tough years after 1975, his limbs were ruined further because of the hard labour of collecting firewood and burning it into charcoal on the mountain near Quy Hòa. Grandpa Thiện felt profoundly humiliated because of his deformities, the leprosy 'marks' fixedly remaining on his body would signal his disease wherever he went.

Grandpa Thiện's limbs, indeed, are badly deformed from leprosy and the hard labour that took its toll on his already damaged body. Many of his fingers and toes had already been amputated either completely or by half, while the remaining half fingers and toes became hard and crooked. Most of the time his truncated hands were black with soil and dirt, since every day he fed the chickens and went out to search for fallen coconut fronds on the ground, cut them into small pieces, and dragged them back home for his wife to burn for cooking.

On one of my first afternoons at Grandpa Thiện's house, I brought him a cup of sweetened iced coffee, bought from a café in front of the hospital. It was a takeaway coffee in a thin, transparent plastic cup that could be thrown away after use. To my embarrassment, Grandpa Thiện confusedly tried different ways to hold the plastic cup with his half-amputated fingers. The plastic cups used for takeaway by this café were not good ones; they were too thin and soft. After trying to pick it up for a while with no results, Grandpa Thiện stopped and left the coffee cup where it was on the table. He seemed embarrassed and there was an awkward moment during which neither of us said anything. Fortunately, we found a way to recover from my gaffe and restart the conversation. To this day, I recall the gulf that my gift had suddenly opened up between me and my elderly respondent. Thinking back to the proverb Grandpa Thiện once shared with me, at that moment I was indeed a duck out of place among the chickens.

After that intensely awkward beginning, I went on to develop a warm and sustained relationship with Grandpa Thiện. I would frequently go and sit with him in the slanting sun of the late afternoon on the porch of his little house. We talked about his life as he tended his chirpy chicks. I still brought him some snacks or drinks, such as soy milk packets, which, as I worked out, he could handle with his fingers.

Ferdinand Tonnies, cited in Zygmunt Bauman (2001), observes that modern community is defined by 'an understanding shared by all its members':

> The community-style, matter-of-fact ... understanding does not need to be sought, let alone laboriously built or fought for: that understanding 'is there', ready-made and ready to use — so that we understand each other 'without words' and never need to ask, apprehensively, 'what do you mean?' (Bauman, 2001:10).

The sense of physical ease and naturalness provided by this condition of mutual acceptance and tacit understanding is all the more palpable in the context of Quy Hòa village as a congregation of people with bodies that inevitably attract attention in the wider society as abnormal or defective. In the atmosphere of the village, one can be oneself, for it is there that such bodily differences are tacitly understood to be normal.

Conclusion

While leprosy stigma in the wider society is slow to change and medical science can offer an only incomplete cure —a biomedical therapy that is highly effective but unable to reverse disfiguration or remove social pain — leprosy-afflicted people continue to fashion a therapeutic life world for themselves in the form of exclusive residential communities such as Quy Hòa. Such leprosy villages constitute a healing environment defined by sameness and equality. Into this world come those experiencing the pain and sadness of 'social death' and a 'spoiled identity' (Goffman 1963), and those who wish to withdraw socially or become invisible to the world of physically intact people. Yet within this life-reinforcing exclusive territory for 'lepers', they are reborn, re-empowered, and revitalised; they are able to express themselves freely as human beings, dignified and equal with everyone else.

Heide Poestges (2011) observes that in the exclusive leper colony in India where she conducted research, members use stigma as a mechanism to create and maintain community membership, and as a strategy to mitigate various social problems induced by their disease. In a related vein, this chapter holds that, ultimately, leprosy-affected people's profound desire for equality and dignity lies at the core of their need for an exclusive social world. The outside society may deny them complete personhood and full dignity as equal human beings; yet they can find comfort and a 'normal' life with a community of people 'of the same kind'. Whereas their leprosy-ruined bodies are feared and reviled outside the village, inside this exclusive territory they return to being normal and equal to other villagers. Sameness in its physical and social aspects constitutes the main healing effect of this community, which offers a comforting and reassuring environment that nurtures social interactions, relationships, and mutual support.

Crossing the border between their village and the outside world, people affected by leprosy continue to realise palpably the difference in their social standing in the two spheres. The curiosity, fear and discomfort occasioned by their presence 'out in life' hurts, but it also reinforces the abundant appreciation for their place 'inside here'. For many, the discomfort engendered by such forays into the world overlays the traumatic memories of exclusion experienced when they first contracted the disease and corroborates the potent sense of their community as a unique sanctuary. It is for these reasons that leprosy villages such as Quy Hòa still exist with great vitality. Residents genuinely cherish the exclusiveness, which also means sameness, of their communities. Susan Burns has similarly noted that Japanese leprosy sufferers embrace the culture of their own exclusion (Burns 2003:116). Writing about leprosy in India, James Staples reflected: 'While ill health might unmake the sufferer's world, in certain contexts — like this one — it also remakes it' (Staples 2003:308).

Quy Hòa is intimately appreciated as 'home', as a shelter, and as a place of rebirth and revitalisation where people can hope to find again things taken away from them by this cruel illness: dignity, faith, hope, care, love, peace, friends, family, and future. Exclusive communities offer a social cure that brings back what sustains a meaningful and fulfilled life. Leprosy villages such as Quy Hòa can heal because they cure the most intrinsic pain of leprosy.

References

Adam, Barry 1978, *The Survival of Domination: Inferiorization and Everyday Life*, Elsevier, New York.

Barrett, Ronald 2005, 'Self-mortification and the Stigma of Leprosy in Northern India', *Medical Anthropology Quarterly*, vol. 19, no. 2, pp. 216–230.

Bauman, Zygmunt 2001, *Community: Seeking Safety in an Insecure World*, Polity Press, Cambridge.

Burns, Susan L. 2003, 'From "Leper Villages" to Leprosaria: Public Health, Nationalism and the Culture of Exclusion in Japan', in Alison Bashford and Carolyn Strange (eds), *Isolation: Places and Practices of Exclusion*, Routledge, New York, pp. 104–118.

Goffman, Irving 1963, *Stigma: Notes on the Management of Spoiled Identity*, Penguin, Harmondsworth.

Hoài Hương 2010, 'Vì một Việt Nam Không có Bệnh Phong' ['For a Leprosy-free Vietnam'], *Báo Công An Thành Phố Đà Nẵng* [*Đà Nẵng City Police Newspaper*], 25 November 2010.

Hồng Hạnh 2010, 'Tiến Tới Loại Trừ Bệnh Phong Khỏi Cộng Đồng' ['Eliminating Leprosy from the Community'], *Báo Điện Tử Chính Phủ* [*Vietnamese Government News Portal*], 24 November 2010.

Howe, Louisa 1964, 'The Concept of Community: Some Implications for the Development of Community Psychiatry', in L. Bellak (ed.), *Handbook of Community Psychiatry and Community Mental Health*, Grune and Stratton, New York, pp. 16–46.

Kelleher, David 1988, 'Coming to Terms with Diabetes: Coping Strategies and Non-compliance', in Robert Anderson and Michael Bury (eds), *Living with Chronic Illness: The Experiences of Patients and their Families*, Unwin Hyman, London, pp. 137–155.

Leerapun, P. 1989, *Health-seeking Behaviour of Leprosy Patients in Northern Thailand*, Mahidol University, Faculty of Social Sciences and Humanities, Thailand (in Thai).

Monnais, Laurence 2008, 'Could Confinement be Humanised?: A Modern History of Leprosy in Vietnam', in Milton J. Lewis and Kerrie L. MacPherson (eds), *Public Health in Asia and the Pacific: Historical and Comparative Perspectives*, Routledge, New York, pp. 122–138.

Poestges, Heide 2011, 'Leprosy, the Key to Another Kingdom', *Leprosy Review,* vol. 82, no. 2, pp. 155–167.

Predaswat, Pimpawun Boonmongkol 1992, 'Khi Thut, "The Disease of Social Loathing": An Anthropology of the Stigma of Leprosy in Rural Northeast Thailand', PhD thesis, University of California, San Francisco.

Redfield, Robert 1960, *The Little Community and Peasant Society and Culture*, University of Chicago Press, Chicago.

Staples, James 2003, 'Disguise, Revelation and Copyright: Disassembling the South Indian Leper', *The Journal of the Royal Anthropological Institute,* vol. 9, no. 2, pp. 295–315.

Staples, James 2004, 'Delineating Disease: Self-Management of Leprosy Identities in South India', *Medical Anthropology,* vol. 23, no. 1, pp. 69–88.

Staples, James 2007, *Peculiar People, Amazing Lives: Leprosy, Social Exclusion and Community Making in South India*, Orient Longman, Delhi.

Tonnies, Ferdinand 1957, *Community and Society*, Courier Dover Publications, New York.

Waxler, Nancy E. 1981, 'Learning to be a Leper: A Case Study in the Social Construction of Illness' in Elliot G. Mishler et. al. (eds), *Social Contexts of Health, Illness and Patient Care*, Cambridge University Press, Cambridge, pp. 169–194.

World Health Organization 1998. *Drugs Used in Leprosy*, (WHO Model Prescribing Information), World Health Organization, Geneva, available at apps.who.int/medicinedocs/en/d/Jh2988e/5.html, accessed May 2015.

5

'The Red Seedlings of the Central Highlands': Social Relatedness and Political Integration of Select Ethnic Minority Groups in Post-War Vietnam

Nguyen Thu Huong

Kon Tum City. Early morning in May 2012. Start of the rainy season. I was on my way to a Bahnar village located in the heart of the city. The road was wide and clean, lined with tall trees and modern buildings that house the People's Committee and various local services — the very nerve centre of the provincial government. Flags and banners in red and gold fluttered in the wind, commemorating the centenary anniversary of the foundation of the province (1913–2013). Further down the road, I saw a dozen men, some squatting on the sidewalk, some standing idly by. Their weather-beaten faces were gloomy, their clothes shabby. These were indigenous Bahnar, not too young or too old, able-bodied males gathering daily at this makeshift 'labour exchange' (*chợ người*), hoping to sell their labour for a meagre wage at some construction sites or plantations in the region. The scene was emblematic of the marginalisation of indigenous individuals in their own territory where their ancestors had settled for centuries, long before the arrival of the Kinh, the French, and the Americans.[1]

In the context of Vietnam, nearly 12 million people, accounting for less than 15 per cent of the total population (General Statistics Office of Vietnam 2010), are classified as ethnic minorities, and, in 2010, they accounted for 47 per cent of the poor (World Bank 2012). Poverty has been decreasing among minority groups in Vietnam's Central Highlands as market-driven opportunities for off-farm labour continue to expand. However, indigenous groups such as the Bahnar, Jarai, and Sedang remain dogged by lower than average literacy and school enrolment rates, poor housing and sanitation, and over-representation in unskilled, poorly paid and unstable agricultural work (Socialist Republic of Vietnam 2013). Despondent scenes such as the improvised Bahnar labour market in Kon Tum are set against a highlands landscape that has been reconfigured by explosive capitalistic resource extraction, the coffee frontier, mining and rubber. Vietnam's central highlanders have been marginalised by world capitalism with frontier characteristics in the wake of *đổi mới*, a process rewarding those with favourable social capital, knowledge of markets, political connections and ties to lowland markets (McElwee 2004).

One set of explanations for this situation points to factors negatively affecting minorities such as the lack of education, of proximity, of cultural familiarity with the dominant Kinh culture, of political capital, and of modern outlook and awareness that tend to deprive them of favourable positions within the state apparatus (Baulch et al. 2010; Rambo and Jamieson 2003). Empirical research in the northern uplands has revealed that the Mường ethnic group is often commended for its ease of assimilation into modern society given its many proximities — linguistic and cultural — with the Kinh ethnic majority (Wangsgard 2009). However, various authors have pointed to the popular discourses about backwardness, deficiency and superstition pertaining to mostly ethnic minorities who reside in the mountains of northern Vietnam and the Central Highlands of southern

1   The preparation of this chapter was made possible with financial and organisational support from the larger project 'Women's Leadership: Empowerment of Women in the Period of International Integration' of the United Nations Development Programme and Ministry of Foreign Affairs of Vietnam, and the 2014 ANU Vietnam Update organisers. The author wishes to thank Philip Taylor, Cao Xuân Tứ, and two anonymous reviewers for their comments on this chapter.

Vietnam (Ngô Thanh Tâm 2015; Turner et al. 2015; Nguyễn Thu Hương 2013; Salemink 2003). Such depictions lend weight to the view that the lowland majority group is upheld as the centre, cultural standard, and model for all ethnic groups (Taylor 2008). Not surprisingly, many upland groups tend to judge themselves by lowland standards and internalise their inferiority (Wangsgard 2009). Nevertheless, it should be borne in mind that members of minorities are not passive subjects; they may not be keen to embrace the workings of the social structure of the dominant group, which have already had a great impact on every aspect of their daily lives.

For its part, the Vietnamese state has played a major role in structuring the avenues for social mobility and inclusion, cultural expression and political participation in the highlands. In general, the state places emphasis on control and assimilation and its equity rhetoric seems secondary to strategic considerations. This approach is reflected in its policy of promoting cultural diversity in Vietnam. In Decree No. 05/2011/NĐ-CP, issued on 14 January 2011, outlining its Action Program for Ethnic Minorities,[2] the government declared that all ethnic people (groups) have the responsibility to respect one another's customs and traditions, and to contribute to building the culture of Vietnam that is progressive and imbued with the nation's identity. It is understood that 'diversity should not compromise national unity' (Lavoie 2011:157), and national minorities have a right to maintain their traditions only as long as they do not pose a threat to the socialist progress of the country. Nevertheless, one may wonder what criteria will be used to determine which traditions and customs of each ethnic group are to be preserved. Along these lines, this chapter will explore how some ethnic groups might be included or excluded from state apparatus in Kon Tum Province because of their past activities during the 'American war'. It should be mentioned that during the *đổi mới* era,

---

2   Programs considered to be 'national targets' are part of the government budget which must be submitted to and approved by the National Assembly, whereas Action Programs are carried out according to availability of funds, proposed by the Finance Ministry and approved by the Prime Minister, mainly from local sources. Centrally directed, national target programs have to be presented to the National Assembly six months beforehand for consideration. The Action Program on Ethnic Minority Affairs somehow reflects the current level of attention the government attaches to ethnic minority issues. More urgent issues are handled under the high-priority National Target Programs which may include poverty alleviation schemes in ethnic minority areas.

the state has been seriously concerned about the spread of evangelical Christianity in the Central Highlands, seeing this as a threat to the country's security (Salemink 2003).

Another set of factors impinging on the experiences of minority peoples in the highlands are the prejudices, attitudes of mistrust, and subtle exclusion strategies of some Kinh people themselves. In other words, minority peoples may be excluded from sociocultural development opportunities through the agency of Kinh people, who may act assertively according to their perceptions and interests in a way that is not in accord with the letter of state policy. For example, undertaking research on the impact of education policies on inter-ethnic and intra-ethnic inequalities in school, Trương Huyền Chi (2011) observes that Kinh teachers' lack of knowledge of their pupils' cultural traditions are due to selective preservation of patterns by the state as well as their own modernist thinking. Teachers in the upland areas often claim that Kinh pupils have a better ability to learn than their minority counterparts (World Bank 2009). Furthermore, the lowland teachers seem to generally attribute the poor performance of ethnic minority pupils to the lack of support from their parents and their inherent poverty (Trương Huyền Chi 2011). Likewise, in state health care service programs in ethnic minority areas, a lack of cultural sensitivity and language barriers among health care workers contribute to misunderstanding and a poor ability to communicate health issues (Bonnin 2013). The historically complex and not always smooth relations between upland ethnic minorities and the majority Kinh contrast with optimistic official framings of these encounters as imbued with sibling-like sentiments of solidarity (McElwee 2008). Arising in a context of internal colonialism, which involves one group dominating another within a single nation state (Evans 1992), majority group attitudes may have the capacity to significantly shape the ways that minority groups apprehend opportunities for social advancement.

A different explanation, and one that I aim to explore in this chapter, is that uplanders might adopt agentive strategies to minimise their involvement in state structures. Here, I am inspired by James Scott's bold reconceptualisation of the politics of minority ethnicity in the entire Southeast Asian massif (Scott 2009). Scott argues that the social structure, livelihood strategies and identifications adopted by highlands actors in the vast region he refers to as 'Zomia' were shaped historically around the desire to avoid being totally and irrevocably absorbed within the lowland state's project. Such an approach has been observed among religiously organised Khmer and Cham communities in the deltaic swamplands of southern Vietnam, whose members often deliberately avoid taking part in activities in the morally profane state and market spheres lest they be negatively judged by their consociates (Taylor 2007, 2014). During wartime, the indigenous ethno-nationalist Barajaka movement among the Central Highlanders was formed in the context of state development policies of forced assimilation, inter-ethnic frictions and social inequities in the highlands (Hickey 2002). Looking at the period after 1975, Salemink (2003) regards the mass conversion to Christianity among Central Highlanders as an attempt to create autonomous space and an attempt to recapture agency. This religious resistance strategy, much like that taken up by the Hmong in uppermost northern Vietnam (Ngô Thanh Tâm 2015), allows marginalised upland actors to determine their immediate living environment at the local and private levels — in particular within the village and within the family.

Accordingly, this chapter shifts the usual focus on uplands–lowlands relations to explore practices of tactical or selective (dis)engagement by the Bahnar people as a modality of agency that differs from those that already have been described in the Central Highlands. Of particular concern is how experiences dating to the 'Vietnam War' of the 1960s and 1970s continue to impact the daily interactions between ethnic groups in the Central Highlands of Vietnam. The chapter examines how the level of participation of some minority groups in social and political activities of the state — mainly run by the Kinh — is related to their wartime experiences. An examination of the relationship between wartime and peacetime experiences offers interesting insights into the complexities in the relations between the minority and majority groups. Related to this, the marginalisation of minority groups can be traced to persisting prejudices and continuing contradictions in majority–minority relations — culturally and historically. By deconstructing these continuing contradictions this chapter engages recent debates surrounding recognition of uplanders' agency (Salemink 2015; Friederichsen 2012; Michaud 2012; Taylor 2008). In particular, it focuses on the agency of these minority groups who, in the face of the overwhelming influence of the majority's culture and state interventionist policies, engage in subtle practices of selective participation. Their practices of tactical withdrawal from positions of responsibility are both historically contingent and gendered, adding further layers to our understanding of the patterning of state power and participation of ethnic minorities in the state project.

In order to elucidate these issues, the chapter is made up of three parts. The first part is based on an ethnographic study of the practices of members of minority groups in accessing education and job opportunities, and on how family relations and other acquaintances affect these practices. The implication explored is that without these relations, access to education and jobs will be extremely difficult. The second part discusses social discourses about differences between the majority Kinh people and minority ethnic groups regarding the lack of representation of members of ethnic minority groups in leadership and management positions in public administration. This is, in part, due to the lack of education opportunity in upland areas, resulting in few minority people being qualified for the jobs available. However, even minority people with revolutionary credentials and good education can still find themselves marginalised if they fail to adapt to the work culture of the dominant group, namely the Kinh. The third part stresses the fact that minority ethnic people are not subservient, passive and inept in making personal choices, as they are so often perceived in Kinh-dominated social discourses. In contrast, they show a high degree of agency in turning these negative discourses to serve their own interests. In particular, by attending to the intricately gendered dynamics of minority self-representation in official governance arenas, it is possible to add sociological texture to the strategic non-participation thesis that has come to engage scholars of state-minority relations in Southeast Asian contexts.

Background

This chapter draws on empirical data collected during three months of fieldwork in Kon Tum Province in 2012. Located in the north of the Central Highlands, Kon Tum consists of one provincial municipality, eight districts and 97 administrative communes/wards. Kon Tum had a population of 432,865 in mid-2009 (General Statistics Office of Vietnam 2009). Over 50 per cent of the population is composed of ethnic minority groups. Of the 25 ethnic groups in Kon Tum, six minority groups are considered as indigenous, including Sedang (mainly inhabiting the districts of Tu Mơ Rông, Đăk Tô, and Kon Plông), Bahnar (mostly living in the city of Kon Tum, and districts of Kon Rẫy and Đăk Hà), and Giẻ-Triêng (concentrated in two districts of Đăk Glei and Ngọc Hồi). The Jarai are based primarily in the district of Sa Thầy, and are also found scattered in some communes of Kon Tum City. Additionally, there are two very small ethnic groups: B'râu in Đăk Mế village of Ngọc Hồi District, and Rơ Măm in Le village of Sa Thầy District. Other ethnic groups settled in Kon Tum under several different migration programs at different periods (Hardy 2003). For the purposes of this study I conducted three months of fieldwork in six selected villages of Bahnar ethnic people in Kon Tum City, and six villages of Jarai ethnic people located along the Vietnam–Cambodia border in Sa Thầy District.

The Bahnar — the largest Mon-Khmer–speaking ethnic group in the Central Highlands — account for about 13 per cent of the overall population in Kon Tum Province. The Bahnar are divided into what are usually regarded as four subgroups: Kon Tum, Rơngao, Jơlơng and Gơlar. The Bahnar Jơlơng group is found mainly in the city of Kon Tum, and in three communes of Kon Rẫy District; the Bahnar Rơngao are found scattered in 29 villages of five communes of Kon Tum City, as well in two communes of Đăk Hà District, and Pô Cô commune of Đăk Tô District; the Bahnar Kon Tum concentrate in four administrative wards and nine communes of Kon Tum City, while the Bahnar Gơlar live mainly in Gia Lai Province. The majority of the Bahnar population in Kon Tum Province is Catholic, a religion first introduced to the Bahnar community in 1848.[3]

The Malayo Polynesian–speaking Jarai are the largest of the upland ethnic groups in the Central Highlands with a population of 411,275 (General Statistics Office of Vietnam 2010). Like their Bahnar counterparts, the Jarai are divided into subgroups known as Chor, Hơdrong, Chưti, M'thur, Aráp, and Tbuăn. Whereas the Jarai live primarily in Gia Lai Province, a small proportion of the Jarai Arap group can be found in the border district of Sa Thầy of Kon Tum

---

3   Charles Keith records that in the 1930s, Kon Tum was created as a separate mission of the French MEP missionary organisation, with its own seminary and bishop. By 1938, Kon Tum was home to 80 Vietnamese Catholic priests (Keith 2012:116–117). There are no available statistics on the present-day Bahnar Catholic population.

Province, and in two communes of Kon Tum City. By 2009, the Jarai population of 20,606 accounted for about 5 per cent of the overall population in the province.

Being quite recent settlers of Kon Tum, the lowland Kinh made up nearly 46 per cent of the overall population of the province in 2009 (General Statistics Office of Vietnam 2010). This figure reflects the general situation in the Central Highlands as a result of various major immigration movements, both as part of official resettlement programs and as independent migrants over different historical eras. As Andrew Hardy notes, the Central Highlands was long perceived as an 'empty' frontier area, destined to absorb population surpluses from the northern provinces (Hardy 2003). This immigration stream accounts for the majority of the region's population increase from 1 million in 1975 to nearly 5.3 million by 2011 (General Statistics Office of Vietnam 2011). Research has shown that the rapid population growth has placed excessive pressure on an already degraded environment (Rambo and Jamieson 2003) and the process of consolidation of ethnic minority lands into state farms have left ethnic minority farmers with insufficient land resources (USAID 2008). The competition for resources and administrative bias towards ethnic Kinh leave indigenous ethnic minorities in the highlands to search for livelihoods in more marginal areas, where they are more exposed to climatic variations and poorer soils (Rambo and Jamieson 2003). Statistics show that ethnic minority households represent 54 per cent of households below the poverty line in Kon Tum (USAID 2008), a province with the highest poverty incidence rate in the Central Highlands region (General Statistics Office of Vietnam 2010).

From a cultural and social perspective, different intensities of migration are associated with different modes of adaptation to the conditions of the Central Highlands. As Andrew Hardy (2003) observes, in the past, people who settled as individuals or families in the highlands of Vietnam tended to adapt to local customs and habits of the majority populations there. However, in the latter half of the twentieth century, new economic zone settlers arrived in large groups. 'They did not have to adapt, and their presence there was intended to bring progress to the highlands to encourage adaptation on the part of the highlanders' (Hardy 2003:229). This approach, together with massive changes in land tenure and population density, are likely to have been contributing factors to widely publicised episodes of unrest in the

Central Highlands in 2001 and 2004 (World Bank 2009:16). A decade later, while doing fieldwork in Kon Tum, I noticed the presence of special military units stationed near communes with high ethnic minority populations that were considered to be 'problematic'.[4] Also the practice of *chào cờ* (flag saluting) on Monday mornings was obligatory for ethnic minority residents. These measures were seen as government efforts to exert social and political control over ethnic groups at the commune level. How these groups react to these measures will be discussed at the end of this chapter. In the following part, I shall discuss the participation of ethnic minorities in the state sector.

Ethnic Minority Participation in the State Sector

In Kon Tum Province, it was reported that in December 2011 the percentage of ethnic minority *cán bộ* (cadres) and *công chức* (civil servants) was approximately 7 per cent, whereas the percentage of ethnic minority *viên chức* (public employees) was about 11 per cent.[5] These quantitative data indicate that representation of ethnic minorities in the state sector is extremely low. Their representation gradually falls at lower administrative levels.

It is worth noting that in a recent survey by UNDP and Vietnam Fatherland Front for the Provincial Governance and Public Administration Performance Index (PAPI) among 30 selected provinces, Kon Tum scored substantially lower than the other 29 provinces (Acuña-Alfaro et al. 2013). The same survey also indicated that Kon Tum performed much lower than other provinces with similar economic status (i.e. Điện Biên, Cao Bằng, Hà Tĩnh). The PAPI survey is based on the experiences and feedback of citizens from various provinces on the performance of governance and public administration. Thus the findings for Kon Tum seem to reflect citizens' negative attitude toward public administration performance. This becomes more evident when we examine the level of ethnic minority

---

4   From information received via locally conducted interviews, the degree of 'problematic' was based on the number of individuals previously known to be involved in incidents occurring in 2001 and 2004.

5   Provincial personnel data provided to the author by Kon Tum Department of Home Affairs, May 2012.

participation in local authorities at commune level. Take the case of Blang ward, for example. Even in a ward where the Bahnar predominate overwhelmingly, in Blang — with a population of 9,723 — the number of minority people in state administrative units is quite low: seven out of 22, or just 30 per cent. This finding is consistent with research elsewhere, which finds that the representation of ethnic minority cadres in the government workforce in the uplands is low (Rambo and Jamieson 2003). This situation would appear to exacerbate existing tensions among local residents, as evident in the comments made by one Bahnar official in the city:

> The ward chairman is a Kinh, cadres in various local services are 90 per cent Kinh. There are just two cadres from ethnic people ... I feel a bit sad. Maybe they think ethnic people cannot do the job, they let the Kinh do it ... They already picked their people. No use talking about it, it makes no sense. We want to take in someone, but they said it's not OK; to get our children in there is difficult, they think we are not qualified.

It is worth noting that most respondents in the research site expressed the wish to get a job in the state sector, since opportunities to get work in the town are very limited. As one research participant commented to the author:

> This village is part of the city. It has little land, young people hire out their labour mainly as porters. Ready anytime. If they could get work [in the rubber plantations or planting trees in the forests] then they could earn money. Here there's nothing.

Moreover, ethnic minority locals often perceive jobs in the state sector as superior 'mandarin jobs' (làm quan), for, compared with lowly agricultural work in the fields, a state sector job provides health insurance and a pension after retirement. These jobs are secure, permanent and much sought after. Trương Huyền Chi (2010) notes that work in the public administration sector is high on the job preference list of the Mnong in Đăk Nông. The desire to have a 'mandarin job' is also prevalent among ethnic minority groups in mountainous areas of Northern Vietnam (Nguyễn Thu Hương and Nguyễn Trường Giang 2011). David Wangsgard (2009) similarly contends that the Nùng Fan Slinh in the northeast of Vietnam tend to believe that the means to achieving popular Vietnamese notions of modernity and development are through wage employment, or other cash-generating activities, becoming Party members or otherwise participating in local governance, and expanding one's social network to include the influential Kinh ethnic majority. From statistical data as well as via conversations with local residents, I found that the number of ethnic minority people who are qualified to apply for state positions are few and far between.

'It is in the Genes [*Gien*]'

On the first day of my visit to a village in the city of Kon Tum, through the introduction of the official in charge of cultural affairs of Kon Tum, I met a lady in her 50s named Moan[6] who the official referred to as a 'main correspondent'. She provided me with a list of villagers working in the public sector and arranged for me to meet them later. It turned out that these persons were all related to her and her family. Miss Moan's daughter-in-law laughed and explained to me that those who worked as state employees in the village 'are all related, as if it is in the genes'. The same pattern occurred in other villages that we visited later. How do we explain this phenomenon and what is meant by 'genes'? On the one hand, family education background serves as a motivation for ethnic minority youth to pursue their studies, as some respondents explained their desire to follow in their parents' footsteps, and to be on the same level, if not do better than them. But we also met state employees of a wholly peasant background who were keen on reaping the benefits of education to improve their social position and the well-being of their families. Another 'gene' no less important is the sociopolitical connectedness enjoyed by a number of local residents owing to their contributions, or those of their families, to the war efforts of the Democratic Republic of Vietnam. This particular factor plays an important role in getting access to education and job opportunities.

From a policy perspective, targets for recruiting local cadres in the 'National project on promoting human resources in ethnic minority and mountainous areas towards 2020' have not been met owing to a lack of students (CEMA 2011:4). Of particular relevance here is the

---

6   Except for the names of administrative units appearing in official documents, all names of persons and locations (under the district level) are pseudonyms in order to protect the anonymity of participants taking part in this research project.

proposed selection policy (*cử tuyển*),[7] whereby the local authority can nominate qualified ethnic minority students to universities, colleges and professional schools without having to pass an entrance exam. These nominees are expected to return to their home districts to work in the public service for a number of years. This is how ethnic minority cadres working at various levels have been trained (Nguyễn Thị Thu Phương and Baulch 2007:24–25). However, it is reported that provinces have rarely met the recruiting target for the proposed selection policy. For instance, provinces reached only 77 per cent of the annual target in 2009 (CEMA 2011).

Findings from this current study reveal that local ethnic communities were rarely informed in a timely manner of the official announcements pertaining to the nomination policy. I was told that it was not unusual for the minorities to receive a call for applications only one day before the official deadline. In such situations, those interested (and qualified) were unable to prepare the required paperwork for their application.

> Only a few people working at the offices in the commune or district know about the information. They keep it for their children or relatives. If these fail to meet the criteria, they don't bother to circulate it; they keep it in the drawer or just throw it away.

Information of this kind is often passed around via social networks and not through official channels:

> A friend of my brother in Kon Tum City told me it's time to apply. I brought the forms to the commune's committee to be certified, they asked me how did I know about it.

Current evidence indicates that some provinces nominate a small number of Kinh students, while others limit the number of students from relatively well-off groups (such as the Thái, Tày, Mường, and Nùng) who can receive nominations (Nguyễn Thị Thu Phương and Baulch 2007). This practice seems to exist in Kon Tum as in the words of a state cadre:

---

7   The two key legal documents governing the nomination policy are Joint Circular 04 in 2001 (Ministry of Education and Training, Ministry of Home Affairs and National Committee for Ethnic Minority Affairs) and Decree 134 in 2006 (Government of Vietnam).

> In recent years some people — children of Kinh big shots [các ông Kinh] — have changed their names and their officially registered addresses [hộ khẩu]. They come to these places and take the jobs available. Because the number of children of ethnic people who qualify for these jobs are few, the Kinh children just fill the slots to meet [recruiting] targets.

Phenomena such as red tape, power abuse, and administrative harassment can be readily observed among the ranks of public servants (United Nations 2004:18). The relationship between civil servants and citizens is not really the relationship between those who serve and those being served, but rather like the kind of 'beg and give' relationship of the old pre-revolutionary days. The situation seems to be worse when it comes to ethnic minorities in mountainous areas. As Terry Rambo and Neil Jamieson observe:

> Many of them [cadres in the uplands] are lowland Kinh assigned against their wishes to remote areas, people who have little motivation to do their jobs well. Not surprisingly problems of corruption and bureaucratic inertia are widely evident. (Rambo and Jamieson 2003:159)

Local people generally concentrate their efforts to get jobs in the fields of education and health care since this is where job opportunities exist due to government policy focused on provision of education and health services to meet the essential needs of local people. Since the livelihood of local people is dependent on agricultural production and related activities, few have the financial means or social connections to branch out to other fields in terms of learning and job prospects. Thus, education and health care are two fields of work that can offer them state jobs. Few parents or young people dream of subjects such as engineering, information sciences, or banking. Only a few students have been selected to follow courses in development economics. For most people, following 'advanced education' outside the province is a far-fetched dream, as one interlocutor observed:

> If we send them to the district or provincial town to study, it's still cheaper than sending them to the big cities. If you want to study economics or banking you have to travel far. There's nothing in the province. And where do you find the money for tuition, room, food? And when you finish you don't know anybody in the banking business to ask for a job.

This apparently negative attitude is rooted in the realistic assessment of the economic situation of the household and the lack of extra-local social connections among local residents. It only reinforces the popular discourse that minority people are only fit for jobs in the health or education sectors — all local jobs — implying that they are not suited for jobs that 'require greater intelligence' or are more competitive. The success of efforts aimed at developing human resources among ethnic minority groups will thus be closely related to the existing social capital of specific communities, groups or individuals in such communities.

Access to local training and work opportunities is constrained by limited social capital, a phenomenon common to some uplands societies in Vietnam. Due to this scarcity of social capital, state efforts to decentralise resource management by returning control over assets into the hands of local communities may be ineffective (Rambo and Jamieson 2003:161–162). From our findings on the ground, most local women currently engaged in the public sector more or less owe their jobs to family or kin relations. More specifically, they are related to local cadres or families who 'have contributed to the revolution': those who supported the war efforts of the Democratic Republic of Vietnam against the United States and their Republic of Vietnam allies. These two factors — social and political capital — play an important role in enabling access to training and job opportunities available for local ethnic peoples. This preliminary study shows that the social capital related to education and training for ethnic groups is quite limited, and the few opportunities available are reserved for the families of those who served on the side of the northern forces during the war against the Americans. This limited social capital is tied up with intricate interpersonal and inter-ethnic relations between the majority Kinh and the minority groups concerned.

Against the multi-ethnic background of the Central Highlands, inter-ethnic relations have been strongly influenced by geo-political and historical factors. Looking at the population distribution of ethnic groups in Kon Tum Province, one can see that the Jarai — most of whom live in Gia Lai Province — are concentrated in the southern-most district of Sa Thầy, while the Bahnar reside mainly around Đăk Bla River in the city of Kon Tum. In line with social discourses about the relative advantages of 'urban' versus 'remote' residence, one may think the 'urban' Bahnar of the city of Kon Tum would fare better in terms of opportunities for social advancement than the 'rural' Jarai in remote Sa Thầy District. But the realities on the ground are quite different. In the case of the Bahnar community in Kon Tum City, they attribute their inferior access to state jobs to their wartime experiences. This explanation implies that those who do not enjoy privileged relationships to power-holders have little chance to benefit from present-day job opportunities. But how have these relationships been shaped? Again, these experiences date back to the time of the 'Vietnam War' when members of some ethnic minorities were allied to the forces of the Democratic Republic of Vietnam. Now they and their children enjoy the fruits of this collaboration. By contrast, members of the Bahnar group living in the city of Kon Tum, where the United States and Republic of Vietnam forces were stationed before 1975, were treated with suspicion by the state after reunification. And, since many of them are Roman Catholic, with their own autonomous history of organisation and education and links to co-religionists abroad, they are not trusted by the state apparatus. As a Bahnar female doctor told us: 'Since they know about my past they deny my [professional] endeavours.'

Similar to observations made by Anne Leshkowich (2008) on the experiences of small traders in Hồ Chí Minh City, past relations still have a bearing on the current life of Bahnar individuals. This reflects what Jayne Werner (2006) has identified as a genealogy of current tensions. Local people told me that in mountainous areas such as Sa Thầy, most people (mainly Jarai) supported the revolutionary cause during the war, whereas the people living in the city of Kon Tum near American and Republic of Vietnam military camps had 'few experiences of support for the revolution'. The general trend is that people currently deployed in leadership positions in the province are from the Sedang, the Jarai, the Giẻ Triêng, and the small Bahnar group from mountainous districts, leaving out members of the larger population of Bahnar people living around the city of Kon Tum.

A Need for Kinh-ness

The study also indicates a primary reason for the absence of members of minority groups in the higher echelons of management positions. Due to the lack of education and training opportunities in uplands areas, few ethnic minority individuals can meet the requirements for those jobs. Their marginalisation is further aggravated by pervasive discourses about sociocultural differences between the majority group (Kinh) and minority groups. It is as though they have internalised a sense of inferiority by persistently measuring themselves, and failing, against 'lowlands' standards. However, even those people who have access to these jobs due to family connections (having made a contribution to the revolution) must still adapt themselves to 'how things work' in the Kinh-dominated bureaucracy and patronage system if they wish to advance their careers. To illustrate this point further, I relate the case of a Bahnar man who I call Mr X. In my fieldwork, I met and talked at length with Mr X, who belonged to the Bahnar group (from a mountainous district), had joined the revolution, and had held various management positions in the public sector:

> At that time it's not that I was awakened to the revolution, I belong to a family participating in the revolution; we hid and nurtured revolutionary partisans. When I was a child, I was an informer ... the revolution chose me. When I got some information I would pass it on to the local cadre [in the occupied zone], I just hung around the village ... I was a member of the secret youth team. The party, the people, the revolution sent the best children, those of families who contributed to the revolution, to the north to be educated, I was one of them. There were 19 of us. It took nine months for us to reach Vĩnh Linh. We kept walking across the Trường Sơn range. The others led the way, I was behind. We were forbidden to break branches, or make the least noise for fear of being discovered. I studied at the Central School for ethnic people. At the beginning I couldn't speak the Kinh language ... At that time there were more than 2,000 people, from Bình Thuận and other provinces, the Khmer, the Mường, the Tày.

For this Bahnar boy, participation in the revolution began by doing liaison work for the Democratic Republic of Vietnam side. This was a turning point in his turbulent life:

> I was fortunate to have been picked by the party and the revolution to have an education ... Before my hair was very long, no one was allowed to cut it. I had to tie it like a chignon. When orders came down for me to cut my hair, we had to offer a pig [to God]. According to local customs to keep one's hair is to preserve the human soul, if you cut it, you're nothing. If you want to cut it you have to sacrifice a cock or a pig and ask for the permission of God [Yang].

Mr X's account echoes the notion of the modern benefits of communism (Goscha 2004) that Vietnamese cadres actively promoted in western Indo-China to win over local support during the war against the French (1945–1954):

> Cadres taught locals how to purify water, cook meat, procure salt, use modern agricultural tools, sew and develop local handicraft industries, even to build their houses differently. The Vietnamese opened up literacy campaigns to transmit the benefits of this new revolutionary civilisation. The Vietnamese taught upland people the importance of hygiene, washing themselves, taking care of their animals and moving them away from their houses. (Goscha 2004:156–157)

All of these methods indicate Vietnamese cadres' discourse of modernity (Goscha 2004) which aimed to bring modernity to these backward peoples by changing their habits and customs in favour of what they saw as superior ones. Mr X continued his narrative about what happened in the post-war years:

> I came and lived here [the city of Kon Tum] since 1994. I was appointed vice director of the boarding school for ethnic people. [Former Prime Minister] Võ Văn Kiệt wanted me to take the director's job but I refused, only wanted to be vice director … He said none of the boarding schools for ethnic peoples has a director belonging to an ethnic [minority] group. At that time I was studying economics at Đà Nẵng, they just put my name up for the director's position. But I said this is a sensitive issue, the local people [ethnic minority people] don't want to get involved, I want to do my best for the country, there should be no distinction between Kinh and ethnic people. The ethnic people don't care much about material things. If the Kinh invite them out to eat or drink, they just go without an afterthought. The Kinh people are calculating, the ethnic people are not like that, they work for the common good.

Other respondents shared similar feelings about the differences in behaviours and attitudes between the Kinh and members of ethnic minority groups in the Central Highlands. Most of them expressed concern regarding the ways that they have to deal with colleagues and superiors — mainly Kinh — noting that, 'if you are straightforward and honest, you cannot move up the career ladder'. How some members of minority groups render the Kinh as 'other' can be discerned in the following remarks made by another former government official:

> Local people like us do not want to get involved in competition
> ... [we are] straightforward, we do not want to misuse privilege.
> The Kinh are different. They calculate every move. The school
> principal and the treasurer divide [the financial resources] between
> them ... I myself don't care, I just want to do my job properly. Before
> I was head of the education service [of the district], there were Kinh
> people there too. When I came to this school, there were more Kinh
> people ... To avoid this problem, I declined the position of school
> principal [offered to me].

This interview excerpt further illustrates that relations between Kinh
migrants and indigenous locals are fraught with prejudice, tension
and inequality (McElwee 2008). Far from erasing ethnic prejudices,
often such interactions accentuate mistrust of others, as long-term
residents see the newcomers as stingy and deceptive, while newcomers
view the locals as simple-minded and ignorant (cf. Taylor 2008:12).
This othering of Kinh migrants as 'calculating' and self-serving seems
to give rise to an unflattering view of the Kinh-run local government.
A Bahnar female doctor explained:

> Formerly the cadres often appropriated land from [local] people. Since
> they were important officials, people were scared of them. However
> people haven't changed their opinion. Once you are a cadre you are
> bound to engage in corrupt activity, they think. Around 1982 some
> local [ethnic minority] people served as government cadres. Some
> cadres like the hamlet head appropriated [public] land as much as they
> pleased. They argued that it was public land but they made it their
> own anyway. After that [the government] appoints no more cadres
> from local [ethnic minority] people.

In the eyes of local residents those ethnic minority individuals taking
part in the government apparatus seem to be 'polluted' by the 'strange'
practices of the Kinh people, and the local government representing
the Kinh-dominated central government is often negatively regarded,
considered to be highly bureaucratic and inefficient as indicated in
the PAPI survey (Acuña-Alfaro et al. 2013) mentioned earlier. It is no
surprise that government jobs are not keenly sought after by some
ethnic minority people in this study.

Furthermore, meeting the criteria of 'having made a contribution
to the revolution' (or being related to someone who did) as well as
being suitably qualified, does not guarantee a smooth ride for ethnic

minority individuals. They also have to show their capacity for 'cultural adaptation' (*thích ứng văn hóa*). As a Kinh administrator who has spent a long time in Kon Tum remarked:

> In the present system you need patronage. If you have no sponsor, there is little chance of moving upwards. Since local people do not join a clique, they are dropped from the system. However, there are those whose [political] background and qualifications are not up to the mark yet still they know how to go along with the system and find a support base to move up the bureaucracy. Once they have secured a solid position, they would bring in family members and friends. Generally speaking, through contacts with the Kinh, they become wiser, they learn the ways the Kinh operate and develop from then on.

From this one can infer that local ethnic people must adapt to the ways things are run by the majority group or be left outside of the power structure. This is similar to the case of Malay Muslims in southern Thailand who do not meet the informally understood criteria for full Thai citizenship (McCargo 2011). As Duncan McCargo argues, being Thai involves a willingness to subsume your ethnicity, language and religious identity to a dominant discourse and mindset of Thai-ness. Malay Muslims fail to pass this basic test, and thus are 'not Thai', despite the fact that they are born in Thailand, hold Thai citizenship, and increasingly speak Thai as a first language (McCargo 2011:14). When identity is linked to demands for political authority and power, ethnicity becomes even more problematic.

In line with McCargo's analysis of the situation in Thailand, Vietnamese citizenship accorded to members of ethnic minorities seems to preclude full social and political participation if they do not embrace major tenets of the Kinh culture. However, the story of Mr X and comments by local residents about cultural differences can also be seen as a form of resistance to the overwhelming influence of the Kinh by way of a method of strategic non-integration. The Kinh, for their part, look at such choices as signs of weakness, or a 'lack of competitive spirit' on the part of ethnic minorities. This finding is consistent with recent studies (Friederichsen 2012; Friederichsen and Neef 2010; Taylor 2008) on the contested interplay between the state and upland peoples in the ongoing processes of marginalisation and integration in Vietnam. This research indicates that while some ethnic minority groups are likely to be excluded from the modern, civilised nation, some of them would like to participate in it. However, the study evidence seems to suggest that 'non-integration can be a reflection of local agency, choice and strategising' (Friederichsen 2012:59). To illustrate the complexity of this process, the following section focuses on the case of women's participation in public activities in selected ethnic minority communes in Kon Tum.

An Interplay of Gender, Ethnicity and Local Politics

During my field trip in Kon Tum, I observed that those attending the weekly community meeting on Mondays under the guise of the flag-raising ceremony were mostly women representing their families. Local cadres used these meetings to propagate government policies on law, education, health, and production. But the high number of women at these meetings does not necessarily correspond to the role or position of these women in the family. Kinh officials explained to me that this active participation reflected the cultural aspects of matrilineal and matriarchal systems among the Jarai, or the bilineal system among the Bahnar. But when I asked these women why their husbands did not attend these meetings, they said the men just did not want to go. The flag-raising ceremony taking place among ethnic minority communities in Kon Tum Province is considered as a good occasion to get women involved in local affairs. However, on looking more closely, we learned that the rather active participation of women in community activities does not necessarily signal an improvement in gender equality. This observation is also made in the World Bank's country report on gender conditions in Vietnam (World Bank 2011). The question is what makes the men stay away from these meetings and how may this be related to notions of masculinity and femininity, of honour, and of power relations among the local community? A villager explained further:

> Only women attend these flag raising meetings. The men don't bother to go. In the ethnic minority villages, the flag raising ceremony is not considered as important, so the women go there. They go home and tell their husbands what happens. They [the men] don't want to hear reports of children's quarrels among the poor households. These things do not concern them. If something concerns their own interests, then they go.

The fact that it is almost exclusively women who attend these meetings reflects a clear gender differentiation in household participation in community activities. Our findings about women's participation in flag-raising ceremonies differ slightly from those concerning women's attendance of meetings organised by the Women's Union or concerning population and family planning as discussed in the World Bank's gender assessment (World Bank 2011). The subjects discussed at these flag-raising meetings not only cover 'women's concerns', such as population control or family planning, but also social, economic and religious issues affecting the whole community. From what we heard from local residents, the near-exclusive presence of women at these civic functions can be traced to an intricate web of social, cultural and economic relations that go beyond the household and the community. These meetings 'bring them nothing' in the sense that they attain no material benefit by attending. From a gender perspective, it is significant that these activities that do not create 'benefit' (material gain), in which women predominantly take part, are considered as 'not important' activities. Men, on the other hand, are understood to engage in matters that are 'important' or 'vital', depending on local perceptions and standards. This has to do with income-generating activities that sustain the household; men have to deal with the outside world and must speak the Kinh language in their daily dealings. It should be noted that subjects relating to the domestic sphere, such as child care and household concerns, occupy a considerable part of the agenda of these meetings, which are conducted in the local language. This language factor is crucial in facilitating the attendance of women at these meetings, where they can communicate readily and feel relatively at ease. As pointed out elsewhere, the main reason preventing ethnic minority women from taking part in activities outside the home is their lack of confidence in interpersonal relations (World Bank 2011).

These meetings are occasions for local officials to reprimand residents or their children — calling them by name — for acts of public disorder such as drunkenness or fighting, school absenteeism, tax evasion, etc. Men consider these public 'denouncements' as humiliating and prefer to stay at home, letting women bear the brunt of official scolding. Some point out that children of local officials who are guilty of similar offences are never reprimanded publicly. I witnessed in another setting this attitude of avoiding 'difficult' or 'awkward' situations on the part of men in some situations and the role played by women. During the last days of our field research, a fight broke out in the village which involved the son of the family who provided us with temporary lodgings. The local police had to intervene and took those involved to the station for questioning. Of course the lady of the house, our 'landlady', had to go to the station to ask for his release and we offered to come along to give her 'moral support'. But she turned down our offer, saying: 'You teachers look like rich people; that won't do. I am dressed like a poor woman, it will work.' And she was right, her son was allowed to go home soon after. It was explained to me later:

> In the village when you have to go to the ward office when something goes wrong, only women go there. Men don't go. They say women do this better, the ward people pity them, and will drop the matter. If you look poor, if you are dressed shabbily, it's better. Men usually drink, they easily lose their temper. If they go there it will cause more problems.

Participation by women in activities outside the home in certain areas of the Central Highlands is not adequately explained by simplistic culturalist interpretations that view such trends as conforming to traditional matrilineal or bilinear family structures. As I have earlier remarked on gender relations among ethnic minority groups in northern Vietnam (cf. Phạm Quỳnh Phương 2012),[8] the participation of men in activities outside the home and their decisions in these matters can be seen as women 'ceding their rights' (nhường quyền) to men, out of common sense, to overcome barriers that women face such as language, means of transport and social skills. In the social and cultural context of the Central Highlands, particularly in the case of the Jarai and Bahnar, such acts of 'ceding rights' — in this case men ceding their rights to women — to get out of difficult situations or gain temporary advantages can be seen as a clever way of exploiting existing discourses on ethnic minorities by playing the underdog (being poor, ignorant, unkempt). However, these extra tasks beyond the usual household chores put the additional burden on women of living up to their presumably important and traditional roles in matrilineal and bilinear societies.

---

8   I was involved as research adviser in the project on gender-related issues among ethnic minority groups in Bắc Kạn in 2011 for the Hà Nội-based Institute for Studies of Society, Economy, and Environment.

From an inter-ethnic relations perspective, these examples are emblematic of the agency displayed by ethnic minority people in the sense that they are not subservient, passive, or lacking in logical thinking as often perceived by the majority Kinh. And even if they may have internalised a sense of inferiority in the face of dominant Kinh culture/civilisation as discussed earlier, they somehow manage to turn negative images about them around to serve their own interests. This sample of Bahnar resistance is consistent with research evidence elsewhere that ethnic minorities have responded to discriminatory policies in numerous — often covert — ways (Michaud 2012:14). For instance, Jean Michaud observes that Hmong individuals in rural communities of Lào Cai province view themselves neither as resisting nor as the submissive victims of domination. Rather, they respond to the official policy of 'selective cultural preservation' with their own strategy of selective acceptance of modernity (Michaud 2009:32), suggesting a certain reservation towards standardisation and a globalising process (Michaud 2012). A study on recent Protestant conversion among Hmong groups in Lào Cai describes the ways in which many Hmong individuals embrace a 'resistant spirit' and resent Kinh contempt for Hmong traditional practices of polygamy and early marriage (Ngô Thanh Tâm 2015). The resilience of Hmong in Vietnam is credited to centuries of neighbourly relations, quarrels, political and economic exploitation, rebellions, invasions, wars, genocides, and flight (Turner et al. 2015). Taylor (2007) notes that Cham Muslim strategies for evading parochial incorporation by the state involve flexible diversification, evident in their ever-shifting household economy mix, discerning local and extra-local mobility, and pluralist ethnic, linguistic, and religious identifications.

By Way of Conclusion

The opening image of a group of Bahnar men — descendants of one of the earliest settlers of Kon Tum — selling their labour in the heart of Kon Tum City can be seen as emblematic of a wider picture of marginality for ethnic minorities in Vietnam. Popular assumptions (held by the majority group) contend that ethnic minorities are less adept at learning. They are also provided with far fewer and narrower higher education and training opportunities. Taken together, this results in ethnic minorities being confined to lower-paid and lower-status local jobs, rather than jobs of a more competitive and rewarding nature. All of this occurs against a backdrop of rapid economic, social, and cultural transformation that has drastically reduced the traditional habitat of minority groups due to massive in-migration of Kinh people and utilisation of the forest for production of commodities to serve the global market. A quarter of a century after *đổi mới* was launched, there is little evidence of the inclusive social and cultural growth for the multi-ethnic nation that was meant to be promoted by state policy. This preliminary study shows that the social capital required for education, training, and job placement for ethnic minority groups is limited, and the few available opportunities for public sector work are reserved for families of those who served on the side of the northern forces during the war against the Americans. It would seem that those who lack access to these privileged relationships have little chance of gaining access to these valued job opportunities. This is evident in explanations by Bahnar people of their current inferior position, with regard to job opportunities and participation in the state sector, which is still strongly shaped by war experiences more than 40 years ago. Particularly with regard to the social and political integration of ethnic minorities in the Central Highlands, entrenched inequalities between the majority group and other minorities have become even wider and the few individuals from minority groups who have somehow climbed out of their own ethnic niches to succeed socially and economically are those who chose to adopt aspects of Kinh-ness.

From the individual accounts in this study, uplanders' non-integration into the mainstream society at times can be perceived as an expression of their rational agency. In fact, members of some ethnic groups might prefer to withdraw or separate from and minimise their involvement in state structures, in order to preserve their sense of honour or masculinity, or perhaps to avoid being shunned by their own peers for seeming too grasping and calculating. This points to a strategy of selective non-participation, which might be explained by a history of mistreatment by and mistrust towards national governments. Some people wish to avoid contamination by the morally profane state and market spheres, and the risk of being negatively evaluated by their consociates for becoming too involved in such activities. They actively try to resist becoming Kinh. Such findings align broadly with what James Scott has termed 'the art of not being governed'

(Scott 2009), while at the same time illuminating the intricately gendered and historically contingent dimensions of such political practices. However, contemporary tactics of selective disengagement also need to be understood as a mode by which minorities actively engage the state, considering that the very categories of difference through which they shape their resistance come to them through a history of state-making and subjectification. These ambivalent and complex dimensions of state-uplander relations have implications for the argument put forward here that the national integration of Vietnam's uplands has been a contested process with deep historical roots. In other words, past experiences of relatedness seem to explain current instances of intentional disconnectedness by some ethnic minority individuals.

References

Acuña-Alfaro, Jairo, Đặng Hoàng Giang and Đặng Ngọc Dinh 2013, 'Governance and Public Administration Performance in Vietnam: A View from Citizens', in *Focus, Vietnam Law and Legal Forum*, May, pp. 5–10.

Baulch, Bob, Hoa Thị Minh Nguyễn, Phương Thu Thị Nguyễn and Hùng Thái Phạm 2010, 'Ethnic Minority Poverty in Vietnam', working paper no. 169, Chronic Poverty Research Centre, Manchester, UK.

Bonnin, Christine 2013, 'Doing Fieldwork and Making Friends in Upland Northern Vietnam: Entanglements of the Professional, Personal, and Political', in Sarah Turner (ed.), *Red Stamps and Gold Stars: Fieldwork Dilemmas in Upland Socialist Asia*, UBC Press, Vancouver, pp. 121–142.

CEMA (National Committee on Ethnic Minority Affairs) 2011, 'Đề Án 'Phát Triển Nguồn Nhân Lực Vùng Dân Tộc và Miền Núi đến Năm 2015 Định Hướng 2020' ['The National Project on Promoting Human Resources in Ethnic Minorities and Mountainous Areas Towards 2020'], CEMA, Hanoi.

Evans, Grant 1992, 'Internal Colonialism in the Central Highlands of Vietnam', *SOJOURN: Social Issues in Southeast Asia*, vol. 7, no. 2, pp. 283–298.

Friederichsen, Rupert 2012, 'The Mixed Blessings of National Integration: New Perspectives on Development in Vietnam's Northern Uplands', *East Asia,* vol. 29, no. 1, pp. 43–61.

Friederichsen, Rupert and Andreas Neef 2010, 'Variations of Late Socialist Development: Integration and Marginalisation in the Northern Uplands of Vietnam and Laos', *European Journal of Development Research,* vol. 22, no. 4, pp. 564–581.

General Statistics Office of Vietnam 2009, *Statistical Yearbook of Vietnam*, Statistical Publishing House, Hanoi.

General Statistics Office of Vietnam 2010, *The 2009 Population and Housing Census*, Statistical Publishing House, Hanoi.

General Statistics Office of Vietnam 2011, *Result of the Vietnam Household Living Standards Survey 2010*, Statistical Publishing House, Hanoi.

Goscha, Christopher 2004, 'Vietnam and the World Outside: The Case of Vietnamese Communist Advisors in Laos (1948–1962)', *South East Asian Research,* vol. 12, no. 2, pp. 141–186.

Hardy, Andrew 2003, *Red Hills: Migrants and the State in the Highlands of Vietnam*, ISEAS Publications, Singapore.

Hickey, Gerald C. 2002, *A Window on a War: An Anthropologist in the Vietnam Conflict*, Texas Tech University Press, Lubbock.

Keith, Charles 2012, *Catholic Vietnam: A Church from Empire to Nation*, University of California Press, Berkeley.

Lavoie, Constance 2011, 'The Educational Realities of Hmong Communities in Vietnam: The Voices of Teachers', *Critical Inquiry in Language Studies,* vol. 8, no. 2, pp. 153–175.

Leshkowich, Anne Marie 2008, 'Wandering Ghosts of Late Socialism: Conflict, Metaphor, and Memory in a Southern Vietnamese Marketplace', *The Journal of Asian Studies,* vol. 67, no. 1, pp. 5–41.

McCargo, Duncan 2011, 'Informal Citizens: Graduated Citizenship in Southern Thailand', *Ethnic and Racial Studies,* vol. 34, no. 5, pp. 1–17.

McElwee, Pamela 2004, 'Becoming Socialist or Becoming Kinh?: Government Policies for Ethnic Minorities in the Socialist Republic of Vietnam', in Christopher R. Duncan (ed.), *Civilizing the Margins: Southeast Asian Government Policies for the Development of Minorities*, Cornell University Press, Ithaca, pp. 182–213.

McElwee, Pamela 2008, '"Blood Relatives" or Uneasy Neighbors?: Kinh Migrant and Ethnic Minority Interactions in the Trường Sơn Mountains', *Journal of Vietnamese Studies,* vol. 3, no. 3, pp. 81–116.

Michaud Jean 2009, 'Handling Mountain Minorities in China, Vietnam and Laos: From History to Current Issues', *Asian Ethnicity,* vol. 10, no. 1, pp. 25–49.

Michaud Jean 2012, 'Hmong Infrapolitics: A View from Vietnam', *Ethnic and Racial Studies,* vol. 35, no. 11, pp. 1853–1873.

Ngô Thanh Tâm 2015, 'Protestant Conversion and Social Conflict: The Case of the Hmong in Contemporary Vietnam', *Journal of Southeast Asian Studies,* vol. 46, no. 2, pp. 274–292

Nguyễn Thu Hương 2013, 'At the Intersection of Gender, Sexuality and Politics: The Disposition of Rape Cases among Some Ethnic Minority Groups of Northern Vietnam', *SOJOURN: Journal of Social Issues in Southeast Asia*, vol. 23, no. 1, pp. 132–151.

Nguyễn Thu Hương and Nguyễn Trường Giang 2011, 'Inept to Study and/or Study for What? Learning Experiences Among Youth Belonging to some Ethnic Minority Groups: Case Studies in Ha Giang, Yen Bai and Dien Bien Provinces', consultancy report submitted to Institute for Studies of Society, Economy and Environment, Hanoi.

Nguyễn Thị Thu Phương and Bob Baulch 2007, 'A Review of Ethnic Minority Policies and Programs in Vietnam', unpublished report submitted to DFID.

Phạm Quỳnh Phương 2012, *Gender, Empowerment and Development: Gender Relations from the Perspective of Ethnic Minorities in Vietnam*, Institute for Studies on Society, Economy, and Environment, Hanoi, available at isee.org.vn/en/Library, accessed 25 October 2015.

Rambo, Terry A. and Neil L. Jamieson 2003, 'Upland Areas, Ethnic Minorities and Development', in Hy Van Luong (ed.), *Postwar Vietnam: Dynamics of a Transforming Society*, Rowman and Littlefield, Oxford, pp. 139–170.

Salemink, Oscar 2003, *The Ethnography of Vietnam's Central Highlanders: A Historical Contextualization, 1850–1990*, Routledge Curzon, London.

Salemink, Oscar 2015, 'Revolutionary and Christian Ecumenes and Desire for Modernity in the Vietnamese Highlands', *The Asia Pacific Journal of Anthropology*, vol. 16, no. 4, pp. 388–409.

Scott, James C. 2009, *The Art of Not Being Governed: An Anarchist History of Upland Southeast Asia*, Yale University Press, New Haven, CT.

Socialist Republic of Vietnam 2013, *Achievements and Challenges in the Progress of Reaching Millennium Development Goals of Vietnam*, New Technology Printing Joint Stock Company, Hanoi.

Stone, Wendy 2003, 'Bonding, Bridging and Linking with Social Capital', *Stronger Families Learning Exchange Bulletin,* vol. 4, Spring, pp. 13–16.

Taylor, Philip 2007, *Cham Muslims of the Mekong Delta: Place and Mobility in the Cosmopolitan Periphery*, NUS Press, Singapore.

Taylor, Philip 2008, 'Minorities at Large: New Approaches to Minority Ethnicity in Vietnam', *Journal of Vietnamese Studies,* vol. 3, no. 3, pp. 3–43.

Taylor, Philip 2014, *The Khmer Lands of Vietnam: Environment, Cosmology and Sovereignty*, NUS Press, Singapore.

Trương Huyền Chi 2010, '"Họ nói đồng bào không biết quý sự học": Những mâu thuẫn trong giáo dục ở vùng đa dân tộc Tây Nguyên Việt Nam' ['"They think we don't value schooling": Paradoxes of Education in the Multi-ethnic Central Highlands of Vietnam'], in Lương Văn Hy, Ngô Văn Lệ, Nguyễn Văn Tiệp and Phan Thị Yến Tuyết (eds), *Hiện đại và động thái của truyền thống ở Việt Nam: Những tiếp cận Nhân học* [*Modernity and Dynamics of Tradition in Vietnam: Anthropological Perspectives*], Vietnam National University Publishing House, Ho Chi Minh City, pp. 361–388.

Trương Huyền Chi 2011, 'Eliminating Inter-Ethnic Inequalities?: Assessing Impacts of Education Policies on Ethnic Minority Children in Vietnam', Young Lives Working Paper 69, University of Oxford, Oxford.

Turner, Sarah, Christine Bonnin and Jean Michaud 2015, *Frontier Livelihoods: Hmong in the Sino-Vietnamese Borderlands*, University of Washington Press, Seattle.

Turner, Sarah and Jean Michaud 2008, 'Imaginative and Adaptive Economic Strategies for Hmong Livelihoods in Lào Cai Province, Northern Vietnam', *Journal of Vietnamese Studies*, vol. 3, no. 3, pp. 58–190.

United Nations 2004, *The Socialist Republic of Vietnam: Public Administration Country Profile*, available at unpan1.un.org/intradoc/groups/public/documents/un/unpan023247.pdf, accessed 10 November 2014.

USAID 2008, 'Vietnam Central Highlands Needs Assessment', USAID, Washington DC.

Wangsgard, David 2009, 'Here we are all Brothers: Gender Relations and the Construction of Masculine Identities in a Nung Fan Slinh Village', PhD thesis, Simon Fraser University, British Columbia, Canada.

Werner, Jayne S. 2006, 'Between Memory and Desire: Gender and the Remembrance of War in Doi Moi Vietnam', *Gender, Place and Culture*, vol. 13, no. 3, pp. 303–315.

World Bank 2009, *Country Social Analysis: Ethnicity and Development in Vietnam*, World Bank, Washington.

World Bank 2011, 'Vietnam Country Gender Assessment', Report 65501, World Bank, Hanoi.

World Bank 2012, *Well Begun, Not Yet Done: Vietnam's Remarkable Progress on Poverty Reduction and the Emerging Challenges*, World Bank, Hanoi.

6

The Struggle to be Poor in Vietnam's Northern Borderlands: Political Metis and Biopower in the Local State Arena

Peter Chaudhry

The state is a pervasive presence in the everyday lives of the people of Vĩnh Thủy commune, a remote and mountainous commune in Vietnam's northern Lào Cai Province.[1] State-owned companies dominate business, the state underwrites agricultural production, and state rituals and state cadre regulate social life in a way unimaginable in urban and lowland areas of the country. But the state's presence is perhaps felt most keenly through the provision of poverty reduction and welfare support to the people of the commune. This support

1   The names of the commune, the district and people in this chapter are pseudonyms. This chapter draws on field research conducted in Lào Cai between 2013 and 2015 as part of my doctoral program at The Australian National University. An international non-governmental organisation kindly supported my application to the provincial authorities to spend time in the commune and I lived there for four months in the second half of 2013. Prior to this, I had spent two months regularly visiting the commune and neighbouring communes in the district. Additional material was collected during visits to other communes in the province and in consultation with key policymakers. I am indebted to Philip Taylor for his extensive comments and suggestions on this chapter and for numerous discussions through which he has helped me to clarify my ideas. I am also grateful to Andrew Walker, and to the two anonymous referees who provided insightful and constructive comments on the chapter.

increased enormously throughout the 1990s and is now a defining feature of the relationship between the state and the people of the northern borderlands.

The increased welfare role of the state has, in turn, led to an increasing bureaucratisation of everyday life. Consequently, local people in the borderlands have necessarily become more knowledgeable about the state and have an increased level of confidence in engaging with officials. As a senior member of the state's ethnic minority affairs committee in Hà Nội remarked to me: 'ethnic minority people are changing, they're making more demands and it's harder to keep them satisfied than it used to be'. Both the ubiquitousness of the state and its changed role in relation to the citizenry has in turn spawned a particular kind of politics, as local people increasingly seek to engage productively with the state for the resources on offer. Inverting James Scott's classic conception of the role of the state and its engagement with the citizenry, Andrew Walker describes this as a shift 'from legibility to eligibility' (Walker 2015).

In Vĩnh Thủy commune, this manifests itself most visibly in the way local people struggle to be recognised by the state as 'poor', and thus eligible for critical government resources. There is a notable lack of stigma attached to being called poor, in contrast to lowland and more urban areas of Vietnam where the term 'poor' (nghèo) has more pejorative connotations. This is perhaps because many people in the commune are classified as either poor or 'near-poor' (cận nghèo).[2] The status is not exceptional and being 'poor' is a classification that is actively sought, as it signals recognition from the state of a right to access resources.[3]

---

2   For the period 2011–15, the rural poor were classified as those with an income below 400,000 VND per person per month (about $20 USD). The rural near-poor were classified as those with an income of between 401,000 and 520,000 VND per person per month ($20–26 USD) (Government decision no. 09/2011/QĐ-TTg).

3   I use the term 'state' here and throughout the chapter to refer to the ensemble of Communist Party and Government of Vietnam organisations, ministries, departments and officials that are responsible for ruling the country today. I make a critical distinction between higher-level state organisations and officials (at the national, provincial and district levels), which I call the centre state, and the 'local state' commune and village-level officials who are the focus of this chapter. I appreciate, though, that the centre state too is not a unitary entity, and that there is significant contestation and conflict between branches of the Party, government ministries and departments, and between different levels of administration (see MacLean 2013 for a thorough discussion on these dynamics). I witnessed this contestation at close quarters as an embedded adviser in two government ministries in Hà Nội from 2008–12.

Increasing integration with market forces is taking place in the northern borderlands, and socioeconomic differentiation and stratification is slowly but increasingly evident in the commune. But it is still fair to say that the vast majority of the people of Vĩnh Thủy have very little, and can rightfully lay claim to being called poor. Indeed, a common observation made in the commune during my fieldwork for this study was that it was only those households that had someone employed as a commune or village official (about 10 per cent of the households in the commune), and who consequently earned a regular government salary, that were categorically not poor. Everyone else could credibly claim to be poor according to the prevailing moral norms of the commune.

Vĩnh Thủy is overwhelmingly populated by ethnic minority people, a common situation in the border areas of northern Vietnam. The commune population is evenly split between Hmông and Nùng ethnic minority households, with each group constituting about 40 per cent of the population overall. The next largest group is the Dao, with 10 per cent, and the remaining households are made up of smaller ethnic groups, such as the Tu'Si, the Pa'Si (also called the Bố Y), and a few Kinh and Tày people. There are 12 villages in the commune and each village is primarily ethnically based, with five of the villages Hmông, four Nùng, and two Dao. Only the central village is ethnically mixed.[4]

The ethnic demographics of the commune are reflected in the formal division of local state power. The allocation of official positions in the local state structure is carefully calibrated through long-standing conventions that are supported by district party and government officials, in order to ensure an equal division of power between the dominant Hmông and Nùng groups. Each of the other ethnic groups receives one position in the local Party-state machinery, but the vast majority of the Party and commune people's committee positions in the local administration are divided between these two ethnic groups. In particular, the two most important positions of Party Secretary and Commune Chairman are always divided between the Hmông and Nùng in the commune.[5] Two family lineages within each group in turn

---

4   The central village is also the most prosperous, with all of the Kinh households living there. The largest village is a Nùng village but with a significant Dao population (about 20 per cent).

5   I discuss this ethnic division of power in more detail in my PhD dissertation and in a forthcoming journal article.

dominate these official positions. They have done so for generations, with power handed on from father to son, uncle to nephew, cousin to cousin.[6] These two networks of power directly encompass a large number of people through kinship and clan ties, but also through relationships of debt, reciprocity, and friendship.

Existing developmental and conceptual approaches to framing poverty reduction processes and ethnic minority agency provide significant insight into understanding the politics of poverty in northern Vietnam, as we shall see. This chapter synthesises and adapts elements of these approaches to offer a hybrid view of post-socialist development in the uplands, a view which emphasises the iterative, practical, and locally embedded ways in which people in Vĩnh Thủy commune exercise political agency. Contrary to the view that ethnic minority people seek to evade or bypass the state, I see evidence that ethnic minority people are actively engaged with the state in complex and varied ways, and are adept at pursuing what Sherry Ortner describes as their own projects 'on the margins of power' (Ortner 2006:142).

This chapter ethnographically explores the manifestation of this political agency through the coming together of two important political processes in the commune. Firstly, the domination by ethnic minority elites, as local officials, of local state power and poverty reduction processes. Secondly, local people laying claim to state resources through the connections they make to these local state officials. Through this engagement, apolitical and technocratic state designs for poverty reduction are adapted and reworked in line with local structures of power as local elites and local people exercise what I describe as a local 'biopower' project, albeit one that feeds off the wider biopolitical project for poverty reduction of the centre state. This local biopolitical project ensures poverty reduction resources are used to foster life in a relatively equitable and harmonious way for those who are connected to power, though with negative consequences for the unconnected. Local people (officials and citizens both) deploy the governmental language of poverty reduction and the associated technologies and classificatory categories of the government in pursuit

---

6   Within the local state apparatus, at the time of my fieldwork, the dominant Hmông lineage directly controlled six of the most important positions in the commune, while the most powerful Nùng lineage controlled seven key positions. There are 22 official positions listed in the commune's manifest of Party-state officers.

of their own projects of power. They are consequently engaged in both shaping, but also being shaped by, the very state categories and governmental processes they are seeking to subvert, or access. What results then is neither a totalising governmentality, nor fully free agency, but a complex, hybrid political entanglement which takes place on the unevenly contoured landscape of power in Vĩnh Thủy commune.

In the next section, I consider the existing literature on the relationship between people, poverty and the state in the ethnic minority periphery, in order to situate my conceptual approach. I then briefly discuss the state's historical project of power in the northern uplands and locate the poverty reduction efforts of the state within this continuum. The importance of these state resources to household efforts at accumulation is highlighted here. The following section discusses the annual poor household census as the principal means for deciding who is classified as poor in Vĩnh Thủy. The section after this considers household strategies for registering eligibility to government poverty reduction resources, followed by a discussion of the condition of 'stasis' that results for those who are left behind in the struggle to be poor. The final section of the chapter draws conclusions from the preceding discussion.

People, Poverty and the State in the Ethnic Minority Periphery

Before engaging in my ethnographic account of the struggle to be poor in Vĩnh Thủy, I wish to reflect upon some of the existing literature on the nature of state development processes and people's agency in the Vietnamese uplands, in order to better situate my critical perspective. I discern three prevalent perspectives in this literature and will discuss each in turn before outlining a hybrid approach through which I intend to present my ethnographic material on the local politics of poverty reduction.

The first prevalent perspective is a state-centric 'developmentalist' view, apparent in the discourse and programming of the government and of international agencies working for poverty reduction in Vietnam. It is apparent in state policy documents for poverty reduction and the projects and programs of international agencies such as the World Bank.[7] According to this view, poverty is an abject condition, objectively measureable and scientifically definable, which results from clearly discernible deficiencies either in the physical and geographical environment, such as the topography, climate, or remoteness of settlements, or of people themselves. In this view, the ethnic minority people of the uplands are hamstrung by elements of their culture and living conditions which roots them in an inert state, and which they can only be liberated from by development and poverty reduction interventions (see Taylor 2008 for a comprehensive critique of this view). Such a view of poverty reduction is critically unreflexive and ethnographically uninformed, resulting from an abstracted and stereotyped construction of the poor. Critically, it fails to recognise how the category of 'the poor' is itself an effect of the very state-prescribed welfare flows intended to address the condition of poverty.

This is not to say that upland people are unaware of living in a state of deprivation, or of inequality. Quite the opposite in fact. Deprivation is well understood and intensely felt, for example, in having insufficient food to last the whole year, in being unable to meet ceremonial and ritual commitments, or in being beholden to others in the community through debt or labour obligations. But state-directed efforts at poverty reduction create a produced status of being 'poor', and this status appears integral to governmental attempts to bring development to the northern uplands, as it enables this development. This will become apparent through the following ethnography. Suffice it to say at this stage that 'poverty' as prescribed by the state is not necessarily abject, as no one particularly wants it to disappear: state officials, government departments, the Party, and international donors are all ennobled through being seen to combat poverty, and those who are prescribed as poor benefit from the resources that are offered. Poverty as prescribed in narrow technocratic and governmental terms appears then to be integral to extending the reach of the state in the northern borderlands of Vietnam.

---

7   This view is perhaps best embodied in the landmark 2000 Vietnam Development Report 'Attacking Poverty' issued by the Government of Vietnam and international donor supporters. This report set the path for poverty reduction in Vietnam for more than a decade.

The second perspective I wish to consider critically informs the critique of state-centric developmentalism described above. According to this view, which I shall call the 'overbearing state' view, state formation at the periphery should be viewed in essentially pessimistic terms, with state agents enacting a colonising process and structuring the space available to local ethnic minority people, restricting the degree to which local agency can be exercised (Leepreecha et al. 2008; Duncan 2004; McCaskill and Kampe 1997). Scholars in the 'overbearing state' tradition observe how governmental schemes are often characterised by inflexible and bureaucratic procedures, and bureaucratic abstraction. Power is concentrated in the hands of bureaucrats and state officials, and the result is the production of indifference, arbitrariness, and unintended consequences for those who live at the periphery of state power (Gupta 2012; Herzfeld 1992; Ferguson 1990).

Writers such as Ferguson and Gupta are at pains to stress the contingent nature of bureaucratic power and emphasise how governmentality can never be totalising and hegemonic. Nevertheless, the outcomes they describe usually involve the indiscriminate destruction of viable local understandings, statuses, and strategies at the periphery. James Scott's early work is notable for the contribution it makes to this view. In his classic work, *Seeing Like a State*, he presents a bleak view of the prospects for human progress under 'high modernist' and totalising state development schemes, socialist ones in particular (Scott 1998). Interestingly, writers on the state in Vietnam have challenged Scott's early dystopian view of the possibilities of agency in the face of state power, showing its limits: Ben Kerkvliet highlighted challenges to the state 'from below' during the state socialist period, through ordinary cadre, and local farmers (Kerkvliet 2005); Ken MacLean wrote about the often ad hoc and contingent way that state socialism evolved (MacLean 2007); and Rupert Friederichsen discussed the incomplete nature of much policy implementation and the local adaptation of policies by northern ethnic minorities (Friederichsen 2012; see also McElwee 2004).

This brings us to the third approach that I wish to consider, which I shall call the 'agentive periphery' view. In Vietnam, this tradition is embodied in strong ethnographic work, which finds that local and 'peripheral' ethnic and grassroots actors have their own standards, resources, dignity, and power. People of the periphery do not wait to be uplifted by state aid, and are not passive, colonised, and reproduced in straightforward ways by state processes and categories. Notable work in this regard includes Turner (2012), Michaud (2012), and Hanh (2008) on the Hmông, Anderson (2007) on the Nùng, and Taylor (2007) on the Khmer. These scholars recognise that the state is a colonising and productive entity, but are sceptical about the determining power of the state in realising statist developmental visions.

James Scott's recent work (Scott 2009) embodies this approach and perhaps takes the agentive periphery view to its furthest extreme, as he characterises the people of the Southeast Asian uplands as state evaders, demonstrating a capacity to avoid colonisation through deploying agentive strategies independent of an overbearing state. But Scott's position is open to critique on the grounds that it romanticises ethnic minorities, and ignores the degree to which local agency itself takes place within and is shaped by governmental categories and processes of state governmentality. Scott's 'state evasion' premise also underplays the degree to which governance is actually desired on the periphery, a critique which is also applicable to other agentive periphery advocates (Turner 2012; Bonnin and Turner 2012).

This notion of state avoidance has been effectively challenged regionally by Andrew Walker's work on northern Thai peasants' engagement with the state, wherein he effectively conflates the stand-off between state and society which is notable in some of the agentive periphery literature (Walker 2012). Holly High too examines the complex and ambivalent ways that rural Lao people engage with the state and poverty reduction programs, highlighting in particular how the state is the focus for rural people's desire, an entity they both fear and long for (High 2014). Walker and High highlight how engaging with the state is not only increasingly unavoidable, but also often desirable in the pursuit of development, broadly understood.

It seems then that drawing a sharp distinction between local and state political cultures is unhelpful in understanding the dynamic and at times contradictory processes at work in the state periphery of northern Vietnam. In particular, our framing needs to reflect the practical and everyday approaches of people situated at the state margins: the way in which they accumulate knowledge and experience in an iterative way to engage with and rework the governmental categories and technologies that are applied in the uplands. James Scott describes this capacity for improvisation and adaptation as '*metis*': 'a wide array of practical skills and acquired intelligence in responding to a constantly changing natural and human environment' (Scott 1998:313). But whereas Scott contends that state power crushes *metis*, I wish to show that in fact in the northwest uplands of Vietnam, *metis* flourishes within the governmental processes of the state, and indeed feeds off these very processes.

Ordering the Periphery as a Continuing Project of State Power

The ethnic minority people of the northern upland region have been misrepresented and misunderstood by both lowland officials and lowland people from colonial times through to the present (Taylor 2008; McElwee 2004). Attempts to impose order upon this mysterious periphery, and render inhabitants 'legible' to the state are correspondingly long-standing, with McLeod describing lowland engagement with the uplands as a succession of 'Confucian, Christian and Communist "civilizing projects"' (McLeod 1999:354). French planners of the colonial era ascribed technocratic categories of governance to the upland peoples they attempted to pacify and incorporate into the colonial state, through narratives of 'civilisation' (*văn minh*) in particular. Modern day state planners have supplemented this with ideas of 'progress' (*tiến bộ*) and 'development' (*phát triển*) — powerful narratives that were also prevalent during the state socialist era in Vietnam (MacLean 2013). In the post-socialist uplands, poverty reduction (*giảm nghèo*) has increasingly become both a key organising and mobilising discourse, and an important technology of rule. Local people are increasingly bound into the state through the receipt of state largesse in the form of poverty reduction support. The modern project for poverty reduction then is part of the long-standing historical continuum of attempting to subdue, civilise and domesticate the people of the periphery and render them productive as modern citizens.

Co-opting influential family groups and their kinfolk into the state-building project has also always been an integral part of the attempt to impose central control over the periphery. French colonial planners attempted to assert their authority through perpetuating a system of domination by local Thai ethnic minority elites in the northwest, in an attempt to rule the uplands through compliant proxies. But whilst a degree of order was imposed in the northern uplands as a result, rule through proxy did not work out wholly as intended for colonial planners, largely as a result of the agency and projects of power of local Thai elites themselves (Le Failler 2011; Lentz 2011). The Việt Minh and the early Democratic Republic of Vietnam, nevertheless, also worked through ethnic elites as they quickly realised that they too needed them in order to extend their writ of rule in the northern uplands. Consequently, Thai domination of other ethnic groups in the northwest continued long after liberation from the French colonial power (Lentz 2011), and rule through ethnic minority elites remains critical to governance in the northern uplands today.

From around 2000, state planners in Hà Nội have been able to mobilise significant amounts of financial capital to invest in the borderlands of the country, principally for poverty reduction. These resources have come from both internal sources and foreign or multilateral donors.[8] Support to perceived 'underdeveloped' areas of the country is of course not new. During the attempts to impose collectivisation in the countryside from the late 1950s until the mid-1980s, the state also sought to provide resources to these areas. This was also the case in the early years of *đổi mới* following the decision to abandon state socialism. Critically, though, state planners in the past were seldom able to follow through on the rhetoric of policy with material support. What is new today is the state's improved capacity to provide the promised poverty reduction resources. Who does and does not get ascribed the status of being 'poor' therefore matters a great deal.

Vĩnh Thủy commune is broadly representative of upland ethnic minority communes in the north of Vietnam generally and receives a large number of government programs for poverty reduction support. In fact, the large number of programs and the complexity of central government provision for poor areas mean that few local Party-state officials in the commune can authoritatively list all of the programs available without first checking commune records. The picture is further complicated by the existence of a number of international donor-supported projects, primarily provided through the World

---

8   This trend of state investment to outlying and 'underdeveloped' regions is not particular to Vietnam alone, and can be seen throughout East and Southeast Asia. See Anderson and Martin (2008).

Bank's Northern Mountains Poverty Reduction Project, and through the international non-governmental organisation that supported my fieldwork, which has provided project support to the commune for more than 10 years.

During the period 2012–13, government programs of support to poor and near-poor households in Vĩnh Thủy encompassed the following: free hybrid corn seed and fertiliser; free rice for the very poor; free roofing and construction materials to build animal stalls (for buffalo and pigs); financial support for education for poor households (with 100 per cent educational support for smaller ethnic groups in the commune, the Pa' Si and Tu' Si); support for paying electricity bills; provision of 50 free chickens along with feeders and associated chicken breeding equipment; free ducks; free pigs as part of a revolving fund scheme; subsidised credit for poor and 'near-poor' households; free roof slates to replace those destroyed by hailstones; a Tết (New Year) holiday payment; and free health insurance and subsidised support to key farmers as part of the agricultural campaigns to promote tea and vegetable production in the commune. There were also a number of schemes to support infrastructure improvements from both central government and donor funds.

The proliferation of state support for poverty reduction means that local people are increasingly reliant upon the resources of the government for their projects of household accumulation. Government resources for poverty reduction, such as seed, fertiliser, credit, and livestock, are one of the only significant forms of capital available in remote rural areas, and thus represent a critical means through which households can structurally transform their well-being and enhance their life chances.[9] The household of Mr Khang in An Trí 2 village illustrates what a difference these poverty reduction resources can make. He has been classified as a poor household in three of the last four years (in the other year, his household was classified as 'near-poor'). Every year he receives several bags of hybrid corn seed and

---

9   The increased provision of state resources to upland areas must, however, be seen in historical context. Increased state provision has occurred at the same time as state policies have closed off many of the livelihood opportunities which upland ethnic minority people have traditionally relied upon. This is most notably the case with forestry and shifting cultivation practices.

fertiliser, sufficient to ensure he is able to grow hybrid corn on almost all of his family land. As a result, he estimates that over the past four years his household has been able to triple its previous income.

He has reinvested much of the money he has made in his children's education, sending his son to one of the district high schools as a boarder. The household also receives an educational support grant which further offsets the cost of his son's education. His wife is involved in the women's group of a successful project run by the international non-governmental organisation to improve the breeding of traditional Hmông black pigs. She has successfully increased the number of pigs they have from a single pig to a litter of six, and she is now able to sell piglets in the commune market twice a year. The family plans to buy a second-hand motorcycle in the next year, with Mr Khang hoping to use the motorbike to travel to the border gate outside the district town to look for labouring work during the agricultural off-season. All of the changes experienced by the household he attributes to being classified as poor: 'Without the support of the government to us as a poor household it would have been impossible to do any of these things.'

The Annual Poor Household Census

The state's presence in the lives of the people of the northern borderlands today appears to be manifested in large part through the programs for poverty reduction support described above. The process of determining who poor households are at the local level is therefore critical. In Vĩnh Thủy commune, this process revolves around a poor household census undertaken annually in October.

In order to carry out the census, commune officers are issued with a dense 107-page guidance manual (*tài liệu hướng dẫn*) by the People's Committee of Lào Cai Province (*Ủy Ban Nhân Dân Tỉnh Lào Cai*). The manual in operation during the time I was doing fieldwork was issued in September 2013. The front cover states the intended purpose as being 'instructions for the investigation of poor and near-poor households in 2013 and health insurance for poor and near-poor people for 2014' ('*Điều tra hộ nghèo, hộ cận nghèo năm 2013 và lập danh sách BHYT ngừoi nghèo, cận nghèo năm 2014'*). It is an exhaustive, highly comprehensive and technical set of instructions for objectively identifying those people the centre state wishes to classify as poor.

The manual contains pages and pages of pro forma tables and corresponding guidance instructions for the completion of information about poor households in the commune. There are two official resolutions (*quyết định*) at the beginning of the manual, establishing the 'Direction Committee' (*thành lập ban chỉ*) along with 'plans' (*kế hoạch*) for the poverty census process and nine different sets of guidance instructions (*hướng dẫn*) to complete the 43 different tables of information contained in the manual. For example, on page 27, guidance sheet B instructs officials in how to go about estimating a household's income (*phiếu khảo sát thu nhập hộ gia đình*). There are four pages of detailed instructions on how to do this, along with references for other instruction documents, resolutions of the Party-state, and the formula for determining which poverty band the household should be placed in, according to income. The manual recognises the difficulties inherent in profiling households in such a detailed way and prescribes a checklist of household assets that local officials should value in order to estimate the income of the poor. This checklist of assets is the primary means through which local officials undertake the annual poverty survey, as we shall see.

The manual also contains detailed lists of provincial- and district-level officials and their allocated tasks and advisory roles in the poverty identification process, and lists the communes in each district of the province which have been classified as 'disadvantaged' or 'advantaged' areas — the overwhelming majority being defined as disadvantaged. The manual serves an important ritual purpose, through sanctioning both the process and the classification of 'poverty' by the state as objective, legitimate, and beyond challenge or reproach. It spatially orders and segments areas in order to project the state's authority and validate the classificatory categories prescribed by state planners. The manual thus imbues the classification process with a higher order sanctity and prescribes 'experts' whose status stems from their position as custodians of this technocratic process of deciding who is poor.

Contradictions Inherent in the State's Poverty Reduction Project

Narratives of poverty and poverty reduction are critical to the centre state's project of power in the uplands. However, the need to project the idea of ever increasing well-being opens up spaces for the agency of local state actors. If district- and provincial-level officials are to be believed, the process of collecting data on the poor and identifying poor households is a rigorously technical process, with each step prescribed in the provincial manual followed exactly and precisely. As the deputy chairman of the District People's Committee confidently asserted to me, there is no higher-level interference with the process and data is simply collated and transmitted upwards in the administrative chain.

But commune officials are in fact given very particular quotas for how many poor people they are expected to take off the poverty list each year. This prescription is not apparent anywhere in the poverty mapping manual, but commune officials disclosed that they do indeed receive specific targets from the district for how many people in poverty they are allowed to have each year, and I have seen such written instructions — confirming this to be the case. These targets drive the poverty identification process much more than the manual itself. Thus, in 2013 the poverty target for the commune was 65.13 per cent, a reduction of 8 per cent from the previous year.

Once this annual poverty reduction target has been received, the percentage reduction is distributed between the 12 villages of the commune, according to population size. Larger villages in the commune therefore have more poor households removed from their quota. Commune officers usually have to identify two to four households in each village which they can remove from the list, and these targets are rigidly enforced by the commune government. Rates of poverty reduction therefore are only loosely correlated (if at all) with the material state of deprivation, rendering the poverty assessment and reporting process meaningless, as the commune reports numbers for poverty reduction only according to the quota they have been set. In a remarkable contortion, one commune officer sought to explain to me the exact match between the target set by the district, and the 'result' of the poverty census process, by asserting that the district understood the poverty situation so well that the target they set corresponded exactly to the 'reality' that was discovered through the poverty census process.

The poverty mapping manual is a symbolic prop of state power: all actors pay lip-service to the manual and the technocratic process it embodies, but also know that collecting all the data required in the way that the manual stipulates would invalidate the poverty reduction target set by government planners, with which they must comply. There is a public ritual of adherence to the manual by both higher- and lower-level state officials, whereby the manual's symbolic power is recognised and respected, but where the process it stipulates has little bearing on the nitty-gritty localised work of deciding who accesses state resources. Many state actors are complicit in this performance, with higher-level officials content so long as the target is adhered to, and local officials careful to revere the manual and the associated higher-level instructions whilst simultaneously effectively ignoring (or bypassing) them. Both lower- and higher-level officials are thus engaged in a process of (mis)representing statistics in particular ways to suit their needs.

The Process of Administering the Poverty Census

Returning to the poverty census process itself, as we have seen, on a practical level, completing a detailed inventory of each household's income and assets would be an enormous and time-consuming operation. What the commune uses instead is a simplified, one-page assessment sheet. The sheet is extremely brief, with no narrative explanation, and simply lists 11 areas for the assessment of a household's assets, with points allocated according to whether the assets exist, and what their value is. At the top of the page there is a space in which the name of the household should be entered, along with the household's registration number. At the bottom of the sheet is a space which the head of the household is expected to sign, to validate the assessment process undertaken by the commune officer.

The 11 assets against which the household's poverty status is assessed are as follows: the total area of the house (in metres squared); the value of the motorbike; the type and value of the bed; whether they have a cupboard, wardrobe, table and chairs and their respective values; the value of any video player and mobile phones; the presence and value of a colour television; ownership of a buffalo, cow or horse; number of pigs owned; presence of a milling machine or thresher; the amount of corn seed available for the next harvest; and the amount of rice seed. In October every year, commune officials undertake the census using this sheet and divide households into one of four categories: poor, near-poor, average, or better-off. The household is supposed to be given a score according to each criterion in the list, and designated one of these four categories.

Only two or three households in the whole commune are considered 'better-off', and only two or three households in each village are given the 'average' status. These households are generally well known and are not surveyed in the poverty census process. All the other households are visited, usually at night when residents are typically at home, and an inventory taken of their assets according to the poverty checklist. I was resident in Vĩnh Thủy during the months in which the commune poverty census took place and accompanied local Party-state officers in their census work over the course of many nights, in different villages in the commune. I observed first-hand the use of the simplified sheet, and the ambiguity it allowed in the process of interpreting and recording assets seemingly 'objectively'. It is this ambiguity that is critical in the local re-working of the state's poverty classification project and the exercise of discretionary power by local powerholders.

Local Party-State Officials and the Census Process

In Vĩnh Thủy commune a handful of chronically destitute households are recognised as being 'poor'. For the remainder of commune residents, though, the official government-assigned classification of being a poor household (*hộ nghèo*) has little to do with an actual state of material deprivation. Rather, being poor or living in poverty is a state-constructed and assigned category. Consequently, intense competition exists amongst commune households to be recognised and officially designated as 'poor' and therefore able to lay claim to the government welfare resources that are so important in transforming household well-being and prospects for the accumulation of capital. Those who end up being classified as poor are not exclusively the most needy, as the poverty classification process is shot through with Ortner's 'projects of power' of commune Party-state officers (Ortner 2006). They shepherd government poverty reduction resources towards family, kin, friends and allies — a very wide and fairly inclusive network.

The key commune Party-state officers involved in the poverty census process are the village head (*trưởng thôn*) and the village mentor (*cán bộ đỡ đầu thôn*). They work as a team to visit each household in the village and undertake the census process, using the one-page inventory form of household assets. Village mentors enjoy a powerful position in the commune system. They are senior commune officers whose role is to supervise and advise the village heads and oversee all aspects of village management and administration. They therefore exert considerable power and influence over village politics and administration. Most village mentors in Vĩnh Thủy are long-standing residents of the commune with powerful family networks behind them, and are deeply embedded as elites in the local system of commune politics.

For their part, village heads have complex motivations for taking up their role. Some village heads are also deeply engaged in commune and village politics, with their own extensive networks of patronage and control. A younger generation of recently appointed village heads have numeracy, Vietnamese literacy, and some training in the government system — skills usually gained through army service. It is these village heads who are most likely to at least attempt to follow the prescribed process for the household poverty census, and who consequently often face difficulties and conflict with entrenched interests within the village and commune.

For those Party-state officials who attempt to follow the prescribed process, the first problem they face is that household livelihoods seldom fit snugly into the centre state–designated income categories. Poverty is not the static state that policy architects envisaged. Rather, household wellbeing is continually in flux. As a newly appointed village head despairingly commented to me during his first year of attempting to do the survey:

> It's very hard to know a household's exact income because it changes all the time. A near-poor household might lose cattle to disease and then they quickly become poor, and similarly a poor household may

get piglets and thus quickly become much better-off. The form asks us to record the household's income at the time we take the survey, but their circumstances can change very quickly, often from day to day.

While a handful of village heads (particularly the newer ones) try hard to complete the process with some form of ritual diligence, others see it as an opportunity to build political capital in the commune and demonstrate their effectiveness to their superiors. One long-standing and entrepreneurial village head explained to me how he had been highly strategic that year in meeting his quota for the number of poor households to be removed from the poor list. He boasted how he had kept a few households 'in reserve' to take off next year's list, so that he would not have to bother too much with the process next year and could demonstrate to the commune leaders that he was quick and effective in carrying out the task. This particular village head is closely aligned through marriage to the dominant Nùng family group in the commune administration, and is also from the largest and wealthiest kin group in his village. He is adept at using the poverty reduction resources of the government to lubricate his village patronage network, with most of his close family and associates officially designated as poor and thus in receipt of the full portfolio of government assistance.

Removing households from the poor list in response to the poverty reduction targets set by the commune is a source of considerable angst to some village heads. They complained that it was extremely difficult to find households to remove from the list. One common strategy is to rotate households off and on the list every year. This was the case with the household of Ms Sèng Thị Sáng in Bình Yên village. She explained that the previous year her neighbour had been on the list and she had not, but that this year she was informed that it would be her turn. Her neighbour had received some asbestos sheeting for her roof during her time on the poor list, but Ms Sáng gleefully related how upset her neighbour was this year when Ms Sáng herself had received 50 chickens as part of a poverty reduction program.

Rotating people off and on the list is a popular strategy for village heads as it ensures their networks can be maintained or even expanded on the promise that a household will receive government support in the future. It is also a means for minimising conflict in the village through ensuring that every household receives government support at some time, irrespective of whether they are 'poor' according to the official classification in any one particular year. Villagers have the belief that their representatives have a responsibility to look after them, should be able to bring outside resources into the village, and will distribute these resources so that every household receives something. These perceptions appear to have deep roots in highland sociality and continue to be important today (see the following discussion of the Hải brothers in Ninh Căn village).

Conflict between the village head and mentor frequently occurs over who should and should not be included or removed from the list. One long-standing village head related to me how he had withdrawn from the census process last year, in protest at the difficulty in deciding who should be taken off the list. He left the decision to the village mentor, at the same time ensuring that he could not be blamed by those who would no longer receive government support. Conflict also occurs when the political projects of local powerholders come up against either the central state's 'technical' project or local conceptions of justice and redistribution, which still persist.

This was the case in one village where I followed the census process closely. The village head withdrew after a dispute with the mentor over a particular household. The village head had wanted to remove the household from the poor list because he claimed they made his life difficult and 'didn't follow village regulations'. The mentor, however, felt the household deserved to stay on the list as they were markedly poorer than many other households in the village. The mentor felt that the village head was being 'too emotional' about the process. In this particular case, the mentor responsible for the census process was also the commune officer responsible for the overall process. He had a reputation for being thorough and trustworthy, and crucially had no family allegiances in the particular village for which he was responsible. This village was also the central village in the commune, and was most open to critical scrutiny. In this case, then, the attempt by the village head to assert his power and authority was unsuccessful, and an alternative conception of redistribution and justice prevailed instead.

The Poverty Census Process as an 'Exercise of Paper Only'

In four of the 12 villages in the commune there was little evidence of the poverty census process actually having taken place at all, though the documentation was completed by the end of October and was filed in the commune office. In terms of physical infrastructure and the relative well-being of village residents, these villages were among the most remote and poorest in the commune. Two of these villages were also Dao villages, with the Dao being political outsiders in the commune, having little representation in the formal power structure, and little ability to demand government resources. The village mentors and village heads in these villages would give vague answers in response to my questions over the progress of the census, and would always defer my requests to join them on their household visits. When I questioned residents of these villages about the poverty census, they had little knowledge of the process. There was no village meeting to discuss and endorse the outcome of the census process as prescribed in the official manual (though this also did not occur often in the other villages of the commune). Shrouding the process in secrecy is therefore an effective strategy deployed by local powerholders to ensure that they can allocate government resources as they please, and frees them from investing time in an otherwise lengthy process, enabling their pursuit of other projects.

Most village mentors have little time for the formal census process, describing it as an exercise 'of paper only'.[10] After one long evening spent visiting households to complete the survey form with the village head and mentor, we relaxed in the village head's house and, after drinking several cups of corn wine, they explained what they really thought of the process:

> In fact we already know who the poor households are in the village. We visit the households only to complete the documentation properly and in particular to get the signature of household heads so that there

---

10   This echoes David Dery's notion of 'papereality', which describes the widening gap in bureaucratic organisations between what is reported and what actually occurs (Dery 1998). MacLean (2013) discusses how this 'papereality' has been central to the operation of the Vietnamese state since collectivisation. The gap between what local officials report and what actually happens contributes to the illegibility of the countryside to central-level officials and manifests distrust between levels of government.

won't be any complaints afterwards. If we don't get the signature then people will always complain that they don't agree with the assessment or that they weren't consulted.

For some village mentors, particularly the most powerful in the commune, the household assessment process is only a formality. One day late in October, I was discussing the poverty census process in the commune office with Mr Nam, the village mentor for Thạch Liêm village and a highly experienced commune officer. There were only a few days left until the process had to be completed, but he had yet to visit a single household in the village. When I asked him how he hoped to finish before the end of the month he replied that he had already identified the households that would be beneficiaries and those that would not. All that he had to do now was visit the village to get the forms signed. Securing the signature of the household head on the poverty census form meant the process was endorsed and valid in the eyes of the state, irrespective of whether the process had been completed as intended. The symbolic and ritual importance of the form thus imbues the process with an authenticity which disguises the operation of particular political forms of long-standing local patronage and reciprocity quite at odds with the 'official' purpose of the census process as prescribed by the higher state.

The Struggle to be Poor: The Politics of Eligibility to State Resources

Complaints over the allocation of government resources provide a constant source of gossip and intrigue in the commune. Countless examples were related to me during conversations with households about who received what, and on what basis they were entitled. For example, Mrs Hồ Ngân Giang, a poor resident of Ninh Điền B village, could not understand why her household did not receive an educational allowance intended for very poor households when a household in a neighbouring village did receive it, despite the household in question not being poor (at least in her view). Mrs Giang's concern reflects the important reality in Vĩnh Thủy commune that state resources nominally intended for the genuinely poor often find their way to those who are substantially better-off.

Local Party-state officials play a critical role in determining the allocation of these government poverty reduction resources, as we have seen, principally through deciding who will be on the poor list. But local people are also actively engaged in the politics of the process, lobbying these local officials aggressively and doing all they can to render themselves 'legible' (or visible) to state decision-makers. Once legible, they can go about establishing their claims for entitlement to government resources through being classified as poor. Partha Chatterjee has described how this form of engagement with the state requires political literacy on the part of the citizenry: an understanding of how the distribution process works and the rules of the game that surround entitlement and laying claim to resources (Chatterjee 2004).

Securing entitlement also requires a level of political capital in being able to establish connections to powerholders. In their struggle to be called poor, Vĩnh Thủy residents exploit all kinds of connections, including those of kinship and marriage, obligations, business connections, and friendship. As one village head observed:

> I get many visitors to my house once people know that the [poverty census] survey is going to start soon. People come and tell me all about their problems and their hardships. They also remind me of the times that they've helped me or my family in the past. They really put me under a lot of pressure.

This pressure comes from both above and below, as he went on to explain: 'I also have to think about people in the commune government too, and what they think. They watch the [survey] process very carefully, particularly if they've got some interests in the village.' During the poverty census process in Vĩnh Thủy, I observed a range of strategies that households used in attempting to establish their credentials as being poor. These can be categorised as follows: concealing resources; leveraging utility, position and status; manipulating government categories; and exploiting the ambiguity of government eligibility criteria. Local Party-state officials are intimately complicit in these strategies and, in the process, ensure that the state remains relevant to the Hmông and Nùng in the commune, and that long-standing practices of inclusion and expectations of mutuality and obligation are met. In what follows, I provide some vignettes from the commune which illustrate how each of these strategies are used.

Concealing Resources

Concealing resources in the intimate environment of a village, where everybody knows everybody else's business, is very difficult. It is particularly difficult to conceal assets from village heads, who make it their business to know what is going on in the village and who has what. Concealment therefore requires a degree of complicity on the part of village officials, either through fear, through a vested interest in benefiting from the concealment, or through a sense of doing right according to prevailing norms of fairness, obligation, and community cohesion.

One night during the census process I accompanied the village head and village mentor to visit a household along the main street of Ninh Điên B village, in the centre of the commune. One of the questions in the checklist required the household respondent to estimate the amount of hybrid corn seed in their possession. The household head reported a minimal amount, in spite of the presence of a large number of corn sacks stacked in the front room which he claimed to be storing for a neighbour. Once we left the house I asked the village head about these sacks and he reported matter-of-factly that the household was engaged in corn trading, a highly lucrative endeavour in the commune. But he had written down the minimal figure as reported by the household head, despite knowing that it was not true. 'What can I do?' he said with a shrug. The household, as I later discovered, was closely related to a senior commune official.

On another occasion I was visiting village Cao Thành A during the census process. I visited the household of a close relative of the village head, Mr Nhã, in the company of the village head and the village mentor. Cao Thành A is one of the more remote villages and the people here are poorer than those in the central villages of the commune. But this house was of sturdier construction and the beds were relatively new, with a cabinet, table and chairs and even floor tiles overlaying the mud floor in the main room, which was unusual in this village. Despite this, the household was marked as poor in the census, as minimal corn seed and household assets were recorded.

I returned to the village several days later and wandered past the house, noting a new motorbike in the front yard, along with a number of bags of fertiliser inside the front door, which had not been present at the time of my previous visit. Casually discussing the household with a neighbour, she wryly noted that two of the sons were currently working in a timber mill in a commune close to the Chinese border, and that they sent back significant remittances every month. These were not recorded during the census process, though the village head (and presumably the mentor) would have been well aware of these contributions to the household income.

On yet another occasion I was participating in the survey process in Ninh Căn village when we arrived at the house of the Hải brothers. Situated on a small plot beside the main path through the village, their house was extremely run-down, almost derelict. There was only an old bed and cupboard in the room in which the boys lived, which was littered with dried corn cobs used to feed the cooking fire. The commune officers related approvingly how the two brothers aged 18 and 15 were both extremely hard workers, working their small piece of land to produce local corn. Their father had died seven years ago and their mother abandoned them soon after in order to remarry in a neighbouring commune. As a result, the older brother had dropped out of school to work the land and care for his younger brother. The attitude of the commune officers towards these boys was paternalistic and caring. They were perceived to be worthy recipients of state support because of their tragic circumstances.

Whilst the boys were clearly 'poor' under any definition of poverty, local or otherwise, the officials were clearly intent on maximising the boys' entitlement as they carefully recorded all of their assets on the census sheet and cajoled them with encouraging questions to ensure they fully reported the hardships they faced, even under-reporting the amount of corn seed stored, as I saw the village mentor write down a far lower figure than the boys themselves had mentioned. The officials waited patiently while the boys tried to find the household registration card, which they eventually located in a dusty drawer, stained and creased. Other villagers would have been reprimanded by the officials for allowing such an important document to deteriorate in such a way, but the officials said nothing, clearly moved by the difficult circumstances in which the two boys were living. In this case, the officials felt obligated to conceal resources and used the process to ensure that the boys were highly legible to the state, in line with widely held moral perceptions in the commune that there is an obligation to look after those who are the victims of circumstances outside of their control.

Leveraging Utility, Position and Status

An example of leveraging position occurred in An Trí 1 village where we visited the household of a teacher at the intermediate school, who had recently moved to the village from another commune. This household held a certificate from the commune office in their previous village, stating that they were a near-poor household. Having recently moved, the household had no agricultural land, which is an important determinant of wealth in the poverty census process, which measures crop production. But both husband and wife were teachers and earned a stable income far greater than the majority of households in the commune. The household had a large refrigerator and ran a well-provisioned store from the front of the house. They also had two motorbikes, one of which was a late model, almost brand-new Honda costing several thousand US dollars. Despite this, the commune officer recorded them as being near-poor. He explained at the time that they had been near-poor in their previous commune and it was difficult to change their status, but there were clearly other factors at work that influenced his decision.

A few nights later, I was drinking corn wine with the village head and mentor after a night of visiting households in the same village and the discussion returned once more to the teachers' household. The mentor was slightly drunk and explained the decision as follows:

> It's really difficult to get teachers to stay in this commune. It's far from Cao Xuyên [the district town] and even further from Lào Cai City. If you're educated, why would you want to live here? We have to make it attractive to make sure that the teachers want to stay.[11]

Although the officials did not reveal the details of what had actually transpired, the implication from our discussion was that the household had successfully leveraged their important position to ensure their categorisation as 'near-poor'. At the same time, the officials involved

---

11 He went on to say, 'In their case both of them are teachers.' By this final statement, I understood him to be saying that this household's utility to the commune was double, as there were two teachers, so it was even more important to keep them happy.

had been willingly complicit, and may have even suggested the classification scenario in order to ensure the teachers stayed in the village to the benefit of the whole commune.

Manipulating State Categories

Another popular strategy deployed by villagers is to manipulate state categories to ensure that the household is recognised as poor.[12] One prevalent way of doing this appears to be 'splitting' the household. While examining completed forms from my household survey I was struck by the number of new households registered just prior to commencement of the poverty census process in October. When I cross-checked with the survey returns for the households in which the newly separate households had previously resided, they invariably recorded a drop in their registered status — i.e. from near-poor to poor, or from average to near-poor or poor. The 'splitting' process always involved a young couple leaving the parental home to establish their own household. However, in practice the newly established household usually took up residence in a simply constructed house located a few metres from the parental home, as new land for house construction in the commune is not easily acquired. In all of the instances of household splitting that I came across, the two households continued to share resources, indeed they often still lived together in the one parental house, with the second house usually of rudimentary construction and remaining unoccupied.[13]

The Hoàng family in Bình Yên village is a case in point. The grandfather explained that the family had decided to split in August of the previous year, with his youngest son and daughter-in-law establishing their own home on the edge of the family compound. The grandfather explained that he had divided his land between his two sons, that he had given them each a buffalo (he had two) and that the three families were now 'separate'. As such, they each qualified

---

12   This was also apparent during the land reform period in Vietnam, with households engaging in this strategy in order to avoid being called 'landlords' or wealthy peasants, and was also apparent during the collectivisation period, during which households manoeuvred to maintain the 5 per cent of land available for individual production. During the decollectivisation period, households also deployed this strategy to maximise the land they could prioritise for production (MacLean 2013).

13   This process of household fissioning may also have been a traditional form of risk management in upland areas.

as 'near-poor' when their assets were registered in the poverty census process. However, all of the corn and rice grown on their land was stored in the loft space of the grandfather's house, he cared for the two buffalos, which continued to be housed in the pens next to his house, and he spent the day babysitting the youngest child of his son while the family worked the land. The recently split family of his youngest son continued to eat their meals in the paternal house, and all of the assets and resources of the family appeared to be pooled in the grandfather's house. If assessed collectively as one household, however, they would have been registered as 'average' and thus not entitled to poverty reduction support.

While the decision to split the household was no doubt genuine and based upon a sincere wish on the part of the younger son to make his own way, in practice they continued to live in one multi-generational household, as the government's concept of a single generation household is anathema to the way the Hmông, Nùng, and other ethnic groups in the commune choose to live. The Hoàng household appeared to recognise the opportunity that 'splitting' provided and went through the process of registering the household as separate, thereby rendering themselves eligible for support as a near-poor household.[14] On their part, local officials do not appear to question this process and simply record the new household and the assets of each household as separate. Local officials appear to flexibly apply local norms to this process of household fissioning, using the government's assumption of discreet and segmented 'nuclear' family clusters against itself. At the same time, through flexibly interpreting the eligibility criteria, government officials appear intent on ensuring that the Hmông (and other groups in the commune) remain engaged and onside with the state, and that the state in turn remains relevant to them.

Exploiting Ambiguities in State Eligibility Criteria

Closely related to the manipulation of government categories is the strategy of exploiting any ambiguity in regulations pertaining to who is eligible to benefit from poverty reduction projects. This ambiguity stems from the fact that some projects and programs do not explicitly

---

14   In order to be recognised, a new household must register with the commune authorities and apply for a new household registration book, which is the most important state document held by people in the commune.

establish who the beneficiaries should be, stating only that the resources should be used for 'poverty reduction'. Local officials thus have the discretionary power to decide upon the allocation of resources. In the case of a project to provide 50 free ducks to households for poverty reduction, local people in Tràng Tôn village successfully exploited the lack of clarity over entitlement to the resources and lobbied the village head to distribute the ducks to every household in half of the village instead. The half of the village that did not receive the ducks subsequently received free chickens under another project in the following year.

In this case, eligibility exploded out from the category of the poor, with state resources that were supposed to be carefully targeted instead going to everyone. In a context where many in the village are indeed poor, this is perhaps a better outcome in the eyes of local state officials, given that it ensures cohesion and adherence to perceptions of what is appropriate and 'just'. It also cements the sense of relevance of the state to those who benefit — an important long-term political goal in the borderlands. The state's targeting of poor households is thus allowed to be subverted by a more locally embedded conception of entitlement, albeit one that reinforces existing hierarchies in the village and bolsters the political projects of the powerful.

'Stasis' and Bypassed Development for the Unconnected

In Vĩnh Thủy commune, important state resources for poverty reduction which the centre state intends to direct to those most in need often end up with those at the local level who are the most politically literate and therefore best able to establish claims upon them. Local commune officials appear to actively facilitate lapses in the official process of identifying the poor for three reasons. Firstly, because many of the beneficiaries are network clients of these officials, by including them in the poor list they bolster their political capital and pool of obligations and indebtedness. Secondly, officials are keenly aware of the need to adhere to long-standing traditions of general sharing, mutuality and cooperation which underpin the operation of harmonious social relations in the commune. Delivering poverty reduction support fulfils the expectations of them as leaders of the two dominant ethnic groups (Hmông and Nùng) to provide for their own. And lastly, dispensing government poverty reduction support is a way of keeping a large number of people engaged with the state, an important expectation placed upon them as local officials by higher up officials in the state hierarchy. This, in turn, ensures that the commune remains peaceful and harmonious and, as an effect if not a goal of state policy, that alternative centres of power and mobilisation around ethnicity — or religion in the case of the Hmông — do not develop.

What ensues is the perpetuation of entrenched hierarchies of power in the commune. This ensures a desired degree of stability and predictability in the commune but has consequences for those who are politically unimportant and often desperately lacking in material resources as a result. These people are largely left behind in the struggle for state resources that I have described. They lack the political skills to render themselves legible and eligible for the state support that would structurally change their lives, such as loans for buffalo (reserved for the 'productive' near-poor), substantial production inputs (they have little land and so are not deemed eligible for this kind of assistance), or a role in pioneering new agro-industrial crops in which the government invests heavily to encourage production.

Paradoxically, a significant shift has taken place in the northern borderlands over the past 10 to 15 years, whereby the state is now able to ensure a minimum level of subsistence and food security for destitute and chronically deprived households. Nobody starves anymore because the state ensures a minimum provision of subsistence for everyone. This was often cited to me as perhaps the most important change to have occurred in the commune over the past 15 years, according to both local Party-state officials and local people.

The household of Mrs Dương Thị Mát from Thạch Liêm village illustrates this well. Her household is one of the poorest in the commune, and she claimed 'if the government didn't support us we'd probably die with nothing to eat'. Over the past few years, the government has provided her with the essentials of food and shelter. She has received timber for reinforcing her ramshackle house, asbestos sheeting to waterproof the roof, and 10 kilograms of rice for each person in her household, which they sell in order to buy enough corn to see them through the hungry season when their own meagre corn supply is finished. The household lacks sufficient land, which is a feature of most chronically poor households in the commune, and this lack of land is also the reason given by local officers for not allocating hybrid corn seed and fertiliser to them. The lack of land also precludes the chronically poor from engaging in the lucrative projects of the commune to plant high-value agro-industrial crops, such as tea and tobacco. The chronically poor are politically unconnected and thus locked in a condition of stasis. They are assured of the basics of food and shelter, but do not have access to state largesse and opportunities which could potentially transform their lives. Instead, these resources go to better off, politically well-connected and politically literate others, which in turn ensures that the political equilibrium of the commune is maintained, along with the social status quo.

The chronically poor appear to fall through the gap between two conceptions of entitlement. They are virtually invisible in the 'moral economy' schema of ensuring social harmony and reciprocity, as they are outside of the important kin lineages and clan networks, and, with little status or influence, they are unimportant to local powerholders. At the same time, the subversion of the government's technocratic poverty survey system, which might have privileged them as key beneficiaries of the full suite of state support, closes off to them the only other possible avenue for the accumulation of resources necessary to structurally transform their livelihoods. Stasis is hard to escape for these chronically poor outsiders who include smaller ethnic groups in the commune (particularly the Dao) which lack political representation in the commune government, and those households amongst the dominant Hmông and Nùng groups who primarily live in the more remote villages of the commune and are outside of privileged networks or family lineages.

This lack of connectedness and inability to render themselves legible means that the powerless are often exploited by commune powerholders. In Cao Thành B village, for example, the very poorest households are eligible for an educational support fee that is supposed to offset the additional costs that households face in sending their children to school. In practice, the very poor never receive the support fee, reinforcing their sense of powerlessness and exclusion. As one woman explained: 'We have to sign every month that we have received the money but in fact the money goes straight to the teachers at the school and we never see it. Even though we sign for it, it's never given to us.' Her friend went on to explain:

In this village the rich families get more things from the government than the poor families. Here they just choose some families who they want to give things to. If they like someone they give things to them. We go along to all of the village meetings but we're not invited to speak. It's always the same people who speak. And we're never told about what things the commune has given the village, and when they will be handed out, and to whom. The village head just tells us that we need to work hard and be nice and if the government has anything he will bring it to us.

Despite facing structural obstacles and serial marginalisation through this lack of connectedness, these disadvantaged and chronically destitute households still aspire to 'play the game' and struggle to render themselves legible to local powerholders. They live within, and are confined by, the prevailing governmental categories that are constructed locally, even though these categories and associated practices are responsible for their continued immiseration. Without social or political capital they have little opportunity to successfully influence these structures to improve their prospects and, as a consequence, state development processes largely pass them by.

Conclusion

This chapter has argued that state discourses of 'poverty' and the practices of 'poverty reduction' that are prevalent in Vĩnh Thủy commune today are contemporary manifestations of the historical project of power of the Party-state in the borderlands: to categorise and regulate ethnic minority people and upland landscapes in a way that renders them amenable to rule. In pursuing this project, state planners today continue the long-standing practice of governance in the uplands, of attempting to co-opt and work through local ethnic elites.[15] In Vĩnh Thủy commune these local political elites exercise power in two registers: they are embedded in the state bureaucracy and act as the local executors of centre state power, but also sustain and grow their own local networks of power and influence in order to meet their local obligations and the expectations of their communities.

---

15 Historically, the Hmông appeared to be one of the groups most subject to domination by ruling elites in the northwest highlands, principally by Thai elites who acted as local brokers for the colonial state. It is also worth noting that the Nùng are classified in Vietnamese state ethnography as a sub-group of the Thai (see Vạn et al. 2000).

State poverty reduction support to the borderlands serves to bind these politically important elites and a large number of upland people to the state, while also allowing them significant local autonomy to exercise power.

The standardised, technocratic construction of the category of 'the poor' that I have discussed in this chapter is the product of the prevalent 'developmentalism' of state planners and their international partners. The narrow policies and practices that they put in place are central technologies of government in Vĩnh Thủy commune, for they permeate everyday life and bureaucratic practice in pervasive ways. At the same time, though, these categories are resolutely local in that they are interpreted, applied and manipulated through the active agency of local state officials and local people. They are deeply embedded in local social and political relations and in prevailing 'moral economy' perceptions, and both shape and are shaped by local values, strategies and statuses — what Bourdieu aptly describes as a process of 'regulated improvisation' (Bourdieu 1977:79). Both the 'overbearing state' and 'agentive periphery' views that I outlined earlier thus appear equally apposite. In fact, processes embodying these different tendencies are entangled and inseparable, laying to rest any notion of a clear separation between distinct state and local political cultures. In a manner evocative of Scott's political *metis* (1998), local officials and local people deploy their accumulated knowledge and experience to dexterously negotiate the governmental categories to which they are subject, with varying degrees of success.

In Vĩnh Thủy commune, the modern state's biopolitical project of fostering life and a productive population through providing poverty reduction support has been reworked by local elites and those in their networks to deploy a local form of biopower of their own. They have colonised the centre state's technocratic and generalised categories, and instead deploy highly personalistic and localised criteria for inclusion. As we have seen, this is made possible through the internal inconsistencies in the centre state's own process which opens spaces for local officials to decide what best constitutes human development for the populace, and who in particular should benefit. Local elites thus exemplify political *metis*, for the ability to act as they do is dependent upon the poverty reduction project of the central state from which they draw sustenance and inspiration. This form of biopower gives local expression to the modern state's standardising, normalising, and regularising logics, but it does so in a way that is simultaneously embedded in and rigorously disciplined by the obligations, standards, and expectations prevalent in local moral economy relations.

Local elites assume primary responsibility for supporting life in the commune through their control of state poverty reduction processes and associated material resources, and commune residents in turn do all they can to ensure that they are connected to and enveloped in this local biopolitical schema. But it is not all encompassing. Those who lack the social and political capital necessary to establish connections to local state powerholders lose out. They lack the political literacy or performative competency to render themselves legible and connected to these powerholders. Consequently, the very system intended to reduce inequality and structurally transform the livelihoods of the chronically deprived — the system for poverty reduction — serves instead only to reinforce their local subordination and perpetuate their continued disconnection.

References

Anderson, James 2007, *The Rebel Den of Nùng Trí Cao: Loyalty and Identity along the Sino-Vietnamese Frontier*, University of Washington Press, Washington; NUS Press, Singapore.

Anderson, Kym and Will Martin 2008, 'Distortions to Agricultural Incentives in China and Southeast Asia', World Bank Agricultural Distortions Working Paper 69.

Bonnin, Christine and Sarah Turner 2012, 'At What Price Rice?: Food Security, Livelihood Vulnerability, and State Interventions in Upland Northern Vietnam', *Geoforum*, vol. 43, pp. 95–105.

Bourdieu, Pierre 1977, *Outline of a Theory of Practice*, Cambridge University Press, New York and Cambridge.

Chatterjee, Partha 2004, *The Politics of the Governed: Reflections on Popular Politics in Most of the World*, Columbia University Press, New York.

Dery, David 1998, '"Papereality" and Learning in Bureaucratic Organisations', *Administration and Society*, vol. 29, pp. 677–688.

Duncan, Christopher R. (ed.) 2004, *Civilizing the Margins: Southeast Asian Government Policies for the Development of Minorities*, Cornell University Press, New York.

Ferguson, James 1990, *The Anti-Politics Machine: 'Development', Depoliticization and Bureaucratic Power in Lesotho*, University of Minnesota Press, Cambridge and New York.

Foucault, Michel 1991, *The Foucault Effect: Studies in Governmentality*, edited by Graham Burchell, Colin Gordon and Peter Miller, Harvester Wheatsheaf, London.

Friederichsen, Rupert 2012, 'The Mixed Blessings of National Integration: New Perspectives on Development in Vietnam's Northern Uplands', *East Asia*, vol. 29, pp. 43–61.

Gupta, Akhil 2012, *Red Tape: Bureaucracy, Structural Violence and Poverty in India*, Duke University Press, Durham.

Hanh, Duong Bich 2008, 'Contesting Marginality: Consumption, Networks, and Everyday Practice Among Hmong Girls in Sa Pa, Northwestern Vietnam', *Journal of Vietnamese Studies*, vol. 3, no. 3, pp. 231–260.

Herzfeld, Michael 1992, *The Social Production of Indifference: Exploring the Symbolic Roots of Western Bureaucracy*, Berg Publishers, New York.

High, Holly 2014, *Fields of Desire: Poverty and Policy in Laos*, NUS Press, Singapore.

Kerkvliet, Benedict J. 2005, *The Power of Everyday Politics: How Vietnamese Peasants Transformed National Policy*, Cornell University Press, New York; ISEAS Publications, Singapore.

Leepreecha, Praseet, Don McCaskill and Kwanchewan Buadaeng (eds) 2008, *Challenging the Limits: Indigenous Peoples of the Mekong Region*, Mekong Press, Chiang Mai.

Le Failler, Phillipe 2011, 'The Đèo Family of Lai Châu: Traditional Power and Unconventional Practices', *Journal of Vietnamese Studies*, vol. 6, no. 2, pp. 42–67.

Lentz, Christian C. 2011, 'Making the Northwest Vietnamese', *Journal of Vietnamese Studies*, vol. 6, no. 2, pp. 68 –105.

MacLean, Ken 2007, 'Manifest Socialism: The Labor of Representation in the Democratic Republic of Vietnam (1956–1959)', *Journal of Vietnamese Studies*, vol. 2, no. 1, pp. 27–79.

MacLean, Ken 2013, *The Government of Mistrust: Illegibility and Bureaucratic Power in Socialist Vietnam*, University of Wisconsin Press, Madison.

McCaskill, Don and Ken Kampe (eds) 1997, *Development or Domestication?: Indigenous Peoples of Southeast Asia*, Silkworm Books, Chiang Mai.

McElwee, Pamela 2004, 'Becoming Socialist or Becoming Kinh?: Government Policies for Ethnic Minorities in the Socialist Republic of Vietnam', in Christopher R. Duncan (ed.), *Civilizing the Margins: Southeast Asian Government Policies for the Development of Minorities*, Cornell University Press, New York, pp. 182–213.

McLeod, Mark W. 1999, 'Indigenous Peoples and the Vietnamese Revolution, 1930–1975', *Journal of World History*, vol. 10, no. 2, pp. 353–389.

Michaud, Jean 2012, 'Hmong Infrapolitics: A View from Vietnam', *Ethnic and Racial Studies,* vol. 35, no. 11, pp. 1853–1873.

Ortner, Sherry B. 2006, *Anthropology and Social Theory: Culture, Power and the Acting Subject*, Duke University Press, Durham.

Rabinow, Paul and Nikolas Rose 2003, 'Thoughts on the Concept of Biopower Today', available at www.lse.ac.uk/sociology/pdf/RabinowandRose-BiopowerToday03.pdf.

Scott, James C. 1998, *Seeing Like a State: How Certain Schemes to Improve the Human Condition Have Failed*, Yale University Press, New Haven and London.

Scott, James C. 2009, *The Art of Not Being Governed: An Anarchist History of Upland Southeast Asia*, Yale University Press, New Haven and London.

Taylor, Philip 2007, 'Poor Policies, Wealthy Peasants: Alternative Trajectories of Rural Development in Vietnam', *Journal of Vietnamese Studies*, vol. 2, no. 2, pp. 3–56.

Taylor, Philip 2008, 'Minorities at Large: New Approaches to Minority Ethnicity in Vietnam', *Journal of Vietnamese Studies*, vol. 3, no. 3, pp. 3–43.

Turner, Sarah 2012, '"Forever Hmong": Ethnic Minority Livelihoods and Agrarian Transition in Upland Northern Vietnam', *The Professional Geographer*, vol. 64, no. 4, pp. 540–553.

Vạn, Dặng Nghiêm, Chu Thái Sơn and Lưu Hùng 2000, *Ethnic Minorities in Vietnam*, Thế Giới Publishers, Hanoi.

Walker, Andrew 2012, *Thailand's Political Peasants: Power in the Modern Rural Economy*, University of Wisconsin Press, Madison.

Walker, Andrew 2015, 'From Legibility to Eligibility: Politics, Subsidy and Productivity in Rural Asia', *TRaNS: Trans-Regional and National Studies of Southeast Asia*, vol. 3, no. 1, pp. 45–71.

7

Thai Entourage Politics in the Socialist State of Vietnam

Ha Viet Quan

Introduction

We arrived at Lò Vi An's house in Châu La Biên,[1] a northwest province, quite late from Hà Nội because the lunch-stop at Châu Quỳnh town took much longer than we had planned. Lò Vi An seemed a bit tired from the rice wine during lunch but he was satisfied with the warm hospitality provided by Cầm Chung, a Thai leader of Châu Quỳnh District, and his entourage. Lò Vi An's house impressed me with its luxurious interior: a big garage, digital security camera system, elevator, and other modern appointments. However, as soon as I crossed the living room with its Western-style furniture, such as a leather sofa, crystal glasses, and gold-plated tea set, I was surprised by the kitchen with its traditional Thai cooking utensils, including several rice baskets (*cam khao*), wooden rice steamers (*mo nuung khao*), and bamboo vegetable steamer (*mo nuung phac*). In a corner of the kitchen, I saw Toàn, an adopted son of Lò Vi An, roasting a piece of dried buffalo skin in a wood-fired stove. As I already knew Toàn, I greeted him and the others in the kitchen by saying how impressed I was by one of the dishes they were preparing: 'Wow! It looks like

---

1 Châu La Biên is a pseudonym. All place names relating to Châu La Biên and the names of Thai cadres and their associates in this chapter are pseudonyms.

we are going to have *nom nang quai* [a Thai-style buffalo skin salad].
It's my Dad's favourite.' Toàn handed up a piece of dried buffalo skin
and asked me in Thai: 'Australians don't eat this special stuff, do they?'
'No, they don't. It is too luxurious for them!' I responded jokingly,
and while we were all chuckling, Toàn introduced me briefly to his
companions as a student studying in Australia. He then turned the
topic to how traditional Thai foods and Thai restaurants are becoming
popular with the Kinh people (Vietnamese) in Hà Nội.

The appearance of Lò Vi An in the kitchen interrupted the story Ly
was telling about her business trip to Hà Nội the previous week.
Ly is Toàn's wife, who I had met once at Lò Vi An's house in Hà Nội.
She looks quite young for the position of Deputy Head of Châu La
Biên Rural Development Department. Dressed like a Kinh, and
speaking Vietnamese, it is nevertheless not difficult to tell that Ly is
a Thai woman because of her strong Thai accent. Lò Vi An sat down
next to me while I was helping Toàn to slice buffalo skin. He took the
kitchen knife from me to demonstrate how to slice it properly. Lò Vi
An then asked Ly, without looking at her, in a mixture of Thai and
Vietnamese: 'Does Trung still drink, Ly? Call him to come here to have
a couple of drinks' (*'Ba Trung kin lau day bo Ly? Gọi nó đến kin lau đi'*).
Ly responded that her brother, Mr Trung, who I came to know later as
her eldest brother and an officer of the Provincial Communist Party of
Châu La Biên, would come for dinner because he too wanted to see Lò
Vi An. Putting his hands on his knees, Lò Vi An slowly stood up, and
scanning around the kitchen and looking at his watch, he announced
as if giving an order, 'Let's make the dinner ready around 6:30pm
guys!', then left.

Lò Vi An was a leading official of Châu La Biên Province, which
is situated in one of the traditional Thai homelands in Vietnam.[2]
He moved to Hà Nội in 2003 to work as head of a national agency.
Like most provincial leaders who are promoted to work at the national
level, his wife and children also moved to live in the capital city.
However, An kept mentioning that he would be going back to Châu
La Biên as soon as he retired from work: 'I don't have any thought that
I could permanently live in Hà Nội. It is too crowded and polluted.'

---

2   The *muang* — glossed here as homeland — is the traditional socio-spatial and political unit
of the Tai in the uplands of mainland South East Asia (Condominas 1990). Historically, within
Vietnam there have been 12 *muang*, known as Sip Song Chau Thai.

That explained why he had spent a lot of money recently renovating his house in Châu La Biên. Even though he works in Hà Nội, Lò Vi An was very well respected in his home town. Talking about his adoptive father's influence in Châu La Biên, Toàn assured me:

> You don't have to worry about your interviews, they all know my Dad so just tell whoever you want to talk with that my Dad [Lò Vi An] says it's OK. If you want to see Thai cadres, I know many of them. They are either our relatives or my Dad's followers [đệ tử], therefore, you will not only be welcome to interview them but also invited to drink!

Indeed, most of the Thai cadres whom I met through Toàn and Lò Vi An during my fieldwork in Châu La Biên are, in one way or another, tightly connected with Lò Vi An. This was the case of Cầm Chung. He told me: 'Without the support of big brother [đại ca] An, I would not be able to achieve what I have today.' Cầm Chung used to work as a planning expert of Châu La Biên Provincial Office before being selected by Lò Vi An to be his private secretary for three years. He was then promoted (with support from Lò Vi An) to be Vice Chairman of Châu La Biên Provincial People's Committee Office, then Chairman of the District People's Committee of Châu Quỳnh District. He is apparently linked with Lò Vi An by a classic patron–client relationship.

However, it seems that Thai cadres such as Cầm Chung, Toàn, Ly, Trung and others in Châu La Biên are not simply tied to Lò Vi An by the traditional patron–client dyadic which, according to Scott's research in Southeast Asia, involves 'a largely instrumental friendship' (Scott 1972:92). They are also connected with him and with each other by primordial bonds such as kinship, ethnicity and language. These ties have been used as a means for Thai cadres to press advantage and maintain autonomy in dealing with the centralised nation-state's administrative structures. The presence of this tight-knit network of Thai cadres in Châu La Biên challenges a prevailing view of Vietnam's socialist state as dominating, monolithic, and assimilatory in its treatment of minority groups (Evans 1992; McLeod 1999; McElwee 2004; Lentz 2011). It also confronts the view that the agency available to Vietnam's ethnic minorities is confined to responses such as ethno-nationalism, religious conversion, passive resistance, and flight (Hickey 1982; Salemink 2003; Taylor 2008; Scott 2009). Instead, the Thai cadres grouping around Lò Vi An comprises an alternative way to advance Thai interests by participating in the state, taking advantage of their positions within the state system, and using the state's resources to achieve their goals and realise positive outcomes.

Studying minority projects in the borderlands, Horstmann and Wadley (2006:19) argue that if anthropologists focus on the concrete interactions between minorities and state power and on the local reworking of national and global scripts, it becomes possible to see how people on the periphery give meaning to and shape their own marginal spaces, and deal with state power. Marginal communities may be able to employ certain existing linkages or develop networks in order to maintain their relative cultural autonomy and to influence state plans in their localities. In another example, the Chinese in Thailand, and in many other countries, are a minority group; however, they continued to dominate the Thai economy through their extensive networks. As Chayan Vaddhanaphuti says: 'Identifying themselves as Thai, having adopted Thai names, embracing Buddhism, they, nonetheless, still retained their Chinese traditions' (Vaddhanaphuti 2005:154).

In Vietnam and in adjacent border areas, some research has been conducted on the vernacular networks of ethnic minorities through religion and trade, such as the translocal networks of minority Cham Muslims in central and southern Vietnam (Farouk and Yamamoto 2008), Hmong women's trade networks in the Sino-Vietnamese borderlands (Turner 2007), and Hmong girls' tourism networks in Sa Pa (Hanh 2008). The scale and vibrancy of these networks contradict the view that ethnic minorities are localised and autarchic, and challenge the image of ethnic minorities as impotent, dependent, or incompetent (Hardy 2005; Taylor 2008). These networks do not necessarily undermine the state's attempts to achieve unification and development, nor do they replicate them; instead, they allow minorities to build up resources and develop their own culture, institutions, and the values that define them. In this research, I do not aim to judge either the national political system or the Thai people in Châu La Biên. Instead, I will recount how the minority Thais in the northwest of Vietnam consolidate their own position, institutions, and values by participating in the state of Vietnam. Since this research is based on the case of a single senior cadre and his entourage, it does not claim to be representative of the behaviour and networks of all Thai elites throughout the northwest of

Vietnam. However, the case does shed light on previously unexamined aspects of the political life of northwest Thai elites that challenge the way the Thai–central relationship has been construed.

This chapter initially looks at the conceptualisation of a Thai leader among Thai cadres in the northwest of Vietnam. It then provides information about his network by asking who its members are, how they are connected, and in what circumstances. The third part analyses the nature of this Thai network and explores how the northwest Thai people domesticate state power to obtain autonomy, dignity, and enrichment within the state of Vietnam. In this section, I explore a mode of entourage politics adopted by northwest Thai cadres, who use their respective positions, powers and responsibilities in the Vietnamese state to support other members and build and preserve influence. The conclusion provides a concise argument about the relationship between the minority Thai group and the state of Vietnam.[3]

Taking Advantage of the State: Conceptions of a Thai Leader

The dinner held at Lò Vi An's house was a great chance for me to approach Thai cadres in Châu La Biên. Among the guests, most of whom were Thai officers working for different provincial departments of Châu La Biên, were two Kinh contractors, who accompanied Lường Trung (Ly's brother) to the feast. Despite the Western-style dining table, the dinner was very traditional, as most of the food was Thai. Lò Vi An invited his brother-in-law Cầm Tuấn, the eldest brother of his wife, to sit at the centre of the dining table with him. After pouring rice wine into two extra cups as wine for ancestors (*lau then*), he tipped wine into Cầm Tuấn's cup and his own, then handed the bottle to Toàn to pour wine for everyone else. Lò Vi An put his little finger into his cup, flicked wine over both his right and left shoulders then said in a mixture of Thai and Vietnamese language: 'Going out to eat fish, going home to drink wine. All are brothers and sisters in

3   The fieldwork on which this chapter is based was conducted over the course of 2013 as part of my doctoral research at The Australian National University, funded by an Australia Awards scholarship. I wish to thank Philip Taylor, Nicholas Tapp, Andy Kipnis, Kim Wells, and the two anonymous reviewers for their valuable feedback and assistance with this chapter.

the family, no one is an outsider so don't be formal: let's finish the first round!' ('*Pay — kin pa, ma — kin lau. Toàn anh em trong nhà cả thôi, không có ai la người ngoài cả, đừng khách sáo. Au heng!*'). He bottomed up his cup after Cầm Tuấn, then showed his empty cup for everyone to follow.

Lò Vi An is the eldest son of an intellectual Thai family (*con nhà nòi*) in Châu Quỳnh, Châu La Biên. His grandfather was a village noble (*phia*) who had supported the Việt Minh during the war against the French,[4] and his father was a high profile Thai leader of the former Administrative Committee of the Northwest Autonomous Zone. Thanks to his father's position in the local state, An and his brothers and sisters had associated with Kinh people from a very early age, so he could speak Vietnamese even before going to school.

In reality, since the early 1960s, as the state of Vietnam implemented its drive towards being a model socialist country, many Kinh teachers were sent up to the northern mountainous areas to build up the general education system for ethnic minority children. Most of them could not speak the local language, and were also unfamiliar with traditional customs and culture, and the highland lifestyle. Hence, the Kinh teachers had to more or less rely on the locals for building schools and mobilising support from local people in the form of foodstuff, labour, and materials for building the schools.

---

4   In scholarship on the northwest Thai region, a common perspective is that Thai nobles tended to follow the colonial French, and were subsequently eliminated as a class or exiled after the revolution. Some scholars of the northwest during the colonial era focus on the role that Thai elites played in sustaining French rule (Le Failler 2011; Michaud 2009; Michaud 2013:66–70). Others see the revolution as essentially a form of Kinh internal colonialism (McLeod 1999). I did not have enough time to investigate this aspect of regional history in depth, but during fieldwork, in addition to Lò Vi An, I met at least three senior Thai officials who also came from noble families and who similarly claimed that their families were Việt Minh followers. Lò Vi An's family history is not necessarily typical, but I would not see it as an isolated case in the northwest region. In reality, many notable northwest Thai leaders from noble families lent their support to the Việt Minh movement, then became senior officials, including Cầm Văn Thịnh, Cầm Văn Dung, Xa Văn Minh, and Cầm Ngoan (for more examples, see Lentz 2011). According to Cam Trong (1978:511–517), there had been a clear strategy on the part of the Việt Minh from 1941–45 to mobilise the noble Thais to participate in the anticolonial movement in Sơn La Province. I would argue that the Thai elites who rallied to the revolution played a vital role in the story of how the lowland-based and Kinh-dominated Việt Minh gained a foothold in the mountainous northwest of Vietnam.

Lò Vi An's Kinh teachers remembered him as a versatile and adept Thai student (*khéo tay, biết làm nhiều việc*) who knew how to build bamboo classrooms, houses, bamboo beds, and other school facilities from local materials. Trần Văn Thuấn, one of Lò Vi An's Kinh high school teachers in Thuận Châu, recalled: 'He was a Thai so he knew how to do things in Thai ways, which we young Kinh teachers couldn't do.' Trần Văn Thuấn also said that he and his colleagues were charged with setting up their own school in Châu La Biên, but they could not speak much Thai language, and most of the Thai people did not speak Vietnamese either. Lò Vi An and a couple of senior students were conscripted into helping the teachers work with the local Thai people in mobilising local kids to go to school, helping kitchen staff to buy foodstuffs from local people, calling for help from local authorities in building classrooms, and so on. It seemed that his local knowledge allowed Lò Vi An to play a much more important role for his Kinh teachers than simply being a Thai student.

In his Thai friends' eyes, Lò Vi An was highly appreciated as a friendly (*hòa đồng*) schoolboy who did not depend on his father's influence (*không ỷ lại/dựa hơi bố*). However, they believed that he had benefited significantly as the son of a man who had been a high profile leader of Châu La Biên since Lò Vi An was a child. He was one of a very few local Thai kids who could speak Vietnamese before going to school. With this language advantage, Lò Vi An was not only a good student himself but was also assigned by his teachers to help other Thai students in his classes. According to his high school friends in Châu La Biên, Lò Vi An was an active Youth Union leader (*cán bộ Đoàn năng nổ*). 'He was also a sporty guy, a good volleyball player. I remembered he used to play volleyball with teachers after classes', a high school friend recalled. Generally, Lò Vi An was remembered by his school friends as a prominent Thai student who came from a noble lineage, spoke Vietnamese well (*thạo tiếng phổ thông*), and had been closely associated with the Vietnamese teachers.

Lò Vi An was sent to study for a bachelor degree at Bắc Thái Pedagogy University after graduating from the Northwest Ethnic Minorities Youth School in Thuận Châu, Sơn La. The path to becoming a cadre of the central planned economy state during the late 1970s and 1980s seemed smooth for An. Firstly, because of educational policies for ethnic minorities in Vietnam (*chính sách cử tuyển*), he did not have to attend the admission exams to go to university like his Kinh schoolmates. It was very common in Vietnam for most ethnic minority students to be sent by their provinces to study at different universities and colleges in line with the fixed quotas set by the central state agencies. Secondly, because of the huge demand for general education teachers in the northwest provinces, Lò Vi An was promptly posted as a lecturer in the newly formed Northwest Pedagogy College in Châu La Biên upon graduation from university.

In the role of lecturer to many local general teachers at the Northwest Pedagogy College, Lò Vi An was widely seen as a young Thai intellectual who not only came from a noble lineage (*con quan*), but also as a well-trained (*được đào tạo bài bản*) Thai cadre of Châu La Biên. He quickly began his political career by taking up the position of Director of the Provincial Education Department of Châu La Biên from the late 1990s. From there onwards, he occupied different positions in the local state of Châu La Biên, such as Chairman of a District People's Committee, Vice Chairman of the Provincial People's Committee, and as one of the top leaders of Châu La Biên Province, before moving to Hà Nội to work at the central level.[5]

There was a rumour in Châu La Biên that Lò Vi An was in fact 'kicked upstairs' to the central level in Hà Nội by his political opponents because of his corrupt activities when he had been a provincial leader. There is also a popular saying in Vietnam about ranking in the government system: 'Better to be the head of a chicken than the cheek of a pig' ('*Đầu gà hơn má lợn*').[6] However, because of the complexity of the political system in Vietnam — namely, relations between the Communist Party, People Council, and the government agencies at different levels — one cannot really ascertain if the rumour is true or not. However, in the eyes of the Thai cadres, Lò Vi An was obviously an influential provincial leader.

Having risen from college teacher to Thai politician, Lò Vi An was a well-respected intellectual Thai leader. Among popular comments that I heard about Lò Vi An, terms such as 'formally educated cadre' (*được đào tạo bài bản*), 'capable official' (*có năng lực*), and 'knowledgeable Thai leader' (*hiểu biết*) were common. Similarly, as a descendant from a Thai

---

5   In order to protect the identity of my key informants, I have listed the positions in which Lò Vi An has occupied in a different order.
6   In English this would be more akin to 'Better to be the head of a dog than the tail of a lion'.

cadre family, Lò Vi An was greatly appreciated for his familiarity with the state of Vietnam. This appears to have been one of his strongest assets as a Thai leader from several viewpoints. Firstly, Lò Vi An was trusted by the state because of his family tradition, his father having been a former leader of the Northwest Autonomous Zone. Lò Vi An was perceived as a Thai leader who had close relationships not only with the top national leaders, but also with the central agencies. Secondly, with his family's contribution to nation-building, his opinions — according to the Thai people — were carefully heard by the central state. Last, but not least, his understanding of the working of the Vietnamese state made him — in the view of local Thai cadres — a capable and worldly-wise Thai official. This helped him take advantage of being a state cadre to fulfil the needs of the local people.

Even though he had been working in Hà Nội for years, An appeared to follow a traditional Thai lifestyle: eating mostly sticky rice and traditional Thai foods, and preferring to speak Thai at home. In Châu La Biên, he was described by local Thai cadres as a leader who cared for both economic and cultural aspects of the province's development. Many Thai cadres compared Lò Vi An to a captain, who had steered Châu La Biên to become the capital province of the northwest territory of Vietnam. He was also very proud of Châu La Biên's cultural and social achievements promoted by the Northwest Culture Fest, which has been held every two years since 2003. He stated:

> I was the one who initiated the Northwest Culture Fest. Without it Châu La Biên Province would not be remembered nationwide and in the minds of national leaders. It is the Culture Fest which promotes the image of Châu La Biên to the country. Being a leader, you have got to know what are the advantages and disadvantages of your province. You have to know that a mountainous province like Châu La Biên, in comparison to other lowland provinces like Bắc Ninh, Hải Phòng and Hòa Bình, can't be famous for its economical potential but for its typical cultural values.

Interestingly, from his own point of view, Lò Vi An considered the Culture Fest as not simply a cultural activity. He seemed to be more proud of his use of the Fest as a political means to attract the attention of outsiders, especially national leaders, to his province.

Lò Vi An's relationship with the central leaders was one of relative strength. In response to my question as to what made Lò Vi An a good leader, the majority of the Thai cadres I met in Châu La Biên believed that Lò Vi An's ability to work with the central agencies was an asset. This aspect was highly valued by the local Thai cadres. They mentioned to me several times that during An's presidency many national leaders had visited Châu La Biên. Lường Trung complained: 'Unlike when the big boss (sếp) Lò Vi An worked here, no top national leaders visit Châu La Biên these days.' According to the local Thai cadres, Lò Vi An's good relations with the administrative centre (quan hệ tốt với trung ương) allowed him to channel state resources to the Thai people. 'He was able to call for many investments from central agencies into Châu La Biên', said Lường Trung. Similarly, Cầm Chung overstated at the lunch-stop at Châu Quỳnh that Châu La Biên should build a statue to Lò Vi An, considering all that he had contributed to the province. He said: 'Very few people know it but I do. He [Lò Vi An] took the advantage of the construction of a major hydropower project to develop massively the infrastructure of Châu La Biên.'[7]

Studying leadership perceptions and attribution of charisma to the leader, Lord and Maher (2002) argue that the power of leaders is fundamentally related to how they are perceived by others, and leaders' characteristics are based on outcomes of salient events. According to Ensaria and Murphy (2003:61), 'a high outcome produces greater attribution of charisma to the leader'. Apparently, the leadership of Lò Vi An was closely associated with the outcomes of the promotion of Thai culture, and infrastructure development in Châu La Biên (when he was working there). His influence was perceived by local Thai cadres as stemming from his good relations with the Vietnamese state, somewhat similar to his school friends' recollection of him as a prominent Thai student who was closely associated with their Vietnamese teachers.

Standing between the Vietnamese state and the Thai people, Lò Vi An appeared as a cultural intermediary or cultural broker who, according to Wolf (1956), Bonacich (1973), Moerman (1969:546), and Szasz

---

7   Sơn La Dam is a concrete gravity dam on the Black River (sông Đà) in Ít Ong, Mường La District, Sơn La Province, Vietnam. It is the largest hydroelectric power station in Southeast Asia. It has a total capacity of 2,400 MW with an expected annual generation of 10,246 GWh. The total cost of the project was $2 billion USD (Bui, Schreinemachers and Berger 2013:537).

(2001), played the role of a middleman. He used his Thai ethnicity to build up his relationships with the Vietnamese state which always needed Thai support for its multicultural project (Ngo 1997:139–141; Nguyễn 1975:9). By acting as a Thai 'foreign minister', symbolising the Thai people to the national state, An was designated authority and power by the Vietnamese state to secure and maintain his leadership among local Thai people. Importantly, his association with the majority Vietnamese did not make Lò Vi An a 'Vietnamised' Thai cadre in their eyes. Instead, by virtue of his notable work achievements such as the Northwest Culture Fest, the province university, and other infrastructure projects, the Thai people in Châu La Biên perceived Lò Vi An as a charismatic leader because he had the ability to deal with and take advantage of the state of Vietnam to fulfil their needs.

Brothers in a Family: The Nature of a Thai Cadre Grouping in Northwest Vietnam

In a car with the engine running, waiting at the clubhouse of a golf course outside Hà Nội, Huy — Lò Vi An's private driver, who is also a distant relative of Lò Vi An's wife — seemed a bit anxious. He mumbled: 'My goodness, what are they talking about that takes so long over there? We can't stop here much longer.' Huy was anxious because he was parked in the pick-up and drop-off area in front of the clubhouse entrance. Lò Vi An had finished playing, but he had met some friends on the way out and had stopped to talk with them. I chatted to while away the time with Huy, who had been driving for Lò Vi An for more than 15 years since he had been posted to Châu La Biên. I heard some interesting observations from Huy during our short conversation:

Me: How often do you and the boss go to Châu La Biên?

Huy: Quite often. Whenever he has free time he returns home [về quê] [Châu La Biên]. When he was renovating his house a couple of months ago, we travelled to Hà Nội — Châu La Biên — Hà Nội almost every week.

Me: Oh. It seems that the boss can't wait to enjoy being in his new house. He must love living in Châu La Biên very much, right?

Huy: Of course, Châu La Biên is his territory. His life is as good as a king in Châu La Biên, because his family, relatives [*anh em, họ hàng*] are all still there. Policemen up there never pull my car over.

Me: Really? I thought he had moved to Hà Nội already so he was no longer in power there.

Huy: Oh. Don't be fooled by the boss [*đừng có đùa với sếp*]. He has had a long-term strategic view about personnel arrangements in Châu La Biên since he was a leader there. Up there, provincial officials are mostly like brothers in a family [*toàn anh em trong nhà*].

Huy's comment made me take notice. The Châu La Biên Thai cadres grouped around Lò Vi An were indeed connected to him mostly by either kinship or adoptive relations. Commonly, they referred to themselves as brothers in a family (*anh em trong nhà*) in speaking both with Lò Vi An and among themselves. Moreover, looking at the daily activities of those Thai cadres, one could also agree with Huy that Lò Vi An, as a Thai leader, had a long-term vision to maintain not only his influence, but also Thai culture in the local state system of Châu La Biên via his entourage. I had a chance to experience these arguments, right at the dinner at Lò Vi An's house, especially when they were discussing implementation of some infrastructure development projects.

Over almost three decades since the economic reform named *đổi mới*, Vietnam has experienced dramatic economic growth, which has led to considerable poverty reduction programmes and policies nationwide (Salomon and Ket 2007; Baulch et al. 2010; Blackburn et al. 2006). Châu La Biên, like most other mountainous provinces in Vietnam, has enjoyed sizable state investments for infrastructure development (Baulch et al. 2012). As a result, the relationship between construction contractors and the local authorities is very dynamic because construction is one of the most profitable businesses in Vietnam (Nguyen and van Dijk 2012). I was told by some private construction contractors that they sometimes accrued a 50 per cent profit out of the total investment budget from infrastructure building contracts. Apparently, infrastructure development is one of the most attractive businesses in the north of Vietnam not only for contractors but also for government officials.

In fact, one of the main topics discussed during dinner at Lò Vi An's house was the government infrastructure development program in Châu La Biên. Lường Trung brought along two contractors to introduce them to Lò Vi An as capable and potential building partners. He wanted Lò Vi An to help them get infrastructure development contracts by using his influence at both central and provincial level. Giving the man sitting next to him a slap on his shoulder, he delivered an endorsement to Lò Vi An:

> Tú [one of the two men he brought to dinner] is the husband of my wife's cousin, and his company has many construction contracts in Laos so they are a very capable construction contractor. More importantly, they are my brothers so they can't escape anywhere. We don't have to worry for anything.

Lường Trung cleverly used the phrase 'they can't escape anywhere', to assure Lò Vi An that the contractors would be responsible for what they do with their contracts. However, it also contained a deep implication that because they are brothers, they would be responsible for sharing any commission derived from the contracts. Lường Trung mentioned several situations in which some contractors had run away after finishing their contracted work. In other words, they did not share the commission with those who had helped them get the contracts. Lường Trung described them as 'unfaithful' people. He said, 'There are many contractors, but many of them are unfaithful. They often kick the bowl that feeds them [*ăn cháo đá bát*].' Signalling Toàn to pour wine for everyone, Lường Trung continued: 'It is very hard to trust outsiders nowadays.' He then proposed that all present share a drink as 'brothers of one family' (*em mời tất cả các anh em trong nhà một chén*), emphasising the contractors' familial relationship to the others in his toast.

Lường Trung and Lò Vi An share an affinal relationship — the former being a brother of Lường Ly, who is Toàn's wife. While Lường Trung was well respected by most of the group's members, Lò Lam, youngest brother of Lò Vi An, described him as an opportunistic man who took advantage of his brother's influence to make money out of many corrupt activities. However, Lường Trung seemed to have gained the trust of Lò Vi An, mostly as a middleman, in carrying out infrastructure development projects in Châu La Biên, where he had no formal position of power.

I had the chance to visit Lường Trung at his well-decorated townhouse in a central street of Châu La Biên City, but I did not have much time to talk with him. I managed to visit Lường Trung again in his Châu La Biên Communist Party office on a cold winter morning around Tết (Vietnamese New Year festival). In contrast with his house, Lường Trung's office was rather simple, with several souvenir pennants from badminton tournaments, a couple of personal merit certificates and other awards hanging on the wall. In an old documents cabinet, there was nothing but some thin books and a jar of herbal wine.

Showing me a warm welcome, Lường Trung poured wine into two teacups, gave one to me and said, 'Tea is useless in this kind of weather; this drink will keep you warm'. I took the cup and sought more information about his relation with Lò Vi An by saying: 'You seem to be very much favoured by the big boss [Lò Vi An]. When we spoke, he appreciated you highly.' Lường Trung responded modestly, 'Oh! We are brothers in a family [*anh em trong một nhà cả*]. But he appreciates you highly too.' We spent more than an hour chatting about his relationship with Lò Vi An and other Thai people in Châu La Biên. Lường Trung appeared to know a lot about the history of Thai people in Châu La Biên as well as in the northwest region of Vietnam, which is rare among the current generation of Thai people. He was very keen to share with me how Lò Vi An was a good Thai leader not only to him, but also to many other Thai cadres. He stressed the fact that, thanks to the leadership of Lò Vi An, Châu La Biên had developed infrastructure — particularly many road improvements. Lường Trung listed Lò Vi An's vision for the expansion of Châu La Biên City, his ideas to build a university and different colleges, turning Châu La Biên into a centre of the northwest area, and a number of other initiatives as valuable achievements. These were all common claims about Lò Vi An's achievements that I had heard before. He closed the conversation by reiterating that, 'Lò Vi An's greatest asset is his strategic view. He is a real big brother to us, who not only supports us, but also connects us together [*quy tụ anh em*].'

Lường Trung was busy during the late morning. A couple of guests came in to say happy New Year and give him some Tết presents. In addition, several calls came in on his landline and cell phone to invite him for lunch. Lường Trung explained to me that he had to deny them all because, 'I promised to drink with a group of Châu Quỳnh District officials at Cẩm Chung's house. We are brothers in a family [*là chỗ anh em với nhau*] so I cannot cancel it.' He invited me to join the lunch with them, by focusing on the 'family connection' again, 'there are no outsiders; all are brothers in a family [*toàn anh em trong nhà*]'. I told him that I needed to inform Toàn and Ly, because they might wait for me for lunch at home (I was staying at Lò Vi An's house). 'Don't worry, I will call them to join us there [Cầm Chung's house] too.' Lường Trung showed his power over Toàn and Ly as their brother by giving them an order to come to the lunch at Cầm Chung's house.

I realised that among the members of the Thai grouping around Lò Vi An, a complex hierarchy enabled some members to wield influence over others. Sometimes the status of a member is based on his or her position in the Vietnamese official hierarchy, but most of the time it is based on their family relations. Ly's relation with Lường Trung is a case in point. As deputy head of a provincial department of Châu La Biên, her position was apparently higher than her brother's in the local state system. However, she had very little power or influence over her brother Lường Trung. Similarly, her husband Toàn had a high position as Vice Director of the Social Policy Bank of Châu La Biên. However, since Toàn is an adoptive son of Lò Vi An, he appeared to have very low status in relation to other members in the group, who he had to address as uncle, aunty, older brother, and so on.

We arrived at Cầm Chung's house in a small street of Châu La Biên City. It was an old house located on a relatively large piece of land. The house even had a little fish pool, a small drying ground in the front, and a separate kitchen house at the back. Because Cầm Chung had been working in Châu Quỳnh District more than 100 kilometres away from his house in Châu La Biên, he did not come home very often. I was told by Lò Vi An that he was expecting to be moved back to the provincial level in early 2014.[8]

Cầm Chung was decanting rice wine into small bottles in the living room, while people were still steaming sticky rice and preparing food in the kitchen. Unlike in the Kinh area in Hà Nội, in Châu La Biên, Thai men are the main cooks when it comes to a big feast or a party.

---

8   According to the latest news I have received from Vietnam, Cầm Chung could not return to the provincial level because of political reasons and had already moved to work for a central agency in Hà Nội with the support of Lò Vi An.

Even powerful leaders in the state system such as Lò Vi An, Cầm Chung, or Lường Trung are likely to be found in the kitchen cooking and preparing Thai dishes. Cầm Chung was delighted to see Lường Trung and I joining the lunch. As I already knew Cầm Chung, I went directly over to give him a hand decanting wine while Lường Trung entered the kitchen with the cooks.

Similar to other feasts in which I participated in Châu La Biên, the lunch at Cầm Chung's house started with a short speech by the host to say that he had not invited outsiders: all the diners were close brothers. I was invited to sit as an honoured guest next to Cầm Chung and Lường Trung, who were the oldest people present. Generally, Thai people in the northwest of Vietnam still observe a hierarchy system, based on age and family relations, to determine the positions of people at a dining table.

Among the group of Thai cadres I met around Lò Vi An, Cầm Chung was one of very few Thais not connected to Lò Vi An through a real family relation. His connection with Lò Vi An began as a patron–client relationship when selected by Lò Vi An to work as his private secretary. Nevertheless, Cầm Chung eventually became like a brother of Lò Vi An since he identified himself as a 'lifetime client' in relation to Lò Vi An. In fact, Cầm Chung was well-cherished not only by Lò Vi An, but his family members as well. In an informal discussion with Lò Vi An's wife in Hà Nội, I remember that she appreciated the connection between Cầm Chung and Lò Vi An because 'it had been tested over the course of time'. She mentioned that even though Cầm Chung's family was in Châu La Biên and he was working as a leader of Châu Quỳnh, he participated in most of the important events at Lò Vi An's house, regardless of whether it was in Hà Nội or Châu La Biên. Lò Vi An said of his bond with Cầm Chung: 'This is a real brothers [pi-nong] relationship of the Thai people', and quoted a Thai saying: 'Brothers are like water, they cannot be cut by a knife; aren't divided even in nine different markets' ('Pi nong tat cong lin, bau khat; toc cau lat bau xia').[9]

---

9   This implies broad geographical dispersion in distant and unfamiliar places, 'markets' referring to higher-level centres or towns that serve a network of villages.

Similar to Cầm Chung, Nguyễn Toàn is connected with Lò Vi An by proven ties of trust. However, familial intimacy and mutual obligation colour the relation between Nguyễn Toàn and Lò Vi An, because he is also a relative of Lò Vi An's wife. Initially, Nguyễn Toàn was adopted into Lò Vi An's family in Châu La Biên basically to help them do housework. In return, he was sent to Châu La Biên High School to continue his education. Having spent most of his younger life living with Lò Vi An's family, Nguyễn Toàn pursued his full family member status as an 'adoptive son' (in Thai: *luc leeng*) of Lò Vi An.[10] The influence of his adoptive father acted to smooth his path to becoming a provincial official.

Lò Vi An has two brothers and two sisters. I know them all personally. Three of them are state cadres, including one vice chairman of a district people's council, one deputy head of division of a local branch of the state bank of Vietnam, and one general director (*giám đốc sở*) of a provincial department. In addition his siblings, Lò Vi An and Nguyễn Toàn wrote down an incomplete interview list comprising 14 other relatives who were provincial and district officials. According to Lò Vi An, the Thai people have culturally a strong connection among relatives. He quoted a Thai saying to describe the connections with his entourage: 'If they are not brothers, they would be sisters; if they aren't consanguineal relatives, they would be affinal relatives; if not cousins on the mother's side, they would be aunties on the father's side' (*'bau ai co noong, bau lung co ta, bau nhinh co sao'*). I could not interview all of those 14 Thai cadres during my fieldwork. However, the list of the Thai interviewees impressed me greatly by presenting a picture of how dominant this Thai extended family could be over the local state of Châu La Biên. In total, they have representatives in leading positions spread out over seven different provincial departments and four districts.

---

10   Similar to the Thai-Lao language term which has been analysed by Keyes (1975), the term '*luc leeng*' means 'child to feed and take care of'. It is somewhat similar to '*con nuôi*' in Vietnamese or 'adoptive son' in English. In accordance with Keyes's analysis, Toàn could also be described as a 'foster child' of Lò Vi An. However, in this research, I prefer to use the term 'adoptive' to describe the process of recruiting and developing members into the grouping of Thai cadres around Lò Vi An.

Contentious Connections

It was not hard to hear comments from local cadres in Châu La Biên that Lò Vi An had arranged for his family members and his followers to hold important positions in Châu La Biên's local state system. A retired provincial leader, one of Lò Vi An's previous political opponents in Châu La Biên, criticised him strongly as 'a corrupted nepotistic leader'. He said, 'Within only the two first years of his presidency, he [Lò Vi An] promoted more than 20 family members and his followers to be provincial department and district leaders. It was unacceptable because this province is not his own kingdom.' Nevertheless, Lò Vi An responded calmly when I discussed those complaints with him. He believed he did not do anything wrong because he simply needed capable staff, who he could trust, to work with. He explained: 'They [his political opponents] complained about it because they know nothing about *ê kíp* [being a team player]. And see, they [persons he promoted] have been working well and are deserving of their positions.'

Discussing his family members' promotion, Lò Vi An contended that 'all decisions were made by a collective board of provincial leaders. I did not sign solely on any of those promotion decisions'. Similarly, Lò Vi Loan — a sister of Lò Vi An — who was general director of a provincial department in Châu La Biên, referred to the saying, 'a hand cannot cover the sun' (*'một tay làm sao có thể che được mặt trời'*), when she asserted that her position was proposed by the Provincial Standing Committee and approved by the Provincial People's Council. In fact, the use of 'collective decisions' is common in politics in Vietnam. It is one of the most popular political tricks used by state officials, making it difficult to find the particular individuals responsible for any given issue. Even at the highest level of Vietnam's political system, Mr Nguyễn Sinh Hùng — the Chairman of the National Assembly — recently raised a very debatable argument that no one, including himself as chairman or any other National Assembly members, can be held responsible for wrong decisions made by the National Assembly. He explained this by asserting that 'the Vietnam National Assembly represents the people so it is the people who are responsible' (*'Quốc hội là dân, mà dân quyết sai thì dân chịu chứ ai?'*) (Linh 2014). Even though Lò Vi An's family members' occupation of positions in the local state of Châu La Biên was criticised strongly, his political opponents could hardly do anything about it, because Lò Vi An had cleverly used the 'collective mechanism' (*cơ chế tập thể*) of the Vietnamese state in forming and strengthening his entourage network.

In general, Lò Vi An was proud of his siblings, especially Lò Vi Loan, who rose up to become a provincial department leader. In conversation among Lò Vi An's family, I heard that Lò Vi Loan had great potential to be promoted as Vice President of the Provincial People's Committee for the next term. To be fair to Lò Vi Loan, who I have known for a long time, she is certainly a smart female Thai leader. Lò Vi An believed that Lò Vi Loan inherited her decisive and determined character — 'like a man' — from their father. Indeed, straightforward as she is, Lò Vi Loan told me clearly via phone when I contacted her for an interview: 'If you want to ask about my work, come here to my office. Otherwise, I will see you at home.' I decided to see her at her office, not simply because of her work, but also because I was curious to know about her work setting. Since she appeared to me as a traditional Thai lady who normally dresses in Thai costume and speaks Thai at home with her family members, I was a bit surprised to find that Lò Vi Loan's office exhibited no trappings of Thai culture except her own personal outfit; as usual, she was dressed in a Thai skirt. Speaking to me in Thai, she said, 'I am going to have a meeting in an hour so you don't have to stand on ceremony like an outsider'.

Since we did not have much time, our conversation went straight to the topic of Thai cadres in Châu La Biên. I asked for her opinion about the criticism of Lò Vi An as corrupt owing to his promotion of so many of his family members to leading positions in the local state. Lò Vi Loan defended him, saying:

> It is politics: opponents criticise you for anything you do regardless of whether it is right or wrong. My brother was in fact too strict with our family members when he was president here. Look at Lò Trang [Lò Vi An's other sister]: she has been deputy head of a division for years. If he had intended to do such a thing [promoting family members], she [Lò Trang] wouldn't still be there now.

However, Lò Vi Loan later confirmed indirectly that Lò Vi An had promoted several family members and followers during the time he had been working as President of Châu La Biên. She argued that the majority of the Châu La Biên Province population is Thai (60 per cent), yet the percentage of Thai cadres in the local government is much lower than that of the population.[11] Hence, 'There was nothing wrong with Lò Vi An's decisions to promote Thai cadres into management positions. Many provincial leaders do the same thing with their families.' I asked her for an example of this and she promptly listed several cases in which the provincial leaders of Châu La Biên used their power to promote their relatives. She even told me the story of an informal negotiation that happened between Lò Vi An and the former Secretary of the Châu La Biên Communist Party for the purpose of promoting and arranging provincial personnel. It sounded as if a lot of informal negotiations had been going on in Châu La Biên between different powerful leaders and/or different clans. For example, she said:

> I am surprised that he [the mentioned retired provincial leader of Châu La Biên] dared tell you about it [Lò Vi An's support to his family members and followers]. His sister-in-law was my deputy [at district level], so he negotiated with my brother that if I moved to provincial level, his sister-in-law should be the one to replace me ... and indeed, she did.

Lò Vi Loan's conversation with me seemed to be more open after we chatted about studying in Australia, as she was planning to send her son to study overseas. She tried to convince me that having family members in the system is very normal and common. According to her, everyone would support their family members, including the nation's top leaders. If they don't have their family members working in the state system, they will support their family members who are working in the private sector to form different business connections. 'Then they might be even more corrupt', she said.

Interestingly, she might have forgotten her youngest brother, Lò Lam, when making this argument. Lò Lam is a case in point, because he was not working for any state agency. He was connected with the group of Thai cadres, including his brothers and sisters, not only by kinship relations but also business relationships. In his early 40s, Lò Lam, according to himself, is literally a 'jobless man', because he does not work for either a state agency or any private company. In Lò Vi An's

---

11   There are currently 21 ethnic groups in the northwest provinces of Vietnam. However, since the Thai people comprise one of the majority indigenous groups of the region, this northwest region was named the Thai-Meo Autonomous Zone from 1955 until 1963. As a consequence, the Thai cadres remain one of the most dominant groups in the local state system in the northwest provinces.

eyes, 'He was over-indulged by my parents. He was spoiled because he got whatever he wanted since he was a boy.' Lò Vi An normally depicted Lò Lam as a failed member of his family because 'he does not belong to any organisation'. Nonetheless, I was curious about what Lò Vi An told me about his youngest brother, and why he kept saying that Lò Lam is a spoiled man.

Having once worked for a local branch of Electric Power of Vietnam, Lò Lam had quit his job in 2002 to work in an infrastructure building firm with his friends. He spoke candidly with me while he was showing me around the town of Châu La Biên, saying: 'Everyone has their own way of life. My ultimate purpose is earning money to raise my family.' Without a doubt, Lò Lam is a wealthy Thai man. He has a big house, drives an expensive car, and was able to send both his children to China to study. His 'money-earning' career seems very successful, in contrast to how he was described by his brother.

I observed that Lò Lam was very well connected, not only with Lò Vi An, but also with other group members. In reality, Lò Lam was working informally for a friend who runs a big construction company. During my second trip to Châu La Biên, Lò Lam even invited me, as his driving companion, to join him and Cầm Chung in travelling to Châu Quỳnh to prepare for a construction bid there. Although he is not a state official like his brothers and sisters, Lò Lam is a practical man who has greatly benefited from the network of Thai cadres grouped around his brother. Similar to what Lường Trung had been doing, Lò Lam basically acted as a broker between state investment officials and private construction companies. In particular, he takes advantage of his family relationships to influence Thai cadres in Châu La Biên to give building contracts to the company. In return, the company had to share its profit with him, and perhaps also to other local authorities via Lò Lam, even though he had nothing to do with implementing those contracts. In short, Lò Lam is an infrastructure construction middleman in Châu La Biên.

In fact, such a 'middleman' — or *trung gian*, *môi giới* or even *cò* in Vietnamese — is quite common. According to Kerkvliet, a problem in village–state relations in Vietnam since the time of de-collectivisation has been that, 'due to insufficient resources and other inadequacies, the actual administrative capacity of the state to coordinate programs and implement policies is considerably less than it would require'

(Kerkvliet 1995:399). Lò Lam's work as a construction middleman in Châu La Biên indicates that the Vietnamese government is still ill-equipped when it comes to running a market-oriented economy. It allows Lò Lam to make himself useful to state officials such as his brothers and sisters, who do not want to be directly involved in a 'sensitive' area like infrastructure development investment, and to private contractors, who cannot otherwise establish their credentials with powerful state leaders. In other words, Lò Lam plays the role of middleman among the Thai people, which, according to the theory of middleman, plugs the status gap between the state and private sector at the local level, acting as broker between them (Bonacich 1973).

Most Thai leaders I met in Châu La Biên, such as Cầm Chung, Lường Trung, Lò Vi Loan, Nguyễn Toàn and Lường Ly, would make a lively endorsement of Huy's statement that 'provincial officials are mostly like brothers in a family'. It is true that most of them are connected with Lò Vi An via a classic patron-client relationship:

> In which an individual of higher socioeconomic status [patron] uses his own influence and resources to provide protection or benefits, or both, for a person of lower status [client] who, for his part, reciprocates by offering general support and assistance, including personal services, to the patron (Scott 1972:72).

However, these persons are also tied to each other within the local state as members of an extended family, which enables them to manipulate the local state and maintain their family influence in Châu La Biên. I found that this grouping of Thai cadres has been effectively using the state of Vietnam as their base, and government policies and programs as their means to strengthen their family connections. By networking with each other, they have been able to practice, maintain, and develop Thai forms of relatedness within the state of Vietnam.

The Thai Cadre Entourage as a 'Fishing Net' of Relations

A formalist depiction of the nature of Vietnamese state authority might easily conclude that it conforms to what Weber has described as legal or bureaucratic authority (Weber 2009:56–65). In principle, the Vietnamese state has long been following the model of a law-based state (*nhà nước pháp quyền*), which is based on a legal authority type with a bureaucratic administrative system (Gillespie 2013:676). In addition, the Vietnamese state is also commonly considered in the literature as an authoritarian regime (Wischermann 2011:7; Joseph 2007), with uniform national institutions that enable the ruling party to project its power homogeneously throughout society in a manner that has been described as 'mono-organizational socialism' (Thayer 2009:3). Koh notes that 'the view that the Vietnamese party-state dominates, leaving very little space for society', has prevailed for some time (Koh 2001:369).

Nevertheless, the network of Thai cadres in northwest Châu La Biên who gather around Lò Vi An reveals greater complexity in the nature of Vietnamese state authority. The connections built up by the cadres, grouped around a senior Thai leader, enable them to exert influence and wield power in a mode that could be called northwest Thai entourage politics. By practising it at the local state level in Châu La Biên, northwest Thai cadres have been flexibly assimilating the Vietnamese state in their locale to a traditional mode of authority that is, according to Weber (2009), generally patrimonial in form, and derived from traditional customs and established norms.

Indeed, Lò Vi An, who was commonly addressed as 'big brother' of the group, used his skill, political influence, and access to state power to shape and connect his family members and followers into an entourage of Thai cadres. With him as the central node person, other members, consisting of about 15 people working in different agencies, were interlinked with each other around Lò Vi An. This Thai grouping consists of a 'meshwork' (Ingold 2011) of related members connected to each other in relations of kinship, adoption, patron–client ties and mutual obligation. Each of them has his or her own ties with the top person, as well as other contiguous members, bringing into form a distinctive constellation of power within the state of Vietnam that is as strong and resilient as a Thai-style fishing net. The nature of this network has several prominent elements, as elaborated below.

One of the most obvious characteristics of this Thai 'fishing net' cadre network in Châu La Biên is the hierarchical relations among its interlinked members. Several factors help identify the status of members, such as age, gender, and position in the state. However, the most dominant factor, which controls their hierarchical positions in the network, is proximity to the leader. For example, Lường Ly, as a younger sister of Lường Trung, basically has a lower status than Lường Trung, even though her position in the local state system is higher. Lò Lam has no official position, but is high in the network. In general, I found through different parties and feasts in Châu La Biên that one of the easiest ways to see the hierarchy among Thai grouping members is by observing their sitting positions around dining tables. It is not much different to traditional Thai seating rules in so-called 'feudal' times, described by Cam Trong several decades ago (Cam Trong 1978:247–248).[12] Accordingly, the closer a person sits to the highest leader of the table, the higher ranking they have in the group.[13]

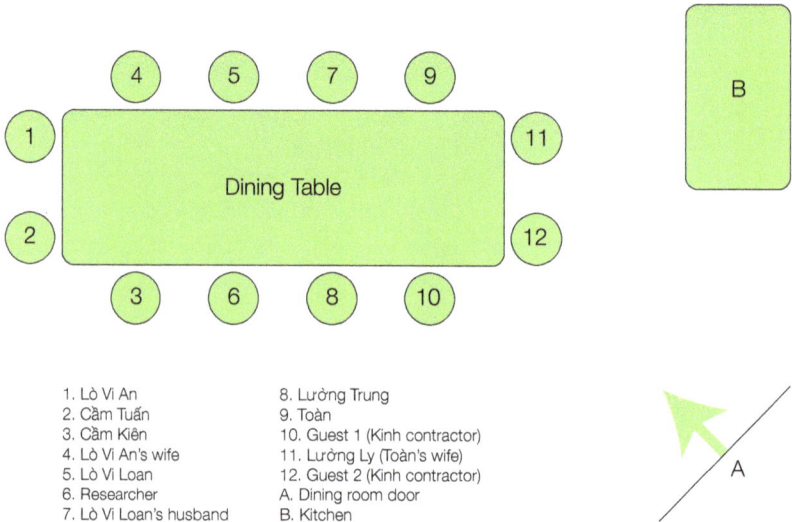

1. Lò Vi An	8. Lường Trung
2. Cầm Tuấn	9. Toàn
3. Cầm Kiên	10. Guest 1 (Kinh contractor)
4. Lò Vi An's wife	11. Lường Ly (Toàn's wife)
5. Lò Vi Loan	12. Guest 2 (Kinh contractor)
6. Researcher	A. Dining room door
7. Lò Vi Loan's husband	B. Kitchen

Diagram 1: Dining positions at Lò Vi An's house.

A second important feature of this Thai entourage is the obligation among members. All members share mutual obligations with both Lò Vi An and other members, including Nguyễn Toàn and Cầm Chung,

---

12   In Cam Trong's (1978) book about Thai people in northwest Vietnam, the author generalises that the term 'feudal time' (*thời phong kiến*) refers to the Chau-Muong administrative system of the Thai people in relation to Vietnam's pre-colonial state and the French colonial state of Indochina before the Vietnamese revolution in 1945.

13   The seat of the highest-status person is normally located opposite the door of the dining room.

whose connections with Lò Vi An had originated in patron–client relations. Here we can find elements of what Scott discerns in his overview of patron–client politics:

> There is an imbalance in exchange between the two partners which expresses and reflects the disparity in their relative wealth, power, and status. A client, in this sense, is someone who has entered an unequal exchange relation in which he is unable to reciprocate fully. A debt of obligation binds him to the patron. (Scott 1972: 93)

In this entourage group, Nguyễn Toàn, Cầm Chung, and Lò Vi An have developed their connections beyond such relations of debt and obligation into kin-like relations infused with sentiment and trust. The 'patron' — Lò Vi An — has assumed the same responsibilities of taking care of Cầm Chung and Nguyễn Toàn as he would his real family members. Obligation weighs most heavily upon the shoulders of the entourage leader, for it is to him that other members of the group look to advance the fortunes of the whole group.

The presence of adoptive members in this group also points to the open, synthetic, and generative nature of this network whose membership criteria are not confined to tradition, inheritance, or ascription alone. Membership and rank in this Thai cadre entourage are earned, consolidated, and reinforced, most notably through displays of loyalty from its subordinate members and of performance from its superordinate leader. As I was to discover, new members can be incorporated into the entourage through invitations to partake in shared meals and drinking sessions, and through inclusive modes of address and collective self-reference, by which means the network can be flexibly extended. Displays of deference, mutuality, and loyalty, as well as facility in the familial idioms of the network, can consolidate one's position in the network, while rank can be enhanced through loyalty and displays of efficacy in navigating the world beyond the entourage and attracting resources to the group. Perhaps the most obvious arena for attaining and symbolising rank in this Thai cadre entourage is the hosting of communal meals, whose size, lavishness, and conspicuously traditional nature earn significant prestige for the entourage leader and bind network members to him.[14]

Of particular note are the strong sentiments of esteem that exist among network members, channelling the loyalties of even far-flung entourage members towards the central node person. For instance, the sincere appreciation by Lường Chung for what Lò Vi An had done in developing Châu La Biên would be more or less comparable to the charismatic type of authority defined by Max Weber as a 'certain quality of an individual personality, by virtue of which he is set apart from ordinary men and treated as endowed with supernatural, superhuman, or at least specifically exceptional powers or qualities' (Weber 2009:329). It would appear that, for many Thais in his region, Lò Vi An embodies qualities of a Southeast Asian-style 'man of prowess' (Wolters 1999) owing to his perceived efficacy as a leader in attracting state investment and enabling careers in his region. Additionally, he embodied in his person the 'magic of the state' (Taussig 1997). By virtue of his father's revolutionary pedigree, his intensive Vietnamese schooling, and his close association with Vietnamese state agents such as Vietnamese teachers and national leaders, he was imbued with the aura of national state power.

A sense of belonging binds the members of the Thai cadres group around Lò Vi An to each other. This sentiment could be considered as one of the prime bases for building trust between network members. This is the gist of Lò Vi An's justification for his decisions to recruit and promote his followers into different important leading positions in Châu La Biên Province. Another example of how belonging is significant to being connected was Lường Trung's insistence on describing two infrastructure development contractors as his 'brothers' during dinner at Lò Vi An's house. Such modes of address and self-reference

---

14 Because of the difference in the density of his social relationships between Hà Nội and Châu La Biên, Lò Vi An felt disappointed in the working environment with his colleagues in Hà Nội during the first years of his posting. Having once been a provincial leader in Châu La Biên, where he had a crowded entourage around not only at work but also at home, Lò Vi An was initially shocked by the fact that he had none of his followers in Hà Nội. According to him, 'there is no feeling (không có tình cảm) among his office mates, and people are cold and too competitive with each other'. One example that Lo Vi An kept mentioning was the difference between his family meals in Hà Nội and in Châu La Biên: 'Whenever I have dinner at home up there [Châu La Biên], we set at least two dining tables for guests. Look at what we have here [Hà Nội], only us [he and his wife] two old people eating together.'

construct a boundary between group members as 'brothers in the one family', and those who are 'outsiders'. Commensal acts of dining and drinking together, and ritual declarations of kinship that accompany such acts further consolidate a sense of togetherness and belonging. The identity of the dishes they consume, often prepared and referred to self-consciously as 'real' or 'traditional' Thai food, also reinforces this sense of belonging. Through these acts, the entourage is given substance as a corporate or inter-corporeal group, whose members routinely provide sustenance for each other and become one of the same substance.

A final feature of this entourage, which was only faintly visible when I conducted my fieldwork, is its apparent portability. In late October 2014, I realised that I had missed three calls from Nguyễn Toàn, who was phoning from Vietnam. A short email from him on the same day, with his working address at the bottom, informed me that he had now started working for a central agency in Hà Nội. During our subsequent phone conversation, I was informed that Lò Vi Loan and her husband would be the next people to move to work in Hà Nội after Nguyễn Toàn and Cầm Chung. Even though both Nguyễn Toàn and Cầm Chung received support from Lò Vi An to move to work in Hà Nội, it is too early to say that Lò Vi An is reforming his Thai entourage right in the heart of a central agency of the Vietnamese state. Nevertheless, these initial moves illustrate the tendency of this northwest Thai entourage to converge around a central node person. This tendency can be observed in the expectations expressed by Lò Vi Loan, during my interview at her office, who was anticipating that Lò Vi An would help to support Cầm Chung to return to the provincial state of Châu La Biên from his position at the district level in Châu Quỳnh.

This description of the elements that make up the Thai cadre network around Lò Vi An provides a sense of the main generative principles underlying Thai entourage politics in the northwest of Vietnam. This grouping of influential Thai cadres is aligned in a ranked meshwork of relations, obligations, and sentiments around a charismatic leader. The entourage around him is characteristically open, flexibly accommodating, markedly performative, and, potentially, has the capacity to extend itself geographically in the wake of its leader's movements.

Conclusion

The strength and resilience of this network of Thai cadres in the heartland of northwest Vietnam leads us to question characterisations of modern Vietnamese state power as homogeneous or monolithic in nature. Researching the Cham and Khmer peoples in southwestern Vietnam, Philip Taylor finds that religious institutions such as Islamic mosques and Theravada Buddhist temples are a compelling nexus of communal authority for these groups that rival the authority commanded by the central state. Many Khmer localities have a historically autonomous quality, with the *wats* functioning as multi-faceted communal institutions and as pivotal nodes between the state and local society (Taylor 2014:17). In this chapter, I use a network of northwest Thai cadres grouped around a powerful Thai leader to illustrate another mode of governance within the Vietnamese state system, one which I call northwest Thai entourage politics. Accordingly, I argue that Vietnam is not a uniform state with a single form of authority, but that the state is a politically aggregate entity comprised of heterogeneous forms of authority.

What I am calling northwest Thai entourage politics comprises several key elements including hierarchy, mutual obligation, openness, performativity, sentiment, belonging, and a tendency of convergence to a central 'node' person. Contemporary Thai people of the northwest also have a relationship with central state power located in Hà Nội which is strikingly similar to that of pre-revolutionary times. In the precolonial era, in spite of offering loyalty to Vietnam's court and engaging in relations with influential centres in neighbouring Thailand, Yunnan, and Laos, the Thai people of Vietnam's northwest for many centuries experienced autonomy under the rule of their local chiefs (McAlister 1967; Cam Trong 1978; Le Failler 2011). From the late nineteenth century when the French seized power from the Vietnamese feudal state, the northwest Thai region came under the rule of the Đèo family, who acted as delegates in the region for French colonial authority, and who even accrued enough power to form their own Tai Federation from 1948 to 1953 'by exploiting the French administrative framework' (Le Failler 2011:63; see also Lentz 2011). In other words, the current situation of northwest Thais has precedents in the past practices of northwest Thai elites who were able to accommodate with the lowland state in Vietnam and act as its delegates to substantively maintain their local power. These research findings suggest that the state of Vietnam is not all powerful in its relations with ethnic minority groups, and that Koh is right when he concludes, 'there is much space in which society can manoeuvre and rework the state's boundaries to society's benefit' (Koh 2001:370).

We have seen that the northwest Thai cadre network cannot be trivialised or explained away as an expression of reactive traditionalism, localism, or disconnection from contemporary state initiatives. It has supple social effects, with the capacity to cast its members into the heart of the Vietnamese state system, and to capture state resources and draw them back to the advantage of network members. The fishing net metaphor used to describe the contours of Thai entourage politics aptly describes these dual processes. The political influence wielded by the Thai cadre network is such that some have alleged it to be corrupt or nepotistic. While potentially such 'special interests' (*nhóm lợi ích*) can be construed as threatening to the modernist principles of rationality, equity, merit, and transparency espoused by the contemporary Vietnamese state, we can question whether political sovereignty is eroded by Thai entourage politics or is, in fact, consolidated by them. Not only does the entourage benefit from the state, but the state benefits from the entourage, which provides a means for the state to articulate with local Thai society, invest in the locality, ensure compliance, and reward performance. Before raising alarm about the erosion of the bureaucratic polity by the operation of this distinctive non-normative network of power, we ought to pose one question: has Vietnamese state power ever been exercised in the northwest uplands in any other way?

References

Baulch, Bob, Nguyen Thi Minh Hoa, Nguyen Thi Thu Phuong and Pham Thai Hung 2010, *Ethnic Minority Poverty in Vietnam*, UNDP, Hanoi.

Baulch, Bob, Hung T. Pham and Barry Reilly 2012, 'Decomposing the Ethnic Gap in Rural Vietnam, 1993–2004', *Oxford Development Studies,* vol. 40. no. 1, pp. 87–117.

Blackburn, Keith, Niloy Bose and M. E. Haque 2006, 'The Incidence and Persistence of Corruption in Economic Development', *Journal of Economic Dynamics and Control*, vol. 30, no. 12, pp. 2447–2467.

Bonacich, Edna 1973, 'A Theory of Middleman Minorities', *American Sociological Review*, vol. 38, no. 5, pp. 583–594.

Bui Thi Minh Hang, Pepijn Schreinemachers and T. Berger 2013, 'Hydropower Development in Vietnam: Involuntary Resettlement and Factors Enabling Rehabilitation', *Land Use Policy*, vol. 31, pp. 536–544.

Cam Trong 1978, *Người Thái ở Tây Bắc Việt Nam* [*The Thai in Northwest Vietnam*], Social Sciences Publishers, Hanoi.

Condominas, Georges 1990, *From Lawa to Mon, from Saa' to Thai: Historical and Anthropological Aspects of Southeast Asian Social Spaces*, Research School of Pacific and Asian Studies, The Australian National University, Canberra.

Ensaria, Nurcan and Susan Murphy 2003, 'Cross-cultural Variations in Leadership Perceptions and Attribution of Charisma to the Leader', *Organizational Behavior and Human Decision Processes*, vol. 92, pp. 52–66.

Evans, Grant 1992, 'Internal Colonialism in the Central Highlands of Vietnam', *SOJOURN: Journal of Social Issues in Southeast Asia*, vol. 7, no. 2, pp. 274–304.

Farouk, Omar and Hiroyuki Yamamoto 2008, *Islam at the Margins: The Muslims of Indochina*, CIAS, Kyoto, Japan.

Gillespie, John 2013, 'Jurifidication of Cause Advocacy in Socialist Asia: Vietnam as a Case Study', *Wisconsin International Law Journal*, vol. 31, pp. 672–700.

Hanh, Duong Bich 2008, 'Contesting Marginality: Consumption, Networks, and Everyday Practice Among Hmong Girls in Sa Pa, Northwestern Vietnam', *Journal of Vietnamese Studies*, vol. 3, no. 3, pp. 231–260.

Hardy, Andrew 2005, *Red Hills: Migrants and the State in the Highlands of Vietnam*, NIAS Press, Copenhagen.

Hickey, Gerald C. 1982, *Free in the Forest: Ethnohistory of the Vietnamese Central Highlands, 1954–1976*, Yale University Press, New Haven.

Horstmann, Alexander and Reed Wadley 2006, 'Introduction: Centering the Margins in Southeast Asia', in Alexander Horstmann and Reed Wadley (eds), *Centering the Margins: Agency and Narrative in Southeast Asian Borderlands*, Berghahn Books, New York, pp. 1–24.

Ingold, Tim 2011, *Being Alive: Essays on Movement, Knowledge and Description*, Routledge, London.

Joseph, Samantha 2007, 'Ethnic Minorities in Vietnam', *Indigenous Law Bulletin*, vol. 7, no. 1, pp. 123–125.

Kerkvliet, Benedict J. Tria 1995, 'Village-State Relations in Vietnam: The Effect of Everyday Politics on Decollectivization', *The Journal of Asian Studies*, vol. 54, no. 2, pp. 396–418.

Keyes, Charles 1975, 'Kin Groups in a Thai-Lao Community', in G. William Skinner and A. Thomas Kirsch (eds), *Change and Persistence in Thai Society*, Cornell University Press, Ithaca, New York, pp. 274–297.

Koh, David 2001, 'State-Society Relations in Vietnam: Strong or Weak State?', in Daljit Singh and Anthony L. Smith (eds), *Southeast Asian Affairs 2001*, Institute of Southeast Asian Studies, Singapore, pp. 369–386.

Le Failler, Philippe 2011, 'The Đèo Family of Lai Châu: Traditional Power and Unconventional Practices', *Journal of Vietnamese Studies*, vol. 6, no. 2, pp. 42–67.

Lentz, Christian C. 2011, 'Making the Northwest Vietnamese', *Journal of Vietnamese Studies*, vol. 6, no. 2, pp. 68–105.

Linh Thư 2014, 'Quốc Hội Là Dân, Dân Quyết Sai Dân Chịu Chứ Kỷ Luật Ai?' ['The National Assembly is the People and who else but They Bear Responsibility for its Mistakes?'], *Vietnamnet*, 11 April 2014, available at vietnamnet.vn/vn/chinh-tri/169988/qh-la-dan--dan-quyet-sai-dan-chiu-chu-ky-luat-ai-.html, accessed 17 November 2015.

Lord, Robert G., and Karen J. Maher 2002, *Leadership and Information Processing: Linking Perceptions and Performance* (second edition), Taylor & Francis, London.

McAlister, John 1967, 'Mountain Minorities and the Vietminh: A Key to the Indochina War', in Peter Kundaster (ed.), *Southeast Asian Tribes, Minorities and Nations*, Princeton University Press, Princeton, pp. 746–770.

McElwee, Pamela 2004, 'Becoming Socialist or Becoming Kinh?: Government Policies for Ethnic Minorities in the Socialist Republic of Vietnam', in Christopher R. Duncan (ed.), *Civilizing the Margins: Southeast Asian Government Policies for the Development of Minorities*, Cornell University Press, Ithaca, pp. 182–213.

McLeod, Mark W. 1999, 'Indigenous Peoples and the Vietnamese Revolution, 1930–1975', *Journal of World History*, vol. 10, no. 2, pp. 353–389.

Michaud, Jean 2009, 'Handling Mountain Minorities in China, Vietnam and Laos: From History to Current Concerns', *Asian Ethnicity*, vol. 10, no. 1, pp. 25–49.

Michaud, Jean (ed.) 2013, *Turbulent Times and Enduring Peoples: Mountain Minorities in the South-East Asian Massif*, Curzon Press, Richmond, Surrey.

Moerman, Michael 1969, 'A Thai Village Headman as a Synaptic Leader', *The Journal of Asian Studies*, vol. 28, no. 3, pp. 535–549.

Ngo Vinh Long 1997, 'Ethnic Pluralism, Multiculturalism and Development in Vietnam', *New Political Science*, vol. 19, no. 1–2, pp. 139–152.

Nguyễn Khánh Toàn 1975, 'Một vài quan điểm cơ bản cần được quán triệt trong quá trình xây dựng danh mục các Dân Tộc Thiểu Số ở Miền Bắc Nước ta' ['Some Fundamental Perspectives to Clarify in Constructing the List of Ethnic Minorities in the North of our Country'], in Bế Viết Đẳng (ed.), *Về vấn đề Xác định Thành Phần các Dân Tộc Thiểu Số ở Miền Bắc Việt Nam* [*The Problem of Identifying Ethnic Minority Groups in Northern Vietnam*], Nhà xuất bản Khoa học xã hội, Hanoi, pp. 3–9.

Nguyen Thuy Thu and Mathijs A. van Dijk 2012, 'Corruption, Growth and Governance: Private vs. State-owned Firms in Vietnam', *Journal of Banking and Finance*, vol. 36, no. 11, pp. 2935–2948.

Salemink, Oscar 2003, 'Enclosing the Highlands: Socialist, Capitalist and Protestant Conversions of Vietnam's Central Highlanders', paper presented to 'Politics of the Commons: Articulating Development and Strengthening Local Practices' conference, Chiang Mai University, 11–14 July 2003, available at dlc.dlib. indiana.edu/dlc/handle/10535/1787.

Salomon, Matthieu, and Vu Doan Ket 2007, 'Doi Moi, Education and Identity Formation in Contemporary Vietnam', *Compare: A Journal of Comparative and International Education*, vol. 37, no. 3, pp. 345–363.

Scott, James C. 1972, 'Patron–Client Politics and Political Change in Southeast Asia', *The American Political Science Review*, vol. 66, no. 1, pp. 91–113.

Scott, James C. 2009, *The Art of Not Being Governed: An Anarchist History of Upland Southeast Asia*, Yale University Press, New Haven.

Szasz, Margaret C. 2001, *Between Indian and White Worlds: The Cultural Broker*, University of Oklahoma Press, Oklahoma.

Taussig, Michael 1997, *The Magic of the State*, Routledge, New York and London.

Taylor, Philip 2008, 'Minorities at Large: New Approaches to Minority Ethnicity in Vietnam', *Journal of Vietnamese Studies*, vol. 3, no. 3, pp. 3–43.

Taylor, Philip 2014, *The Khmer Lands of Vietnam: Environment, Cosmology and Sovereignty*, NUS Press, Singapore.

Thayer, Carlyle 2009, 'Vietnam and the Challenge of Political Civil Society', *Contemporary Southeast Asia*, vol. 31, no. 1, pp. 1–27.

Turner, Sarah 2007, 'Trading Old Textiles: the Selective Diversification of Highland Livelihoods in Northern Vietnam,' *Human Organization*, vol. 66, no. 4, pp. 389–404.

Vaddhanaphuti, Chayan 2005, 'The Thai State and Ethnic Minorities: From Assimilation to Selective Intergation', in Kusuma Snitwongse and Scott Thompson (eds), *Ethnic Conflicts in Southeast Asia*, ISEAS Publications, Singapore, pp. 151–166.

Weber, Max 2009, *The Theory Of Social and Economic Organization*, Free Press, New York.

Wischermann, Jörg 2011, 'Governance and Civil Society Action in Vietnam: Changing the Rules From Within — Potentials and Limits', *Asian Politics and Policy*, vol. 3, no. 3, pp. 383–411.

Wolf, Eric R. 1956, 'Aspects of Group Relations in a Complex Society: Mexico', *American Anthropologist*, vol. 58, no. 6, pp. 1065–1078.

Wolters, Oliver William 1999, *History, Culture, and Region in Southeast Asian Perspectives*, Cornell Southeast Asia Program Publications, Ithaca, New York.

8

Searching for a Khmer Monastic Higher Education in Post-Socialist Vietnam

Philip Taylor

In 2015 I met a 32-year-old man from a small village in Trà Vinh, a province of the Mekong Delta which is home to many of Vietnam's ethnic minority Khmer. He had grown up in a family of landless farmers in a village that only recently had been connected to a sealed road. Like many Khmer students in this remote and impoverished province, he had dropped out of state school after only five years, and his Vietnamese was not good. He had, however, studied for several years in temple schools in his district where, while ordained as a monk, he had learnt to read and write Khmer. The Buddhist temples in his home province are linked in an educational network comprising 144 campuses that provide schooling in numerous subjects up to Grade 12. Despite its size and sophistication, this autonomous, religious-based education network is relatively obscure, even among Vietnamese people, for the education it provides is entirely in Khmer.

After we had exchanged preliminary greetings in Khmer, he astonished me by breaking into fluent English. Details of an unusual biography emerged. In 2000 he had graduated from the top level of the monastic system but, unsatisfied with the narrowness of the curriculum, he had crossed the border illegally to Cambodia to continue his studies. He wanted to learn more about history, he said. At that time,

Vietnam did not have a university for Khmers and his elderly Pali teacher had advised him to go to Cambodia, saying that he would learn nothing about his Khmer heritage in Vietnamese state schools. While still ordained as a monk he studied Khmer literature and English for Buddhism for his BA in the main Buddhist university in Phnom Penh. Four years later, a laywoman sponsored him to do further studies in Thailand. He learnt Thai and did his MBA in the English language. Then he returned to Phnom Penh where he disrobed, married, and started work as an office manager in an English-speaking foreign firm. He now owns a car and a house in Phnom Penh and does charity by raising money for scholarships for poor Khmer Krom students. His biggest regret is not being able to work in his home province, owing to the fact that he had left his birth country illegally.

The story of this young man illustrates the capacity of higher education to promote mobility into the urban middle class. By 2015, it was becoming common for Khmer people from disadvantaged rural areas of the Mekong Delta who had been through state schooling to establish themselves in large Vietnamese cities, although it was still rare to meet people from such a background working as a manager in an English-speaking office, let alone owning a house and car. The most intriguing feature of this man's impressive story of social mobility was that he had not studied beyond the primary level of state school, had never resided in a Vietnamese urban area, and was scarcely literate in the national language. Yet he had two post-secondary degrees, had studied in two capital cities, and was fluent in two foreign languages. His remarkable passage out of rural obscurity had proceeded via a vernacular education network that connects the Khmer-speaking margins of the Mekong Delta to the metropolitan centres of Theravada Asia. For 16 years he had studied and resided in the temples of this transnational network, his living and study costs provided by Khmer Buddhist laypeople. Tellingly, however, his story also can be read as a failure to progress in Vietnamese-speaking educational and social spheres. Not only had he failed to exit the ethnic bubble in which Vietnam's Khmer minority are enclosed, his illicit educational voyages had eroded his employment prospects in his home village, resulting in a demotion in his status even in narrowly local terms.

The vernacular Buddhist education systems of the Theravada world are defined by this tension between parochialising and cosmopolitan characteristics. In Thailand, monastic education played a key role in the 'integrative revolution' (Geertz 1963) and was used by a centralising Thai state to promote identification with a transcendent national polity and supplant alternative local, religious or ethnic identifications (Keyes 1971; Tambiah 1976). Similar concerns informed the French colonial effort in Cambodia to propagate a standardised notion of Khmer identity in the curriculum used in Buddhist temple schools. The purpose of such efforts was to inculcate in students a sense of loyalty to the French protectorate of Cambodge and replace attachments to Siam as a civilisational centre. Such a project was conceived and coordinated through the auspices of the Buddhist Institute in Phnom Penh, which served as the headquarters for formulating the curriculum, training teachers, and disseminating curricular materials (Edwards 2007).[1] These activities shed light on the paradoxical uses of Buddhist education institutions as centres for the inculcation of transcendent subjectivities that, contradictorily, serve to parochialise their subjects and foreclose alternative transcendent attachments.

Often the impetus to construct such institutions has been a moment of cultural crisis. For instance, Anne Hansen traces the inception of the modern system of Buddhist learning in mid-nineteenth-century Siam to King Mongkut's doubts about the validity of his own ordination, which set him to amassing the knowledge and expertise that would enable him to authenticate his status as a Buddhist cleric. Similarly, the nineteenth-century monastic pioneers of the Khmer Buddhist higher education system who repatriated the new Siamese learning to Cambodia did so out of the dire sentiment that their tradition had been denuded and debased after decades of war and occupation (Hansen 2007:49–50, 84–96). Key Khmer contributors to the Buddhist Institute were beset by a premonition that their cultural and religious tradition was about to be extinguished by mass conversions to the new Cao Đài faith centred in Vietnam (Edwards 2007:197–209). These institutions that set Buddhist education on new foundations crystallised the solutions forged by a founder figure to a crisis of cultural reproduction and renewal. They emerged in an era when the legitimacy of the old was threatened by the new, in zones such as former royal capitals and

---

1   Justin McDaniel has described concurrent initiatives in the French protectorate of Laos to redesign monastic learning so as to neutralise the appeal of Siamese Buddhist education among Lao student monks and promote identification with the cultural and spatial construct of French Indochina (McDaniel 2008:38–52).

urban centres where cultures were in collision, and they issued from the cultural elites of the old order for whom the need to find new modes of legitimacy was at its most urgent.

If we adopt the perspective of students, we see such institutions in a different light. Scholars have noted that the monastic educational networks that centred on Bangkok and Phnom Penh were used by youths from peripheral rural regions as an avenue of social mobility (Wyatt 1966; Kalab 1976). The Buddhist universities of Bangkok served as stepping stones for disadvantaged rural students to gain access to the wealth of specialised knowledge and employment opportunities that exist in the metropolitan centre (Kabilsingh 1986). From the vantage point of late nineteenth-century Cambodia, the Siamese metropolis obtained a very different significance as a charismatic centre that exerted a magnetic pull over students as a symbol of modernity, the pure source of culture, magical texts, and enlightened teachers (Hansen 2007:79–96). The central node of these monastic educational networks thus served an exemplary centre that offered students the experience of authentic self-knowledge, transcendence, or salvation. Drawing a leaf from the experience of Muslim Southeast Asians who travelled to Mecca on educational journeys, we can postulate that for Theravada Buddhists, pilgrimages to their own metropolitan institutions of higher learning conferred distinction, power, and an aura of the sacred upon those who returned from such sites.[2] In short, these institutions derive their vitality from the periphery itself for which they serve, in one guise or another, as the charismatic centre.

The situation is more fragmented for the Khmer Krom, an ethnic and religious minority in Vietnam with complex historical relations to several states (Taylor 2014). As in other Theravada Buddhist contexts, the Khmer Krom have a vernacular education system centred on a network of Buddhist *wats*, which, among other purposes, serve as local schools and as a pathway to advancement in wider society. Despite long-standing linkages to religious centres in South and Southeast Asia, the Khmer Krom live in a country where Theravada Buddhism is a minority creed and has never attracted significant state patronage. As former subjects of the Khmer kingdom, they identify culturally with Khmers in Cambodia, while they are divided from

---

2   On the Hajj pilgrimage from Southeast Asia, see Tagliacozzo (2013).

modern Cambodia by a political border. As citizens of Vietnam, they are compelled to enrol in state education whose focus has been to inculcate a sense of belonging to a nation whose centre lies in faraway Hà Nội. With religious, cultural and political affiliations that seemingly pull in different directions, it is of interest to know what significance the Khmer Krom attach to these disparate civilisational projects, and what role has been played by their vernacular educational institutions in connecting or disconnecting them from the plurality of centres under whose sway they come.

In the second quarter of the twentieth century, a concerted effort was made by the French to draw the hundreds of Khmer temple schools in the Mekong Delta into the orbit of the Buddhist Institute in Phnom Penh, which both disseminated ideas of their membership in a Khmer cultural tradition and served as a peak destination for their educational journeys. With the demise of colonialism in the mid-1950s, the institutional link to Cambodia was severed. However, during the decades of nation-building and war in Vietnam, numerous Khmer Krom students and monks continued to undertake educational pilgrimages to Cambodia. With the rise of communist states in Indochina in 1975, monastic education in both countries was plunged into a severe crisis. In Cambodia, it disappeared. In Vietnam, repressed by the government, and with a curriculum that offered students no prospects for advancement in the broader society, the Khmer monastic education system faced extinction.[3] After a crisis lasting 30 years, several initiatives were launched by Khmer monastics in Vietnam to fight their way out of parochialisation and irrelevance, relink Khmer temple schools in Vietnam to peak educational destinations in the Theravada Buddhist world, and stimulate a flow of students.

Coming to a head in the first decade of the twenty-first century, such initiatives gave rise in quick succession to no less than three alternative higher education destinations: in Thailand, Cambodia, and within Vietnam itself. This sudden multiplication of higher education pathways after three decades in which none had existed offers revealing insights into the numerous actors and contradictory pressures that shape the Khmer monastic field in Vietnam. Each of these pathways attracts a significant number of students, which signals

---

3   The situation of monastic education in socialist Laos after 1975 is discussed by Justin McDaniel (2008:52–68) and Martin Stuart-Fox (1996).

the thirst that exists among Khmers in Vietnam for higher education, and the willingness of Khmer students to try different ways to achieve it. Examining the relative popularity of these different routes offers a sense of the competing desires that shape these educational quests. The fact that the most-trodden route is illegal and that the officially sponsored route is the least favoured suggests that the government's ability to steer monastic education from the top down is limited. Similarly, Khmer monastic authorities' attempts to craft an entirely new educational pathway have attracted only limited support from state authorities and individual students. By tracing the educational journeys taken by Khmer Krom students, one can understand the ambitions and frustrations that shape from below the institutional contours of Khmer monastic higher education in Vietnam.

This chapter describes the search for a viable monastic higher education pathway for the Khmers of Vietnam's Mekong Delta. Charting the decline and partial rehabilitation of Cambodia as their peak educational destination, it also documents the alternative destinations that have emerged over the course of the last decade. By focusing on the agency of state authorities, monastic leaders, and students, the chapter shows how the field of monastic higher education has been shaped in a negotiation between multiple actors with competing priorities. Having once been oriented towards Cambodia as the peak destination of their vernacular tradition, Khmer Krom students now enjoy tenuous access to a variety of educational centres, none of which satisfies the aspirations nursed by them, or by religious or state elites, for Khmer higher education in Vietnam.[4]

---

4   This chapter draws on research conducted in Vietnam and Cambodia over multiple visits between 1999 and 2015 funded by the Australian Research Council and ANU College of Asia and the Pacific. I thank David Chandler, John Marston, Roger Casas, and Sango Mahanty for their comments and assistance with this chapter. Conversations with numerous Khmer Krom intellectuals, monks, abbots, and political leaders provided me with valuable insights into the concerns that have informed a long history of monastic educational reform. Collected life histories of students spanning 70 years of educational travel to Cambodia and observation of activities in many learning institutions gave me a sense of the aspirations and frustrations that have informed student's selection of educational options.

Closing the Educational Route to Cambodia

The Khmer Krom, or ethnic Khmer people of Vietnam, number over a million and live primarily in the Mekong Delta of southern Vietnam (Taylor 2014). They have a deep-seated historical connection to Cambodia, dating to when the Mekong Delta was part of the Khmer kingdom. Even after the Mekong Delta came under Vietnamese and French administrative control, Khmers of this region continued to be integrated culturally with Khmers in Cambodia. One feature of this integration was an education system based in Theravada monasteries that was identical to that found in Cambodia. A French report in 1903 observed that in every Khmer Buddhist temple in the province of Trà Vinh, a monk was in charge of educating local children to read and write Khmer and to do basic maths. In the early 1880s, a system of public schools had been set up by the colonial authorities 'to propagate the French language and serve as an instrument of civilisation', but these schools were mostly attended by 'Annamite' (ethnic Vietnamese) children. The report notes that the task of getting Khmers into state schooling was 'delicate, owing to the fact that Khmer fathers preferred their children to study under a monk in the local temple' (Société des Etudes Indochinoises 1903:41–42).

Despite this apparent conservatism, major changes to the monastic education system occurred during the colonial period. Around 1930, the French began to introduce in selected temple schools in Cochinchina the renovated temple school model that had been introduced in Cambodia. According to Louis Mallaret, by 1944, there were 209 schools of this type in Cochinchina, with a total of 7,274 students, of whom 1,093 were girls (Malleret 1946:29). As Penny Edwards notes, the curriculum in these schools included textbooks on Khmer history, geography, language, and other secular subjects that had been developed under the auspices of the Buddhist Institute in Phnom Penh (Edwards 2007:177–182). This curriculum promoted ideas about Cambodian history, culture, and geography that were to become foundational to nationalist ideas about Cambodian identity. Between 1929 and 1933, noted Phnom Penh-based monastic leaders Ven. Huot Tath and Ven. Chuon Nath travelled to Cochinchina on tours of inspection, establishing schools and distributing books

(Edwards 2007:188–190; Harris 2009:107–108). For the next half century, Khmer monastery schools of the Mekong Delta had the same curriculum and used the same textbooks as those in Cambodia.

By the 1930s, Khmer monks from the Mekong Delta were travelling to Cambodia to undertake teacher training and higher studies. Malleret notes that monks who taught in the renovated temple schools in Cochinchina would go to Phnom Penh, Trà Vinh, and Sóc Trăng to undertake vocational teacher training (Malleret 1946:29). Harris mentions that, in 1931, some 30 Khmer Krom monks spent a year in Cambodia to undertake teacher training for the reformed Buddhist schools (Harris 2009:108). Khmers from Cochinchina also studied for longer periods of time in the protectorate's two elite educational institutions, the École Supérieure de Pali (Pali high school, established in 1922), and the Buddhist Institute (established in 1930). A well-known instance of this was the founding member of Cambodia's communist movement, Tou Samouth. Born in Trà Vinh in 1915, he was educated as a Buddhist monk at the Buddhist Institute in Unnalom Monastery, Phnom Penh, where he also taught Pali until the mid-1940s (Kiernan 1981:163).[5] In the course of my own research in Vietnam, I met an elderly man from Sóc Trăng who had ordained and studied Pali and French in the École Supérieure in Phnom Penh for 30 years, from the 1940s to the 1970s. One man born in Trà Vinh in 1925 had studied French and Khmer in Trà Vinh for seven years, after which he was ordained and went to Phnom Penh, where he studied for another four years in Wat Unnalom. Another man born in Kiên Lương in 1940 had studied Sanskrit, Pali, French, and English in Phnom Penh for four years, from 1959–63.

Of the 25 Khmer Krom people whose biographies of educational travel to mid-twentieth-century Cambodia I collected, around half had gone to study in state schools. Cambodia was attractive to the Khmer Krom as an educational destination because instruction was in Khmer and French rather than in Vietnamese. By the end of the Second World War, there were only 19 official Franco-Khmer elementary schools in the whole of Cochinchina (Malleret 1946:29), and just one lower secondary school, in Cần Thơ. Meanwhile, Cambodia had several

---

5   Another Trà Vinh-born founding member of Cambodia's communist movement, Achar Mean, later known as Son Ngoc Minh (b. 1920), also taught in Unnalom Monastery in the early 1940s (Kiernan 1981:163).

secondary and higher-level studies institutions, such as the College Preah Sihanouk in Kompong Cham, the Lycée Sisowath in Phnom Penh,[6] and the Teachers' College in Phnom Penh.[7] In the 1940s and 1950s, several of my elderly interlocutors had gone on to higher-level studies in Cambodia after completing elementary or lower secondary Franco-Khmer schooling in Cochinchina. Others went directly to Cambodia to study at elementary level. These state school students tended to come from moderately wealthy to wealthy families. I also met many Khmer Krom who, after South Vietnam was founded as a republic in 1955, had studied in state schools at the primary and secondary level in the provinces of Kompong Thom, Kampot, Takeo, Kompong Cham, and Phnom Penh.

Cambodia was attractive to Khmer Krom students because of the vibrancy of its Khmer-language public sphere, the breadth and depth of its labour market, and, after 1960, the haven it offered from conscription and war in Vietnam. Having completed their studies in the monastic or secular streams, many Khmer Krom students remained in Cambodia to work and assume social leadership positions. The best-known exemplars of this trend are the Cambodian political leaders Son Ngoc Thanh (b. 1908), Tou Samouth (b. 1915), Son Ngoc Minh (b. 1920), Ieng Sary (b. 1929), and Son Sen (b. 1930), all of whom were born in Trà Vinh then lived and worked for the rest of their careers in Cambodia. I met several elderly Khmer Krom who had commenced their education in temple schools in the Mekong Delta, and spent the 1960s and 1970s teaching in Cambodia. Some became distinguished teachers and abbots in Buddhist temples. Others taught foreign languages in state schools in Phnom Penh, Battambang, Takeo, and other places. Obtaining skilled work of this kind in the urban centres of Cambodia was an exceptional accomplishment for the children of farming families from a marginalised minority in the Mekong Delta. We see here a good example of the role of the monkhood in Khmer society as an avenue of social mobility (Kalab 1976). The opportunity for social advancement provided by monastic education undoubtedly was one of the factors that made ordination attractive to rural youths.

---

6   One of its alumni was Khmer Rouge leader Ieng Sary, born in Trà Vinh in 1929. He commenced his studies in 1945.

7   Khmer Rouge leader Son Sen, born in Trà Vinh in 1930, commenced studying there in 1946.

Not all of these students stayed in Cambodia. When they graduated from higher studies, many returned to Vietnam to work, teach, marry, and assume leadership positions in the monastic system and wider society. Those who had studied in Cambodia returned with their prestige and position in the Khmer community considerably enhanced. Of the 15 returnees whose biographies I collected, two went on to lead the monastic resistance against the South Vietnamese regime in the 1960s, two became special forces commanders, and three assumed high-level positions in the new regime after 1975, while others became respected abbots, meditation teachers, and ritual specialists. Two disrobed, married, and returned to farming. They also made a critical contribution to reproducing the monastic education system. All but one of the returnees contributed to teaching subjects such as Pali and Khmer literacy and foreign languages to the monks and lay children in their local temples.

Such educational passages came to an abrupt end in 1975 when Communist regimes came to power throughout Indochina. In Democratic Kampuchea, the Khmer Rouge emptied the cities and terminated diplomatic relations with many countries. Their peasant troops closed down schools, destroyed books, banned the speaking of foreign languages, and put to death many intellectuals. The monkhood was terminated, temples were used as storehouses and granaries, and former monks and teachers were disrobed and put to work along with urban and educated people, planting rice and undertaking agrarian earthworks in collective farms. People identified as Khmer Krom were persecuted and eliminated (Kiernan 1996; Chandler 2008; Harris 2012). I was told about several Khmer Krom teachers and abbots who had stayed on in Democratic Kampuchea and later perished under the Khmer Rouge.

Vietnam's communist resistance movement had worked closely with Khmer Krom monastic leaders during the Vietnam War. This alliance had helped keep Khmer monastic education functioning in Trà Vinh and other provinces in the face of repression by the South Vietnamese state. However, once the communist government assumed formal power in southern Vietnam in 1975, efforts were made to reduce the hold of monasteries in Khmer life. Khmer monks were required to undertake heavy agrarian labour, and the alms round was suppressed. A systematic attempt was made to terminate the monastic education program by confiscating books, forbidding classes, and imprisoning monks who continued to teach. Through determined covert actions and tight solidarity, and under the leadership of communist-affiliated clerics and officials, Khmers managed obstinately to continue their classes for up to 10 years after liberation. However, in the mid-1980s, the Vietnamese government cracked down, arresting teachers, abbots, and the educational resistance movement's leading figures, several of whom died mysteriously in jail. The monasteries were raided and surrounded, and all teaching came to a halt, for up to 10 years in some localities.[8]

In the late 1980s, classes in the Khmer monastic education program reopened in attenuated form. The initial classes were small and low-key and were conducted in select monasteries in remote parts of Trà Vinh Province where Khmer Krom members of Vietnam's communist party were concentrated. The new curriculum consisted of 12 religious and Khmer-language subjects.[9] Gone were the subjects of Cambodian geography, history, and civic morality and citizenship, as well as French and English. Students had to contend with the complete absence of Khmer-language texts and classroom study materials, which had been confiscated and destroyed in the period before 1985. Initially, teachers transcribed study materials into notebooks from memory or surviving texts, which were then repeatedly copied by hand. By the late 1990s, study texts for all 12 grades of the syllabus were being smuggled furtively from Cambodia and endlessly re-photocopied, replenishing monasteries in Vietnam with a reservoir of faint and sometimes illegible facsimiles of the original Cambodian texts.

When classes recommenced, they drew critically on the resources of Khmer intellectuals who had survived the crackdown and had remained in the country. Hundreds of members of the Khmer Krom intelligentsia who had participated in the resistance movement had fled the country. Many survivors were too cowed to resume a life of educational service. Initially, classes were taught from memory by weather-beaten lay teachers who returned to classrooms from the rice fields. In this culturally sparse environment, the cultural knowledge

---

8   Brief references to this resistance movement and crackdown can be found in Harris (2009). This compressed summary draws on interviews conducted with numerous participants in the movement, which I hope to be able to write up on another occasion.

9   These included Khmer literacy, grammar, reading, dictation, composition and maths; Buddhist doctrine, history and monastic law; Pali literacy and grammar; and Pali–Khmer translation.

possessed by those who had once studied or spent time in Cambodia was prized and became a crucial element in the regeneration of Khmer monastic education in Vietnam. However, these were people who had been in Cambodia long ago, and thus the bridge to that country they represented was vestigial.

In post-Khmer Rouge Cambodia, the monkhood had been reconstituted in the early 1980s (Keyes 1994; Marston 2014), but ordinations were tightly restricted for the remainder of that decade and only in 1989 was the first Buddhist primary school in Cambodia officially reopened (Sovanratana 2008:258–259). Buddhist education in Cambodia began its renaissance in the 1990s, with the opening of a high school in 1992 and the reopening of Preah Sihanouk Raja Buddhist University in 1999. By 2005, Cambodia could count 555 Buddhist primary schools, 23 Buddhist secondary schools, and two Buddhist universities (Sovanratana 2008:259–264). Secular higher education institutions in Cambodia were revived and restructured in the 1990s under the country's internationally sponsored reconstruction. In the next decade, the number of universities and colleges mushroomed with the entry of numerous private education providers. By 2007, there were 62 higher education institutions in Cambodia, of which 40 were private. Three decades after the Khmer Rouge had almost wiped out the country's intellectual elite, higher education in Cambodia was again booming, with 45,000 students enrolled in a great array of degree programs in public, private, and religious institutions (Chealy 2009:154–160).

The cultural and educational renaissance underway in Cambodia did not go unnoticed among the Khmers of the Mekong Delta. Senior abbots and Khmer government officials making approved official trips brought home news of Cambodia's reconstruction. Via relatives and news media, Khmers in the Mekong Delta were able to follow the news of the rebuilding of temples, the resurgence of education, Cambodia's vibrant cultural and festive life, the explosion of publications, media and arts, the growth of international tourism, and reconstruction of museums and ancient monuments. By the late 1990s, monks who had completed the monastic high school level in Vietnam were also contemplating the prospects of further education. With the opening of Buddhist universities in Phnom Penh, Cambodia again beckoned as an appealing higher education destination.

However, at that time Khmer Krom monks were prohibited from travelling to Cambodia to study. Applications for passports and travel permits were denied or inexplicably held up indefinitely. Monks who applied were told that it was impossible to travel to Cambodia; their lives would be endangered, for Cambodia lacked laws and security. Monks who went to Cambodia to study would be breaking the law. When I began conducting research in Trà Vinh in the late 1990s, the bans on Khmer Krom monks travelling to Cambodia was one of the most heated topics of conversation. I was often told of monks who had tried to go illicitly but had been arrested at the border. Some had made it into Cambodia but had been arrested and defrocked on their return. Those who returned from an illegal sojourn in Cambodia were punished in other ways, invited by the police for questioning, surveilled, denied permission to take up residence again in their home temple as a monk, or denied work or promotion.

As one monk told me in 1999, being a Khmer monk is what made it hard to go to Cambodia, rather than being Khmer per se:

> The government now tolerates trade, or the movement of people with business or investment projects: anything which is of purely economic benefit to Vietnam. However, they never give permission to Khmer monks.

> They are worried that because monks have the time to study their culture and their country's history, meet with other monks and discuss their situation, they are more likely to engage in politics. They might meet up with the Cambodian government and opposition and take part in resistance to Vietnamese rule. Since traders and small business people haven't the time or the education to develop a broad picture of their people's plight they don't represent the same threat. These restrictions are what the government calls 'precautionary' measures. In fact monks here are too afraid to take part in such activities.

Only in the mid-2000s were Khmer Krom monks permitted to travel to Cambodia, on a tourist visa, but the period of time they were allowed to stay there was short. Travelling for the purpose of study remained out of bounds. As one group of student monks from Trà Vinh told me in 2005, the reason Vietnam prevents Khmer monks from travelling to Cambodia to study is that the government probably does not want them to be influenced by the environment of anti-Vietnamese politics in Cambodia.

Consequences of Closing the Cambodian Study Route

The ban on monks continuing their studies in Cambodia aroused in Khmer Krom students an intense sense of being denied access to crucial aspects of their cultural heritage. Aware that the curriculum they had studied had been shorn of several important subjects, many suspected that they lacked adequate knowledge of Khmer culture and society and about the history of the localities they called home. Thus many had cause to doubt that they truly knew who they were, let alone being able to claim status as well-educated people. Having had access to only a handful of photocopied school textbooks during their years of monastic study, many students yearned for exposure to a fuller spectrum of Khmer-language texts in the disciplines they had studied. All were aware that in Cambodia, the Khmer language was the medium of a diverse and dynamic public sphere and media, popular culture, and the arts. As opposed to Vietnam, where Khmer script had no purpose other than as a subject for study by Khmers in their temples, in Cambodia the written word was living, functional and highly developed and central in many walks of life. Many student monks I spoke to expressed regret that by being denied the opportunity to study in Cambodia, they were deprived of complete and authentic experience of their own culture.

At the same time, closure of the border prevented monks who wished to specialise intensively in the study of Buddhism from accessing high-quality education in that field. In late 2006, monks in Trà Vinh who aspired to deepen their understanding of Buddhism told me:

> The monastic schools in Cambodia are better than those in Vietnam because they concentrate on Pali, Sanskrit, Buddhism, Buddhist history, and Pali–Khmer translations. Here, Khmer language and culture subjects take up a large part of the curriculum because these subjects are not taught at all outside of our temples. Plus Cambodia has two Buddhist universities that allow one to specialise more deeply in Buddhist subjects.

A number of Khmer Krom monks have enrolled to study in the Buddhist university in Hồ Chí Minh City, which reopened in the 1980s, following its closure in 1975, and now offers undergraduate and post-graduate level courses. However, this option was not considered satisfactory by the Khmers with whom I spoke, since the instruction and curricular study materials are entirely in Vietnamese. They noted that emphasis in the curriculum is on the development of Mahayana Buddhism as a Vietnamese national tradition, and on Buddhism in Vietnamese history and culture. Khmer students identified this institution as concentrating on Vietnam's religious and cultural heritage at the expense of their Khmer traditions, without necessarily providing them with an adequate Buddhist studies education.

The closure of the monastic route to Cambodia also closed down the most convenient option available to Khmer people wishing to advance their education in non-religious subjects. In 2003, I spoke to a monk in Wat Chantarangsay in Hồ Chí Minh City who was undertaking studies in computer science and English in an urban university. To gain entry to the university, he had to study in the Vietnamese state system for 12 years, in addition to the many years he had studied as a monk in the Khmer and Buddhist system. Around that time, scores of Khmer monks were accessing secular Vietnamese higher education in this way. However, the temple where he was staying — one of only two Khmer *wats* in the city — was small and crowded, and he found learning the Vietnamese language difficult. He told me it would have been much easier for him to study in Cambodia, whose proximity, shared language and culture, and large number of temples, colleges and alms-providing laypersons in its urban centres made it an ideal place for Khmer youths to further their studies.

The closure of the educational path to Cambodia deprived the Khmer Krom monastic education system of well-trained teachers. Although individual monks can and do make their way to Cambodia, it is very hard for them to return home. If they do return, they must disrobe and are not allowed to teach. Similarly, teachers and monks from Cambodia are not allowed to teach in Khmer monasteries in Vietnam. Hence in the 1990s to the late 2000s, monastic educators were drawn exclusively from people who had studied in Cambodia prior to 1975, or those who had studied in Khmer temple schools in Vietnam — at most to high school level. As a result, Khmers in Vietnam were denied the opportunity to interact with teachers with advanced religious or secular knowledge or functional literacy in their own language. Increasingly, Khmer students in Vietnam were taught by teachers whose only knowledge of written Khmer came from the small set of textbooks used in the monastic classroom.

Many people I spoke to bemoaned the deterioration in the intellectual capacity of the Khmers in Vietnam that these policies have brought about. A senior monk in Hồ Chí Minh City with whom I spoke in 2010 was despairing about his people's low educational level:

> Khmer Krom students are far from meeting international standards and from gaining admission to study overseas. Hardly any Khmer Krom students have MAs or PhDs.

> Their level of Pali and religion is also very low. All of the talented, knowledgeable teachers have died. Some have gone overseas. No one is left to pass on knowledge to the next generation. Because there are so few knowledgeable monks and *achars* left — educated *achars* are working in the rice fields — there are few people who could teach the next generation or guide the development of a better educational system.

> Trà Vinh alone has a strong Pali and Buddhist studies program. In the provinces of Cà Mau, Kiên Giang, and An Giang, such a program is practically non-existent. But Trà Vinh is strong only in knowledge of the Pali sutras and monastic law. In these respects they are as strong as or even stronger than monks in Cambodia. Yet no new research is being done there or deeper investigation into the religion, language, and law. Quite likely there is not a single Khmer monk in Vietnam who could prepare an original composition in Pali — for example, describing the layout and activities of a typical Khmer temple. On the other hand, Thailand has scores of people who have done in-depth PhD research into Buddhism.

> By contrast too, Vietnamese Mahayana students study to a high level, have PhDs, do research, hold conferences, study abroad, and they have good access to and do well in secular subjects as well.

Ultimately, the closure of the route to Cambodia threatened to have an impact on ordinations. Until the mid-1970s, ordination in Vietnam provided monks with knowledge that had utility in neighbouring Cambodia. It provided rural youths with a way to loop through Cambodia's urban centres, where they could deploy their knowledge to their advantage or accumulate more to repatriate to their home communities. Denial of these opportunities led to the marginalisation of ordination in Vietnam as a means for Khmer social and economic advancement. Related to this was students' lack of any sense of where their education might take them, or how it might relate to a world beyond their villages, given that the border to Cambodia was closed after 1975. Lacking these elements, Khmer monastic education in Vietnam risked becoming a closed system that failed to bring in any new ideas. Unable to engage with the outside world or change with the times, Khmer monastic education was in danger of becoming sterile and defunct.

The Search for a Peak Educational Destination

The closure of the border to Cambodia had major implications for the survival of the monastic education system and for Khmer cultural reproduction in Vietnam. It denied Khmer intellectuals in Vietnam access to the perceived source and centre of their culture. It terminated a well-trodden educational route that Khmer students in the Mekong Delta had taken to the peak destinations of their vernacular tradition. It denied Khmer communities in Vietnam access to a means by which their members had long been able to gain local distinction and attain leadership, thus closing down a traditional avenue of social distinction within the Khmer-speaking world of Vietnam. It also undermined the entire Khmer monastic system in Vietnam, threatening to make it obsolete as the vestigial launch pad for a leap into higher learning and social position.

The closure of the monastic route to Cambodia created serious problems for Vietnam as well. Although the government had permitted the reopening of monastic schools and turned a blind eye to the illicit importation of Khmer-language textbooks, the ban on monastic educational travel to Cambodia became a focal point of ethnic Khmer dissatisfaction with the government. Ever since I began my research in 1999, complaints about this measure have been intense, bitter, and consistent. The bans were cited widely as proof that the Vietnamese government lacked interest in Khmer culture, educational self-improvement, freedom of religion and mobility, local tradition, and the sanctity of monks. The removal of a peak destination for education was taken as evidence that the government's plan for its Khmers was to keep them ignorant and to stifle the emergence of self-aware, conscious, and enlightened Khmer individuals, thereby making it easier to assimilate the Khmers.

In 2006, in apparent response to these concerns, the Vietnamese government moved to set up a high-level Khmer Buddhist Studies Institute in Vietnam that would teach Buddhist and Khmer studies subjects at the university level. Several high-ranking Khmer abbots in provinces of the western Mekong Delta are credited by their peers with pushing forward this initiative. The site selected for the institute was in Ô Môn District of Cần Thơ Province, a rural fruit-growing area of formerly dense Khmer settlement not far from the Bassac River whose Khmer population had largely been dispersed by the wars from the 1940s to the 1970s. Its main campus was in Wat Polthisomrong, a temple beside the Ô Môn market with very small grounds, where a dormitory of 23 bedrooms and some small classrooms were constructed in 2007. A second campus was designated in Wat Sanvoar, just a kilometre or so away, in a rural area whose lower population density and available land would allow the school to expand in size.

The institute was officially opened in mid-2007 when the first intake of 63 monks began their four-year higher-level Khmer and Buddhist studies course. The students came from many provinces; over a third were from Trà Vinh. All of them were ordained monks. They had already studied for at least five years in monastic schools and had a strong foundation in Pali, Khmer, and religious subjects.[10] The eight or so teachers came from several provinces, mostly from Sóc Trăng. Two of the teachers from Trà Vinh had undertaken MA-level Buddhist studies overseas.[11] The curriculum comprised 25 subjects. They included a variety of religious subjects, no less than six language subjects, some computing, history, and social science subjects, and subjects on Khmer culture, arts, and literature.[12] The students told me that English and Sanskrit were the most difficult subjects for they had little prior exposure to them. The students in the first intake finished their degree in 2010 with exams and a mini thesis.

Abbots in the Ô Môn area played a leading role in mobilising funds and labour for construction of the school buildings in Wat Polthisomrong. Much of the labour to build the dormitory and classrooms was

---

10 According to the students with whom I spoke at the institute in July 2010, the numbers of students by province were: 24 Trà Vinh; 12 Sóc Trăng; 9 Kiên Giang; 9 Vĩnh Long; 3 Cần Thơ; 2 Bạc Liêu; 2 An Giang; 1 Hậu Giang; 1 Cà Mau.

11 One teacher did his MA in Buddhism in Sri Lanka, the other did his MA in Buddhism in Maha Chulalongkorn, Thailand.

12 The languages studied were Thai, English, Vietnamese, Sanskrit, Pali, and Khmer.

contributed by local laypeople, with fees paid to building contractors only for specialised tasks. A contribution of $1,000 AUD was made by a Khmer family in Australia. Contributions were also made by Khmer Krom now living in America and Canada. Locals also chipped in. The Abbot of Wat Polthisomrong told me that some single donations of $100–200 AUD made by local families were major contributions, given local families' limited means. He said the government also had promised to match those funds obtained from Buddhist laypersons. If followed through, he said, the contribution from the government would be 50 per cent. The state also granted some 10 or 12 hectares of land to the school at the Wat Sanvoar campus to construct a larger and permanent facility.

There was some pride and optimism among Khmer Krom abbots and monks at the founding of this institute, which bore the name 'The Khmer Buddhist Studies Institute of Southern Vietnam' (in Khmer, *Wicia Stan Butisasana Khmer Vietnam Khang Thbon*). One leading abbot said it was one of just four Buddhist institutes in Vietnam, the others being in Hà Nội, Huế, and Sài Gòn. It was the first university-level institute for Khmers in Vietnam. Before it was founded, Khmer monks who wanted to study to a higher level had to attend the Vietnamese Buddhist University in Hồ Chí Minh City. The leading Khmer abbots of the three largest Khmer-populated provinces were on its governing board. One of them, who said he was the deputy head of the institute, told me with emotion that its founding showed how much the Communist Party of Vietnam cared for Khmers.

Nevertheless, the institute has also attracted widespread criticism from Khmer Krom monastic leaders and educators. Most lamented the small size of the school, cramped in the grounds of one of the region's smallest temples, which greatly restricted the scope of the school, leaving no space for it to develop. Several also commented to me on the length of time it was taking to establish a larger and more permanent facility on a second campus, giving rise to a view that official commitment to the institute was diffident. Many suggested that the government had skimped in its support for the project by selecting an obscure location where the land was cheap and relying on co-contributions from poor Khmer laypeople. Development of the new campus was delayed by lack of government funding. Also indicative of official disinterest was the lack of people with higher-level degrees to teach at the institute. If better teachers were to be found, Khmer people would have to come up with the money themselves to send people overseas to gain an appropriate education. Meanwhile, the institute is not given the money it needs to recruit adequately trained teachers.

The main criticism of the institute was its location in a remote rural area, which was a matter of universal disappointment and occasional despair. Those I spoke with considered it strange and inappropriate for such a high-level institute to be based in such a location. Acceptable facilities or services are not available locally to support university-level studies. All of the teachers have to be brought in from outside, and few quality teachers could be attracted to reside long-term in such a remote location. Just as importantly, no other colleges are available locally that could extend students' range of study options. The present campus is deep in the countryside, away from anywhere that high-level Khmer students want to be. They already have spent their whole lives in the countryside and the present location does not allow them to expand their knowledge in line with the challenges and imperatives of a modern society. The site is not even in a Khmer neighbourhood, which limits its integration into Khmer social and cultural networks, and it is situated far from the demographic centre of the Khmer population in Vietnam.

All of the leading Khmer monastics I consulted thought that the institute should be in the centre of a major city where there is better access to books, services, and teachers appropriate to the range of courses taught at this high level. All thought Hồ Chí Minh City (*Prey Nokor*) was the most appropriate place. This was what originally had been proposed. The leading abbot of one province told me that after conferring among Khmer monks and abbots, the South Vietnamese Khmer Buddhist monks association proposed to Vietnam's Religious Affairs board (*Ban Ton Giao*) to establish the Khmer Buddhist Studies Institute in Hồ Chí Minh City. However, he said:

> The board rejected the proposal, as did the People's Committee of Hồ Chí Minh City. They said the proposal would cost too much. Sài Gòn lacked space and the land for the institute would be too expensive. Instead, they suggested that the institute should be better located in Cần Thơ, which is the economic and cultural hub of the Mekong Delta and in the middle of all the provinces where Khmer people live. Eventually, however, the site selected was not in Cần Thơ City but in the countryside, 20 kilometres away from Cần Thơ. Ô Môn is not in any way a hub for the region. Why put it in Ô Môn rather than closer

to the centre of Cần Thơ where far better teachers and services would be available and monks would be able to study other subjects like computing, English, and the like in urban college campuses?

Several senior monks vented their frustration at the government's response to their suggestions for the location of the high-level Khmer institute. Leading abbots told me that they had put the suggestion to the Committee for Ethnic Affairs (*Ban Dan Toc*) to locate the university in a major city, but they were not heeded. This committee and the religious affairs committee were the responsible authorities. The National Buddhist Association was not helpful either, nor were the metropolitan governments. One monk assured me that '10 out of 10' abbots will tell you that they are sad about this outcome. Many abbots continue to insist that the Vietnamese government can and should find the money to build a campus in either Hồ Chí Minh City or Cần Thơ. Perhaps the best indication of the unpopularity of the government's initiative is that the second intake of students at the Institute in Ô Môn, in 2011, consisted of just 30 students.

The Thai Connection

Khmers are not permitted to travel abroad to study. If they are desperate to do so, they can sneak across the border with Cambodia. But then they have to sneak back as well. Either way, if the police catch them, they will be thrown in jail for a very long time. The government says that those Khmer travelling abroad are seeking to engage in 'politics'. But Vietnamese are free to do so.

This criticism was delivered to me in 1999 by a monk in one of the biggest monasteries in Trà Vinh Province. In this and following years, I frequently heard Khmer monks speak of the serious lack of educational opportunities that Khmers in Vietnam confronted both in their traditional monastery system and the state system. Many people I met, old and young, conveyed to me their sentiments of intense anger at the oppression and mistreatment to which Khmers were subject, and their despair about the imminent demise of Khmer identity and culture. Abbots and monks sketched a claustrophobic scenario of being entombed within a Vietnamese-dominated world in which, slowly but surely, they were being suffocated.

However, this monk offered a ray of hope. He showed me the picture of one local monk who had managed to make it to Thailand. He was depicted studying Buddhism in a class of Thai monks. My host said indeed this individual had made it to Thailand, but he was not able to return.

In the early 2000s, I began to hear stories about Khmer monks who were studying Buddhism in Myanmar, Sri Lanka, Thailand, and even further afield. Persistent stories were told of one monk from Trà Vinh who was studying Buddhism in Sri Lanka. The abbot of another monastery was studying Buddhism in Myanmar. The legal status of these educational journeys was unknown. However, people speculated that the Vietnamese government would allow Khmer students to study in Myanmar because, like Vietnam, Myanmar had an authoritarian government that restricted freedom of expression and therefore Khmers residing there could not learn or say anything that was critical of the situation of the Khmers in Vietnam. Sri Lanka was so far away that monks who were studying there posed virtually no threat to the government.

The exploits of these monks were the subject of much discussion and admiration. One was described as a genius. He was noted for his exceptional intelligence, knowing five to six languages, some of which he had been able to master in a matter of months. In one week he had been able to learn the contents of an entire three-month course in computing. Another story, told to me in 2003 by student monks in Wat Somroang Ek, seemed to muddle the details of another monk's educational itinerary. The abbot of their monastery, they said, had been studying overseas in Canada for three years. He had completed the 12 years of Pali education in Trà Vinh, graduated from Year 12 of the state system, spent several years studying in Sài Gòn and in Hà Nội, studied for three years in Myanmar, and, they thought, he also had studied for a few years in Australia. 'His life is devoted to education alone.' They estimated that he had spent 30 years of his life studying.

The stories engendered an outpouring of hope. They outlined a potential pathway of educational mobility. They suggested that, by ordaining and studying Buddhism, it was possible to make it overseas; foreign locations were accessible, and they were attainable to those with the aptitude and dedication. The stories of these successful overseas educational journeys alleviated many Khmer people's sense that their lives, consciousness, and futures were to be confined exclusively to what Vietnam had in store for them. The possibility of studying abroad, however remote it may have been, captured the imagination of a great many monks and inspired in them the ambition to eventually make it overseas to study Buddhism. So many times did I hear monks express the aspiration to study overseas that it cannot be discounted as a significant factor behind the decision of many to ordain and to persist in the program of monastic studies.

In the mid-2000s, I began to see signs that the dream of overseas study was being realised. The new focus was Thailand. In 2006, I spoke with a group of monks in a monastery in Trà Vinh town. The monks wanted to practice English with me. One from Trà Cú had been ordained for ten years. His English was very good. He was also learning Thai and told me that he was planning to go to Thailand to study Buddhism for three years. When I returned to the temple the following year I was told that two of the monks I had met last time had departed for Thailand. Three of the monks were now speaking quite good English. They would also go to Thailand. 'This is a new place to study', they said. 'Five years ago, no Khmer monks were studying in Thailand.'

Increasingly, I heard stories of monks from a range of temples in Trà Vinh who had gone to study Buddhism in Thailand, or were preparing to do so. In 2006, monks told me that 12 Khmer Krom monks were currently studying Buddhism in Thailand. In September 2008, I was told that altogether 50 monks from Vietnam were studying in Thailand. In January 2013, the leading abbot of Trà Vinh Province reported that so far, over 100 students from Trà Vinh had studied in Thailand. The most popular destination is the Buddhist University Maha Chulalongkorn, in Bangkok, although Khmer Krom monks have also studied in universities in Chiang Mai and Surin.

The attraction of Thailand as a higher education study destination lies in the perception that Theravada Buddhism has reached a uniquely high level of development in that country. Monks told me that Thailand is a good place to study Buddhism because Buddhism is the state religion of Thailand and Buddhist education thus receives strong patronage from the state. New research is being done there, for example, transcription of the Pali sutras which are held in abundance in Buddhist monasteries, and deeper investigation into the religion, language, and law. Thailand has many people who have done PhD research into Buddhism. The country also appeals as a global centre or hub for Buddhism. One monk who was planning to study in Maha Chulalongkorn told me that this university teaches monks from Myanmar, Laos, Cambodia, Thailand, and Sri Lanka.

Nonetheless, it is clear that what is sought in these educational pilgrimages is broad-spectrum knowledge in secular subjects as much as of Buddhism itself. The opportunities it presented to study English and other non-traditional subjects at a high level was an important reason for Thailand's appeal. Monks in their early 20s in Wat Kompong Nikrodh said that the advantage of studying in Thailand or Myanmar over Cambodia is that the language of instruction is English. As the senior Pali teacher of another important Trà Vinh monastery told me:

> Four of my former students are now studying in Thailand. They have sought permission to study there for four years. They live in a monastery, still ordained as monks, and study English in a college in Bangkok. That is what they are there for. They want only to study 'outside' subjects like English, especially, and computing.

Thailand is considered a modern, sophisticated country where the quality of teaching is high. In 2010, I met a monk in rural Trà Vinh who had studied in Thailand for four years. He spent two years in Chiang Mai and two years in Maha Chulalongkorn. He studied English, Thai literature, and Buddhism. 'In Thailand, Buddhism is very advanced. The quality of teaching is high.' He had many foreign teachers in Chiang Mai, spoke English remarkably well, and was now teaching it in his home temple.

Another factor that works to the advantage of Thailand is the pressure the Vietnamese government is under from Khmer Krom people to provide them with reasonable educational options. As one monk noted, many monks yearn to study in Cambodia, where they can study in Khmer and take both Buddhist and non-Buddhist subjects. However, Cambodia is closed off as a path for higher studies because of political conditions. Internally, the government has been far from successful in providing an option of equivalent quality for higher-level education in Khmer studies or Buddhism. And few Khmer Krom monks are attracted to studying in Vietnam's own Buddhist universities, because of the markedly Vietnamese flavour of the curriculum, and Khmer monks' perceptions about discrimination within Vietnamese Buddhism against Khmer Theravada monks and practices. As student monks in a Trà Vinh monastery noted, the Vietnamese government is forced to allow monks to study in Thailand since it has failed to provide any other alternatives for their higher education.

Also having an effect on monks' study destinations are shifts in Cambodian official policy. Monks in Phnom Penh told me that, prior to 2007, monks from Trà Vinh frequently snuck across the border to Cambodia to continue their Buddhist education at high school and university levels. This illicit movement was tolerated by the Cambodian government, and the Cambodian Sangha abetted the flow by recognising the monastic studies program in Trà Vinh as a prerequisite for entering Cambodia's Buddhist universities. The peak was around 2007, when there were perhaps as many as 300 Khmer Krom students in monastic schools in Phnom Penh. However, demonstrations by Khmer Krom student monks in both Vietnam and Cambodia in that year led the Cambodian government to restrict the flow. The Cambodian Sangha withdrew its recognition of the Khmer monastic studies program in Trà Vinh as a prerequisite for higher-level studies in Cambodia. Monks told me that this had an immediate effect on the flow of Khmer Krom monks to Cambodia to undertake higher-level Buddhist studies. Now it is only Thailand that recognises the Vitchear Alai (high school) qualification in Trà Vinh, so many monks from Trà Vinh go straight into Buddhist university in Thailand.

A leading abbot of Trà Vinh Province told me that Thailand is the route preferred by the Vietnamese government for Khmer Krom monks to pursue university education. The state issues permits and passports to students, and it is easy for them to return to Vietnam to teach and work since this route is officially sponsored. It is also the path promoted by Vietnam's Khmer Buddhist association as the best option available at the present time. One of the reasons for the association to promote this route is to build up a cadre of teachers who will be able to teach in the temple schools.

The principal factor that puts a limit on studying in Thailand is the cost. Since the youths who take this route are exclusively from impoverished rural families, usually with only a fraction of a hectare of ricelands to their name, they have to rely on outside sources of funding. The first Khmer Krom monk to study overseas in the post-war years was sponsored by laypeople in the United States. He did his

English-language MA in Buddhist philosophy at the Buddhist and Pali University of Sri Lanka (established in 1981) in Colombo, and lived in Sri Lanka for nine years. He was ordained as a monk the entire time, staying in a monastery in Colombo. Many of the students who travel to Thailand similarly must rely on sponsorship from a wealthy layperson. Student monks from one famous temple in Trà Vinh told me that the abbot has paid for students to study in Thailand. But they are under bond. After returning from Thailand, the monks must teach in the temple for an equivalent length of time to repay the debt. Some excellent students also receive sponsorship from the Theravada Buddhist monks association.

However, as monks who contemplate the alternatives frequently observe, the problem with Buddhist higher education overseas is that one has to be wealthy to pursue it. If one is not among the few supported by the association, one has to pay transport costs, which are very expensive. Local institutions may allow monks to stay in the temple for free and one can rely on the alms round for meals, however, a host of additional expenses exist, such as for supplementary food and drinks, study materials, fees for additional study, and water and electricity fees. To prepare for study in Thailand, a monk has to study English and Thai for several years and arrange his own papers. Unless he finds a generous sponsor, a typical rural youth cannot afford these studies.

Nonetheless, the opening of a path to higher education in Thailand has had notable revitalising effects on the Khmer monastic program in Trà Vinh. It charged the whole enterprise with newfound purpose for monks to know that their studies in local monasteries had currency in the world beyond. Ordination provided them with the means to attain distinction according to criteria which had universal significance, and gave them hopes of gaining access to an arena of prestigious modernity. For a people who consider themselves imperilled by the Vietnamese institutions that envelop them, Thailand offers an escape route, an alternative path for development and self-realisation that is felt to be autonomous from the designs of the Vietnamese state. It also has unleashed unexpectedly a boom in the study of the English and Thai languages in temples deep in the countryside. And it gave new rigour to the study of Buddhist subjects, for these were to be emphasised in the Thai monastic curriculum.

This new pathway also has significant limitations. As already noted, such travels are not subsidised by the state, and the high cost of getting to Thailand means that only a few community-supported positions are available each year. Additionally, the investment in money and time in studying English and Thai are considerable, and put the option beyond the reach of the vast majority. All said, the Thai option is significantly more costly and less accessible than the traditional path to higher education in Cambodia, which is closer and does not require additional linguistic preparation. However, the major disadvantage of studying in Thailand is that it does not provide any opportunities for studying Khmer at a higher level, learning more about Khmer culture and history, or gaining practical experience in Khmer as a sophisticated functional language. One leading abbot who was instrumental in forging the option of studying in Thailand confided to me his regrets that the emphasis in Thailand is on studying Buddhism, while there is no emphasis on historical and Khmer cultural heritage subjects. Such a pathway therefore runs the risk of turning the Khmer monastic education system in Trà Vinh into a foundational religious studies course, rendering as extraneous the Khmer cultural literacy subjects that many believe to be the most crucial elements of the monastic studies program.

Pilgrimages to the Cultural Centre

Considering the inadequacies of these options for higher monastic education, it is not surprising that many student monks in Trà Vinh continue to regard Cambodia as the best destination for undertaking higher-level studies. Despite the illicit nature of such journeys, the likelihood of being arrested or surveilled on one's return, and the risks to employment opportunities and one's status as a monk, many student monks choose to make the journey. It is widely known in Trà Vinh that many monks have left for Cambodia to undertake higher-level studies. One of the top abbots in the province, who holds an important official position, described it as the 'private route' (*pleu aecachun*), deliberately refusing to call it illegal, but distinguishing it from the officially sanctioned route to Thailand. He had no doubt that more monks from Trà Vinh were studying in Cambodia than in Thailand or elsewhere, and he told me calmly that this was understandable, since Cambodia was the traditional destination for monks from this province to pursue their higher-level studies.

Over a period of years of visiting Phnom Penh, I met many Khmer monks from Vietnam who were studying in the capital city's higher education institutions. Most came from Trà Vinh, although monks from Vĩnh Long and Sóc Trăng were also well represented. I could not obtain official statistics, but in 2012 the consensus was that several hundred Khmer Krom monks were currently enrolled in educational institutions in Phnom Penh. They resided in many monasteries, some of the largest concentrations being in Wat Maha Muntrey, Wat Potum Wattey, Wat Somraong Andeth, Wat Unnalom, Wat Tuol Sangke, Wat Uttara Wattey, Wat Langka, and one unregistered Khmer Krom temple. Like the many thousands of student monks from rural Cambodia residing in Phnom Penh monasteries, the monks observed standard monastic routines while also studying full time. Some were repeating Buddhist secondary school years in the temples, while others were undertaking educational programs outside the *wat*. They were enrolled in a remarkable range of undergraduate and graduate programs, including in Phnom Penh's two Buddhist universities, and in numerous secular state and private colleges and universities where they studied a great variety of subjects.

Every one of these intelligent and serious people, the cream of Trà Vinh Khmer society, had crossed the border into Cambodia illegally. Their stories of cross-border travel were frequently adventurous. The story of Luk Sone provides an example.

Luk Sone resides in one of Phnom Penh's famous inner city temples. He comes from Trà Cú District in Trà Vinh. He is the oldest of seven children. His younger brother, a lay student, is in the temple with him. The rest of his family is back at home. He came to Cambodia in 2002 because he wanted to study at a university. The quality, level, and resources for Khmer education in Vietnam were too low for him to study further than the fourth year of the Butikah Saksa program. When he crossed the border, he went with a travel organiser, to whom he paid 900,000 VND to arrange his travel. He went in a group by bus. When he got to the border, he removed his upper torso robe and put on a shirt, coat, pants, and a hat to conceal his monastic appearance, keeping on only his lower body robe — by keeping that on he remained ordained. He did not carry travel papers. Some of the money he paid was used to facilitate informal cross-border passage arranged by the tour operator.

All of the Khmer student monks I met in Phnom Penh had crossed the border furtively, avoiding the border posts by detouring around them or by disguising their monastic identity. They were reluctant to describe the specifics of their journeys when other monks were present, either explaining that it was very difficult to talk about the topic, or falling silent when I probed for details.

The Khmer Krom student monks I met in Phnom Penh in 2009–13 were products of the monastic education program in Trà Vinh. Most had been monks for over 15 years, having first ordained in the mid-1990s. The typical biography was of a man from a poor rural family who ordained in his early to mid-teens, having already studied Khmer literacy in the temple in the evenings or summer breaks, or while engaged as a temple boy (*khmeng wat*). After a year's probationary ordination, they had entered the monastic program, completing both the intermediate and high school stages, or seven years in total, in the period between 1995 and 2005. Some then continued teaching literacy or higher-level subjects in their home temples. They were good students and were ambitious to study further, but had reached the upper limits of the Khmer-language monastic education available in Vietnam.

Like Luk Sone, many told me that they had come to Cambodia in order to continue Buddhist studies at the university level. Members of this cohort had completed their monastic schooling in Vietnam prior to the founding of the Khmer Buddhist studies institute in Ô Môn or the opening of the path to Thailand as a viable destination for university-level studies. Several of them had enrolled in one of the two Buddhist studies universities in Phnom Penh — Preah Sihanouk Reach, run by the Mahanikay order, and Preah Sihamoni Reach, run by the Thommayut order — both located close to the Royal Palace. Each had a four-year undergraduate program which taught standard subjects such as the monastic code, Pali–Khmer translation, and Buddhist history — at a deeper level than was taught in Trà Vinh — along with subjects such as philosophy, Sanskrit, comparative world religions, and Buddhism in Khmer literature, which, prior to 2007, were not taught in Vietnam. They each also offered graduate level studies which required students to complete a thesis under supervision. Hence these students' reason for coming to Cambodia was to progress to a higher level of study than was locally available, in a place, format and language accessible to poor rural youths, and in a locality that for generations had been a peak destination for Khmer-language monastic education.

Also prominent among the reasons given for travelling to Cambodia was to undertake studies in secular subjects. I met Khmer Krom monks in Phnom Penh who were enrolled in English, accounting, computing, tourism, agricultural development, and educational management courses at the undergraduate and graduate levels. Their opportunities for studying such subjects in Vietnam were practically non-existent. Coming from Khmer-dominated rural areas of the Mekong Delta, where state schooling at all levels was weakly developed and of poor quality, most had only elementary-level Vietnamese schooling, and their Vietnamese language was very basic. The tough entry requirements, costs, and distance and unfamiliarity of Vietnamese colleges and universities posed intimidating barriers to gaining a high-level secular education. By contrast, such options were within reach in Cambodia, where student monks were supported by laypeople and resided free of charge in temples close to a range of educational institutions which used their mother tongue as a language of instruction. As in Thailand, the monkhood served as an avenue of social mobility for poor rural youths who would otherwise lack opportunities for worldly advancement (Wyatt 1966; Tambiah 1976). Such instrumentalist reasons were not inconsistent with monastic vocations for, as one monk put it, the essential purpose of ordination is to gain knowledge.

For many Khmer Krom students, Cambodia beckons as a cosmopolitan centre, a place where foreigners brush shoulders with Khmers, where international languages are widely spoken and can be learned easily. One monk from the backwater village of O To Tung in Kompong Spien had been in Phnom Penh for six years. When I met him in 2012 he had been studying English for four years. He told me that his primary reason for coming to Cambodia was to study English, and explained how he had come to this decision: 'When I was ordained, some monks from my home temple came home from Cambodia to visit and they were speaking in fluent English. It created a strong impression in me and I wanted to speak this language as well as them.'

A significant underlying reason for monks wanting to undertake higher education in Cambodia in either the 'religious' or 'secular' streams is the unique opportunity it provides to improve their capacity in their native language. Courses and assignments at this level push students to a very high standard of written and spoken Khmer, take them into specialised realms of expression and vocabulary not commonplace in rural communities, give them knowledge of the etymological roots of their language, and expose them to new expressions. In addition to the huge range of texts used in the classroom is the plethora of media, popular books, and signage all around them in this Khmer cultural metropolis. This is a highly significant factor for students for whom the only examples of Khmer writing are the handful of photocopied texts from Cambodia used in temple schools. Khmer people in Vietnam live in a social environment devoid of written Khmer, where Khmer is a pedagogic language rather than a language of functional cultural citizenship, and where all debates, laws, and discussions are conducted in Vietnamese. Students value the depth, breadth and dynamism of this rich and immersive linguistic experience and access to the metropolitan centre of their language.

More important still, and common to all students, is the nature of study in Cambodia as a quest for cultural identity. Many of them expressed doubts about the integrity of the Khmer monastic education program they had been through in Vietnam. A monk who had come to Cambodia to study in the secondary level of the monastic curriculum told me:

> The most important subject for me is Khmer. It is the main reason I came here to study. In the monastic studies program in my province, Vietnamese language and content are mixed in with the Khmer curriculum. Few books in Khmer language are available for study or deeper research. And one cannot study subjects such as Khmer geography or history. Thus Khmer people cannot learn about their origins [*daem kamnaat*], their identity. Also, Khmer morality and culture are not taught unlike in the monastic curriculum in Cambodia. The quality of monastic education is higher in Cambodia. Classes in the monastic curriculum are broader [*bauk tu lie chien*].

Another monk had completed 12 years of the Khmer Buddhist monastic curriculum in Trà Cú District Trà Vinh, epicentre of the Khmer studies program. He then taught what he had learnt to novices and young Bhikku in his temple. After three years he wanted to study further, so he asked his abbot for permission to travel to Cambodia, and the abbot agreed. He did not ask permission from the authorities, because they would not grant it. So he crossed the border illegally:

> I wanted to study in Cambodia because the Vietnamese government tightly restricts what can be learnt in Khmer schools. In fact, only seven subjects can be taught in the monastic high school in Vietnam, half as many as in Cambodia. Several subjects are forbidden, such as history and geography. And the content of the allowable subjects is greatly restricted. The depth and breadth of subjects in Cambodian schools is much greater. I know this because I have studied in both places. The Vietnamese government does not want the Khmer Krom to know about their history because if they do they will feel anger, sorrow, pity and will demand to do something about it. They will join together to ask for their country back.

I spoke with several abbots and university lecturers in Phnom Penh temples who agreed Khmer Krom monks had a mixture of motivations for studying further. However, the most pressing one is to learn more about their culture, their language.

One senior monk who lectures at Preah Sihanouk Reach Buddhist University said that there are many Khmer Krom students at his university. 'They are more accomplished [*boukae*] than student monks from Kampuchea. They work very hard. Most monks from Kampuchea Krom want to study in Cambodia.' The Khmer Krom students at his university come from all provinces of Kampuchea Krom. Those from Trà Vinh (*Preah Trapeang*) are highly represented. He commented:

> The monks in Preah Trapeang are very strong [*khlang*]. They are like Buddhist soldiers. Their desire to protect their culture is very strong. They have a sense that they alone can prevent the loss of Khmer culture. Girls too study in the Buddhist program for the same reason. It is quite rare for girls in rural areas of Cambodia to attend the Buddhist studies program.

We can see that Cambodia continues to act as a powerful magnet for Khmer Krom monks who see it in multiple respects as a highly desirable educational destination. The knowledge that can be obtained in Cambodia is judged to be broader, deeper, and more reliable and pure than what can be gained in Vietnam. The educational pilgrimage to Cambodia provides self-knowledge about one's origins and language, and an immersive experience in modern Khmer cultural trends that cannot be obtained elsewhere, be it in Vietnam or Thailand. It provides exposure to contemporary and practical forms of knowledge that otherwise are inaccessible.

Impossible Returns, Lasting Divides

Having made the journey to Phnom Penh for an education, many Khmer Krom see no reason to return to Vietnam. For instance, one person from Bạc Liêu came to Cambodia because he wanted to study English. He told me that the quality of English teaching and learning in Cambodia is much better than in Vietnam. He came as a layperson and ordained for eight years while studying, because he wanted to be a monk. Ordination also allowed him access to free accommodation in a conveniently located urban temple, as well as donations from laypersons. Then, when he graduated, he left the monkhood, married and bought a house in the suburbs of Phnom Penh. He now works selling medicinal oil (*prieng ktchol*) in various places in the capital.

A monk from Vĩnh Long, residing in a central city temple, told me that the quality of secular education in Cambodia is better than in Vietnam. That, in addition to the paucity of Khmer-language books and the lack of a robust university-level Buddhist studies course in Vietnam, is why he came to Phnom Penh to study, crossing the border illegally to do so:

> For Khmer Krom, it is easier to get a good education in English and other subjects in Cambodia than in Vietnam. Plus for Khmers there are many more work opportunities in Cambodia. For an educated Khmer person, it is very difficult to get good quality jobs in Vietnam.

He told me that he definitely will not return to live or work in Vietnam, even to retire, although he misses his family. One reason for this thinking was the lack of work opportunities in Vietnam. However, in addition, as a monk who has studied in Cambodia, he would be impeded in making a living in Vietnam — he would be suspected and restricted in obtaining work for the government, as a teacher, or in the business sector.

As this comment indicates, gaining access to this centre of knowledge has high costs. Having broken the law in crossing the border without official permission, student monks are unable to return to Vietnam.

Monks say they would be arrested or persecuted by the police if they attempted to return. In all probability, it is not the small infraction of an illegal border crossing that makes them vulnerable to prosecution, but the threat they pose to the Vietnamese order. Having amassed new knowledge about their culture, history, and origins, they have made themselves into a resource that has the potential to threaten the prevailing regime of truth in their homeland. For them to display their cultural competencies in Vietnam would challenge the Vietnamese pedagogic order, for it would demonstrate that officially prescribed channels of educational mobility are not necessarily the best way for the citizens of the Mekong Delta to gain an education.

One of the unexpected consequences of this educational movement to Cambodia is that nearly all the monks who have followed this path have renounced Vietnamese citizenship, and have sought and obtained Cambodian citizenship and passports. They have charted plans for permanent residence in Cambodia, and have no intention to return to live or work in Vietnam. Superficially, this switch in citizenship might seem like a sign of their blind devotion to Cambodia, or to their own educational careers, and could be read as their abandonment of their Khmer compatriots who live in Vietnam. In actuality, the reverse is true. Ironically, it is the desire to return home to visit family, attend ceremonies, and maintain relations with their former teachers and peers that has led them to take out Cambodian citizenship. The only way they can return home and avoid persecution by the Vietnamese authorities is as the citizen of another country, under the protection of its embassy and of international law.

The ability for Khmer Krom monks to obtain Cambodian passports for travel to Vietnam appears to be a relatively new development. It possibly dates to around 2010, for I did not hear about it before then, and before 2010 I had never met a Khmer student monk in Vietnam on a return trip from Cambodia. However, in the years 2011–14, I met several Khmer Krom student monks who had travelled home on short visits using a Cambodian passport. They went to visit family, attend funerals, pick up funds, or attend the Khmer New Year, Pchum Ben, and Oc Omboc festivals. One told me he goes back once a year for about 10 days at a time. The experience is never comfortable:

> I have been back to my village several times but only because I have a Cambodian passport. If I did not have it, I would be in big trouble with the police. Even so, when I visit, the police always approach me

and ask all sorts of questions. The local police are contacted by the higher authorities and told that I am a bad person who committed a crime by leaving the country illegally. As a result, they always follow me and question me. You mightn't realise you are being observed when sitting, talking and laughing with a group of monks. But after you leave them, they are questioned by the police. As a result people are very reticent about what they say to me when I visit.

This was confirmed by another student monk: 'Now we have Cambodian passports, we can visit home, but are followed by police everywhere we go. This happened to me when I visited my home town for a week. I was followed every single day.'

While short, heavily policed home visits are allowed, student monks are deterred from making longer visits. None of them thinks it would be possible to return home to work as a teacher or in any other capacity. This assessment was echoed by a leading Cambodian Buddhist university lecturer who had worked with scores of such students:

Khmer monks from Vietnam who study in Phnom Penh never return to Vietnam to live and work. They can go back to visit for a few days but if they try to stay longer they are followed and questioned. They are suspected of being involved in politics and spreading information about history and forming a network with nationalists in Cambodia.

One monk told me that he would like to go back to Vietnam and teach, but the police would not allow anyone who has studied in Cambodia to do so, because such people know too much.

And what they know would cause their students to rise up and protest against the government. The government wants people to forget their history. It would be very difficult for him to return.

He knows of just one person who returned, but that person disrobed.

As a result of these acute sensitivities, a significant number of the most talented, ambitious, and knowledgeable Khmer Krom people have left Vietnam and are unable or unwilling to return. Pending a shift in Vietnamese government policy, which seems unlikely, those monks who travel to study in Cambodia are destined to remain there for the rest of their lives. In consequence, they are unable to repatriate their knowledge and experience, be that in Khmer culture, Buddhism, or other areas of expertise. This situation has led to the pooling on one side of the border of numerous culturally competent Khmer Krom people who are able to contribute to Cambodia's cultural and political life. On the other side of the border, Khmers in Vietnam lack a viable means to reproduce their cultural tradition and hence are deprived of the means to achieve cultural equivalence with respect to their counterparts in both Cambodia and Vietnam.

This comes as a significant cost to Vietnam, in the form of a brain drain affecting one of the country's largest minority groups, which loses the benefits of the social reinvestments that would flow from the return of these students and their repatriation of a variety of forms of valuable knowledge. In response, the Vietnamese government has had to build up an alternative infrastructure of secular educational institutions in order to replace what it has dismantled. At the same time, in order to counter the accusation that the closure of the educational route to Cambodia is designed to assimilate the Khmers, the government has had to keep in place a Khmer-language education system that mirrors the Cambodian national system. Ironically, the price to be paid for detaching the Khmer Krom from Cambodia's cultural sphere is tending to the faithful reproduction of Cambodian-style cultural institutions within Vietnam itself. It is difficult for the Vietnamese government to compete respectably on this terrain, and thus it is permanently vulnerable to the criticism that denying the Khmer Krom educational access to Cambodia has deprived them of access to social mobility, traditional and modern knowledge, religious expertise, and the ability to reproduce themselves socially and culturally.

References

Chandler, David 2008, *A History of Cambodia* (fourth edition), Silkworm Books, Chiang Mai.

Chealy, Chet 2009, 'Higher Education in Cambodia', in Yasushi Hirosato and Yuto Kitamura (eds), *The Political Economy of Educational Reforms and Capacity Development in Southeast Asia: Cases of Cambodia, Laos and Vietnam*, Springer, Netherlands, pp. 153–165.

Edwards, Penny 2007, *Cambodge: The Cultivation of a Nation, 1860–1945*, University of Hawaii Press, Honolulu.

Geertz, Clifford 1963, 'The Integrative Revolution: Primordial Sentiments and Civil Politics in the New States', in Clifford Geertz (ed.), *Old Societies and New States: The Quest for Modernity in Asia and Africa*, Collier-Macmillan, London, pp. 105–157.

Hansen, Anne 2007, *How to Behave: Buddhism and Modernity in Colonial Cambodia*, University of Hawaii Press, Honolulu.

Harris, Ian 2009, 'Theravada Buddhism among the Khmer Krom', in Khmers Kampuchea Krom Foundation, *The Khmer-Krom Journey to Self-Determination,* Khmers Kampuchea Krom Foundation, Pennsauken, NJ, pp. 103–126.

Harris, Ian 2012, *Buddhism in a Dark Age: Cambodian Monks under Pol Pot*, University of Hawaii Press, Honolulu.

Kabilsingh, Chatsumarn 1986, 'Buddhism and National Development: A Case Study of Buddhist Universities', in Bruce Matthews and Judith Nagata (eds), *Religion, Values and Development in Southeast Asia*, ISEAS Publications, Singapore, pp. 62–81.

Kalab, Milada 1976, 'Monastic Education, Social Mobility and Village Structure in Cambodia', in David Banks (ed.), *Changing Identities in Modern Southeast Asia*, Mouton, The Hague, pp. 155–169.

Keyes, Charles 1971, 'Buddhism and National Integration in Thailand', *Journal of Asian Studies*, vol. 30, no. 3, pp. 551–567.

Keyes, Charles 1994, 'Communist Revolution and the Buddhist Past in Cambodia', in Charles Keyes, Laurel Kendall and Helen Hardacre (eds), *Asian Visions of Authority: Religion and the Modern States of East and Southeast Asia*, University of Hawaii Press, Honolulu, pp. 43–74.

Kiernan, Ben 1981, 'Origins of Khmer Communism', *Southeast Asian Affairs*, pp. 161–180.

Kiernan, Ben 1996, *The Pol Pot Regime: Race, Power and Genocide in Cambodia Under the Khmer Rouge, 1975–79*, University of California Press, Berkeley.

Malleret, Louis 1946, 'La Minorité Cambodgienne de Cochinchine', *Bulletin de la Société des Etudes Indochinoises*, vol. 21, pp. 19–34.

Marston, John 2014, 'Reestablishing the Cambodian Monkhood', in John Marston (ed.), *Ethnicity, Borders, and the Grassroots Interface with the State: Studies on Southeast Asia in Honor of Charles F. Keyes*, Silkworm Books, Chiang Mai.

McDaniel, Justin 2008, *Gathering Leaves and Lifting Words: Histories of Buddhist Monastic Education in Laos and Thailand*, University of Washington Press, Seattle.

Société des Etudes Indochinoises 1903, *Monographie de la Province de Tra-Vinh*, Imprimerie L. Menard, Saigon.

Sovanratana, Khy 2008, 'Buddhist Education Today', in Alexandra Kent and David Chandler (eds), *People of Virtue: Reconfiguring Religion, Power and Moral Order in Cambodia Today*, NIAS Press, Copenhagen, pp. 257–271.

Stuart-Fox, Martin 1996, *Buddhist Kingdom, Marxist State: The Making of Modern Laos*, White Lotus, Bangkok.

Tagliacozzo, Eric 2013, *The Longest Journey: Southeast Asians and the Pilgrimage to Mecca,* Oxford University Press, Oxford.

Tambiah, Stanley 1976, *World Conqueror and World Renouncer: A Study of Buddhism and Polity in Thailand against a Historical Background*, University of Cambridge Press, Cambridge.

Taylor, Philip 2014, *The Khmer Lands of Vietnam: Environment, Cosmology and Sovereignty*, University of Hawaii Press, Honolulu; NUS Press, Singapore.

Wyatt, David 1966, 'The Buddhist Monkhood as an Avenue of Social Mobility in Traditional Thai Society', *Sinlapakon,* vol. 10, no. 1, pp. 41–52.

9

Described, Inscribed, Written Off: Heritagisation as (Dis)connection

Oscar Salemink

Preamble

In 2011, UNESCO inscribed the fourteenth-century Citadel of the Hồ Dynasty in Vietnam's Thanh Hòa Province on the World Heritage List, thereby both recognising and rewarding Vietnam's efforts in conserving the archaeological site, as well as obliging it to meet UNESCO's official conservation standards. In an article titled 'Hồ Citadel the Site of a Modern Conflict' in the English-language newspaper *Việt Nam News* of 8 June 2014, Deputy Director of the Centre for Conservation of the Hồ Dynasty Citadel World Heritage, Nguyễn Xuân Toán, lamented that local people continued to 'build houses and other civil works' in the area, in violation of conservation regulations, and in spite of awareness-raising meetings. The district authorities do not wish to forbid construction of houses within certain limits, but have a plan for the gradual removal of cultivation fields from the site, and according to journalist Hồng Thúy, local people would be happy to move if they receive adequate compensation. The conflict referred to in the title is, therefore, not just a conflict between the Conservation Centre and local people, but between the centre and the district authorities, with Mr Toán complaining that 'the Centre for Conservation of the Hồ Dynasty Citadel World Heritage does not have the authority to mete out punishments on violators when they detect infringement of the site'. Mr Toán is supported by the Ministry of Culture, Sports and Tourism in Hanoi: 'Management and preservation at the site will not improve unless the centre's power is enhanced, said Deputy Director of the Ministry of Culture, Sports and Tourism's Cutural Heritage Department, Nguyễn Quốc Hùng'.[1] The news report construes this as a conflict between two government agencies — district authorities and heritage management authorities — but the conflict is over the power to evict local inhabitants whose livelihood practices are, since 2011, branded 'an infringement of the site'; local people are enemies of conservation.

Introduction

The 'heritage conflict' reported above suggests that the proclamation of heritage affects people living with or close to that heritage in various ways; it might result in their dispossession of land, objects, or the product of their labour. Since the 1993 inscription of the former imperial capital of Huế on the World Heritage List, Vietnam has made great efforts to have its cultural heritage recognised by UNESCO as world heritage. Belatedly, beginning with its monumental heritage (Huế town, Hội An town, Mỹ Sơn temple complex, the Imperial Citadel of Thăng Long, Citadel of the Hồ Dynasty), natural heritage (Hạ Long Bay, and Phong Nha Kẻ Bàng National Park), and mixed heritage (Tràng An Landscape Complex), Vietnam has more recently focused on its 'Intangible Cultural Heritage' (abbreviated by UNESCO as 'ICH'). In 1994, Vietnam hosted UNESCO's first ICH 'expert meeting', on the cultures of ethnic minorities and of Huế. Even before the ICH lists were formalised, in 2003, the year of the ICH Convention, *nhã nhạc* court music from Huế was recognised as a cultural treasure, and in 2005 the gong music (*không gian văn hóa cồng chiêng*) of ethnic minorities in Vietnam's Central Highlands. In addition, since 2009, Quan họ, Ca trù, Xoan and Đơn ca tài tử, Ví and Giặm singing, and the Gióng Festival of Phù Đổng and Sóc temples, and the Worship of the Hùng Kings in Phú Thọ have been inscribed.

---

1   vietnamnews.vn/in-bai/255933/ho-citadel-the-site-of-a-modern-conflict.htm, accessed 16 November 2014.

In this chapter, I propose to look at Vietnam's rapid heritagisation since 1993 in terms of connection and disconnection with reference to the inspirational ideas about spectacularisation in Guy Debord's pamphlet *The Society of the Spectacle* (1994). For Debord: 'The spectacle is not a collection of images; it is a social relation between people that is mediated by images' (Debord 1994:4).[2] For Debord, modern industrial society is 'fundamentally spectaclist' in the sense that the spectacle has become autonomous in two senses. On the one hand, spectacularisation is based on the separation between spheres of production and consumption, which is akin to Marx's alienation of workers from the product of their labour, leading Debord to argue that the spectacle is a visual reflection of the social order. On the other hand, spectacle refers to the separation between reality and image, between thing and sign, where the image becomes the end-product of the 'dominant system of production', and where the spectacle is 'the visual reflection of the ruling economic order', and 'aims at nothing other than itself' (Debord 2002:§14). But at the same time the separation gets blurred, because 'when the real world is transformed into mere images, mere images become real beings', and 'wherever *representation* becomes independent, the spectacle regenerates itself' (Debord 2002:§18, original italics) as the visualisation, self-indulgence and enjoyment of power.

For Debord:

> *Separation* is the alpha and omega of the spectacle. The institutionalization of the social division of labor in the form of class divisions had given rise to an earlier, religious form of contemplation: the mythical order with which every power has always camouflaged itself. Religion justified the cosmic and ontological order that corresponded to the interests of the masters, expounding and embellishing everything their societies *could not deliver*. In this sense, all separate power has been spectacular ... The general separation of worker and product tends to eliminate any direct personal communication between the producers and any comprehensive sense of what they are producing. With the increasing accumulation of separate products and the increasing concentration of the productive

---

2   Debord's book contains 221 numbered paragraphs of varying length — from one sentence to half a page — and it is to these paragraphs that I refer. There exist many different English translations of this book, which is notoriously difficult to translate. I use two different translations (Debord 1994, 2002).

process, communication and comprehension are monopolized by the managers of the system. The triumph of this separation-based economic system proletarianizes the whole world ... In the spectacle, a part of the world presents itself to the world and is superior to it. The spectacle is simply the common language of this separation [which] is experienced by the producers as an *abundance of dispossession* (Debord 2002: §25, 26, 29, 31).

Heritage is arguably a Debordian spectacle, in the sense that something that was an object to use, a place to live, a place of worship or an object to worship, or a ritualised event, becomes an image of such cultural sites, objects or practices representing the past. Temporally speaking, part of the attraction of heritage lies in its claim to represent the past and to point the way towards the future. In a recent essay, I suggested that heritagisation constitutes an appropriation of the past and thus an attempt to control the future by certain elites that alienate other groups in the process, as well as an attempt to control the economic value of the commoditised heritage, in the world's biggest economic industry, tourism (Salemink 2014). Thus, heritagisation does not only involve a connection with the nation, but simultaneously instigates a twin movement of separation, namely between the cultural sites, objects and/or practices, and their spectacular image; and between the sites, objects or practices, and their producers, makers, authors and/ or performers. Thus, heritagisation as a formally ritualised connection with the nation paradoxically comes at a price of local disconnection from the cultural site, object, or practice that is officially labelled cultural heritage. In this chapter, I argue that the heritagisation of cultural sites, objects, and practices effectively disenfranchises the cultural communities involved from the legacy that they formed over years of cultural and ritual labour, as other players — cultural experts and scientists, state agencies, tourist companies — effectively take over the management and organisation of the heritage for their own benefit. In other words, as particular cultural sites, objects and practices are connected nationally and internationally through a process of heritagisation, their constituencies paradoxically become disconnected from that part of their legacy as outsiders take over. Thus, movements of connection and disconnection operate simultaneously or consecutively at different levels. In other words, the description and inscription of heritage sites, objects and practices result in the writing off of the constituent communities as viable and reliable cultural agents.

I unfold my argument about simultaneous and subsequent connection and disconnection through heritagisation in the following sections. The next section discusses the concept of heritagisation as it emerged during the global heritage 'boom'. The subsequent section, 'Intangible Cultural Heritage in Vietnam', briefly describes the history of UNESCO-certified heritage in Vietnam. This will be followed by three sections looking more closely into one specific intangible cultural heritage, namely the 'Space of Gong Culture' and its cultural subjects situated in the still contentious Central Highlands as well as their role in the 'Worship of the Hùng Kings' in Phú Thọ Province. In a final section, I offer some reflections on heritagisation in Vietnam in terms of connection and disconnection, of incorporation and separation, of instrumentalisation and dispossession.

Heritagisation as a Global Process

In 1996, David Lowenthal published his influential book, *Possessed by the Past: The Heritage Crusade and the Spoils of History*, in which he tried to come to terms with the overnight ascendancy of heritage, and offered partial answers to the question of why heritage labels, claims, and practices had become so pervasive, so ubiquitous   how all sorts of different *legacies* have become heritage; how heritage is connected up with a particular understanding and use of the past through history; and how it generates rivalry, competition, and conflict. Lowenthal placed emphasis on the partisan use of heritage claims for presentist purposes, and on what I would probably call aspects of faith in and sacralisation of specific historical narratives about the past.

In his recent *Heritage: Critical Approaches*, Rodney Harrison (2013) also speaks of the ubiquity of heritage and of the heritage boom in 'late modernity', but rather than as a fixation on the past, Harrison interprets this heritage boom 'as a creative engagement with the past in the present' which helps us shape our future (Harrison 2013:4). Heritage, then, is a 'relationship between people, objects, places and practices', and 'is concerned with the various ways in which humans and non-humans are linked by chains of *connectivity* and work together to keep the past alive in the present for the future' Harrison (2013:4– 5, original italics). In a chapter on 'Late-Modernity and the Heritage Boom', Harrison points to globalisation, migration, and demographic changes; deindustrialisation in the West and the rise of the 'knowledge economy'; the emergence of travel, leisure, and 'experience' as marketable commodities; and the commercialisation of the past as factors in the emergence of a 'heritage boom' after the Second World War, but especially since 1970. This heritage boom went hand in hand with a pervasive process of heritagisation, by which 'objects and places are transformed from functional "things" into objects of display and exhibition' (Harrison 2013:69). Although Harrison seeks to contextualise the 'heritage boom' in a particular condition of 'late modernity', he fails to draw attention to the simultaneity of the global heritagisation process with the neoliberalisation of the global economy, starting in the United States under Reagan and the United Kingdom under Thatcher. I will return to this connection later.

The concept of heritagisation was coined by Robert Hewison in his book *The Heritage Industry: Britain in a Climate of Decline* (1987), in which he refers to the heritagisation of certain sites. This spatial meaning was picked up by Nikki Macleod (2006), Melanie Smith (2009), and since then a host of other scholars, who use the concept of heritagisation with reference to certain sites and places — i.e. tangible cultural heritage — usually in Europe. But in a 2007 article in *Current Anthropology*, Breidenbach and Nyíri draw attention to the differential effects of the process of 'global heritagisation' of certain heritage sites (Breidenbach and Nyíri 2007:322) in terms of affecting the 'consumption' of nature and heritage in post-socialist Russia and China. They assert that the globalising narrative of World Heritage must be read in the context of distinctive national contexts — a valid observation for Vietnam as well. But heritage is not just about pedagogy (about how to preserve, how to be a proper citizen) and consumption (of heritage sites and practices).

Beyond the notions of instrumentality that the notion of heritagisation calls forth, Yaniv Poria (2010) draws attention to the effect heritagisation produces among visitors, who may or may not have a (tenuous) link with the community linked to, or owning, the heritage site. He does so while analysing visual displays of heritage sites, and the 'stories behind the picture' that are conveyed through such visual displays. A different meaning of heritagisation was suggested by Kevin Walsh (1992) in his *The Representation of the Past: Museums and Heritage in the Postmodern World*, in which he speaks not only of a transformation of certain spaces (in terms of aestheticisation), but also of the past.

Heritagisation involves an ahistoric aestheticisation of the past, which as a result has only 'few local associations or affiliations'. Still referring to heritagisation in spatial terms, he also includes temporal ('past'), representational ('aesthetics'), and constituency ('community') dimensions in his discussion.

To my knowledge, the spatial connotation of heritagisation in terms of heritage sites remained dominant — if poorly elaborated — until Regina Bendix published 'Heritage Between Economy and Politics: An Assessment from the Perspective of Cultural Anthropology' (Bendix 2009). Although refraining from a strict definition, Bendix offered the most comprehensive treatment of heritagisation to date, based on the intuitive notion that it refers to the elevation of particular objects (art, monuments, landscapes, memorial sites) and practices (performances, music, rituals, and related cultural practices and memories) to the status of heritage as something to be consciously preserved for present and future generations. This process is necessarily selective, as not all cultural memory will gain this status. Her work is not only interesting in that she explicitly includes intangible cultural heritage in her discussion, but also because she points to some of the necessary transformations brought about by the canonisation of certain places and practices as heritage: the strategic invocation of tradition and authenticity; the projection of identity and cultivation of symbolic capital; the contestation of heritage values; and the symbolic work of marketing. Bendix also notes that the temporal and social axes of heritagisation move closer together. Along the temporal axis, whereas in the nineteenth and early twentieth centuries only historical sites referring to a distant past were seen as heritage, these days contemporary phenomena such as industrial heritage, digital archives, and, indeed, intangible cultural heritage are seen as worthy of heritage recognition. Along the social axis, whereas past heritage practice focused on elite structures (temples, royal compounds), now labour class and ethnic minority cultural practices could officially be labelled heritage. As cultural heritage becomes an object inviting or requiring action from society, the economy and politics, heritagisation involves not only a process of canonisation (or 'ennobling') of cultural practice, but also of its instrumentalisation. Bendix specifically mentions competition and quality control through evaluation (Bendix 2009).

In this connection I would like to mention two other recent essays that are relevant for this topic. In 'World Heritage and Cultural Economics', Barbara Kirshenblatt-Gimblett (2006) discusses some of the paradoxes underlying the global 'world heritage' programme, in the sense that especially intangible cultural heritage is on the one hand unique — and uniquely tied to a particular group or community of people — and on the other hand universal — in the sense of a heritage for humanity, to be mediated and managed by the nation. Kirshenblatt-Gimblett does not use the term heritagisation, but rather the term metacultural operation, which similarly involves codification practices and the development of 'universal standards [that] obscure the historically and culturally specific character of heritage policy and practices' (Kirshenblatt-Gimblett 2006:19). Distinguishing between tangible cultural heritage dealing with objects, and intangible cultural heritage dealing with living subjects, often ethnic minorities, she then asserts that such cultural subjects — the 'culture carriers' of UNESCO — are bearers of cultural rights, as a subset of the universal human rights. But where culture becomes evaluated, valued and valuable, these rights are in jeopardy, as their valuation — the value that these people attach to their heritage — becomes entangled with the cultural, historical or artistic valorisation by outside experts and, ultimately, the (potential) economic value in terms of cultural economics, especially tourism.

In 'Indigenous Cultural Heritage in Development and Trade: Perspectives from the Dynamics of Cultural Heritage Law and Policy', Rosemary Coombe and Joseph Turcotte discuss the ICH regime from the vantage point of international law, trade and property. They assert that:

> The new emphasis on inventorising ICH, reifying it, assigning appropriate caretakers for it, and investing in capacity-building to develop local expertise, arguably constitutes a new regime of power which poses both promise and peril for the local communities and indigenous peoples deemed to bear the distinctive culture that these new regimes seek to value. (Coombe and Turcotte 2012:304)

In other words, because of the entanglement of different systems of valuation — by practitioners, cultural experts, state officials, and markets — at different levels (local, national, transnational, and international), ICH recognition can be a mixed blessing for those communities that are 'bearers' — but perhaps no longer 'owners' —

of the cultural practice deemed intangible heritage. These connections between culture — including cultural heritage — and possessive (individual, collective and/or indigenous) subjects who claim rights over or property of cultural 'objects' have been studied critically and comprehensively by Rosemary Coombe in a series of books and articles (Coombe 1998, 2005, 2009, 2011a, 2011b, 2013). The combined effect of these studies is to denaturalise both (cultural) subject and (cultural) object by treating these as constituted by their mutual connection; the discursive, practical and performative aspects of these connections — as claims, rights, identifications, etc. — allow Coombe to persistently question and politicise such relations.

Summing up, we can see that during the last decade the concept of heritagisation made headway, amongst others in critical heritage studies (for example, Smith 2006) and in the burgeoning anthropology of heritage (for example, Bendix 2009). In French scholarship, the notion of patrimonialisation is more common than heritagisation in English (Isnart 2012; Mauz 2012), which in its most bare-bones meaning refers to the making of heritage where such claims have been absent in the past, with reference to natural or cultural landscapes, objects like monuments, or particular practices and forms of knowledge. Such places, objects, practices, and knowledge may have been considered as part of a particular legacy by a group of people, carried over from one generation to the other, but the label of heritage does something different. Heritage involves claims by others for recognition of such legacy having extraordinary value which may be local, national or global — or, more often, all at the same time. In other words, the label of heritage assigns certain value to places, things, and practices. In the contemporary world, heritage claims invariably bring in cultural experts outside and beyond the local population to assess and evaluate the heritage values of the places, things, or practices under consideration. And heritage claims invariably bring in the state as the arbiter, guarantor, and protector of heritage. The global model for heritage practices is given by UNESCO, which assigns special responsibilities to the state, even though such heritage is often not always seen as representative of that state, but of particular localised 'communities'. As pointed out in countless studies, heritagisation brings in not just the state, but also the market, as the label of heritage — especially, but not exclusively, World Heritage — functions as a certification label and hence as a brand name in domestic and international tourist markets.

In fact, states — both national governments and local authorities — are often motivated by ideas of prestige but also of economic gain by capitalising on the heritage label. In other words, the value of heritage is not simply cultural or intangible, but financial as well, suggesting a process of commoditisation in spite of all professions of disinterestedness (cf. Coombe 2005, 2009, 2013). In the next section, I investigate the emergence of the concept, discourse, and practice of intangible cultural heritage in Vietnam.

Intangible Cultural Heritage in Vietnam

The term 'Intangible Cultural Heritage'[3] was introduced in Vietnam by UNESCO, which in 1994 sponsored two back-to-back 'expert meetings' in Vietnam on the intangible cultural heritage of ethnic minorities and the culture of the imperial city of Huế. I was invited to participate in an 'International Expert Meeting for the Safeguarding and Promotion of the Intangible Cultural Heritage of Minority Groups in Việt Nam' (Hà Nội, March 1994), and became the *rapporteur* for the meeting and editor of the resulting volume (Salemink 2001).[4] ICH was then a new concept within UNESCO, and was very much in line with the Lévi-Straussian concept of culture long dominant within UNESCO (Eriksen 2001; see also Arizpe 1998).[5] A new subdivision for

---

3   According to the 2003 Convention for the Safeguarding of the Intangible Cultural Heritage, the intangible cultural heritage — or living heritage — is the mainspring of our cultural diversity and its maintenance a guarantee for continuing creativity. The convention states that the ICH is manifested, among others, in the following domains: oral traditions and expressions (including language as a vehicle of the intangible cultural heritage); performing arts (such as traditional music, dance and theatre); social practices, rituals and festive events; knowledge and practices concerning nature and the universe; and traditional craftsmanship. The 2003 convention defines ICH as the practices, representations and expressions, as well as the knowledge and skills, that communities, groups and, in some cases, individuals recognise as part of their cultural heritage (see www.unesco.org/culture/ich/index.php?pg=00002, accessed 11 August 2008).
4   Subsequently, I was involved in cultural heritage work as editor of a UNESCO volume on Vietnam's minorities; as grantmaker on behalf of the Ford Foundation; as participant in international workshops on the 'Gong cultural space' intangible heritage in Pleiku (2009) and on the Hung Kings in Phú Thọ (2011); and as advisor for the UNESCO-sponsored research project on 'Safeguarding Intangible Cultural Heritage and Development in Vietnam' carried out by GS Lê Hồng Lý, TS Nguyễn Thị Hiền, TS Đào Thế Đức, and TS Hoàng Cầm under the auspices of GS Nguyễn Chí Bền of VICAS (2012).
5   Claude Lévi-Strauss (b. 1908) was a very influential French anthropologist whose work on cultural diversity formed the philosophical basis for much subsequent 'urgent' or 'salvage' anthropology which aimed to record and, if possible, save 'cultures' before they became 'extinct' (i.e. changed), a practice for which the concept of intangible cultural heritage was intended to give legitimacy.

intangible cultural heritage was established in Paris, largely funded by Japan and staffed by Japanese officials (Ms Noriko Aikawa was the Director of the Intangible Cultural Heritage section of UNESCO during those years). At the time, the (linguistic/anthropological) notion of intangible cultural heritage constituted an experimental departure from the established (historical/archaeological) practice of heritage conservation focusing on material objects.[6]

The interest in ICH in Vietnam only caught on, however, after the official UNESCO recognition of a growing number of world heritage sites resulted in a phenomenal boost in tourist visits and in national pride.[7] From 2003 onward, nine 'elements' — in the terms of UNESCO — from Vietnam were inscribed on the Intangible Cultural Heritage List. I have argued elsewhere that the process of claiming and recognising heritage status in Vietnam is a political process at various overlapping and interacting 'levels', involving local political ambitions within a national context, as well as national political and cultural interests in an international arena. This process invokes the artistic and academic authority of national and transnational 'experts', and results in the appropriation and the uses of 'intangible cultural heritage' in the Vietnamese context, with reference to local, national-level, regional, and international political discourses (Salemink 2007 and 2013a; see also Smith 2006; Thaveeporn 2003). Locally, heritage claims can be interpreted as a way to respond to certain political demands or — alternatively — to seek the promotion of a region. Nationally, the politics of heritage help establish political legitimacy for Vietnam's capitalist orientation under a Communist Party. Internationally, UNESCO recognition puts Vietnam on the global radar screen as an old civilisation and venerable culture. In this policy process, the Vietnamese state does not act as a monolithic entity but rather constitutes an arena of contestation in which conflicting interests are played out and resolved; still, the outcome of these contestations inevitably integrates perceived national interests into one discursive frame, namely that of an 'authorised heritage discourse' (cf. Smith 2006; see below) which frames (local) heritage as national.

---

6   I do not discuss natural heritage in this chapter, because the effects of nature conservation on local populations (relegated to 'bufferzones') have been analysed abundantly (see, for example, Büscher 2013).

7   In 2010, the Imperial Citadel of Thăng Long was added to the list, and in 2011 the Hồ Dynasty Citadel. In 2014, the Tràng An karst landscape was inscribed.

A recent report commissioned by UNESCO Vietnam suggested that the label of heritage is a double-edged sword; based on field research in four heritage sites in Vietnam, the authors speak about selective preservation, invention of tradition (with reference to the saying 'bỏ cũ, xây mới' ('abandon the old, build new')), and theatricalisation of cultural practice — something that is connected to the spectacular quality of heritage. Sometimes heritage status does bring good results in terms of preservation, ownership, management, and benefit sharing — as reported for Hội An — but often it leads to the disenfranchisement of local communities. And the concept of heritagisation shows that this latter aspect is perhaps inevitable, as the label of heritage — certainly of UNESCO World Heritage — turns what was once simply a local cultural practice into a site of outside intervention and policing: once their cultural practice is canonised as heritage, local people are no longer in exclusive control of that cultural practice which they largely organised and managed on their own in the past. Instead, local and national authorities, UNESCO officials, cultural experts, tourism developers, and larger, outside publics become 'stakeholders' in the process of evaluation, validation, and valorisation (Lê Hồng Lý et al. 2012; see also Lê Hồng Lý and Nguyễn Thị Phương Châm 2014). In the next sections I will focus on the 'Space of Gong Culture' in the Central Highlands as ICH.

The 'Space of Gong Culture'

In 2005, the 'Space of Gong Culture' (không gian văn hóa cồng chiêng) of ethnic minorities of Vietnam's Central Highlands was proclaimed a 'Masterpiece of the Oral and Intangible Heritage of Humanity', and after the ratification of the International Convention on Intangible Cultural Heritage in 2008 it was transferred to the new ICH List of 'Intangible Cultural Heritage in Need of Urgent Safeguarding'. The gong music that accompanies ritual events such as funerals and other life cycle rituals, as well as agricultural rituals and feasts among the ethnic minority groups in Vietnam's Central Highlands (and among similar ethnic groups across Vietnam's borders and ethnic groups in mountainous parts of coastal provinces), is undeniably special. The clear ringing sounds of the gongs, the beautiful melodies, and the intricate shifting rhythms act to mesmerise, bringing the listener or dancer into a state of trance. The comparison with Indonesia's rich local — both folk and court — traditions of gamelan music has often been made, but in Vietnam each gong in the carefully tuned set is held up and struck by a separate person, in tune and in rhythm with each other.

Although beautiful and entrancing, this ritual music is deemed to be under threat. It is slowly disappearing from everyday ritual life in Vietnam's Central Highlands. The older generation does not always pass on the skill to the younger generation, who may have lost their interest in the music, turning to modern music instead. Children go to school and learn to read, write and calculate in a future-oriented expectation to become modern citizens rather than peasants living by the rhythm of the passing seasons, attuned to the spirits surrounding them, and following in the footsteps of their ancestors before them. Children might no longer pass their evenings sitting around the hearth and listening to the old folks telling their stories — perhaps one of the famous epics of their group — but they might be sitting around the television, looking at Korean soap operas and Vietnamese or Western pop music. The rapid disappearance of gong ritual music from everyday life in the Central Highlands constituted the motivation for UNESCO to adopt this practice as one of the first projects in its intangible cultural heritage campaign (cf. Salemink 2001).

But gong music is also on the way out because the precious gong sets are disappearing, like so many other cultural or artistic objects that were once prized and used in the Central Highlands — and among highland minorities and Kinh people too. Since the first time I came to the Central Highlands in 1991, I have been offered gong sets for sale, as well as antique jars or other prize items. I have never taken up these offers, but I do know that many collectors, traders, and tourists — both Vietnamese and foreign — are eager to buy such items at low prices. I have noticed that upon returning to the Highlands after an absence of years, people no longer had possession of such items, even if these were family heirlooms. Sometimes sold, sometimes extorted during times of hardship in return for some money or rice, sometimes even stolen: outside various Highlands villages I have been shown graveyards from where famous grave statues had been stolen, to end up in boutiques in Hà Nội or Hồ Chí Minh City and eventually in overseas 'exotic art' and ethnographica shops and collections. Here, the UNESCO validation of the cultural or artistic value of gong music for humankind translates ironically into enhanced commercial value of the cultural objects (musical instruments, statues, traditional woven fabrics) connected with the gong culture and a consequent dispossession of these artefacts.

In other words, gong ritual music — or more broadly, 'gong culture', in UNESCO jargon — does not exist in a vacuum. There is always a wider ecological, economic, social, political, cultural and religious context in which such music is being practiced, performed, and passed on to younger generations, and in which this music obtains its meaning for players and audiences. This broader context is captured in the word 'space' in the 'Space of Gong Culture' which UNESCO aims to safeguard through its inscription in the World Intangible Cultural Heritage List. Thus, with the UNESCO proclamation of the Space of Gong Culture as part of the world's intangible cultural heritage, two wide-ranging and diffuse concepts are combined to be safeguarded: 'space' and 'culture'. Both these terms, however, are not self-evident, not immediately clear, and highly contested in artistic, academic, and public debates. Moreover, depending on how it is defined, safeguarding the Space of Gong Culture seems like a formidable, perhaps impossible task, amid the rapid change enveloping Vietnam, especially the Central Highlands. In the following paragraphs, I seek to unpack both terms, 'culture' and 'space'.

When investigating the Space of Gong Culture, it is necessary to have a clear concept of what we mean by 'culture'. The work of 'safeguarding' implies keeping things — objects, spaces, practices, meanings, environments – as they are, for use, display or performance in the future. The backdrop to this endeavour is the assumption that the work of time changes these 'things', and this change threatens to make these things disappear, or at least to reduce or dilute them. Thus, the work of safeguarding presupposes an opposition between tradition and modernity, whereby the traditional cultures of ethnic groups are thought to be replaced by a modern, more or less global culture. According to this analysis, traditional culture is gradually or rapidly disappearing, and the responsibility of scientists such as professional anthropologists and other scholars would be to describe and create a record of what belongs to this culture and what is characteristic of this culture. But once a 'traditional culture' has been described and authenticated through this kind of ethnographic research, any social and cultural change can only be conceived of as a dilution of this authentic, traditional culture. Thus, safeguarding the threatened cultural heritage of minority groups becomes an essentially conservative operation of trying to stop the work of time.

The problem with this view of culture is that it reifies and essentialises culture. Culture is seen as a collection of 'things' or attributes containing essential characteristics of a particular ethnic group. The classic definitions of culture by early anthropologists, such as Edward Tylor (1871), describe culture as a sum of things that pertain to a particular group of people — a 'tribe', nation, or ethnic group. This view of culture corresponds with the style of the 'holistic' ethnographic monograph that was predominant for a long time. Usually, such monographs contained chapters on environment, livelihood and material culture, on kinship, on religion and rituals, and on leadership and (non-state) politics, in an attempt to speak exhaustively and authoritatively about the 'whole' culture. Based on research in one or a few villages of a 'whole' group, the author would claim the authority to speak not just of the culture of village 'X' but of the culture of group (tribe, clan, *ethnie*) 'Y'. In the past, such an author would exclude references to the incorporation of such groups into wider networks of state and market which emerged in the colonial and postcolonial contexts, and which made such anthropological research possible and imperative at the same time. And although the field research would usually be limited to one or two years, the style of ethnographic description would cut out the work of time by employing the 'ethnographic present', as if the practices observed and described were unchanging and timeless. Hence, safeguarding 'culture' would almost imply the stopping of time, or at least the reification and ossification of certain cultural objects and practices as museum pieces, to be shielded from the work of time.

In other words, although research provides only a local and temporal snapshot, in his or her reports and publications the researcher would implicitly claim that the locally specific observations represented a whole group, and that the temporally specific observations stood for an unchanging tradition — both in combination denoting the culture of group 'Y'. It is this notion of culture which seems to dominate the conceptualisation of culture by UNESCO — the embodiment of global cultural politics — which since the 1980s has consistently celebrated and endeavoured to protect the world's cultural diversity. This is clearly illustrated by the debates surrounding the authoritative 1995

UNESCO report entitled 'Our Creative Diversity' which had been prepared by the World Commission on Culture and Development. This report triggered condemnation from anthropologists, who criticised the inconsistent but often essentialist definition of culture underpinning the report and its recommendations (Wright 1998; Arizpe 1998; Eriksen 2001). In contrast with UNESCO's static and essentialist view of culture, most present-day anthropologists and cultural scholars worldwide see 'culture' not as a bounded collection of 'things' connected with a clearly delineated ethnic group, but as an ever-changing process with fuzzy boundaries. Thomas Hylland Eriksen (2001) traced the Lévi-Straussian notion of cultures (plural) as isolated islands in the UNESCO Commission's discourse. Eriksen observed the tendency to link 'culture' to 'indigeneity', and emphasised the problematic tension between universal concepts of individual rights and communitarian notions of rights implied in culture as necessarily collective, localised, and hence exclusive. This tension can also be seen in the history of cultural claims and rights in Vietnam's Central Highlands — the designated space for gong culture — as I argued in 2006 (Salemink 2006).

But for gong music in the Central Highlands, the concept of 'space' was wedded to 'culture', thus making the arena of safeguarding and intervention even more fuzzy. The concept of 'space' may refer to the 'cultural space' in which ritual gong music and dance is enacted and is meaningful because it refers to the larger context from and in which gong ritual music obtains its meaning for the diverse local communities where it developed. Throughout the Central Highlands, Gong ensembles play a role in various rituals and public ceremonies that were closely linked to daily life and the cycle of the seasons. Thus the Space of Gong Culture, the variety of ethnic groups represented within that culture, and the continued participation of community members in gong ensembles is very different from, say, the more restricted contexts and audiences of Huếst *nhã nhạc* court music. The Space of Gong Culture thus encompasses a musical genre, born in the ritual life of highland communities, usually tied to seasonal (agricultural) and life cycles. Developed in a diversity of customs and ritual contexts, gong culture is congruent with the linguistic and ethnic diversity of the region. The instruments themselves, made from a mixture of bronze and silver, are not cast by highland people but purchased from long-distance traders and produced in far-away regions.

Writing about the UNESCO concept of 'cultural landscape', which combines a spatial category with the adjective 'cultural', Rosemary Coombe states:

> the addition of the category of cultural landscape to the World Heritage List in 1992 was crucial for legitimating the heritage of local communities and indigenous peoples … that later became formalised in the ICH Convention and that has arguably spread as a norm of customary international law into international heritage protection policy more generally. (Coombe 2013:377)

It may have been the intention of some UNESCO staff at the time to contextualise gong ritual music in its wider cultural and spatial settings,[8] but this worked out differently in the Central Highlands. After all, 'space' may have different meanings from 'cultural space' alone. For starters, 'space' has a clear geographic connotation, as it circumscribes the places where the cultural practices are supposed to take place. This spatial circumscription refers to the Tây Nguyên region, currently made up of the five provinces of Kontum, Gialai, Đắk Lắk, Đắk Nông, and Lâm Đồng. In that sense, it is also a political space, denoting the five administrative units now making up the Tây Nguyên region of Vietnam. It leaves out the upland districts in surrounding coastal provinces where the same or similar ethnic minorities live with similar gong musical practices, and it leaves out regions in Cambodia and Laos with ethnic groups that are equally similar or the same, but living across the Vietnamese border. The political character of the 'gong space' is also brought out by the fact that Tây Nguyên is an integral part of Vietnam's national territory, with the Vietnamese Government filing the dossier for UNESCO inscription and ultimately responsible for safeguarding this heritage.

But 'space' refers also to the ecological, economic, and social space that forms the context for gong culture, along with myriad other cultural practices, and as a subtext and context to the cultural space of gong culture, the ecological, economic, political, and social space are changing extremely quickly. In other words, the Space of Gong Culture is predicated on the changing landscape of Tây Nguyên. Rather than being bounded, both 'space' and 'culture' in the 'Space of Gong Culture' are fluid categories, reminiscent of the changing and

---

8   Personal communication, Dr Frank Proschan.

changeable 'scapes' (technoscape, financescape, ideoscape, ethnoscape, mediascape) by which Arjun Appadurai (1996) denoted the processes of change, interaction, migration, blurring, and hybridisation that influence lifeworlds as a consequence of global flows. In the next section, I briefly indicate — rather than describe and analyse — the social and economic changes that contextualise and influence gong culture in Tây Nguyên.

Changing the Tây Nguyên Cultural Landscape

While 'space' refers to the multifaceted landscape where gong culture is located, efforts at safeguarding are taking place against a background of displacement, loss, and dispossession that have drastically affected the lifeworlds of these communities. Cultural transmission was severely disrupted during almost four decades of intermittent warfare (1942–79), resettlement and defoliation. These disruptions continued into the period of socialist modernisation, which brought further resettlement in the name of modernity, but have accelerated as the Central Highlands have been rapidly drawn into global economic and cultural circuits. For example, Vietnam's Tây Nguyên almost overnight became a hotspot of globalisation, producing much of the world's coffee, tea, pepper, cashew, and rubber in smaller or larger commercial farms. While this changed the physical (ecological, economic, infrastructure) landscape, the demographic, social, and cultural landscape was changed almost beyond recognition. Lacking the space to venture into much ethnographic detail here, I propose an analysis of the current situation with emphasis on the post-1975 period, in particular, on the market reform period known as đổi mới, or 'renovation'. After a period of socialist collectivism, the market reforms have resulted in rapid capitalist development and high economic growth in much of Vietnam, including Vietnam's Central Highlands. Simultaneously, the introduction of market reforms in the late 1980s often had dire consequences for the indigenous ethnic minority groups who regard the region as their 'ancestral domain' and who embody the gong culture. In this section, then, I shall briefly indicate recent developments in Vietnam's Central Highlands in terms of a process of multidimensional transformation of the physical environment, of the economic system, of the religious beliefs and practices, and of subjectivities.[9]

From a marginal region in 1975, with a majority of the (indigenous) population engaging in subsistence farming through clan- or village-based rotational swidden cultivation and some trade, in the first decade of the second millennium the Central Highlands became fully integrated into the world market as a major cash-crop producing region. In just 10 years it became the world's second-largest coffee producing region, saturating the global coffee market with robusta coffee and causing a temporary worldwide slump in coffee prices. Vietnam's Central Highlands are also among the world's top three producers of rubber, pepper, and cashews. These cash-crop plantations and gardens were set up mostly by ethnic Việt lowlanders who migrated *en masse* to clear land and set up coffee gardens (now being diversified to include tea, pepper, rubber, cocoa, and cashews) in tracts of forest and savannah, or in old swidden fields. At the same time, rivers valleys are used for hydropower projects, while remaining forests with economic or ecological value are designated as national parks, nature reserves, or protected forests. More recent developments promise even more sudden, incisive and disruptive transformations to the Space of Gong Culture as part of the Central Highlands are presently transformed into a 'bauxite space' of strip mining, which is highly detrimental to the local ethnic groups and hence to the 'safeguarding' of the Space of Gong Culture. In other words, from a situation of low population density and more or less environmentally balanced rotational swidden cultivation embedded in managed forests, a massive environmental transformation has changed the face of the landscape and the nature of the natural resources through deforestation, zoning and exploitation of natural resources.

This environmental transformation is linked with a complete economic transformation predicated on concepts of private land ownership, on capital inputs, on technical know-how and on market access and individual calculation which are at odds with traditional subsistence-oriented agricultural and ritual practices predicated on collective — or at least communal — arrangements among indigenous

---

9   The following sections are based on Salemink (1997, 2002, 2003a, 2003b, 2004).

central highlanders. Whereas some lowlander in-migrants have become *nouveau riche* (and others went bankrupt in adverse market conditions), many indigenous communities and (extended) families have no use for the official division in forest land and agricultural land (a useless distinction for traditional swidden cultivators). Nor does the concept of private land ownership (promoted through a land allocation program backed by western donors and big development banks) hold much promise for most highlanders, because the plots are too small for subsistence farming. They often lack the capital and knowledge to invest in cash-crops with long-term return — hence the frequent sale of official land titles by highlanders who then move deeper into the forest or become economically dependent on their in-migrant neighbours (Salemink 1997).[10]

Since 1975, many highlanders have abandoned their traditional community religions (often glossed as 'animist') which were highly localised in the sense that deities and spirits often housed in specific sites (mountains, rivers, forest groves, single trees or stones) in a 'Durkheimian' sacralisation of the physical environment. With the transformation of the physical environment and its appropriation by outsiders without respect for its sacred nature, these localised religious beliefs and practices gradually lost their sacral character and significance along with the environment in which they acquired meaning. At the same time, changes in agricultural practices and in the (ethno-demographic) composition of the population rendered rituals progressively meaningless. On top of that, many rituals simply became too time- and resource-intensive, given the general environmental degradation and the economic impoverishment of the indigenous population. Faced with increasingly meaningless and burdensome rituals, many highlanders have abandoned their traditional religion and adopted a new one: Evangelical Christianity. Introduced and propagated without much success by American evangelical missionaries before 1975, Evangelical Protestantism has become the existential safe haven of a large part of the indigenous population since the capitalist market reforms in the 1990s. This massive religious transformation sets them apart from the ethnic Việt lowlanders, but sacralises a new lifestyle imposed by the exigencies of capitalist development — austerity,

---

10   This section is, of course, a generalisation, as the situation tends to vary according to locality and ethnic group. However, the occurrence of widespread unrest in February 2001 and April 2004 over issues of land ownership and religious freedom confirms this general analysis.

moderation, frugality, thrift, calculus, and individual responsibility — under the auspices of transnational modernity. And like the other transformations, this religious transformation cannot simply be rolled back or even stopped.

The last type of transformation, then, concerns highlander subjectivities, or sense of personhood. During the 'collectivist' period of 'socialist construction' in reunified Vietnam (1975–85), the Communist Party attempted to create 'New Socialist Person' (*Con người Xã hội chủ nghĩa Mới*), who would be different from 'Traditional Person' in that the latter's loyalties lay with the family, local group, and class, whereas 'New Socialist Man' would widen his horizon, subject his own desires to the goals of the state, and selflessly work to fulfil these goals. These attempts to create new socialist people were actively resisted, sabotaged or simply ignored in most parts of Vietnam, and certainly in the Central Highlands, where indigenous highlanders were singled out as primitive, backward, superstitious, or even reactionary. But the market reforms of the 1980s triggered the demise of 'New Socialist Man' and provoked the rise of a new type of person whom we might call 'New Capitalist Man', characterised by what Daniel Bell (1996) calls the 'cultural contradictions of capitalism'. In the realm of production, capitalism puts a premium on (Weberian) frugality, calculus, and deferral of gratification. Whereas in the realm of consumption, capitalism promises immediate gratification of social, cultural, and economic desires (Bell 1996:54–76).

In other words, capitalist culture thrives on the promise of absolute wealth and the hedonistic fulfilment of desire — the promise of finding paradise in consumption. Capitalism holds out the promise of an earthly paradise, but through consumption rather than production. Consumerism is not a concept that one would easily associate with Vietnam's Central Highlands. Yet with integration into the global market, highlanders too are confronted with the imagery of wealth and consumption through the mass media, advertisement, tourism, and conspicuous lifestyles. They are now inescapably confronted with a new vision of modernity — a capitalist modernity, held up as a paradise in the making through consumption. I have never encountered anyone in Vietnam or elsewhere who did not wish to partake in the promises of material consumption, except for explicit religious reasons (in the narrow sense). But like transcendental religions, such as Buddhism or Christianity, capitalism requires a project of personal transformation of the 'reverse Weberian' type. On a personal level, capitalist reforms are aimed at instilling a frugal, calculating and individualistic mentality — or, in the Vietnamese Central Highlands, turning clan-based and community-oriented subsistence farmers into individualistic agricultural entrepreneurs. Whether they continue to be farmers or day-wagers, they will be dependent on the market for their survival and thus have to conform to the exigencies of the market.

Central Highlanders Facing Intangible Cultural Heritage Practices

In this situation of wide-ranging ecological, economic, religious, and subjective transformations, the basis for community-based ritual life which UNESCO calls 'gong culture' is disappearing fast. In an economy that puts a premium on competitive individual — or at least household — performance, the community solidarity that underpinned agricultural ritual is perennially under threat. With livelihoods less and less based on the subsistence swidden agriculture of 'eating the forest' (cf. Condominas 1982), the cosmological environment as the context for ritual action ceases to have meaning, and the agricultural cycle changes with the new cash crops introduced. Many people lack the resources to invest in ritual, making them feel permanently in debt *vis-à-vis* their deities and hence at risk of hazard. In this situation, many highlanders opt for a new, more individualist and scripturalist religion with completely different liturgical ritual: Christianity. With the conversion to Christianity, the performance of gong music during life cycle rituals is no longer a matter of course, and is sometimes even actively condemned as 'pagan' by followers of the new religion. The cultural transmission of knowledge of ritual and gong music skills to younger generations is becoming difficult in this context.

While Christian highlanders condemn their 'pagan' past, the Vietnamese regime condemns highlander Christianity. In January 2001 and April 2004, many highlanders demonstrated in some of the major towns in the Central Highlands such as Pleiku and Buôn Ma Thuột, as well as in some of the more remote districts such as Chu Xe in Gialai Province. Their demands concerned freedom of religion and land rights, but were articulated overseas by the anti-communist diaspora organisation Montagnard Foundation as a call for 'Dega' autonomy — Dega being a new, politicised ethnonym for the indigenous groups of Vietnam's Central Highlands. This putative association with Dega diaspora politics triggered a strong repression of highlander political and religious articulations. One of the frequently reported political responses were attempts by security personnel to force people to recant their Christian confession and to perform specific versions of 'pagan', non-Christian rituals — indeed, the very rituals that in the times of high socialism were branded backward, superstitious, unhygienic, and wasteful. I have discussed the dynamics of rights claims, protests, and repression elsewhere (cf. Salemink 2006); here I shall focus on Vietnam's official response in terms of cultural politics. Just one month after the 'first' protest in 2001, Vietnam's government gave the largest grant for social science research in its history — the equivalent of $1 million USD — for researching, collecting, recording, translating, analysing, and publishing the long epics of the Central Highlands. The project was managed and carried out by the Institute of Folk Culture Studies of the Vietnam Academy of Social Sciences, which over the years published well over 60 volumes of epics. The dossier for the UNESCO inscription of the Space of Gong Culture was prepared in 2004, right after the second protest during Easter 2004. Just like the forced recantations of Christianity, the sudden conservationist cultural policies were predicated on religious and ritual practices that highlanders had already abandoned or were in the process of abandoning.

In other words, what was called (intangible) cultural heritage in the 2000s, were religious concepts and cultural and ritual practices that had been condemned and suppressed by successive political regimes as backward and superstitious, and which had been rendered practically unsustainable by the disruptive ecological, economic, demographic, political, and cultural transformations in the Central Highlands. Given the deep politicisation of both Christian conversion and official cultural politics in Tây Nguyên, the label of heritage being given to largely abandoned cultural practices creates much tension within communities and between communities and state agencies. This is one of the dilemmas facing the gong practice among the Lạch group in Lâm Đồng, as noted by the UNESCO report on 'Safeguarding and Promoting Cultural Heritage against the Backdrop of Modernization'

(Lê Hồng Lý et al. 2012). Many Christians refused to play the gong, or even to possess a gong set, seeing it as an instrument of the devil. In places where an accommodation could be reached between Christian liturgy and gong music, the report found that the official predicate of 'heritage' bestowed by the state or by UNESCO incited local actors or even national agencies to make investments or 'improvements' that contradict the idea of heritage preservation;[11] that disenfranchise local communities who used to be in control of the cultural practice now dubbed heritage; and that privilege outside actors or interests (tourism, economic, political) which conceive of intangible cultural heritage as a spectacle.

This brings us back full circle to Guy Debord's analysis of the *Society of the Spectacle*. In the case of ICH, people themselves become a spectacle, just like the celebrities analysed by Debord (1994) and Rosemary Coombe (1998); but where celebrities become individual brands, central highlanders become collectively branded through the validation and certification processes undertaken or overseen by UNESCO. In the case of gong culture, it is specific ritual labour which used to acquire meaning within the setting of a restricted ritual community — and perhaps a slightly wider but vernacular ritual constituency — but which becomes a spectacle validated by outside experts and consumed by outside audiences of officials and tourists. As a spectacle — but not a ritual — such ICH becomes spectacular in the sense that aesthetic and performative aspects are privileged over substantive signification as ritual. This spectacularisation of the practice is predicated on external notions of 'improvement' that seek to make the performance shorter, louder and wilder — often in a context of artistic competition.

I witnessed examples of the latter at the 'International Conference on Economic and Social Changes and Preservation of the Gong Culture in Vietnam and the Southeast Asian Region' in Pleiku, 9–11 November 2009, which took place in the context of an international gong music festival organised by Vietnam's Ministry of Culture, Sports and Tourism to celebrate the UNESCO inscription of the Space of Gong

---

11   In the late 1990s, the former director of the Huế Monuments Conservation Centre, Mr Thái Công Nguyên, showed me how he shortened the *nhã nhạc* court music scores, which in their original form were too long and hence 'boring' to watch by tourists. He conceived of that as an improvement. (I could give many examples of such improvements.)

Culture one year earlier. The opening ceremony was a loud, pompous, mass-mediated performance choreographed by Vice-Minister and People's Artist Lê Tiến Thọ, in which a swirling mass of hundreds of dancers, musicians, and drummers as well as some elephants performed a mockery of the quiet ritual gong music for an audience of officials and guests, local people and — via television — the nation. But an opening ceremony is often a grandiose event, certainly in Vietnam, and hence not necessarily representative for — in this case — gong music itself. But the festival itself had the format of a competitive music meeting, in which more or less professional gong troupes from different ethnic groups, provinces, and even countries performed in a competitive atmosphere, inducing the troupes to perform in ever more spectacular fashion — often adding drums to the performance as well. In such a context, gong music becomes professionalised, meaning that it is entirely taken out of the ritual context of the village community and is performed by semi-professional artistic troupes for outside audiences. As I noticed in my paper to the conference, what was missing in this movement of cultural decontextualisation from the ritual community and recontextualisation in a tourist context was any attempt to recontextualise gong music in a different ritual context, namely of church liturgy.[12] Highlander Christians and Vietnamese state officials seemed too suspicious of each other to allow that to happen — with some Bahnar Catholic groups the proverbial exception as they incorporated gong music into church liturgy.

This can be interpreted as an instance of possessive cultural nationalism (cf. Handler 1985, 1991; Coombe 1998) in the sense that a particular cultural object — in this case practice — is seen as the property not of an individual (for example, an author or an artist), but of a collective. Whereas UNESCO seeks to ascribe ownership of ICH to specific cultural groups, in practice, the cultural practices that go under the label of heritage become the property of the state, which assumes the responsibility to protect, preserve, and manage the heritage. In this case, the heritagisation of gong culture amounts to a process of large-scale cultural dispossession. This happens first of all because of the wholesale ecological, economic, demographic, cultural, and cosmological transformation of the Tây Nguyên landscape, which works as a classic movement of enclosure in Karl Marx's sense of the

---

12   I made a similar observation in Salemink (2009).

term. Secondly, the state performs a mockery of highlander gong culture in which highlanders have no say and from which they are largely absent. Thirdly, to the extent that highlanders perform, they are turned into a spectacle, devoid of ritual meaning and dispossessed of the product of their ritual labour. And fourthly, highlanders are practically prevented from reintroducing gong music into their new liturgical rites and thus from recontextualising it into their own ritual communities. Although the state is not directly implicated in the loss (sale, theft) of cultural objects such as gong sets (see Van Dat 2009), this does happen with reference to other ICH in Vietnam, such as the Worship of the Hùng Kings.

When I visited the Hùng King Festival in the 1990s, it was largely a local affair, organised by ritual leaders from villages surrounding the Nghĩa Linh mountain, for a ritual constituency consisting largely of local people from Phú Thọ Province — especially young people for whom this was an occasion for courting and dating. In the 2000s, the festival had become a large-scale affair: the *ngày giỗ tổ Hùng Vương* became a national holiday in Vietnam, marking the 'origin of the nation' before the historic Chinese occupation (but, ironically, it was the first national day to be calculated by the Sino-lunar calendar (*ngày 10 tháng 3 âm lịch*)). It attracted large crowds from all over Vietnam, but especially high-level political officials from Hà Nội and the province, who assumed leading ritual roles as well. When I attended the festival on 10–12 April 2011 — in connection with a campaign for UNESCO inscription — I visited some of the temples in the surrounding villages that had been responsible for part of the rituals and had kept some of the ritual objects in those temples. Not only had the local committees been deprived of their responsibilities, but also of some of the original objects. (In another case, the cultural authorities substituted the 'old' ritual objects for new ones in the rituals themselves, which meant that the temples could keep the original items but not use them anymore in the rituals.) Dispossessed of their ritual responsibilities, local villagers were still expected to show up at the festival, but more as props in a ritual choreography directed by outsiders.

This blatant ritual dispossession found its match in another, involving dance troupes from the Central Highlands. The Hùng Dynasty coincided with the Đồng Sơn bronze drum civilisation, which is claimed by Vietnam as well other countries and regions, such as Yunnan (cf. Han Xiaorong 1998, 2004), as its national cultural property. Given the superficial resemblance of the iconography on the bronze drums with stereotypical styles and scenes in the Central Highlands, it is assumed that contemporary central highlanders are similar to proto-Việt from the time of the Hùng Kings, and hence the contemporary ancestors of the Kinh (Salemink 2008:161–162). At any rate, such Tây Nguyên drum troupes are aesthetically convenient performers at the Hùng King Festival, but in this way they are denied coevalness with our times (cf. Fabian 1983) and locked up in an imagined past. They are robbed of their contemporaneity with us, which at once legitimises the dispossession of their distinctly un-modern cosmological landscape — characterised as irrational, unscientific and uneconomic — and legitimises the denial of their right to choose a modern religion.

Conclusion: Connection and Disconnection, Incorporation and Dispossession

Heritagisation — understood in its minimal meaning, namely as branding of sites and cultural practices as heritage — is a worldwide process, and the last two decades have witnessed an upsurge in heritage practices. Much of that was led by the efforts of UNESCO, but as an inter-governmental organisation UNESCO is little more than the sum of its parts — the member states — which all have their own reasons to be engaged in heritage. Worldwide, heritagisation emerged simultaneously with neoliberal governmentality (see also Coombe 2013); in Europe with the rise of identity politics against the backdrop of globalisation, immigration and EU expansion; and in Vietnam with its integration into the region and the global market. Paradoxically, this infatuation with the past — in the form of dead (monumental) or living (intangible) heritage — is a by-product of late modernity, as Barbara Kirshenblatt-Gimblett (2006) argues. Because the label of heritage connects localities with nationally and internationally 'authorised heritage discourses' (cf. Smith 2006), the process of heritagisation is fraught with paradoxes, especially with reference to intangible cultural heritage.

Intangible cultural heritage denotes living culture, but simultaneously reifies and objectifies it. It embraces the local communities ('culture bearers'), but leaves the evaluation and valuation process to outside experts and agencies, with reference to global rather than local cultural standards. It instrumentalises cultural practices because it usually suits the agendas of outsiders — intellectuals and cultural experts, local authorities, national governments — to recognise certain such practices as cultural heritage. It turns cultural practices and the people involved in those into spectacles, and hence into sites of outside intervention, assessment and accountability. It creates a new, bigger — national or international — public for cultural practices that might once have been reserved for their own community, often in the form of heritage tourism. It changes the environment of heritage practices by allowing that outside public — in the guise of tourists, state officials, experts, researchers and media — to come and see (or hear, smell, feel) these heritage practices. It generates economic benefits in the world's largest economic sector — tourism, of which heritage tourism is an important part (cf. Hitchcock et al. 2010) — that are necessary to maintain the cultural practice in changing circumstances but that might not be shared with the community (even though all ritual practice requires material investment). Heritagisation — at World Heritage, Intangible Cultural Heritage, and state levels — celebrates the local, the unique, the specific, and the authentic, but brings in the global, which — according to UNESCO — is the major threat to cultural diversity. In order to combat some of the perceived negative effects of globalisation, more globalisation is called forth, and local communities are subjected to outside gazes and interventions.

Heritagisation — especially of 'intangible culture' or 'living' cultural practices — turns the 'culture bearers' into spectacles, while dispossessing them of their ownership over their cultural objects and lives. First, as Guy Debord intimated, the spectacularisation of places, objects, people, and their practices (which is inherent to heritagisation) is predicated on a representational alienation — a disconnection between self and image — which is the price for connecting one image — as spectacle — to larger, state- and market-dominated arenas. Second, temporally speaking, the attraction of heritage lies in its claim to represent the past and to point the way towards the future, as I have argued elsewhere (Salemink 2014). Heritagisation, then, constitutes an appropriation of the past — often in the form of narrative monopolisation — and thus an attempt to control the future by certain elites at the expense of other (alienated) groups that become disconnected from the present and the future through the portrayal of them as the 'living past'. Third, spatial connections and disconnections occur when state- and market-operated incorporations of heritage sites, objects, people and practices link spatially marginal people to central agents and agencies that articulate an 'authorised heritage discourse' (cf. Smith 2006) which marginalises the people living close to, or embodying, the heritage. Finally, in terms of a class analysis, heritagisation — as suggested through my reading of the work by Guy Debord — constitutes a form of separation and hence alienation of the cultural sites, objects, practices, and knowledge from the people who produced, managed, or embodied these products of their ritual labour. Paraphrasing David Harvey (2005), heritagisation can be interpreted as another form of accumulation by dispossession in a neoliberalising world that attributes financial value, commoditises and commercialises everything. While connected to a national and global cultural market, UNESCO's 'culture bearers' become disconnected from their culture turned spectacle.

Paradoxically, heritagisation comes at the price of local disconnection from the cultural site, object, or practice that is officially labelled cultural heritage. The spectacularisation of culture that is intrinsic to the label of 'Intangible Cultural Heritage' separates local communities from their cultural practices, as other players — cultural experts and scientists, state agencies, tourist companies — effectively take over the management and organisation of the heritage for their own benefit. These communities are effectively disenfranchised from the legacy that they have formed over years of ritual labour. Thus, movements of connection and disconnection operate simultaneously or consecutively at different levels. In other words, the description and inscription of heritage sites, objects and practices result in the writing off of the constituent communities as viable and reliable cultural agents.

References

Appadurai, Arjun 1996, *Modernity at Large: Cultural Dimensions of Globalization*. University of Minnesota Press, Minneapolis.

Arizpe, Lourdes 1998, 'UN cultured [Letters]', *Anthropology Today*, vol. 14, no. 3, p. 24.

Bell, Daniel 1996 [1976], *The Cultural Contradictions of Capitalism* (20th anniversary edition), Basic Books, New York.

Bendix, Regina 2009, 'Heritage Between Economy and Politics: An Assessment from the Perspective of Cultural Anthropology', in Laurajane Smith and Natsuko Akagawa (eds), *Intangible Heritage*, Routledge, London and New York, pp. 253–269.

Breidenbach, Joana and Pál Nyíri 2007, '"Our Common Heritage": New Tourist Nations, Post-"Socialist" Pedagogy, and the Globalization of Nature', *Current Anthropology*, vol. 48, no. 2, pp. 322–330.

Büscher, Bram 2013, *Transforming the Frontier: Peace Parks and the Politics of Neoliberal Conservation in Southern Africa*, Duke University Press, Durham.

Condominas, Georges 1982 [1957], *Nous avons mangé la forêt de la Pierre-Génie Gôo (Hii saa Brii Mau-Yaang Gôo): Chronique de Sar Luk, village mnong gar (tribu proto-indochinoise des Hauts-Plateaux du Viet-nam central)*, Flammarion, Paris.

Coombe, Rosemary 1998, *The Cultural Life of Intellectual Properties: Authorship, Appropriation, and the Law*, Duke University Press, Durham and London.

Coombe, Rosemary 2005, 'Legal Claims to Culture in and against the Market: Neoliberalism and the Global Proliferation of Meaningful Difference', *Law, Culture and the Humanities*, vol. 1, pp. 35–52.

Coombe, Rosemary 2009, 'The Expanding Purview of Cultural Properties and their Politics', *Annual Review of Law and Social Science*, vol. 5, pp. 393–412.

Coombe, Rosemary 2011a, 'Cultural Agencies: "Constructing" Community Subjects and their Rights', in Mario Biagioli, Peter Jaszi and Martha Woodmansee (eds), *Making and Unmaking Intellectual Property*, University of Chicago Press, Chicago, pp. 79–98.

Coombe, Rosemary 2011b, 'Possessing Culture: Political Economies of Community Subjects and their Properties', in Mark Busse and Veronica Strang (eds), *Ownership and Appropriation*, Berg Publishers, London, pp. 105–127.

Coombe, Rosemary 2013, 'Managing Cultural Heritage as Neoliberal Governmentality', in Regina Bendix, Aditya Eggert, Arnkia Peselmann and Sven Meßling (eds), *Heritage Regimes and the State,* University of Göttingen Press, Göttingen, pp. 375–387.

Coombe, Rosemary J. with Joseph F. Turcotte 2012, 'Indigenous Cultural Heritage in Development and Trade: Perspectives from the Dynamics of Cultural Heritage Law and Policy', in Christoph B. Graber, Karolina Kuprecht and Jessica C. Lai (eds), *International Trade In Indigenous Cultural Heritage: Legal and Policy Issues,* Edward Elgar Publishing, Cheltenham, pp. 272–305.

Debord, Guy 1994 [1967], *The Society of the Spectacle,* New York, Zone Books, available at www.antiworld.se/project/references/texts/The_Society%20_Of%20_The%20_Spectacle.pdf, accessed 19 November 2014.

Debord, Guy 2002 [1967], *The Society of the Spectacle,* new translation by Ken Knabb, available at www.tacticalmediafiles.net/mmbase/attachments/47184/sos.pdf, accessed 19 November 2014.

Eriksen, Thomas Hylland 2001, 'Between Universalism and Relativism: A Critique of the UNESCO Concept of Culture', in Jane K. Cowan, Marie-Bénédicte Dembour and Richard A. Wilson (eds), *Culture and Rights: Anthropological Perspectives,* Cambridge University Press, Cambridge and New York, pp. 133–147.

Fabian, Johannes 1983, *Time and the Other: How Anthropology Makes its Object,* Columbia University Press, New York.

Han Xiaorong 1998, 'The Present Echoes of the Ancient Bronze Drum: Nationalism and Archaeology in Modern Vietnam and China', *Explorations in Southeast Asian Studies,* vol. 2, no. 2, pp. 27–46.

Han Xiaorong 2004, 'Who Invented the Bronze Drum?: Nationalism, Politics, and a Sino-Vietnamese Archaeological Debate of the 1970s and 1980s', *Asian Perspectives,* vol. 43, no. 3, pp. 7–33.

Handler, Richard 1985, 'On Having a Culture: Nationalism and the Preservation of Quebec's Patrimoine', in George W. Stocking (ed.), *Objects and Others: Essays on Museums and Material Culture,* University of Wisconsin Press, Madison, pp. 192–217.

Handler, Richard 1991, 'Who Owns the Past?: History, Cultural Property, and the Logic of Possessive Individualism', in Brett Williams (ed.), *The Politics of Culture*, Smithsonian Institution, Washington DC, pp. 63–74.

Harrison, Rodney 2013, *Heritage: Critical Approaches*, Routledge, London and New York.

Harvey, David 2005, *A Brief History of Neoliberalism*, Oxford University Press, Oxford.

Hewison, Robert 1987, *The Heritage Industry: Britain in a Climate of Decline*, Methuen, London.

Hitchcock, Michael, Victor T. King and Michael Parnwell (eds) 2010, *Heritage Tourism in Southeast Asia*, NIAS Press, Copenhagen.

Isnart, Cyril 2012, 'Les Patrimonialisations Ordinaires: Essai d'images Ethnographiées', *Ethnographiques,* vol. 24, Juillet, available at www.ethnographiques.org/2012/Isnart, accessed 17 October 2015.

Kirshenblatt-Gimblett, Barbara 2006, 'World Heritage and Cultural Economics', in Ivan Karp, Corinne Kratz, Lynn Szwaja and Tomas Ybarra-Frausto (eds), *Frictions: Public Cultures/Global Transformations*, Duke University Press, Durham NC, pp. 161–201.

Lê Hồng Lý, Đào Thế Đức, Nguyễn Thị Hiền, Hoàng Cầm, and Nguyên Chí Bền 2012, Bảo tồn và phát huy di sản văn hoá trong quá trình *hiện đại hoá. Nghiên cứu trường hợp tín ngưỡng thờ cúng Hùng Vương (Phú Thọ), hội Gióng (Hà Nội), tháp Bà Poh Nagar (Khánh Hòa) và văn hoá cồng chiêng của người Lạch (Lâm Đồng)* [*Safeguarding and Promoting Cultural Heritage against the Backdrop of Modernization: Case Studies of Beliefs and Worship Regarding the Hùng Kings (Phú Thọ Province), the Gióng Festival (Hanoi), Poh Nagar Tower (Khánh Hòa Province) and the Gong Culture of the Lạch People (Lâm Đồng Province)*], UNESCO, Hanoi.

Lê Hồng Lý and Nguyễn Thị Phương Châm (eds) 2014, *Di Sản Văn Hóa Trong Xã Hội Việt Nam Đương Đại* [*Cultural Heritage in Vietnam Contemporary Society*], NXB Tri Thức, Hanoi.

Lowenthal, David 1998 [1996], *The Heritage Crusade and the Spoils of History*, Cambridge University Press, Cambridge.

Macleod, Nikki 2006, 'Cultural Tourism: Aspects of Authenticity and Commodification', in Melanie Smith and Mike Robinson (eds), *Cultural Tourism in a Changing World: Politics, Participation and (Re)presentation*, Channel View Publications, Clevedon, pp. 177–190.

Mauz, Isabelle 2012, 'Les Justifications Mouvantes de la Patrimonialisation des Espèces "Remarquables": L'exemple du Bouquetin des Alpes', *Ethnographiques,* vol. 24, pp. 1–18.

Poria, Yaniv 2010, 'The Story behind the Picture: Preferences for the Visual Display at Heritage Sites', in Emma Waterton and Steve Watson (eds), *Culture, Heritage and Representation: Perspectives on Visuality and the Past*, Ashgate, Farnham, pp. 217–228.

Salemink, Oscar 1997, 'The King of Fire and Vietnamese Ethnic Policy in the Central Highlands', in Ken Kampe and Don McCaskill (eds), *Development or Domestication? Indigenous Peoples of Southeast Asia*, Silkworm Books, Chiang Mai, pp. 488–535.

Salemink, Oscar (ed.) 2001, *Diversité Culturelle au Viet Nam: Enjeux Multiples, Approches Plurielles* (Mémoire des peuples), Éditions UNESCO, Paris.

Salemink, Oscar 2003a, *The Ethnography of Vietnam's Central Highlanders: A Historical Contextualization, 1850–1990*, London, Routledge Curzon; Honolulu, University of Hawaii Press.

Salemink, Oscar 2003b, 'Enclosing the Highlands: Socialist, Capitalist and Protestant Conversions of Vietnam's Central Highlanders', paper presented to 'Politics of the Commons: Articulating Development and Strengthening Local Practices' conference, Chiang Mai University, 11–14 July 2003, available at dlc.dlib.indiana.edu/dlc/handle/10535/1787.

Salemink, Oscar 2004, 'Development Cooperation as Quasi-religious Conversion', in Oscar Salemink, Anton van Harskamp, and Ananta Kumar Giri (eds), *The Development of Religion, the Religion of Development*, Eburon, Delft, pp. 121–130.

Salemink, Oscar 2006, 'Changing Rights and Wrongs: The Transnational Construction of Indigenous and Human Rights among Vietnam's Central Highlanders', *Focaal: Journal of Global and Historical Anthropology,* vol. 47, pp. 32–47.

Salemink, Oscar 2007, 'The Emperor's New Clothes: Re-fashioning Ritual in the Hue Festival', *Journal of Southeast Asian Studies,* vol. 38, no. 3, pp. 559–582.

Salemink, Oscar 2008, 'Embodying the Nation: Mediumship, Ritual, and the National Imagination', *Journal of Vietnamese Studies,* vol. 3, no. 3, pp. 257–290.

Salemink, Oscar 2009 'Where is the Space for Vietnam's Gong Culture?: Economic and Social Challenges for the Space of Gong Culture, and Opportunities for Protection', conference paper presented to International Conference on Economic and Social Changes and Preservation of the Gong Culture in Vietnam and the Southeast Asian Region, Pleiku City, Vietnam, 9–11 November.

Salemink, Oscar 2013a, 'Appropriating Culture: The Politics of Intangible Cultural Heritage in Vietnam', in Hue-Tam Ho Tai and Mark Sidel (eds), *Property and Power: State, Society and Market in Vietnam*, Routledge, New York and London, pp. 158–180.

Salemink, Oscar 2013b, 'Is there Space for Vietnam's Gong Culture?: Economic and Social Challenges for the Safeguarding of the Space of Gong Culture', in Izabela Kopania (ed.), *South-East Asia: Studies in Art, Cultural Heritage and Artistic Relations with Europe*, Polish Institute of World Art Studies and Tako Publishing House, Warsaw and Torún, pp. 127–134.

Salemink, Oscar 2014, 'History and Heritage — Past and Present: Thinking with Phan Huy Lê's Oeuvre, in Trần Văn Thọ, Nguyễn Quang Ngọc, and Philippe Papin (eds), *Nhân Cách Sử Học* [*A Historical Personality*], NXB Chính trị Quốc gia, Hanoi, pp. 547–568.

Smith, Laurajane 2006, *Uses of Heritage*, Routledge, London and New York.

Smith, Melanie 2009, *Issues in Cultural Tourism Studies*, Routledge, Oxon and New York.

Thaveeporn, Vasavakul 2003, 'From Fence-breaking to Networking: Interests, Popular Organizations and Policy Influences in Post-socialist Vietnam', in Benedict Kerkvliet, Russell Heng, and David Koh (eds), *Getting Organized in Vietnam: Moving in and around the Socialist State*, ISEAS Publications, Singapore, pp. 25–61.

Tylor, Edward B. 1871, *Primitive Culture: Researches Into the Development of Mythology, Philosophy, Religion, Art, and Custom* (two volumes), John Murray, London.

Van Dat 2009, 'Sacred Gong Culture in Need of Spiritual Revival', *Vie Van Dat,* 23 September.

Walsh, Kevin 1992, *The Representation of the Past: Museums and Heritage in the Postmodern World*, Routledge, London.

Wright, Susan 1998, 'The Politicisation of "Culture"', *Anthropology Today*, vol. 14, no. 1, pp. 7–15.

10

Geographies of Connection and Disconnection: Narratives of Seafaring in Lý Sơn

Edyta Roszko

An unexpected sea breeze coming from the north on a Friday morning in June 2014 promised a bit of respite from the heat on Lý Sơn Island, located about 30 kilometres offshore from Quảng Ngãi Province in Vietnam and 123 nautical miles (ca. 228 km) from the Paracel Archipelago.[1] Every Friday and Saturday, I sipped my morning coffee in one of the local café shops near the port, updated myself on village affairs, and observed the stream of Vietnamese tourists flowing from the ship onto the seashore. Most of them were taken by cars to newly built hotels and small guesthouses that quickly filled up with organised tour groups, mainly from Hà Nội and Hồ Chí Minh City. Due to China's repeated confiscation of Lý Sơn's fishing vessels and harassment of their fishermen, Lý Sơn Island had become

1   The research for this chapter was funded by the People Programme (Marie Curie Actions) of the European Union's Seventh Framework Programme (FP7/2007–2013) under REA grant agreement no PIEF-GA-2012-326795. This paper is also partially based on a 12-month period of ethnographic fieldwork conducted in 2006–07 in Lý Sơn, which received financial support from the Max Planck Institute for Social Anthropology in Halle. The author also wishes to acknowledge support from the 2014 Vietnam Update organisers and particularly thanks Philip Taylor for his close reading and many invaluable comments that have greatly improved this chapter. Oscar Salemink, Li Tana, and the two anonymous readers also deserve special mention for their thoughtful comments on the chapter.

a putative symbol of 'defending sovereignty' over the 'East Sea' — the Vietnamese name for the South China Sea (Roszko 2015) — and became a destination for tourists eager to show their solidarity with the islanders who bore the brunt of the defence of the nation's sovereignty.

A group of eight women in their late 50s who I met that Friday serve as an example of a new style of patriotic tourism in coastal areas that has become increasingly popular among urban Vietnamese. This kind of tourism — which is both secular and ritual — involves travelling to the country's islands in order to experience the sea environment, food, and patriotism through entertainment and commemorative activities in spaces designated and designed by the state for remembering. The eight retired correctional police officers (*công an điều chỉnh*) from Hà Nội, Nha Trang, Buôn Ma Tuột, and Pleiku arranged with Lý Sơn authorities to meet with selected 'poor fishing families' and award a small sum of money to children who had achieved high grades in the village school. Following a new patriotic slogan, 'the whole Vietnamese nation turns to the sea' (*cả Việt Nam hướng về biển*), these women told me that they considered Lý Sơn Island to be the 'navel of the nation' (*rốn bao của cả nước Việt Nam*) and wanted to express their solidarity with local fishermen, whose months-long detention by China had been widely covered in Vietnam's national media. In Vietnam's traditional conception of the human body, the 'human body [is] a microcosmic reproduction of the vast dynamic forces at work in the universe' (Marr 1987:28), and the navel is considered the centre of the body. By calling Lý Sơn Island the navel of the nation, the erstwhile 'excentric' island has become the imagined centre of the country's geo-body.

How could a marginal place such as Lý Sơn Island become the nation's navel in so few years?

Introduction

Although there are historical records of the presence of Lý Sơn Islanders on the Paracels acting on behalf of a Vietnamese polity (see Lê Quý Đơn 1972; Bộ Ngoại Giao Uỷ Ban Biên Giới Quốc Gia 2013), the conflict with China over the South China Sea has opened up a new maritime frontier that did not exist before — at least not in the same manner. Back in 2006 when I carried out my doctoral fieldwork, few people had heard about Lý Sơn, and I observed few Vietnamese or foreign tourists visiting the island. However, eight years later, the conflict over the Paracel (Hoàng Sa) and Spratly (Trường Sa) archipelagos, with repercussions at local, national, and international levels, had inscribed the island at the centre of Vietnam's history and geography, and as the destination for thousands of Vietnamese tourists from all over the country. For many Vietnamese, the island was at the centre of a re-imagined map of the nation's territory, which now included both the land and the sea. Considered as a historic and contemporary stepping stone to the far-flung Paracels, Lý Sơn found itself in the middle of Vietnam's imagined maritime and territorial geo-body, as brought out, for instance, in iconographic depictions of Vietnam's map in daily televised weather reports. Lý Sơn thus became a figurative cartographic navel of the national geo-body.

The reason for this discursive connection between Lý Sơn and the Paracels can be traced back to the sixteenth and seventeenth centuries, and throughout the nineteenth century, when specific seafaring communities, including from Lý Sơn, were given the right to collect goods from wrecked ships in exchange for the best share of the spoils for Vietnam's rulers, thus giving both rulers and fishermen a material stake in and presence on the Paracel islands (Wheeler 2006). This connection was formalised through the Hoàng Sa (Paracel) navy, which consisted of sailors recruited from Lý Sơn Island (Lê Quý Đôn 1972:210). Many of the Hoàng Sa sailors died at sea and their bodies were never returned to their relatives, giving rise to special ritual and memorial practices in Lý Sơn.

In the context of tensions with China over competing claims over the South China Sea during the early 1990s, the Vietnamese State turned its attention towards Lý Sơn as a valuable source of information about the sailors of the Hoàng Sa and Trường Sa navies (Roszko 2010). A few years later, it issued a directive establishing a memorial site for the two flotillas. Facing rival claims from China to sovereignty over the archipelagos, the Vietnamese Party-state chose to frame its strategy not in economic terms, but with reference to historical and emotional stories of Vietnamese sailors who had sacrificed their lives at sea. Through gradually revealed family genealogies which are expected to shed new light on Vietnam's putative long-standing sovereignty in the Paracel and Spratly archipelagos, members of Lý Sơn lineages have worked hard to recentre their marginal(ised) locality on the imagined map of the national territory — this time including the sea.

Historian Dian Murray (1988:4) points out that uninhabited islands constituted little concern for neo-Confucian states such as China or Vietnam, where sovereignty was typically defined in terms of human habitation and social organisation. According to this view, the Paracels and Spratlys were considered by Chinese and Vietnamese imperial governments as a maritime hazard for safe navigation rather than as an integrated part of national territory. This changed in postcolonial times. The colonial encounter had a transformative effect on many Asian states, which were pushed to recognise the need for creating their own national geo-body — both the territory and the nation — through mapping, and thus crafting an outline of the map as a national symbol (Winichakul 1994; Roszko 2015). The current conflict with China over the South China Sea evokes strong emotions in Vietnam, where many people assert feelings of affection for the 'ancestral' grounds of the — largely uninhabited and uninhabitable — islands and islets of the Hoàng Sa (Paracels) and Trường Sa (Spratlys). As I describe elsewhere, repeated Chinese seizure of Vietnamese vessels and the detention of Lý Sơn fishermen has been widely covered in Vietnam's mass media in the last five years, adding fuel to an already heated mediated debate about the disputed archipelagos in the South China Sea (Roszko 2015). At the same time, by designating officially approved spaces for expressing feelings of national pride, the Vietnamese state uses all possible means to encourage Vietnamese people's identification with the expansion of Vietnam's territory to include the contested waters in the South China Sea.

Against the backdrop of the South China Sea dispute, this chapter examines what kind of shift in subjectivities is required of Lý Sơn people to navigate the state's project and new economic opportunities that have emerged with the growing national interest in the island's historical and cultural heritage. How does the Lý Sơn community actively recentre itself on the imagined map of the nation's geo-body in its desire to become part of the modern world? As I demonstrate, people in nationally significant sites such as this have their own agendas and interpretations of history that favour local identities over all-embracing state visions (O'Connor 2003:271). In order to capture these processes at work, I open my discussion by exploring territorial imaginaries associated with 'Vietnameseness' and spiritual and hierarchical boundaries between two modes of life — farming and fishing. In the subsequent section, I focus on the islanders' gradual marginalisation in post-revolutionary Vietnam and their various aspirations to break their provincial status as fishermen by claiming the identity of traders and explorers as a way of life. In the final section, I analyse how Lý Sơn villagers position themselves in the context of Vietnam's novel rhetoric that redefines the country from a rice-growing culture to a maritime nation. Ultimately, I suggest that islanders seek to produce their own version of locality against the backdrop of the territorial dispute and their victimisation by the Chinese coastguard, widely projected in the national media.

Territorial Imaginaries

Colonial sources produced influential territorial imaginaries of Vietnam, centred on the terrestrial rice-growing Red River Delta as 'the cradle of Vietnamese civilisation'. This era is also the source of the cliché of the Vietnamese village as a politically autonomous, socially homogenous corporate community surrounded by a hedge and rice paddies (for example, Gourou 1936, 1940; McAlister and Mus 1970; Kleinen 1999). Moreover, the classic tripartite division of Vietnam into North, Centre, and South, metaphorically characterised by '"two rice baskets on a pole" — to describe the agrarian rich North and South held together by the poor but hard-working Centre' is still alive in many historical accounts (Wheeler 2006:129–130). Keith Taylor (1998:971) has spoken against the 'pan-Vietnamese village morphology' that produces the hierarchy defined as 'Vietnamese' and points out different ways of acting Vietnamese that existed through space and time. Taylor's (1998) critique of representations of Vietnamese history, culture, and territory as affirming unity and continuity is echoed in the work of Charles Wheeler (2006), Li Tana (2006) and John Whitmore (2006) and their attention to the coast. By conceptualising the littoral as a fluid rather than solid zone they offer a new perspective on Vietnamese society seen from the sea. Like the littoral, which is in a constant state of flux, this society must be seen as fluid and flexible as well (Pearson 1985, 2003).

My own ethnographic work in coastal communities shows that potent intersections of religion, economy, politics, and ecology are particularly visible in such a contact zone where the state struggles to establish and increase its presence (Roszko 2011). The very idea of 'Vietnameseness' tends to underplay the regional, historical, and cultural differences, and to marginalise places such as Lý Sơn Island that are seen as representing an extreme, unusual, and unsettled situation that does not stand for the imagined Vietnamese territory and nation. The spatial marginality and ambivalence of such communities remains a major concern of the state, which tries to incorporate them through various cultural agendas and development programs, such as the already mentioned patriotic tourism. For instance, after several ports in China started to operate regular tours to the disputed Paracel archipelago, Vietnam's Ministry of Culture, Sports and Tourism responded by approving an ambitious project aiming to develop Vietnam 'into a strong sea-based country, enriched by sea' and protect national sovereignty.[2] In the context of an imagined or real threat from China, many urban Vietnamese book tours to unpopular islands that were previously only loosely connected to the Vietnamese geo-body in order to — at least once in their life — experience the fatherland as seen from the sea.[3]

In response to uneven access to education, healthcare, or basic infrastructure, along with China's exclusionary claims on resources in the South China Sea, Lý Sơn people appropriate and capitalise on these national and geopolitical narratives in order to reproduce and relocate their locality in a desired way. The commemoration related to Hoàng Sa, which more recently has received the status of 'national heritage', provides the opportunity for Lý Sơn villagers to demonstrate the historical and communal value of their genealogies and temples, and reshape and redefine their local narratives and social identity beyond the category of fishermen. According to local family records (*gia phả*) the first 15 Việt families came from the mainland in 1609, divided land between them, and established two villages, An Hải and An Vĩnh,

---

2   www.hanoitourist.com.vn/english/sea-travel/1817-sea-and-islands-a-driving-force-for-vietnam-tourism-development, accessed 4 September 2015.
3   english.vietnamnet.vn/fms/travel/12151/marine--island-tours-chosen-to-show-patriotism.html, accessed 4 September 2015.

which nowadays form two communes.[4] However, a source of anxiety for the islanders was the awareness that the Việt people on Lý Sơn Island were only the latest residents in a long history of settlement, and that archaeological evidence indicates that the Cham civilisation was present prior to the Việt arrival on Lý Sơn. Islanders assuaged such unsettled feelings by seeking to convey a sense of genealogical continuity with the mainland. During my conversations with the islanders, many of them betrayed a sense of awkwardness about the previous Cham presence, which is indisputable taking into account archaeological evidence. A Lý Sơn villager told me:

> In the past, Bình Thuận was the place of origin for the Cham people but from there they spread to central parts entering Đà Nẵng and Quảng Nam. In Lý Sơn there was not so many of them, so [the land] out here was intact. There was no one to have an exchange with at all. For that reason in the sixteenth and seventeenth century the Việt people occupied Champa and stayed there. Well, back then, people from all provinces were moving in and out … to other provinces. There were also people here [on the island] and the Cham also came here but then [Việt] occupied the islands. After that [Cham] did not come here anymore, they were not able to [laughing] … The Việt caught crabs, fish and snails which they ate through the day to survive. When more Việt occupied the island and stayed here the civil harmony began with Champa people.

When I asked what he meant by the 'civil harmony with Champa', he replied:

> Still, there were a few Champa people here, they lived on this land. After those regarded as Champa died, they did not enter the island anymore, they were gone so the Việt people flocked together here.

The passage quoted above is not an isolated example of the awkwardness associated with the previous Cham presence on the island. It reveals an immediate defensive reaction by islanders who tried to convince me of the absence of Cham people at the time when their ancestors arrived on the island. Despite the historical evidence that Champa consisted of several coastal states which occupied the south-central

---

4   See, for example, *Gia Phả — Hộ Võ Văn* (Family annals — *Hộ Võ Văn*) kept by the Võ Văn lineage, An Vĩnh Commune, Lý Sơn District, Quảng Ngãi Province or *Gia Phả — Hộ Phạm Văn* (Family annals — *Hộ Phạm Văn*) kept by the Phạm Văn lineage, An Vĩnh Commune, Lý Sơn District, Quảng Ngãi Province.

coast of Vietnam from the end of the first millennium BC (Southworth 2004; Vickery 2009; Hardy 2009), many islanders maintained that the Cham were originally concentrated only in the southern part of Vietnam, in present-day Bình Thuận Province. Many villagers claimed that those Cham who stayed on the island gradually vanished and, generally, the Việt people outnumbered them. In this way, Lý Sơn people wanted to clear up any doubts about their identity, the rights over the land, or possible violence in the settlement process on the island. Yet, the surnames such as Mai, Đinh, Tiêu, etc., suggest that the Vietnamese migrants on Lý Sơn Island intermixed with the Cham natives (very few of whom still lived in the area). In the process — masking their Cham origin — the descendants of these inter-ethnic marriages absorbed and retained most of the beliefs of the agrarian villages from which their Việt forefathers had come.

While contemporary residents took possession of islands as Việt territory by means of a Việt-centric settlement history, villagers were grappling with the problematic notion of Cham predecessors, which unsettled their sense of territoriality. Indeed, as some authors argue, control over territory 'is not only about use or power; it is also about meaning, claiming, consolidating, legitimacy' (Vaccaro, Dawson and Zanotti 2014:3). Intriguingly, we obtain a very different understanding of how villagers emplace themselves in Lý Sơn history by considering their ritual relations with the Cham spirits that are to this day worshipped in many temples on the island. The ritual relationship with these spirits, predicated on the existence of a more powerful spiritual domain, was maintained through the ritual 'buying or renting land' (*lễ tả thô*) (Li Tana 1998:131; Tạ Chí Đài Trường 2005:264). Right into the twentieth century, the inhabitants of Lý Sơn performed a 'ritualised bargain' through a local 'sorcerer' with a Cham ancestral couple, Chúa Ngu Ma Nương, and made lavish sacrifices in order to keep the land fertile (cf. Li Tana 1998:131; Tạ Chí Đài Trường 2005). One of the oldest inhabitants of Lý Sơn Island described the ceremony concerning land ownership in the following words:

> In the past, the North of Lý Sơn belonged to the Cham Kingdom [Chiêm Thành]. Our Kinh forefathers fought with the Cham Kingdom who were defeated and had to leave their land. The land remained and it was sacred [*linh thiêng*]; if our ancestors who wanted to inhabit it refused to worship them [the Cham deities] they would bring serious illnesses upon the village. That is why the forefathers installed an altar

[on the old Cham territory] for a wife and husband Chúa Ngu Man Nương. The couple managed the land and every five years the village organised the ritual of 'request for land' during which many oxen and buffalo had to be offered to keep peace. The ceremony was great and lasted several days and nights. The sorcerer [*phù thuỷ*] was invited too. He called the couple and asked them if they were satisfied with the offerings. If they said 'yes' they could stop but if they said 'no' they had to continue to make sacrifices of animals. The land belonged to them, without the offerings the village would be punished. If the husband required five pigs they would give him exactly five pigs. When queried about this they responded: 'the husband was easygoing but to satisfy his wife was very difficult!'

By performing the large ceremony for the Cham spirits, such as the Uma Goddess and Chúa Ngu Ma Nương,[5] the newcomers established themselves not only as rightful patrons of the new land but also tacitly apologised for taking this land away from the Cham natives. As the new owners of the territory they ritually accommodated the fact that other inhabitants once ruled over the land and its fertility. Through ritual procedures the spirits were pacified and incorporated into the pantheon of the new dominant community that gained local power.

The new experience of the sea and the encounter with Cham civilisation prompted the Việt on Lý Sơn Island not only to adopt foreign spirits and beliefs into their own religious practices but also to willingly experiment with the material culture of their predecessors. Việt migrants learned seafaring techniques from the Cham and even the structure of their ships followed Cham principles (Li Tana 1998:112; Pham, Blue and Palmer 2010; Pham 2013). Local family annals (*gia phả*) provide information from the seventeenth to the nineteenth centuries that, due to the excellent seafaring capacity of the islanders, many were recruited by the feudal state to collect precious sea products and goods from wrecked ships in the Paracel and Spratly archipelagos. The eighteenth-century Vietnamese historian Lê Quý Đôn (1972:210) reported the case of Vietnamese sailors who were allowed to move to Lý Sơn and were granted royal concession to explore the sea. Such practices were not unique to Vietnam, but also took place in other regions of Southeast Asia. In his interesting account on eighteenth- and early nineteenth-century migration and

---

5   Uma Goddess is the name for the Hindu Great Goddess Paravati, usually associated with mountains. Chúa Ngu Ma Nương is a Cham spirit of a husband and wife.

trade practices of 'sea people' in Southwest Kalimantan, Atsushi Ota (2010:69) writes that during this period many migrants, called 'pirates' by Europeans, established their communities in the coastal areas and 'were engaged in various profitable activities such as trade, fishing, and cultivation, supplemented by occasional raids on traders, fishermen, and the villagers'. By calling these maritime migrant communities 'sea people', Atsushi Ota (2010:69) makes an interesting point that those communities were 'within the political reach of states and settled under state rulers' approval, but they were not completely politically integrated, maintaining privileges in certain activities, such as settlement in certain places and plundering'. This resembles the case of Lý Sơn, with its loose connection to the mainland's political apparatus. As already mentioned, this connection was formalised as the Hoàng Sa and Trường Sa navy, consisting of villagers recruited from Lý Sơn Island who operated in the vicinity of the Paracels and Spratlys, which today constitute the fishing grounds of Lý Sơn fishermen (Lê Quý Đôn 1972:203, 210).

The Dichotomy Between the Land and the Sea

Trần Quốc Vượng (1992:29) notes that in pre-colonial and colonial Vietnam, fishing was a despised occupation and fishermen constituted one of the most marginalised groups in society. Landless, without roots in the village and living in areas close to the sea and rivers, fishermen were discriminated against and deprived of the spiritual and material means offered by the village. The dichotomy between the land and the sea that constitutes Lý Sơn society is expressed in the two emic terms: *làng* and *vạn*. Traditionally, *làng* or 'village' constituted the territorial unit of Vietnamese society, with the political and ritual system localised in the *đình* (communal house), and represented a land-based lifestyle. In the *đình,* villagers spiritually ensured good harvest for the upcoming year through the worship of those who first broke the land under the plough (*tiền hiền*) and the founders of the village (*tiền hậu*).[6]

---

6   In central and southern Vietnam, communal houses were characteristically erected in honour of the *tiền hiền* and the *tiền hậu*: those who first broke the land under the plough and the founders of the village. Where the communal house was a northern *đình* it was a shrine for the village guardian spirit. The guardian spirit of the village, or *thành hòang*, worshipped in the northern *đình* could be either a historical or a mythical person.

Generally, in central Vietnam, *vạn* referred both to a self-ruling fishing organisation and to a territorial unit with its own religious system localised in the *lăng*, a temple for the cult of a seafaring guardian spirit — the Whale. The fact that *lăng* means 'tomb' speaks volumes about fishermen's concerns, as if through propitiating the Whale Spirit they sought protection rather than seeking to ensure and control the fertility of land and, hence, the village.

Lack of arable land and inability to grow rice is an important detail that sheds new light on the formation of categories such as *làng* and *vạn* in Lý Sơn. In the face of serious physical constraints to growing rice, islanders still tried to reproduce the hierarchical division between farmers and fishermen that they knew from the mainland. Coming from the northern coast of Thanh Hóa, Nghệ An, and Hà Tĩnh, some of the 'founders' and 'great lineages' might have had the lower status of fishermen, but in the new setting, by taking advantage of being first, they established themselves as a superior *làng*. The recognised descendants of the 'founders' formed dominant lineages and an unofficial channel of grassroots administration — chiefs of hamlets (*xóm*) and sub-hamlets (*lân*) — that operated as 'patrilineages' of the village. Other lineages that were ranked alongside the 'founders' but did not win the same power were those whose precursors came shortly after the founders; these lineages were called *tộc lớn*, or 'great lineages'. This hierarchical stratification survives on the island until today and is displayed in religious and ritual practices. All of these groups recorded their genealogies (*gia phả*) in the ancestral halls of individual lineages. Others, who might have been fishermen or peasants, were not admitted to the *đình* order and did not share equal rights as village members because they arrived much later than the 'founders' and 'great lineages' and did not have access to free land. They were required to obtain permission from the 'founders' or 'great lineages' to buy a plot of land and build a house on the territory of the village, but even in such cases they were not considered legitimate village members. Denied village membership, they joined forces and formed a *vạn* with its own civil code, although still subordinated to the village.

In contrast to mainland central Vietnam, where fishing communities occupied sandy dunes and could be easily distinguished from agricultural villages with their surrounding rice fields, fishing and farming settlements on Lý Sơn Island merged because of the lack of arable land for rice cultivation. More precisely, the two 'municipalities' of An Vĩnh and An Hải were established in the seventeenth century as two *làng*, but shared their territory with two *vạn*: Vĩnh Thạnh and An Phú. Vĩnh Thạnh *vạn* was positioned within the territory of An Vĩnh village, while An Phú *vạn* overlapped with An Hải village. This arrangement survives today. Those who formed a *làng*, however, could not claim superior status on the basis of investment in rice cultivation; nor could they produce the crop that would rescue the village from starvation in times of famine. Unable to keep strict physical boundaries between the *làng* and the *vạn*, *làng* members of the two villages nurtured these separate categories through ritual and ceremony, and through claims that their ancestors were the first settlers on the island who tamed the new 'wild' land and founded the villages.

Drawing on the annals and local narratives, we know that the Hoàng Sa and Trường Sa navies that collected and traded goods from wrecked ships consisted of those who were members of the founding lineages and those who belonged to the organisation called *vạn*. Moreover, according to An Vĩnh temple's records, the *vạn* in Lý Sơn was more than just a fishing organisation; above all it was a trading organisation (*vạn giao thương*), a point that I will develop in more detail later.[7] The popular saying that fishermen 'soak up wealth like a sponge' (*giàu bọt nước*) hints at the perception that their profit was not morally justified when compared with the hard work of preparing the soil for cultivation (Nguyễn Duy Thiệu 2002:118). Coastal settlements were seen as the frontier of pirates and smugglers who could always find a good hideaway somewhere along the South China coasts (see, for example, Watson 1985; Murray 1987; Kleinen and Osseweijer 2010). Michael Pearson (2003:6) wrote:

> [p]irates and fisherfolk are ubiquitous, the former to be seen as macroparasites, human groups that draw sustenance from the toil and enterprise of others, offering nothing in return, the latter equally predatory, for unlike peasants they extract but do not cultivate, take but do not give.

---

7   See the Hán-Nôm document of Vĩnh Thạnh vạn in An Vĩnh commune, Lý Sơn Island.

In this sense, fishermen were regarded by the agriculturalists as a 'world apart', a group living in the margins of society, 'savages' and 'barbarians', who did not really represent the traditional Vietnam (Nguyễn Duy Thiệu 2002).

In his classical monograph on Malay fishermen, Raymond Firth (1964) demonstrated that in coastal areas, fisherfolk often live side by side with people of other occupations, including farmers with whom they maintain economic and frequently intimate relations. Pearson (1985:3) goes a step further by stating that 'land and the sea intertwine in complex and various ways', arguing that we must avoid seeing the people living on the shore as totally land- or sea-oriented. Indeed, Lý Sơn's cosmology looks both to the mainland and to the sea as sources of livelihood and as cosmological and sovereign centres. Yet the example of Lý Sơn shows that they dichotomise two modes of life — farming and fishing — even though in everyday life they might mix the two activities. The two vernacular terms — *làng* and *vạn* — appeared in almost every conversation with villagers, indicating that they recognise a social difference between the land and the sea. The distinction between the two territorial domains was manifested in the erection of two separate temples — *đình* and *lăng* — which marked spiritual and hierarchical boundaries between the land-based village and the fishing community.

Nevertheless, such distinctiveness between sea and land activities preserved in the social and religious organisations of the Lý Sơn society does not exclude the possibility that these two types of community are in a constant state of flux. The example of Thiên Y A Na — a Vietnamised Cham Goddess of Pô Nagar who is believed to secure the livelihood of the fishermen on the seashore — well illustrates this phenomenon. Whenever I attended anniversary ceremonies for Thiên Y A Na in An Hải village, I was always astonished by the large number of fishermen who visited her temple and took part in religious observance. While in this temple, the *làng* carried out an important ritual aiming to ensure the fertility of the land. I also witnessed fishermen sacrificing to the goddess — once they gave two, or even three, fine pigs. They explained that when the goddess blessed them with good catches or they escaped a Chinese coastguard they gave back to her more than was expected. The ceremonies always took place in the late evening, enduring for many hours and ending with a feast before the sun broke the darkness.

However, the *làng* was not always happy with the ostentatious sacrifices made by the *vạn*, and in some cases tried to regulate this matter. According to local narratives, in Lý Sơn at the beginning of the nineteenth century, farmers found a whale beached on the shore just opposite the temple of the Goddess of Five Elements (*Bà Chúa Ngũ Hạnh*) which belonged to the village An Vĩnh. The villagers decided to include the seafaring deity in their spirit pantheon. The fishermen's organisation of Vĩnh Thạnh protested and claimed rights to the beached whale. However, the farmers refused to yield and they strongly believed that the Whale Spirit chose their village to send rain in time of drought and to improve crops. Subsequently, the two communities of farmers and fishermen reached a compromise by building two separate temples called the Outer Dune Temple (*Lăng Cồn Ngoài*) and the Inner Dune Palace (*Dinh Cồn Trong*) to venerate the Whale Spirit, which was revered by fishermen and farmers alike under his full name 'Great and Cruel General of the Southern Sea' (*Nam Hải Dạ Sa Đại tướng quân tôn thần*). It was decided that the fishermen's anniversary celebration would precede the one organised by the farmers but it could not be held without the presence of the village elder — the ritual master of high sacrifice and representative of the founding lineage and hence a farmer — as a sign of the *vạn's* respect for the village. In June 2007, I took part in the ceremony organised by the *vạn*. I witnessed that the *vạn* was not allowed to offer a pig, as this sacrifice was reserved for the *làng*, and instead was only permitted to present a chicken to the divinity.

In saying that the islanders cognitively dichotomise the sea and the land, we should not associate their sense of territoriality with hierarchy, as enshrined in a permanent and immutable situation and structure (Kirsch 1973:35). Lý Sơn society is subject to a continuous process of change due to the ever-changing ecological, political and social conditions of its environment. Thus, the structure of the *làng* and the *vạn* in Lý Sơn is not permanent and static but constantly adapting to current situations. With a growing global demand for marine products and the global consequences of the South China Sea dispute, fishermen started to play a more important role in the village ritual domain to which the *vạn* had no previous access. Like in the past, when the feast in the *đình* served to increase status differences within the village, today the *vạn* uses the same means in order to earn 'permanent prestige and status relations' as well as social recognition (cf. Kirsch 1973:17). Renovating temples, appropriating the traditional right of the agricultural village to sacrifice pigs, and sponsoring village agricultural rituals became means of displaying their ritual 'potency' and thus their growing status in the Lý Sơn community. Each lavish sacrifice made by fishermen in agricultural temples served as evidence of their good catches and their material well-being and hence their spiritual 'reward'. By resisting the exclusive ritual control of the *làng*, they turned the tables on the old hierarchy.

This recent enhancement of fishermen's economic position *vis-à-vis* the farmers and their ritual investment in agricultural temples reveals the complexity of local territorial imaginaries and the dichotomy between the land and the sea. It also suggests that fishermen are not just a disadvantaged group, but that they exploit the situation in order to demonstrate and cultivate their prestige in response to the changing political and economic context. This observation goes to the heart of Taylor's (1998) argument that different modes of acting Vietnamese exist through time and terrain. Instead of looking at Lý Sơn villagers exclusively through the lens of the homogenising narratives of the nation, region, or historical process, it is worth remembering that they constitute not monolithic but rather heterogeneous entities entangled in complex relations in which they construct themselves within and across international, national, and local interests (Appadurai 1996).

Cosmopolitan Connections

Lý Sơn villagers proudly talked about their ancestors' engagement with other societies, and their extraordinary mobility and adventurous explorations to contest and change their present status as a remote or 'sea-locked' and 'outlandish' fishing community. Indeed, mobility and commercial networks between Cham, Chinese, and Việt across the South China Sea were long standing.[8] Prior to Việt colonisation in the seventeenth century, Lý Sơn had been an important part of a network of wells providing fresh water to Cham sailors and foreign ships (Hardy 2009). Throughout the seventeenth, eighteenth, and nineteenth centuries, the Hoàng Sa and Trường Sa sailors capitalised on various cosmopolitan and commercial links in the South China

---

8   For the region of the Mekong Delta, see Taylor (2007).

Sea by gathering gold, silver, swords, ivory, porcelain, cloth, wax, and other goods from the wrecked ships in the Paracels and Spratlys, and supplementing them with a large quantity of mother of pearl, snail, tortoise, and sea cucumber, which were submitted to the royal court in Huế. The sailors were allowed to keep a significant part of the harvested marine produce for their own profit (Lê Quý Đôn 2006:155). The impressive and well preserved ancestor house built during the reign of the Minh Mạng Emperor (1820–41) by the family of Mr Tư (b. 1930)[9] — the uncle of my host on Lý Sơn — bears testimony to the extraordinary profits derived from that trade and extensive maritime networks that connected Lý Sơn villagers and Chinese. During their voyages to the Paracels, the Hoàng Sa and Trường Sa sailors occasionally met Chinese fishermen on the high seas and exchanged information (see, for example, Lê Quy Đôn 1776:82b–85a in Nguyễn Q. Thắng 2008). In the nineteenth and twentieth centuries, some Fujianese or Hainanese who ventured into the Nanyang region (present-day Singapore, Malaysia and Indonesia) to procure their catches of the sea cucumber (*hải sâm*, *bêche-de-mer*) stopped in Lý Sơn to obtain fresh sweet drinking water and peanut oil for cooking. Mr Tư revealed that generations of his family had built their wealth on the lucrative trade that involved the sea cucumber — a highly appreciated delicacy among Chinese. For a long time, Lý Sơn villagers did not develop a taste for sea cucumber, but knew how to process the marine animal in order to sell the product in Hội An — a former Cham port that from the seventeenth century onward attracted many Chinese as well as Japanese, Muslim, and European merchants.

Under French colonial rule, the Hoàng Sa and Trường Sa flotillas ceased to exist, but the seafaring capacity and trading profession of the islanders enabled their voyages to the south where they continued to explore new markets and expand their world and networks through translocal and transregional trade. The Lý Sơn seashore and adjoining waters were rich in fish, snails, sea urchins, and sea cucumbers, and provided trade for many. As the *vạn* in Lý Sơn functioned as a trading organisation, islanders traded with the mainland and sold whatever they caught and farmed: beans, peanuts, and — most famously — fish sauce, peanut oil, and fishing nets made of a special tree fibre (*cây gay*) grown on Lý Sơn. An informant from Lý Sơn explained that in the

---

9   All personal names are pseudonyms.

1930s his late father had worked as a 'trader assistant' (*lái phụ*) for one of the boat owners (*chủ tuyền*) on the island, travelling southward on the winter monsoon and returning northward with the summer monsoon. In November (lunar calendar), the northerly wind began blowing and in the following few months Lý Sơn people sailed to Sài Gòn for the Lunar New Year. The trip south was to buy rice, which was essential for Lý Sơn people's livelihood. The father of my informant did not travel alone but was accompanied by a group of other sailing boats that followed him. En route, he made two important trade deals: he bought sugar (*đường phên*) in Quảng Ngãi and salt in Sa Huỳnh, and relied on established trade networks in Quy Nhơn, Nha Trang, and Hà Tiên. Disembarking in Sài Gòn or Cà Mau, he and the rest of his crew offered themselves as labourers to the French or Chinese, which gave them additional income for the purchase of rice. During March, the wind began to change course to a northerly direction, signalling the time for the return trip. In early summer, with a full load of rice, the group sailed in a northerly direction along the coast, passing different ports on the way. Since medicinal plants (*thuốc nam*) were highly sought after by islanders, Cham traders were welcomed on board, embarking at the port of Bình Thuận and remaining on board until reaching the island. The father of my informant would stop again in Sa Huỳnh to buy salt for resale in Lý Sơn. However, reaching home did not mean that the voyage was complete. Taking advantage of the southerly wind, he would resume his journey northward through the ports of Hội An and Huế where he would typically purchase blocks of jackfruit wood, for building ancestral houses, and Chinese porcelain, which was highly sought after by Lý Sơn islanders.

The outbreak of the First and the Second Indochina Wars brought new political and economic pressures to the Lý Sơn people, who were trapped between two forces: the National Liberation Front and US troops. The strategic location of the island was used by the Vietnam Naval Forces — a command of the US Navy — to control passing ships and trawlers in the South China Sea but also by communist guerrillas to hide stolen weapons, for example. Lý Sơn fishermen were occasionally used by the Vietnam Naval Forces in military missions to the Paracels. However, in contrast to the mainland, Lý Sơn's geographical position enabled it — to some extent — to avoid the turmoil of war. Importantly, most of the island's religious structures survived the two Indochina wars, giving both the provincial authorities and the local community a clear stake in recovering local commemoration of Hoàng Sa and Trường Sa sailors and applying for national recognition of this ceremony. In the eyes of Lý Sơn villagers, this commemoration was testimony that they were not backward but using their trading skills and the seafaring capacity that connected them with the rest of the world. Forty-nine-year-old Lý described this in the following words:

> Previously Lý Sơn people used to go on sailing boats and, I think, because of that, having only sailing boats they were still able to go to the Paracels. They kept sailing to the Paracels not because of the royal order, which at that time was just a small part of their activities, but because the Paracels were located on the Silk Road, the trade route of, for example, Chinese, Dutch, Spanish, Portuguese; all kinds of people were passing there, so they [Lý Sơn people] followed that route and its trade up to the Paracels. There the Hoàng Sa flotilla was responsible for collecting things such as guns, steel or porcelain ... I am telling you some families in Lý Sơn if they traded they would get very rich. Lý Sơn was very rich so that the guiding principle of Lý Sơn [people] in that time was 'to get rich one must do trade' [*muốn làm giàu phải đi buôn*], or, as they put it, 'without trade there will be no prosperity' [*Phi thương là bất phú*] with the meaning that in order to get rich you must engage in trading, so those in Lý Sơn who did trade were economically better off.

When Lý said that villagers went to the Paracels regardless of the royal order, he meant that the islanders always had to strategise and seek various opportunities to make a living. He later added that Lý Sơn fishermen would continue to go to the Paracels or Spratlys without consideration for the state's position for the same reason, because this is one of the very few options available to them to earn their living.

While Lý sentimentally talked about the previous economic cosmopolitanism of islanders and their prosperity, he also depicted the dramatic changes and desperate years brought at the end of the Second Indochina War. The islanders' mobility and trading networks were severely restricted after the reunification of Vietnam in 1975, particularly in the period of the collectivist subsidy economy which lasted from 1977–86. Lý Sơn villagers reported shortages of basic necessities such as rice, sugar, and salt, which had to be brought from the mainland. To sail to Quảng Ngãi they needed to obtain special permission from the local authorities. Such permission specified clearly how many days they were allowed to stay away. On the day of the trip, their names would be called loudly by the authorities and only after presenting a valid document would they be allowed to embark on the small motor boat. The islanders recalled that the boat was filled with more people than it could properly accommodate, and many were forced to remain crouched or in an uncomfortable position for eight or more hours until reaching Sa Kỳ. Villagers still managed to smuggle local products, such as garlic and onion, to sell on the black market in Sài Gòn in order to buy rice to take home. Hidden in baskets full of vegetables, the rice was then illicitly transported by the boat to the island. Villagers recalled that they had so little rice that they cooked it with sweet potato in order to fill their stomachs. It was during this period that Lý Sơn people sought to ensure their livelihood by capitalising on their seafaring skills.

In 1982, Mr Nha (b. 1948) was the first fisherman on the island to make a daring journey to the Paracels — using a simple administration map stolen from the local People's Committee office. Later in the same year he guided another seven fishing boats. Navigation systems or nautical charts were not available at that time, as the local government feared that fishermen might seek to escape the country by sea. Initially, in the Paracels, the fishermen caught mainly flying fish (*cá chuồn*) which could be preserved using salt, but one year later when the technology became more accessible, they expanded their fishing territories, catches and methods. Fresh fish from the Paracels and Spratlys was transported to Đà Nẵng, where ice was also obtained. However, along with the new market opportunities that appeared, most Lý Sơn fishermen chose to sell their catch to local women traders in Đông Ba market in Huế. In 1989, Lý Sơn's fish trade was ultimately moved to Sa Kỳ port — the closest point between the mainland and Lý Sơn — where it began to operate under the Border Guard Command (*Công an Biên phòng*) which provided the logistical facilities for the development of the local fish market.

In the early 2000s, due to regular fishing expeditions to the Paracels and Spratlys and a diving technology that uses compressed air, Lý Sơn fishermen were able to collect the sea cucumber in deeper waters, and the old trade in the Chinese delicacy underwent revival. With the booming fishing market, some of the Lý Sơn people who in the late 1960s and 1970s emigrated to Quảng Ngãi, Nha Trang, or Sài Gòn saw opportunities for profitable business. They bought marine products from Lý Sơn fishermen and sold these to exporters, often of Sino-Vietnamese origin. The exporters provided credit to these intermediate traders who, in turn, were able to connect with fishermen. Initially, the cargo of sea cucumber, shark fin and, occasionally, turtle and turtle-shell and sea urchin, was sent to urban markets in central and southern Vietnam for export to China and Cambodia, but more recent destinations include ports in northern Vietnam. In the north, out of sight of customs patrols, fish and various marine products from Lý Sơn are traded across the border at fishing villages of Móng Cái and transferred to Chinese fishing vessels at sea, or transported directly by Sino-Vietnamese traders to Guangxi, Guangdong Province, or to Hainan Island.

This thriving trade of marine goods has been caught between two opposing forces — the liberalisation of cross-border trade between China and Vietnam, and the simultaneous enforcement of borders on the sea. Already under French colonial rule, China had begun to show interest in the uninhabited islands of the Paracels and Spratlys, and to assert claims over them. But it was not until decades later, in 2001, that China first denied Lý Sơn fishermen rights of use to fishing grounds which for generations they had considered their own. In 1982 — the year in which Lý Sơn people recommenced their trips to the Paracels and deep-sea fishing began — the legal regime of an exclusive economic zone (EEZ) came into force as a new provision of the International Law of the Sea. Until then, national borders at sea did not concern Lý Sơn fishermen, but with the enforcement of the EEZ they found themselves accused of entering restricted zones illicitly. As the economic, political, and military powerhouse in the region, China's expansion of an exclusive coastal economic zone resulted in the enforcement of a seasonal fishing ban, the seizure and detention of Vietnamese fishermen, and the destruction of their vessels by Chinese patrol ships. China's introduction of a map (in 2009) that engulfed virtually the entire South China Sea further exacerbated tensions and incidents in the region, in spite of a common history of commerce and exchange, and a shared understanding of marine life as common property (Roszko 2015). As the tensions over the Paracels and Spratlys worsened, occasionally erupting into anti-Chinese protests across the country, Lý Sơn villagers preferred to maintain a low profile for their trading activities with China.

The status of Lý Sơn as a restricted border zone impels Lý Sơn villagers to strategically preserve those memories of economic cosmopolitanism that figuratively bring the island closer to Vietnam's ancestry and fatherland, simultaneously obscuring those shared with the Cham or Chinese. In doing so, they selectively underline that Lý Sơn Island was not an isolated place, but one situated at the crossroads of the Silk Road trade routes that spanned China, Hainan, Nanyang, and the rest of the world. Articulating alternative accounts of their ancestors' engagement in long-distance voyages at sea, local markets, and commercial networks, Lý Sõn people conveyed an implicit protest against their dramatic domestication and reductive narrative representations brought about by a centrally planned economy after 1975 and the politicised South China Sea dispute. As a result, these proud and skilful sea navigators and traders with cosmopolitan economic networks — who once did not hesitate to advertise to the royal court in Huế about their risky but profitable operations at sea — became reduced to mere fishermen.

Staging Citizenship on the South China Sea

Seeking to become part of the modern world, the people of Lý Sơn have begun to contest their island's marginal location and seek to represent it as a strategic link between Vietnam and the disputed maritime areas to the east. By claiming that they are historically and emotionally bound not only to their natal villages on the coastal mainland, but also to the dispersed islets of the Paracels where their ancestors worked and died during marine operations, they projected their own meaning of territoriality. In Lý Sơn people's highly localised perception of the nation's territory, the modern border line shifted from the island to the Paracels and Spratlys, expanding and making Lý Sơn a virtual centre of Vietnam's territory, now comprised of both land and sea.

Being marginalised and economically left behind after the re-unification of Vietnam in 1975, Lý Sơn fishermen and farmers aspired to be recognised as translocal and 'cosmopolitan' subjects whose identity in previous centuries was built on extensive trading networks, and the experience of far-distance travel and exploration, rather than exclusively on fishing. As Nina Glick-Schiller and Andrew Irving (2015) show, cosmopolitanism is an ongoing process that allows those who feel provincialised and marginalised to be attentive to global processes without compromising their local interests. In the case of Lý Sơn, recentring the country's geo-body became a matter of integrating the mainland territory, the two disputed archipelagos, the familiar system of ancestor worship, their cosmopolitan economic networks, and the sacrificed Hoàng Sa soldiers into a new rendition of the imagined nation.

Capitalising on a newly discovered patriotism among islanders and consciousness about protecting 'ancestral lands' in the 'East Sea', in 2014 the Vietnamese Ministry of Culture, Sports and Tourism selected Lý Sơn Island — considered a vanguard of Vietnam's sovereignty — to host the national exhibition of Vietnam's and China's historical maps, under the slogan 'Paracel and Spratly Islands belong to Vietnam — legal and historical evidence'. Most of the maps presented at the exhibition in a local museum were collected from various antiquarian bookshops around the world by Trần Đình Thắng — a young Vietnamese who was born in Vietnam but raised in a foreign country. With the aim of raising morale among local fishermen and local soldiers stationed on the island, the exhibition on Lý Sơn was marked by the attendance of representatives of the Vietnam Naval Forces, central and local state authorities, and guest of honour Trần Đình Thắng. The event was accompanied by a staged performance, including dance and patriotic songs, and widely broadcast in the national media.

Until recently, the region of the Red River Delta in Vietnam was seen as the undisputed cradle of civilisation and representative of Vietnam's 'authentic' wet rice culture. However, the international debate over the South China Sea caused a significant change in rhetoric in Vietnam which redefined Vietnam from a rice-growing culture to a maritime nation (*nước biển*). Discursively, these territorial and mental shifts were marked by stories about the most recent 'turn towards the ancestral sea islands' (*hướng về biển đảo quê hương*) and the idea of Vietnam as a *'nước biển'* (literally 'sea country', but more accurately 'sea-oriented country'), which is a contemporary invention of tradition that discursively places Vietnam in Tony Reid's (1999) Malay World. Propaganda posters recently arranged at the front entrance to the local museum on Lý Sơn Island are part of that effort. The most interesting slogans proclaimed: 'Vietnam is a maritime country' (*'Việt Nam là một quốc gia biển'*), 'The island is a home and the sea is a homeland' (*'Đảo là nhà biển là quê hương'*), and 'Each Vietnamese is a citizen of the sea' (*'Mỗi người Việt Nam là một công dân biển'*). While fishermen had previously been portrayed mainly in terms of socialist production — next to agriculture and forestry — the most recent Vietnamese state rhetoric turns Vietnamese fishermen into the heroic vanguards of national sovereignty in the 'East Sea'. Novel expressions of national identity and citizenship can also be seen in T-shirts bearing the slogan 'Vietnamese nation is determined to preserve each plot of the Vietnamese land and sea islands' ('*Dân Tộc Việt Nam Quyết Tâm Gìn Giữ Từng Tấc Đất và Biển Đảo Của Việt Nam*'), or 'Vietnam turns toward the East Sea' ('*Việt Nam hướng về Biển Đông*'). These T-shirts became increasingly popular among many young Vietnamese tourists in Lý Sơn who wanted to publicly express their identification with fishermen and the sea.

I opened my paper with a vignette about a group of eight patriotic former policewomen who wished to express their solidarity with poor fishing families, who were suffering for the sake of the nation, through an act of compensation. Ironically, most of the families selected for the meeting with the former policewomen depended on agriculture and not the sea for their livelihood, as month-long fishing operations in distant waters required considerable expenditure on gear, vessel, fuel, and reserves of food. In spite of the diversity of livelihoods found on the island, the women saw its inhabitants exclusively through the prism of the highly politicised character of the South China Sea dispute. Pointing to a cultural and economic gap between those on the mainland and those on the island, they perceived the inhabitants of Lý Sơn as 'nothing but sea people' ('*người dân biển thì thế thôi*'), and knowing hardly anything beyond living off the sea (*biết chỉ làm biển thôi*). Without help from the state — which was, for these women, an educator and patron of progress — the coastal areas such as the islands could not be developed. The women contested the islanders' way of being Vietnamese, as certain customs on the island made them anxious — for example, they considered it unhygienic that many graves were located in the vicinity of human habitation. Although the women's mission was to encourage fishermen to 'cling to the sea, cling to the fishing grounds to defend national sovereignty' ('*bám biển, bám ngư trường để bảo vệ chủ quyền tổ quốc*'), they agreed that one could hardly consider Lý Sơn to be an attractive place to live, let alone a tourist destination. One of the women said: 'A touristic place is one of rest, entertainment and fun but there is nothing here' ('*nơi du lịch là nơi nghỉ ngơi, giải trí và vui vẻ và ở đây chẳng gì có*'). Her remark about the islanders' pronunciation, which she found incomprehensible and odd, cast the islanders as somehow less authentically Vietnamese in comparison with the more 'representative' culture of northern Vietnam.

Vietnamese tourists' image of Lý Sơn as a navel of the nation was very much shaped by national media and recent tensions between China and Vietnam over the disputed waters in the South China Sea. Moreover, the media publicised contradictory images: on the one hand advertising Lý Sơn as a holiday destination with charming beaches, on the other hand underlining the island's defence position and praising the extraordinary bravery of its inhabitants living under constant threat from China. As a result, many mainlander tourists imagined the island as a highly militarised place located somewhere in the vicinity of China, but soon experienced the absence of electricity[10] and medical facilities, the conversion of beaches into garlic and onion fields, and the islanders' 'incomprehensible' pronunciation. Taken together, these elements contributed to the perception of Lý Sơn as remote: a geographical and cultural backwater more suitable for a short, single visit rather than a longer stay. Most tourists perceived the islanders as an undeveloped fishing community bravely standing at the forefront of national sovereignty, in the very middle of Vietnam's land mass and the sea, including the Paracel and Spratly archipelagos.

Lý Sơn people were aware of these various perceptions about them and that they were seen as strange, odd, and at times funny. They felt uncomfortable about mainlanders' remarks about their local accent. For example, while they tended to appreciate my adoption of their local pronunciation, they immediately warned me that I was not allowed to speak 'Lý Sơn language' on the mainland, because they sensed that mainlanders would make fun of them. While they understood that the island's location made it a vanguard of Vietnam's sovereignty, attracting thousands of tourists and opening new economic opportunities, they still became upset if the national media stretched this picture too far. They were afraid that it might scare tourists and give a wrong impression of the island as a dangerous place. They were especially wary of crowds of journalists and local researchers who spent only a day or two on the island, chasing stories about fishermen victimised by a Chinese coastguard, or chasing elders and their family records. An outspoken islander woman expressed her opinion that real poverty on the island rarely attracted attention. Another fisherman complained that some journalists lost interest when they learned that the damage

---

10   At the time of fieldwork, between May and July 2014, the installation of a submarine cable providing power supply to Lý Sơn Island was under construction. Electricity only became widely available on the island in October 2014.

to his fishing boat came not from a Chinese coastguard but from a short circuit. Others who renovated old guesthouses or built new ones worried about their business and wanted the island to be seen as a modern, safe, and attractive place for tourists. Situated on 'a tricky double edge — both cutting and peripheral' (Chu 2010:26), Lý Sơn people worked hard to recentre their marginal(ised) locality within the categorical order of the modern nation-state's cartography (Malkki 1992) by projecting themselves as cosmopolitan subjects. While they willingly shared with other Vietnamese a sense of being a 'navel of the nation' by claiming a twofold status, as an integral part of Vietnam and as part of the Paracel archipelago, they searched for their own context in the process of constructing their place within the nation's historical narrative and territorial map.

Conclusion

In his analysis of the local consequences of the international conflict known as the Taiwan Strait Crisis on Jinmen Island, Michael Szonyi (2008) vividly shows effects of militarisation slipping into the daily life of people and individual imaginations. Yet, in cartographic iconographies of Vietnam, it is the sea and its islands that have become conspicuously visible in arenas as varied as posters, stamps, logos, and museum exhibitions. In these changing aesthetics of the nation, the continental landmass becomes ex-centric and the margins become centred, culminating in the rendition of Lý Sơn as the navel of the nation. The island became a symbol of heroic sacrifice in the name of all Vietnamese citizens, who started to identify themselves with the 'Vietnamese waters'. In the case of Lý Sơn, this aesthetic shift is accompanied not by militarisation but by a changing geography of affect (Navaro-Yashin 2007) by which people who have never been on the Paracels or Spratlys claim a deep emotional bond with these 'ancestral' places and the desire to defend their 'sovereignty'. This affect is performed in a wide variety of ways: walling Lý Sơn Island against Chinese; emotional demonstrations in the streets of Hà Nội or Hồ Chí Minh City against Chinese occupation of 'ancestral' seas; and mainlanders showing solidarity with islanders — supposedly victimised by Chinese vessels — through patriotic tourism, donations and cultural campaigns. The changing geography of affect creates new spaces for interaction not just between state and society, but between different ways of acting Vietnamese. The affect provoked by the 'ancestral land' of the deep sea, fishing practices, new maps of the national geo-body, new development plans, and a new style of patriotic tourism in Vietnam's coastal areas illustrates the multitude of ways in which people respond to local and global economic and political discourses. In this same sense, the submarine cable that connected Lý Sơn Island with the national grid and provided a steady power supply in 2014 has been rendered not only as an item of cultural and socioeconomic development, but as an act of maintaining security, national defence, and sovereignty.[11]

Thinking about the economic cosmopolitanism of Lý Sơn people requires recognition that cosmopolitanism is about various groups of people whose actions are situated in different political, economic, and social niches, and who are driven by contradictory goals. The islanders' expanding universe — embedded in and shaped by global competition for resources in the South China Sea — was largely based on their local experience of long distance commercial fishing and trading, which has been interpreted by a large part of the Vietnamese population as Lý Sơn's determination to exercise Vietnam's sovereignty. Indeed, Lý Sơn's fishermen and farmers began to tie their identity to the state emergency in connection with the Paracels and with Lý Sơn Island's geopolitical role in this international dispute. However, the narratives about Lý Sơn's translocal and transregional connections to the sea could be read as villagers' desire to go beyond the image of their heroic and geopolitical role in the South China Sea that reduces them to the 'suffering subject' (Robbins 2013). In their desire to be modern, progressive, and attractive for the tourist industry, they seek to stage their own roles in this global dispute. Even though they might complain about enclosures and appropriations of terrestrial and maritime commons, and about the way they are being depicted as uncivilised and not-quite-Vietnamese, they often embrace the opportunity to take centre stage and become the centre of the nation for the eyes of the world to see — if only temporarily. The domestication and instrumentalisation of maritime populations in performances of and for the nation paradoxically draws the periphery

---

11   See, for example, www.vietnambreakingnews.com/2014/03/contract-inked-on-power-supply-for-ly-son-island/, accessed 31 August 2015.

into the centre. For a short-lived moment, Lý Sơn people could be confident that their dispossession can be read as a sacrifice — willing or unwilling — for being the navel of the nation.

References

Appadurai, Arjun 1996, *Modernity at Large: Cultural Dimensions of Globalism*, University of Minnesota Press, Minneapolis.

Atsushi Ota 2010, 'Pirates or Entrepreneurs?: Migration and Trade of Sea People in Southwest Kalimantan c. 1770–1820', *Indonesia*, vol. 90, pp. 67–96.

Bộ Ngoại Giao Uỷ Ban Biên Giới Quốc Gia 2013, *Tuyển Tập các Châu Bàn Triệu Nguyễn về Thực Thi Chủ Quyền của Việt Nam trên Hải Quần Đảo Hoàng Sa và Trường Sa* [*Collection of Official Documents of the Nguyen Dynasty on the Exercise of Sovereignty of Vietnam over the Paracels and Spratlys Archipelagoes*], Nhà xuất bản tri thức, Hanoi.

Chu, Julie Y. 2010, *Cosmologies of Credit: Transnational Mobility and the Politics of Destination in China*, Duke University Press, Durham and London.

Firth, Raymond 1964, *Malay Fishermen: Their Peasant Economy*, Routledge and Kegan Paul, London.

Glick-Schiller, Nina and Andrew Irving 2015, *Whose Cosmopolitanism?: Critical Perspectives, Relationalities and Discontents*, Berghahn, New York and Oxford.

Gourou, Pierre 1936, *Les Paysans du Delta Tonkinois: Étude de Géographie Humaine*, Éditions d'Art et d'Histoire, Paris.

Gourou, Pierre 1940, *L'utilisation du Sol en Indochine Française*, Centre d'Études de Politique Étrangère, Paris.

Hardy, Andrew 2009, 'Eaglewood and the Economic History of Champa and Central Vietnam', in Andrew Hardy, Mauro Cucarzi and Patrizia Zolese (eds), *Champa and the Archaeology of Mỹ Sơn (Vietnam)*, NUS Press, Singapore, pp. 107–126.

Kirsch, A. Thomas 1973, *Feasting and Social Oscillation: A Working Paper on Religion and Society in Upland Southeast Asia*, Cornell University, Southeast Asian Program, Ithaca.

Kleinen, John 1999, 'Is There a "Village Vietnam"?', in Bernhard Dahm and Vincent J. Houben (eds), *Vietnamese Villages in Transition: Background and Consequences of Reform Policies in Rural Vietnam*, Passau University, Passau, pp. 1–41.

Kleinen, John and Manon Osseweijer (eds) 2010, *Pirates, Ports and Coasts in Asia: Historical and Contemporary Perspectives*, ISEAS Publishing, Singapore; International Institute for Asian Studies, Leiden, Netherlands.

Lê Quý Đôn 1972 [1776], *Phủ Biên Tạp Lục [A Compilation of the Miscellaneous Records When the Southern Border was Pacified]*, vol. 1, Phủ Quốc Vụ Khạnh Đặc Trách Văn Hóa, Saigon.

Lê Quý Đôn 2006 [1776], *Phủ Biên Tạp Lục [A Compilation of the Miscellaneous Records When the Southern Border was Pacified]*, vol. 1, Nhà xuất bản văn hóa thông tin, Hanoi.

Li Tana 1998, *Nguyễn Cochinchina: Southern Vietnam in the Seventeenth and Eighteenth Centuries*, Cornell Southeast Asia Program, Ithaca, New York.

Li Tana 2006, 'A View From the Sea: Perspectives on the Northern and Central Vietnamese Coast', *Journal of Southeast Asian Studies*, vol. 37, no. 1, pp. 83–102.

Malkki, Liisa 1992, 'National Geographic: The Rooting of Peoples and Territorialisation of National Identity among Scholars and Refugees', *Cultural Anthropology*, vol. 7, no. 1, pp. 24–44.

Malkki, Liisa 1995, 'Refugees and Exile: From "Refugee Studies" to the National Order of Things', *Annual Review of Anthropology*, vol. 24, pp. 495–523.

Marr, David G. 1987, 'Vietnamese Attitudes Regarding Illness and Healing', *The Vietnam Forum*, vol. 10, pp. 26–50.

McAlister, John T. and Paul Mus 1970, *The Vietnamese and their Revolution*, Harper and Row, New York.

Murray, Dian H. 1987, *Pirates of the South China Sea 1790–1810*, Stanford University Press, Stanford, CA.

Murray, Dian H. 1988, *Conflict and Coexistence: The Sino-Vietnamese Maritime Boundaries in Historical Perspective*, Center for Southeast Asian Studies, University of Wisconsin, Madison.

Navaro-Yashin, Yael 2007, 'Make-believe Papers, Legal Forms and the Counterfeit: Affective Interactions between Documents and People in Britain and Cyprus', *Anthropological Theory*, vol. 7, no. 1, pp. 79–98.

Nguyễn Duy Thiệu 2002, *Cộng Đồng Ngư Dân ở Việt Nam* [*Fishers Communities in Vietnam*], Nha xuất bản khoa học xã hội, Hanoi.

Nguyễn Q. Thắng 2008, *Hoàng Sa Trường Sa Lãnh Thổ Việt Nam: Nhìn Từ Công Pháp Quốc Tế* [*Vietnam's Paracels and Spratlys Territory: The View from International Law*], Nhà xuất bản tri thức, Hanoi.

O'Connor, Richard 2003, 'Founders' Cults in Regional and Historical Perspective', in Nicola Tannenbaum and Cornelia A. Kammerer (eds), *Founders' Cults in Southeast Asia: Ancestors, Polity, and Identity*, Yale University, Southeast Asia Studies, New Haven, pp. 269–312.

Pearson, Michael N. 1985, 'Littoral Society: The Case for the Coast', *The Great Circle: Journal of the Australian Association for Maritime History*, vol. 7, no. 1, pp. 1–8.

Pearson, Michael N. 2003, *The Indian Ocean*, Routledge, London and New York.

Pham, Charlotte 2013, 'The Vietnamese Coastline: A Maritime Cultural Landscape', in Satish Chandra and Himanshu Prabha Ray (eds), *The Sea, Identity and History: From the Bay of Bengal to the South China Sea*, Society for Indian Ocean Studies, Delhi, pp. 94–137.

Pham, Charlotte, Lucy Blue and Colin Palmer 2010, 'The Traditional Boats of Vietnam, an Overview', *The International Journal of Nautical Archaeology*, vol. 39, no. 2, pp. 255–277.

Reid, Anthony 1999, *Charting the Shape of Early Modern Southeast Asia*, Silkworm Books, Chiang Mai.

Robbins, Joel 2013, 'Beyond the Suffering Subject: Toward an Anthropology of the Good', *Journal of the Royal Anthropological Institute*, vol. 19, no. 3, pp. 447–462.

Roszko, Edyta 2010, 'Commemoration and the State: Memory and Legitimacy in Vietnam', *Sojourn: Journal of Social Issues in Southeast Asia*, vol. 25, no. 1, pp. 1–28.

Roszko, Edyta 2011, 'Spirited Dialogues: Contestations over the Religious Landscape in Central Vietnam's Littoral Society', PhD thesis, Martin Luther University, Halle.

Roszko, Edyta 2015, 'Maritime Territorialisation as Performance of Sovereignty and Nationhood in the South China Sea', *Nations and Nationalism*, vol. 21, no. 2, pp. 230–249.

Southworth, W. 2004, 'The Coastal States of Champa', in Ian Glover and Peter Bellwood (eds), *Southeast Asia: From Prehistory to History*, Routledge Curzon, London and New York, pp. 209–233.

Szonyi, Michael 2008, *Cold War Island: Qumoy on the Front Line*, Cambridge University Press, Cambridge.

Tạ Chí Đài Trường 2005, *Thần, Người, và Đất Việt* [*Deities, People and the Land of Việt*], Nhà xuất bản văn hoá thông tin, Hanoi.

Taylor, Keith 1998, 'Surface Orientations in Vietnam: Beyond Histories of Nation and Region', *The Journal of Asian Studies*, vol. 57, no. 4, pp. 949–978.

Taylor, Philip 2007, *Cham Muslims of the Mekong Delta: Place and Mobility in the Cosmopolitan Periphery*, University of Hawaii Press, Honolulu; NUS Press, Singapore; NIAS Press, Copenhagen.

Trần Quốc Vượng 1992, 'Popular Culture and High Culture in Vietnamese History', *An Interdisciplinary Journal of Southeast Asian Studies,* vol. 7, no. 2, pp. 5–38.

Vaccaro, Ismael, Allan Charles Dawson and Laura Zanotti 2014, 'Negotiating Territoriality: Spatial Dialogues Between State and Tradition', in Allan Charles Dawson, Laura Zanotti and Ismael Vaccaro (eds), *Negotiating Territoriality: Spatial Dialogues Between State and Tradition*, Routledge, New York and London, pp. 1–20.

Vickery, Michael 2009, 'A Short History of Champa', in Andrew Hardy, Mauro Cucarzi and Patrizia Zolese (eds), *Champa and the Archaeology of Mỹ Sơn (Vietnam)*, NUS Press, Singapore, pp. 45–60.

Watson, James L. 1985, 'Standardizing the Gods: The Promotion of Tien Hou (Empress of Heaven) Along the South China Coast 960–1960', in David Johnson, Andrew Nathan and Evelyn Rawski (eds), *Popular Culture in Late Imperial China*, University of California Press, Berkeley and Los Angeles, pp. 292–324.

Wheeler, Charles 2006, 'Re-thinking the Sea in Vietnamese History: Littoral Society in the Integration of Thuận-Quảng, Seventeenth–Eighteenth Centuries', *Journal of Southeast Asian Studies*, vol. 37, no. 1, pp. 123–153.

Whitmore, John K. 2006, 'The Rise of the Coast: Trade, State and Culture in Early Đại Việt', *Journal of Southeast Asian Studies*, vol. 37, no. 1, pp. 123–153.

Winichakul, Thongchakul 1994, *Siam Mapped: A History of the Geo-Body of the Nation*, University of Hawaii Press, Honolulu.

Contributors

Philip Taylor is Senior Fellow in the Department of Anthropology, College of Asia and the Pacific, The Australian National University (ANU), and Editor of the *Asia Pacific Journal of Anthropology*. He has been conducting research in the Mekong Delta since the early 1990s. He has authored and edited numerous books and scholarly articles on history, religion, ethnicity, economy, and environment in Vietnam. His latest book, *The Khmer Lands of Vietnam*, was co-published in 2014 by NUS Press, NIAS Press, and University of Hawaii Press. At ANU, he supervises PhD students working on Vietnam and Southeast Asia. Along with ANU Vietnam studies colleagues, he has been involved with organising the Vietnam Update series since 2003.

Hy V. Luong is Professor of Anthropology at the University of Toronto. He is the author, editor, and co-editor of nine books. His recent publications include *Tradition, Revolution, and Market Economy in a North Vietnamese Village, 1925–2006* (University of Hawaii Press, 2010); *Urbanization, Migration, and Poverty in a Vietnamese Metropolis: Hồ Chí Minh City in Comparative Perspectives* (edited volume, National University of Singapore Press, 2009); *Hiện đại và động thái của truyền thống ở Việt Nam: Những cách tiếp cận Nhân học* (*Modernities and the Dynamics of Tradition in Vietnam: Anthropological Approached*), (two edited volumes, National University of Ho Chi Minh City Press, 2010); and *The Dynamics of Social Capital and Civic Engagement in Asia* (co-edited with Amrita Daniere, Routledge, 2012). Luong is currently working on social capital, rural-to-urban migration, and sociocultural transformation in Vietnam.

Nguyen Thi Thanh Binh is Head of the Việt-Mường Ethnic Research Department in the Institute of Anthropology, Hanoi. She received her PhD from The Australian National University in 2010. She has published several refereed articles on social change in rural

Vietnam, and has undertaken research on topics such as migration, social transformation, and land conflicts. She obtained a grant from the International Foundation of Science, Sweden, to research urbanisation on the outskirts of Hanoi and is currently completing book chapters on this project. She convenes courses in anthropology at Vietnam National University and the Academy of Social Sciences, and supervises graduate students in anthropology.

Linh Khanh Nguyen is a PhD candidate in Cultural Anthropology at the Maxwell School of Citizenship and Public Affairs, Syracuse University. She came to the US to study as a Freeman scholar and graduated *summa cum laude* with high honours in Sociology from Hobart and William Smith Colleges. Her dissertation research is currently funded by the Bucerius PhD Scholarships in Migration Studies. Her research interests include social inequality and its articulations through movement, gendered movement and morality, and displacement in place.

Yen Le is Lecturer in the Department of Vietnamese Studies, University of Social Sciences and Humanities, Vietnam National University, Ho Chi Minh City. She completed her PhD in Anthropology at The Australian National University in 2015. Her thesis concerns people affected by leprosy in Vietnam, and draws on long-term ethnographic fieldwork conducted in communities of leprosy sufferers in central and southern Vietnam. The thesis won the Sir Raymond Firth Prize for Anthropology in 2014 and a chapter earned the prize for best graduate essay from the Vietnam Studies Group of the Association of Asian Studies. Yen's research interests include stigmatised diseases, care, the body, and personhood. She has presented her research findings to the Asian Society for the History of Medicine, the Singapore Graduate Forum on Southeast Asian Studies, and at annual conferences of the Australian Anthropological Society.

Nguyen Thu Huong is Lecturer in Anthropology at Vietnam National University, Hanoi. She is also affiliated with Lund University as a Postdoctoral Research Fellow on a research project — led by Helle Rydstrom and funded by the Swedish Research Council — on 'Gendered Violence in Emergency Settings in Pakistan, the Philippines, and Vietnam'. Her recent publications include 'The Politics of Sexual Health in Vietnam' (with Tine Gammeltoft) in *The Routledge Handbook of Sexuality Studies in East Asia* (Routledge, 2015); 'At the Intersection of Gender, Sexuality, and Politics: The Disposition of Rape Cases among some Ethnic Minority Groups of Northern Vietnam' (*Sojourn*, 2013); 'Whose Weapons?: Representations of Rape in the Print Media in Modern Vietnam' (*Journal of Vietnamese Studies*, 2012); and 'Rape Disclosures: The Interplay of Gender, Culture and Kinship in Contemporary Vietnam' (*Culture, Health and Sexuality*, 2012).

Peter Chaudhry is a PhD candidate in the Department of Political and Social Change, The Australian National University (ANU). Before resuming his studies in 2012, Peter worked for 15 years as a researcher and public policy specialist for NGOs, bilateral and multilateral agencies, and the United Nations. From 2008 to 2012 he was an embedded adviser in Vietnam's Ministry of Labour and Social Affairs, and the State Committee for Ethnic Minority Affairs, in Hanoi. At ANU he served as convenor of the Vietnam Update in 2015. His interests lie in political ethnography and processes of modern state building at the margins of Southeast Asia's modern nation states.

Ha Viet Quan is a PhD candidate studying Anthropology and Public Policy at The Australian National University. He obtained his masters degree in Development Studies from the Kimmage DCS, Holy Ghost College of Dublin, Ireland, in 2008. Having worked for the Committee for Ethnic Minority Affairs (CEMA), a ministerial agency of Vietnam, since 2002, Ha Quan has been involved in numerous poverty reduction and development policies, projects, and programs for ethnic minorities. His main research interests are public policies for ethnic minorities, with a focus on the relations between minority groups and the Vietnamese state.

Oscar Salemink is Professor in the Anthropology of Asia at the University of Copenhagen. He received his doctoral degree from the University of Amsterdam, based on research on Vietnam's Central Highlands. From 1996 to 2001, he was responsible for grant portfolios in higher education, arts and culture, and sustainable development in Thailand and Vietnam on behalf of the Ford Foundation. From 2001 to 2011, he worked at VU University in Amsterdam, from 2005 as Professor of Social Anthropology. His current research concerns religious, ritual, and heritage practices in everyday life in Vietnam and the East and Southeast Asian region. His recent book-length publications include *Colonial Subjects* (University of Michigan Press, 1999); *Vietnam's Cultural Diversity* (UNESCO Publishing,

2001); *The Ethnography of Vietnam's Central Highlanders* (University of Hawaii Press, 2003); *The Development of Religion, the Religion of Development* (Eburon, 2004); *A World of Insecurity: Anthropological Perspectives on Human Security* (with Thomas Hylland Eriksen and Ellen Bal, Pluto Press, 2010); the *Routledge Handbook on Religions in Asia* (co-edited with Bryan S. Turner, Routledge, 2014); and thematic issues of *History and Anthropology* (1994), *Focaal: European Journal of Anthropology* (2006), and the *Journal of Southeast Asian Studies* (2007).

Edyta Roszko is Marie Curie Research Fellow at the School of Government and International Affairs of Durham University and Postdoctoral Researcher at the Department of Cross-Cultural and Regional Studies of the University of Copenhagen. Prior to taking up posts at Durham and Copenhagen, Edyta spent several years researching in Vietnam and at the Academia Sinica in Taiwan. Her doctoral thesis focuses on coastal communities in Central Vietnam and the multifaceted contestation over the religious landscape in the context of changes in the ecology, the economy, and in politics. Edyta has recently been pursuing her interest in fishermen's perceptions and actions in relation to territory, in connection with their 'mental maps' by working on European Union and Danish Research Council–funded projects that aim to build a more informed approach to territoriality and local communities' attempt to protect the environmental foundation of their livelihoods. Edyta has been published in *Journal of Social Issues in Southeast Asia* (2010), *East Asia: An International Quarterly* (2012), and *Nations and Nationalism* (2015).

www.ingramcontent.com/pod-product-compliance
Lightning Source LLC
Chambersburg PA
CBHW050806270326
41926CB00026B/4574